D0879172

Deconstructing Sacramental Theology and Reconstructing Catholic Ritual

Deconstructing Sacramental Theology

and

Reconstructing Catholic Ritual

Joseph Martos

RESOURCE *Publications* • Eugene, Oregon

Resource Publications
An Imprint of Wipf and Stock Publishers
199 W. 8th Ave., Suite 3
Eugene, OR 97401

www.wipfandstock.com

ISBN 13: 978-1-4982-2179-5

Manufactured in the U.S.A.   06/08/2015

Unless otherwise noted, all translations are those of the author.

To all those who made this research possible,
from the medieval monks who laboriously copied ancient manuscripts
to the contemporary computer scientists who made it possible
to digitize and download the writings of the past.

And to Gary Macy, who helped me access those writings.

Thoroughly understand what it is to understand, and not only will you understand the broad lines of all there is to be understood but also you will possess a fixed base, an invariant pattern, opening upon all further developments of understanding.

—Bernard Lonergan, *Insight: A Study of Human Understanding*

Contents

Preface | ix

Introduction | xiii

A Note about Footnotes | xvii

I. The Construct: Scholastic Theology and Sacramental Doctrine | 1

    1. Catholic Doctrine in Church Documents | 2

    2. Scholastic Sacramental Theology Before Vatican II | 15

    3. Scholastic Sacramental Theology After Vatican II | 31

    4. Conclusion | 39

II. Construction: The Naïve Development of Sacramental Theology | 41

    1. Sacramental Theology in Historical Perspective | 42

    2. Sacraments in a Literal Reading of the Scriptures | 44

    3. Sacraments in the Writings of the Church Fathers | 48

    4. Sacraments in Medieval Theology | 56

    5. Sacraments in Modern Theology | 63

    6. Conclusion | 68

III. Deconstruction: A Critical Analysis of the Theological Development | 70

    1. Sacraments in the Christian Scriptures | 71

    2. Sacraments in the Second and Third Centuries | 100

    3. Sacraments in the Christian Roman Empire | 123

    4. Sacraments in the Dark Ages | 160

    5. Sacraments in the High Middle Ages | 171

    6. Complex History and Theological Method | 212

Contents

IV. Reconstruction: Sacraments in the Future | 220

    1. Symbols and Meaning | 221

    2. Meaning and Context | 224

    3. Reality and Symbol | 230

    4. Dimensions of meaning | 236

    5. Toward an Authentic Future | 244

    6. Sacraments and Sacramentality | 278

A Summary of the Argument | 282

Bibliography | 303

Index of Names | 307

Preface

DECONSTRUCTION IS A TERM often associated with Jacques Derrida and other post-modern philosophers who have attempted to reveal structures hidden in language that surreptitiously privilege some things over others, and to show thereby that what people think is objectively the case may be a pre-conditioned way of looking at it. More broadly, the term can be used to name a type of analysis that takes apart conceptual structures such as philosophies and theologies in order to expose logical inconsistencies or conceptual flaws. The first three chapters in this book are a work of deconstruction in the latter sense. The fourth chapter is an attempt to begin reconstructing something—in this case a theology of sacraments—to replace a theology that has been shown to be incoherent.

Not that Catholic sacramental doctrine or scholastic sacramental theology are internally incoherent. Indeed, their internal conceptual coherence contributed to Catholicism's ability to defend itself against Protestant critiques since the sixteenth century, as well as its ability to explain the moral and spiritual dimensions of religiosity to the members of the Church until the mid-twentieth century. For over four centuries (and for longer, if one traces scholastic theology to the schoolmen of the high Middle Ages) Catholic thinking about the sacraments was logically self-consistent as well as consistent with Catholic life as it was experienced by the faithful.

In one way, however, Catholic sacramental thinking was inconsistent with its origins. In quite a different way, it has recently become inconsistent with Catholic life as it is experienced by people who regard themselves as faithful members of the Church.

Today the origins of Catholic sacramental doctrines can be researched with a depth and breadth that was impossible before the advent of the computer. On the internet it is possible to do simple word searches of English translations of all the important Christian writings from the second to the sixteenth century. Using specialized CD ROMs (compact disks with files stored in read-only memory) it is possible to do sophisticated word searches in Greek and Latin. Moreover, it is now possible to access any word or phrase in the Bible in virtually any language (and in a wide variety of English translations) as quickly as it takes to type a few keystrokes.

By examining key words and phrases from their first appearance in the scriptures, to their use by ante-Nicene authors, to their adoption by the great fathers of the church, to their interpretation by the medieval schoolmen, and finally to their affirmation by the Catholic bishops at the Council of Trent, it becomes clear that in some crucial cases the last iteration of those words and phrases had little in common with their earliest iteration. The Tridentine church was triumphantly certain that its beliefs and practices were solidly founded on biblical revelation and patristic faith, but sometimes what biblical and patristic authors had in mind was quite different from what the ecclesiastical guardians of the faith defined as dogma. It can therefore be demonstrated today, in a way that was not feasible before the technological innovations of the twenty-first century, that there are fundamental inconsistencies between sacramental doctrines formulated in scholastic terminology and the ancient documents regarded as foundational. Catholic sacramental doctrine, therefore, expressed as it is in overwhelmingly scholastic terms, is actually not consistent with many of the biblical and patristic sources on which it claims to be founded. In other words, it is historically incoherent.

Moreover, sacramental doctrine has in recent decades become what one might call experientially incoherent. Catholics in earlier centuries could see that their religious practices reflected the teachings of the Church. For example, baptism was understood to be necessary for salvation, and so babies were baptized as soon as possible after they were born. Stillborn infants were conditionally baptized in the hope that the soul had not yet left the body, and children unlucky enough to die unbaptized could not be buried in consecrated ground. Following the same sort of thinking, great missionary efforts were mounted to bring baptism and the faith to pagan peoples outside of Europe in order to save their souls. Today the Church still teaches that baptism is necessary for salvation, but children who die before they are baptized are no longer regarded as unsaved, nor does the Church insist that people who practice other religions are condemned to hell.

Similarly, Sunday worship in the past consisted of attendance at the Holy Sacrifice of the Mass, at which the priest did not have to preach and the people did not have to receive communion in order for the sacrifice to be validly offered. The high point of the service was the transubstantiation of bread and wine into the body and blood of Christ, whose real presence could be felt after the consecration of the mass. In addition, the Blessed Sacrament, as the consecrated bread was called, was reserved in a richly decorated tabernacle on the altar so that Christ could be venerated in person at any time of the day or night. Today the mass is still called a sacrifice in church documents, but by and large Catholics do not think of what they do in church as attending a sacrifice. The high points for most people are the homily (if it is a good one) and the receiving of communion, but many church-going Catholics no longer regard the Eucharist as the actual body and blood of Christ, nor do any but the most devout make visits to the Blessed Sacrament.

In the past, the sacrament of penance was understood to be needed for the remission of sins, especially mortal sins—and all sins of a sexual nature, even impure thoughts, were regarded as mortal sins. For this reason, and also because receiving the Blessed Sacrament in a state of impurity was regarded as a sacrilege, Catholics regularly went to confession before receiving holy communion at mass. Catholics understood that if they died with a mortal sin on their soul they would go straight to hell, even if their body was buried in a Catholic cemetery, and so they prayed for the grace of a happy death and hoped to receive the sacrament of extreme unction shortly before closing their eyes for the last time. Today, the Church's official position on sin and confession is not much different from what it was, but Catholics do not think about sin the way that their parents and grandparents did, nor do they go to confession frequently, nor do they regard the last rites as important for their eternal salvation.

Likewise, marriage and ordination used to be seen as lifelong commitments, for indeed they were. With few exceptions, Catholics who got married stayed married until they died, and the clergy were said to be "priests forever according to the order of Melchizedek." Today the Church still teaches that marriage is indissoluble, but all Catholics know other Catholics who have been divorced and remarried, often without first having obtained a legally required annulment. Moreover, there is a shortage of priests, partly because of the numbers who have left the priesthood, partly because the requirement of celibacy dissuades men who would like to marry, and partly because sex scandals have tarnished the priestly office. The Catholic doctrine about holy orders has not changed, but today it is difficult for many to believe that priests have unique supernatural powers.

All of this adds up to what can be termed a lack of coherence between Catholic sacramental theology and the lived experience of all but the most conservative and devout Catholics. Liberal Catholics and ordinary church-goers either see that sacramental doctrine and practice do not really match, or they do not pay enough attention to notice the discrepancies.

How this has come about is the topic of this study. The shorter explanation for the discrepancies is that the current incoherence between theology and practice is rooted in the historical incoherence between sacramental theology and its origins. The longer explanation follows.

Introduction

CATHOLICS GENERALLY DO NOT advert to the fact that they use the word "sacrament" in two senses. In the first sense of the word, a sacrament is a liturgical ritual such as a baptism or a religious wedding ceremony. In the second sense of the word, a sacrament is something that is administered and received during the performance of the ritual, as when we talk about administering the sacrament of baptism or receiving the sacrament of marriage.

Theologians and canon lawyers, however (especially those who write about sacraments), are very aware that the word "sacrament" is used in two senses, but like specialists in any field they tend to move from one meaning of the word to the other rather smoothly. Moreover, most of their professional interest is in sacraments as administered and received. Theologians discuss matters such as the meaning and importance of the sacraments that are received; canonists discuss matters such as what is required for validly administering and receiving the sacraments. With regard to sacramental performances, however, the professionals who focus on the ritual aspect of sacraments are primarily liturgists.

Although the above does not present a detailed or nuanced taxonomy, it is sufficient for the purpose of introducing (or reminding) the reader of the two meanings of the word "sacrament" in Catholic usage, and for suggesting that this ambiguity may be the source of problems in the Church.

Some of these problems are pastoral, such as those that arise when Protestants who invite Catholics to take communion in their church are prohibited from receiving communion in a Catholic church. Even if the two liturgical rituals (sacraments in the first sense) are similar, the understanding of the received sacraments is different. Increasingly, however, many of the problems are broadly ecclesiological in the sense that they affect the Church's well-being. In the 1960s priests began to leave the active ministry for a variety of reasons, but the traditional understanding of holy orders made it difficult for the Vatican to address this problem by ordaining married men and possibly women to the priesthood. In the 1970s participation in the sacrament of penance plummeted despite a modernization of the private rite. In the 1980s bishops who had used the public rite in a pastoral manner were ordered to discontinue that usage, with the result that many who wanted to participate in the public rite to become practicing Catholics again found themselves excluded from the life of the Church once more. In the 1990s the shortage of priests led to a decline in the administration of anointing of the sick. In the new millennium that same shortage is making the Eucharist less available to Catholics around the world.

Consider some discrepancies between theory and practice in the church. In theory, Catholics who receive the sacrament of confirmation are fully initiated into the church, yet they have no rights or responsibilities that are different from those of the merely baptized. In theory, those who are baptized, married or ordained enter a state that is permanent and irrevocable, yet Catholics leave the church, divorce and remarry, and depart the priesthood with statistical regularity. Similar things can be said about the discrepancies between different ecclesiologies. Juridically-minded clergy can think of the institutional church in terms of who is able to administer and receive the sacraments, while laity who know little of canon law tend to think of their parish church in terms of interpersonal relationships and a sense of community. As a result, Catholics who are in canonically invalid marriages have to hide their status if they want to receive communion or participate in parish ministries.

It is my belief that some of these problems are related to "sacrament" when it is used in the second sense of the word. Behind that usage is a Latin term that is translated in more technical theology books as the symbolic reality or the sacramental reality. The Latin term itself is *sacramentum et res* (literally, sacrament and reality), which can also be written as *res et sacramentum* (reality and sacrament). In either form, it has been a common term in sacramental theology since the thirteenth century.

That term and the concepts behind it made a great deal of sense in medieval society and they worked quite well in scholastic theology. They still work well in scholastic theology to the extent that conceptual systems are static sets of terms and relations, but they do not make nearly as much sense in contemporary society, as already suggested. One could say that today they work well in theory but not in practice, or that in practice they have become dysfunctional. This is different from saying that scholastic sacramental theology is false, for like any theory, scholastic theology can be true within certain parameters. Analogously, an earth-centered picture of the universe can be said to be true within the limits of naked-eye observations of the heavens. What has happened is that the parameters have shifted, and so traditional Catholic sacramental theory is not as applicable to the known world as it used to be. Hence the problems.

To say it another way, theologians in the Middle Ages invented an explanation that made sense of the religious rituals in their culture and of the personal experiences associated with those rituals. For example, they saw infants being baptized, they saw people attending mass, and they saw adults getting married or being ordained in religious ceremonies. They also perceived the baptized as being saved from hell, they had religious experiences associated with the eucharist, and they sensed the spiritual power of priests. Moreover, biblical and patristic texts suggested what an acceptable explanation might look like, and ancient philosophical texts suggested how physical actions could have spiritual effects. *Sacramentum et res*, as a key term in an explanatory construct, helped scholastic theologians understand how baptism bestowed grace, how bread and wine became the body and blood of Christ, how single people became married couples, and how priests acquired supernatural gifts.

Building on the aforementioned analogy, astronomers in the ancient world invented an explanation that made sense of what they saw in the sky by day and in the heavens by night. The idea that the earth was stationary, that the sun and moon were round bodies that circled it, and that the stars were lights affixed to the dome of the heavens made intuitive sense to everyone. But astronomers, using only naked-eye observations, were able to chart the movements of wandering stars or planets, and to propose a theory to explain those movements: the planets, like the sun and moon, revolved around the earth, but at greater distances. It was an explanation that fit the facts that were available at the time.

Centuries later, when the telescope was invented and more accurate observations could be made, the geocentric model of the heavens was first questioned, then discredited, and finally replaced with a heliocentric model that put the sun at the center and made the earth one of the planets. Similarly, the scholastic explanation of how sacraments work lasted for centuries, but in the face of new observations about Catholic rituals and the experiences associated with them, that theology has begun to be questioned. Nonetheless, the Catholic Church's sacramental doctrines remain stuck in the Middle Ages, in Aristotelian philosophical categories, and in ritualistic performances that have little relevance for many Catholics' lives. Although the Second Vatican Council opened a door to change, real change has not occurred because of the hierarchy's belief that the way things looked in the thirteenth century is the way they still look—or at least ought to look. It is time to discredit that belief and to prove, using documents from the history of sacramental theology, that the *sacramentum et res* is an idea whose time has gone.

In order to offer a thorough treatment of this serious matter, this book's approach will be somewhat circuitous. Chapter one will establish the claim that Catholics use the word "sacrament" in two different senses, and it will summarize sacramental theology as it was taught in Catholic seminaries and universities prior to the Second Vatican Council. To the extent that this theology is still found in the Catechism and the Code of Canon Law, and to the extent that it underlies recent Vatican documents, the scholastic approach to sacramental theology has influence even today. Chapter two will give a historical overview of the developments that culminated in the creation of scholastic sacramental theology. Documents from the first centuries of Christianity will reveal the development of the notion of a non-material or metaphysical reality that is conferred and received through ritual means. A continuation of this examination in the Middle Ages will show how a number of ideas become combined in the general concept of *sacramentum et res* in the scholastic drive to develop a systematic approach to theology, and it will show how the concept fit neatly into the medieval culture of Christendom and later into the modern culture of Tridentine Catholicism. Chapter three will re-examine the same development but from a more critical perspective. It will conclude that the concept of *sacramentum et res*, far from being the timeless entity that the scholastics believed it to be, is actually a concept that is closely related to one form of religious culture. If this is the case, then the concept becomes less relevant (and more dysfunctional) in cultures that are further removed from medieval and Tridentine Catholicism.

Readers who are willing to accept the argument in chapter three, which dismantles the conceptual structure of Catholic sacramental theology, may regard the first two chapters as unnecessary. Others may object, however, saying that what is deconstructed in chapter three is not Catholic theology but a cheap imitation of it, a flimsy hodge-podge of ideas put together so that it can be easily taken apart. In anticipation of such objections, every pertinent biblical, patristic and doctrinal text is examined in chapter one in order to demonstrate clearly the intellectual strength of the scholastic system both as an internally coherent set of ideas and as totally plausible explanation of Catholic practice during the Church's Tridentine era. Likewise, the historical evolution of Catholic thinking about sacraments is presented in chapter two in order to show how and why, at each step of the way, the developments that occurred were intelligent and reasonable, for they were appropriate to what was known about the scriptures and other important writings at the time. Churchmen assumed that ancient texts could be interpreted in ways that made sense to them, regardless of what the texts originally meant. Lacking historical consciousness, they could not be aware that earlier cultures and practices may have been significantly different from their own. If chapter one demonstrates the intellectual strength of the scholastic system, chapter two demonstrates its historical credibility, given the limitations of what the schoolmen knew about the past, and given the philosophical frame of reference within which they worked.

A word remains to be said about chapter four, which is different from the others in a number of ways. Whereas the first three chapters present and analyze the scholastic synthesis, chapter four suggests the possibility of an entirely new approach to sacramental theology, if not a new synthesis. The first three chapters are therefore heavily peppered with footnotes documenting the claims that are made, but the fourth chapter is only lightly salted with references to information with which readers may be unfamiliar. The first three chapters are theological and historical, locating scholastic sacramental theology in its Tridentine context, and then looking two times at the scriptural, patristic and medieval contexts out of which it arose. In contrast, the fourth chapter is philosophical and imaginative, beginning with a phenomenological analysis of symbol and meaning, moving through a critical conception of what is real, and concluding with the imagining of new possibilities for Catholic sacraments that meaningfully symbolize what is real in the lives of individuals and communities.

Readers who are unfamiliar with church history, with sacramental theology, or with Greek and Latin, are advised to read in advance the summary of the argument that begins on page 282, either in its entirety or in sections, as they proceed through this somewhat densely written book.

A Note about Footnotes

SOME ACADEMIC READERS WHO looked at the manuscript prior to publication expressed dissatisfaction with certain aspects of the footnoting. In particular, they would like to have seen more references to scripture scholarship in the biblical sections, more references to historical works in the patristic, medieval and modern sections, and more references to the social sciences and ritual studies in the section on meaning in liturgy and worship. There are reasons why such footnotes were not supplied.

The first reason is that much of the research contained here is original. The vast majority of references are therefore to primary sources in Greek and Latin and not to secondary sources. Moreover, since researching *Doors to the Sacred* in the late 1970s, I have looked at and taken notes on virtually every book published in English about the sacraments and sacramental theology. Very few of them provided information that was pertinent to my argument. For example, every book about the sacraments and scripture translates the words πνεῦμα ἅγιον as "the Holy Spirit," and never as "a holy spirit," despite the absence of the definite article in almost half the places where those words appear in the New Testament. And there is no book about medieval theology that points out that the schoolmen mistakenly interpreted *sacramentum* in biblical and patristic texts as referring to sacraments as they existed in the Middle Ages. The pertinence of these observations will become apparent in chapter three.

Another reason is that part of this work's argument rests on a premise that is not largely accepted in the academic world. The premise is that ideas do not come from nowhere. Thus, if it cannot be shown that an author derived an idea from something that had been written before, I consider the possibility that the idea came from an insight into the author's own experience. When the apostle Paul wrote about spiritual gifts, for example, it is likely that what he said derived from his observation of charismatic behavior in others and even from the experience of charisms in himself. Similarly, when the medieval schoolmen wrote about such things as contrition for sins, the presence of Christ in the Eucharist, and the exercise of priestly powers, it is plausible that in many places they were relying on their observations of Christian religious practices as well as on their own religious experiences, especially when they said things that cannot be found in other texts. With few exceptions, books about the history of the sacraments make little reference to the social world or spiritual lives of ancient and medieval authors.

In those places where readers might want to find additional information about what is said herein about the history and theology of the sacraments, I have here and there provided references to my own books and to others that are readily available in libraries. These footnotes should be regarded as being supplied for convenience and background, not as trying to prove what is found in the text.

The reason why there are no references in chapter four to theories of meaning put forth by social scientists is that I have not found such theories helpful for envisioning the future of sacraments and sacramental theology. Instead, I have relied on insights gleaned from my own experience of meaning and meaningfulness in religious worship, and I have offered explanations that will hopefully make sense to readers in light of their own experience. Ultimately, the verification of what I have written is to be found not in other books but in the minds of those who read the chapter.

I

The Construct

*Scholastic Theology and Sacramental Doctrine**

ALTHOUGH CATHOLIC THEOLOGIANS HAD been thinking systematically about sacraments since the High Middle Ages, the Catholic magisterium did not begin to make organized statements about them until circumstances made it necessary to publicly formulate the content of the Catholic faith. In the fifteenth century, a diplomatic effort to reunite the Orthodox and Catholic churches required each side to present its sacramental doctrines to the other. Although the reunification effort was not successful, it left a helpful record of what the magisterium believed was essential to the Catholic position. A century later, the Protestant Reformation compelled the creation of a more detailed presentation of Catholic beliefs because much of the reformers' energy was directed against what they perceived as abuses in sacramental practice and absurdities in sacramental theory. The Council of Trent's dogmatic pronouncements and ecclesiastical reforms were so far reaching that they defined Catholic teaching and practice for four centuries, in what came to be called the Tridentine era.

According to Catholic doctrine, a sacrament is an ecclesiastical ritual which, when properly performed, has supernatural effects. In the case of the Eucharist, the effect is to change bread and wine into the body and blood of Christ. In the other six cases—baptism, confirmation, penance (now called reconciliation), extreme unction (now called anointing of the sick), marriage, and ordination—the effect is received by those for whom the sacrament is performed. Any sacramental effect is a gift from God—χάρισ in Greek, *gratia* in Latin—commonly referred to as grace in English, or even supernatural grace.

This simple schema is complicated by the fact that sacraments are also said to be received, that is, one of the effects of any sacramental ritual is also called a sacrament. In the case of the Eucharist, the sacrament produced by the words of consecration is the body and blood of Christ, traditionally referred to as the Blessed Sacrament. In the other six cases, the primary effect is a supernatural gift that enables the recipient to

---

* For an abstract of this chapter, please read the summary of the argument that begins on page 282.

receive other supernatural gifts. For example, a person who receives the sacrament of baptism is enabled to receive additional sacraments. Theoretically, then, if an unbaptized couple were united in a Catholic wedding, they would not receive the sacrament of marriage despite having gone through a sacramental ritual.

In the Middle Ages, theologians developed a way to explain the relationship between the two types of sacraments. The sacrament that is the ecclesiastical ritual was called *sacramentum tantum*, meaning only a sign or just a symbol. The sacrament that is received was called *sacramentum et res*, literally meaning sign and thing but connoting something like symbol and reality. Thus the Eucharist, as *sacramentum et res*, was regarded as both a sign of Christ's presence and the reality that it signified. The six received sacraments were spiritual signs that the recipients were different from other people (for example, ordination signified that a priest was different from a lay person) but they were also real in the sense that they enabled the recipients to do things that others could not (for example, a priest could consecrate the Eucharist and forgive sins).

The conceptual construct that became Catholic sacramental doctrine was assembled over the course of centuries and was given dogmatic form by the Council of Trent. In this chapter, the pieces of that construct are presented in a somewhat chronological order, beginning with the term *sacramentum* itself, pointing out its ambiguous reference to both a ritual and as something received. It will then introduce various terms such as grace and character, and it will present the basic doctrine for each of the seven sacraments.

1. Catholic Doctrine in Church Documents

The Council of Trent (1545–1563), convened by Pope Paul III in response to the Protestant Reformation, was largely concerned with defending the Catholic doctrine on the sacraments and with eliminating abuses in worship and other church practices. The intellectual frame of reference within which the council fathers thought and spoke was that of medieval scholasticism. It was not necessarily the scholastic system of Thomas Aquinas, or Thomism, but it was a generally Aristotelian system of thought and analysis that had been introduced to European schools of philosophy and theology in the twelfth century. Philosophical scholasticism had fallen into disfavor by the fifteenth century, and theological scholasticism had been corrupted by legalistic and magical thinking, which is one reason why it was rejected in the sixteenth century by the Protestant reformers. The council did not address all Catholic beliefs and practices but only those that had been attacked or rejected, with the result that Trent's decrees on the sacraments were never comprehensive. Nevertheless, they became the points of doctrine that were emphasized by the Catholic counter-reformation, and they tended to dominate Catholic thought during the modern centuries. For example, Trent's focus on the mass as a sacrifice, the real presence of Christ in the Eucharist,[1] and communion under the species of bread alone neglected scripture and preaching in Christian worship, and that neglect continued until the twentieth century. Moreover, the council often formulated Catholic doctrine in scholastic terminology, for example, teaching that the *substance* of bread is changed into the *substance* of Christ's body even though the *species* of bread remains.[2]

The scholastic way of thinking was taken for granted by modern or Tridentine Catholicism. In 1879 Pope Leo XIII recognized the prominence of St. Thomas Aquinas among the scholastics, making Thomism normative in Catholic philosophy and theology until the Second Vatican Council (1962–1965). The Church's many laws were first codified into a single set of definitions and rules in 1917, and many of the code's definitions and directives concerning the sacraments used scholastic terminology. Even when it was revised in 1983, the Code of Canon Law still spoke of sacraments as being administered and received—a terminology which, though not introduced by the medieval schoolmen, was systematically used by them.[3] Likewise, the 1994 Catechism, although not uniformly scholastic in its sacramental terminology, retains a number of scholastic elements such as the concept of a sacramental character (a type of *sacramentum et res*) that is conferred by certain sacraments.[4]

In summarizing scholastic sacramental theology, it might be helpful to begin with the basic elements that are found in expressions of Catholic doctrine. In addition to the sources already mentioned, use will be made of the Catechism of the Council of Trent (the basis for the Baltimore Catechism, with which many older Catholics are familiar), the 1917 Code of Canon Law, Ludwig Ott's *Fundamentals of Catholic Dogma* (a standard reference work prior to Vatican II), and Bernard Leeming's *Principles of Sacramental Theology*.[5]

1. In this work, the word "eucharist," when it refers to the Blessed Sacrament, understood as the real presence of Christ, is regarded as a proper noun and as such is capitalized. When the word is used in other contexts (e.g., biblical passages, patristic references to a ritual meal, and Protestant theology), it is regarded as a common noun and is left uncapitalized. By convention, the adjective "eucharistic" is always written in lower-case letters.

2. Council of Trent, Decree on the Most Holy Eucharist, ch. 4; found in Henricus Denzinger and Adolfus Schönmetzer, eds., *Enchiridion Symbolorum: Definitionum et Declarationem de Rebus Fidei et Morum* (Freiburg: Verlag Herder, 1963), 1642; also in John F. Clarkson et al., eds., *The Church Teaches: Documents of the Church in English Translation* (St. Louis, MO: B. Herder Book Co., 1964), 722. Since the writing of this chapter, a Latin-English edition of *Enchiridion Symbolorum* has been published as *Compendium of Creeds, Definitions, and Declarations on Matters of Faith and Morals*, edited by Peter Hünermann, Helmut Hoping, Robert L. Fastiggi, Anne Englund Nash, and Heinrich Denzinger (San Francisco: Ignatius Press, 2012). The numbering of the conciliar texts is the same as that found in the earlier Latin edition, used here.

3. See, for example, *Code of Canon Law: Latin-English Edition* (Washington, DC: Canon Law Society of America, 1983), 840–48.

4. *Catechism of the Catholic Church* (Città del Vaticano: Libreria Editrice Vaticana, 1994), 1121 and elsewhere.

5. *The Catechism of the Council of Trent*, Translated by Rev. J. Donovan (New York: Christian

a. Doctrinal Pronouncements

Some scholastic terms appear repeatedly in Catholic sacramental doctrine, and can be said to be presupposed by the doctrines themselves. That is, the terms were in the Christian theological vocabulary at the time when the official teachings were formulated, so they were used in the sense then commonly understood.

One of these key terms is the word, "sacrament," in Latin, *sacramentum*. Originally a translation of the Greek word, μυστήριον, for a long time *sacramentum* had a somewhat vague meaning and a rather broad extension. Augustine famously defined it as a sacred sign, and early scholastics defined it as a sign of something sacred,[6] so the word could be extended to include a wide variety of church rituals, religious symbols, liturgical feasts, and mysteries of faith. By the mid-twelfth century, usage of the word had narrowed somewhat. Hugh of St. Victor (d. 1141) proposed that the word be used only for visible or material signs that contain an invisible or spiritual gift or grace. Peter Lombard (d. 1160) argued that a sacrament "properly so called" is an outward sign that has a visible likeness to an invisible grace and is also a cause of that grace.[7] Lombard restricted the use of the term to seven church rituals that spanned the Christian life from birth to death, and by the time of the Second Council of Lyons (1274) both this understanding of sacrament and their enumeration were accepted by the hierarchy.[8]

Similarly, scholastic terms such as cause and effect, potency and act, matter and form, natural and supernatural, substance and accidents, power and virtue, confer and receive, salvation and justification, character and grace were used in ways originally proposed or refined by medieval theologians. Other terms such as *ex opere operato*, valid and invalid, licit and illicit, marital bond and marital contract were legal terms primarily used in canon law, but they found their way into theological writings and church documents as well. Thus when reading these words in doctrinal statements, they need to be taken in the sense used by the scholastics from the Middle Ages to the modern period, and not in a sense that they might seem to have in contemporary English.

Although the sacraments had been enumerated by the Second Council of Lyons, the Council of Florence (1438–1445) was the first to present a Catholic definition of sacraments. The council had been convened to attempt the reunification of the Orthodox and Roman churches, which had by this time been in schism for almost four hundred years. After listing the seven sacraments (by then traditional in the west, but not yet accepted in the east), the Decree for the Armenians (1439) compared

---

Press Association Publishing Company, no date, but probably c. 1830); Ludwig Ott, *Fundamentals of Catholic Dogma*, trans. Patrick Lynch (St. Louis, MO: B. Herder Book Co., 1962); Bernard Leeming, *Principles of Sacramental Theology* (Westminster, MD: Newman Press, 1956).

6. *The City of God*, 10.5. Ott, *Fundamentals*, 325.

7. Hugh of St. Victor, *The Sacraments of the Christian Faith*, 1.9; Peter Lombard, *Sentences*, 4.1. See Ott, *Fundamentals*, 326.

8. See Denzinger, *Enchiridion Symbolorum*, 860; Clarkson, *Church Teaches*, 660.

the sacraments of the Old Law (i.e., Jewish religious rituals such as circumcision and animal sacrifices) with those of the Christian dispensation, saying,

> . . . our sacraments both contain grace and confer it on those who receive the sacraments worthily. . . . All these sacraments are brought to completion by three components; by things as matter, by words as form, and by the person of the minister effecting the sacrament with the intention of doing what the Church does. And if any one of these is lacking, the sacrament is not effected. Among these sacraments, there are three, baptism, confirmation, and holy orders, which imprint on the soul an indelible character, that is, a certain spiritual sign distinguishing the recipient from others. Hence, these are not given more than once to one person. The other four do not imprint this character and may be repeated.[9]

In this passage, the word "sacraments" and pronouns that refer to sacraments appear a number of times. But what are the sacraments to which they refer? In some places, the word refers to religious rituals. In other places, the word refers to sacraments that are received, and in those places it cannot mean religious rituals for it makes no sense to talk about receiving liturgical performances. As it stands, then, the text is ambiguous, and the referents are not always easy to discern, even though some of the referents are clearly different from others.

- When the decree speaks of sacraments of the Old Law, it clearly means religious rituals, for it observes that these sacraments "did not cause grace but were only a figure of the grace that was to be given through the Passion of Christ."[10]

- But, according to the council fathers, "our sacraments both contain grace and confer it on those who receive the sacraments worthily." Here the first occurrence of "sacraments" is ambiguous, but it most likely means religious rituals, for it is in a sentence contrasting Jewish and Christian rituals. The second occurrence of "sacraments" almost certainly means spiritual realities of some sort: first, because they are what make the seven sacraments of the New Law different from those of the Old Law, which could only prefigure the Christian sacraments; and second, because although material things are received in some Christian sacraments (e.g., baptism, Eucharist, and extreme unction), nothing material is received in others (e.g., penance and matrimony), so the received sacraments cannot be material elements.

- When the document says, "All these sacraments are brought to completion by three components," it is speaking of religious rituals, for it is only the rituals that contain a material element (e.g., water, bread, oil), a formal element (i.e., ideas expressed in words), and an intentional element (wanting to do what the Church

---

9. Clarkson, ibid., 663. See Denzinger, ibid., 1310.
10. Ibid.

wants to do). Received sacraments would not seem to have such components.

- Moreover, when the text says, "And if any one of these is lacking, the sacrament is not effected," it is clearly referring to the sacrament (i.e., the spiritual or non-material reality) that is produced as a result of the ritual action. One does not speak of a ritual being effected or produced, and it would not make much sense to say that if one of the components of the ritual is lacking, then it is not a ritual at all.

- The next sentence starts out speaking of sacraments as church rituals (baptism, confirmation, and holy orders) but it then notes that they "imprint" an indelible character or a spiritual sign "distinguishing the recipient from others."

- The character is clearly something that is received, for the text states that they "are not given more than once to one person." As we have already observed, spiritual realities that are administered and received through church rituals are called sacraments in traditional Catholic terminology. So the character is being thought of as a sacrament of some sort.

- The last sentence quoted above refers to sacraments in both senses, for it says, "The other four [i.e., church rituals] do not imprint this character [i.e., a spiritual reality] and may be repeated."

The remaining paragraphs in the Decree for the Armenians summarize the Roman Catholic teaching, as it stood in the mid-fifteenth century, on each of the seven sacraments.[11] As we shall see later when scholastic sacramental theology is discussed more fully, doctrinal pronouncements such as these do not contain all the details of a fully developed theology (for example, it does not explain how the character is to be understood as an alteration of the soul), but it does contain enough scholastic elements to demonstrate that the council fathers were thinking and writing in scholastic categories.

A century later, the seventh session of the Council of Trent (1547) condemned a number of positions taken by various Protestant reformers, and in doing so it affirmed a number of teachings of the Council of Florence, namely,

- There are seven sacraments of the New Law.[12]

- They contain the grace that they signify, and they confer that grace on those who receive them if they do not obstruct the grace in some way.[13]

- Three sacraments (baptism, confirmation and holy orders) imprint an indelible character or spiritual sign on the soul of the recipient, for which reason these sacraments cannot be repeated.[14]

---

11. See Denzinger, ibid., 1314–27.
12. Denzinger, ibid., 1601; Clarkson, ibid., 665.
13. Denzinger, ibid., 1606; Clarkson, ibid., 670.
14. Denzinger, ibid., 1609; Clarkson, ibid., 673.

In addition, the council taught that if the minister "observes all the essentials that belong to effecting and conferring the sacrament," the sacrament is produced even if the minister is in a state of mortal sin.[15] Trent's reason for this affirmation was to counter the Protestant claim that true sacraments could not be produced by sinful ministers, but our reason for citing it here is to note that sacraments in the sense of spiritual realities are said to be either *effected* or *conferred*. This is because, in the scholastic way of thinking, the sacramental reality of the body and blood of Christ is said to be effected (i.e., produced as an effect) by the act of pronouncing the words of consecration, but the sacramental realities of the other six sacraments are said to be conferred (e.g., matrimony, holy orders, absolution) when their respective rituals are properly performed.

Trent went on to publish canons or rules of faith about all seven of the sacraments, but the only ones that interest us here are those that are directly or indirectly connected with the idea of a received sacrament that is both symbolic and real, i.e., the concept of *sacramentum et res*. Such canons are always written in a condemnatory formula, beginning with the words, "If anyone would say" (*Si quis dixerit*), and ending with the words, "may he be accursed" (*anathema sit*). It will better suit our exposition, however, to extract the Catholic doctrine and present it in a straightforward manner, as we did above. Thus, for example if there were a canon that read, "If anyone would say that baptism is not a sacrament instituted by Christ, may he be accursed," we would recast the wording more positively as, "Baptism is a sacrament instituted by Christ."

None of the Protestant reformers questioned the existence of baptism or its institution by Christ (cf. Matt. 28:19), but two things they did argue about were its relation to salvation and the notion of rebaptizing those who had been baptized earlier in life. Thus the council declared the following:

- Baptism is necessary for salvation.[16]

- Those who renounce their faith and later repent should not be rebaptized.[17]

- Those who were baptized in infancy, when they were too young to make an act of faith, should not be rebaptized.[18]

The theological reason for not rebaptizing had already been presented in the general canons on the sacraments, namely, that there are sacraments which imprint an indelible character on the soul and which therefore cannot be repeated. The idea here is not that the church ritual cannot be repeated, for the physical action could certainly be performed, even if doing so were contrary to canon law. (The Anabaptists were rebaptizing quite regularly!) Rather, the idea is that baptizing a second time would

---

15. Denzinger, ibid., 1612; Clarkson, ibid., 676.

16. Denzinger, ibid., 1618; Clarkson, ibid., 691.

17. Denzinger, ibid., 1624; Clarkson, ibid., 697.

18. Denzinger, ibid., 1626; Clarkson, ibid., 699.

not confer the sacrament of baptism again, or to say it perhaps a little more clearly, performing the ritual over would not confer the sacramental reality a second time. For if the sacramental reality (the baptismal character) is indeed permanent or indelible, then going through the baptismal ritual again would not give people anything that they did not already have. It would be like putting a second (and identical) tattoo on top of a first.

The necessity of baptism for salvation was affirmed to counter the claim of some Protestants (who cited scripture passages such as John 3:5, Rom. 3:22, and Eph. 2:8) that salvation required faith at the time of baptism, and that therefore infant baptism is of no avail. Note, however, that the council's claim is not that baptism is all that is needed for salvation. Note too that "salvation" is left undefined, but it can be taken to mean the soul's going to heaven after death, for that is the meaning the word generally had for Catholics in the Middle Ages and the early modern period.

Confirmation often gets short shrift in church documents. Trent devoted only three canons to this sacrament, affirming that it is a true sacrament, that some power (*virtutem*) can be attributed to the sacramental anointing, and that the ordinary minister of this sacrament is a bishop.[19] As with baptism, the sacramental character bestowed in confirmation was treated earlier, in Trent's general treatment of sacraments.

Eucharist, on the other hand, received extensive treatment, not only because it is central to Christian faith and worship but also because the reformers attacked a number of traditional Catholic beliefs and practices. First and foremost of these was the doctrine of real presence, the teaching that Christ is really present in the sacrament, which was expounded in eight chapters and eleven canons.

- "[I]n the blessed sacrament of the Holy Eucharist, after the consecration of the bread and wine, our Lord Jesus Christ, true God and man, is truly, really, and substantially contained under the perceptible species of bread and wine." Here the doctrine of real presence is formulated in very scholastic terminology, saying that Christ is substantially (*substantialiter*) contained (*contineri*) under the appearances (*species*) of bread and wine. The word "substantially" is used in opposition to Protestant claims that Christ is present in a symbolic or figurative fashion (*in signo vel figura*) or by his power (*virtute*). In other words, the consecrated elements are a sacramental reality (*sacramentum et res*) for they are both truly Christ and truly a sign of his presence, and hence, a blessed sacrament.[20] Note, however, that the technical term, *sacramentum et res*, does not appear in the council documents, although the concept (as we shall see later) is clearly in the scholastic tradition.

- Christ "instituted this sacrament at the Last Supper."[21] Although pious Catholic

---

19. Denzinger, ibid., 1628–30; Clarkson, ibid., 708–10.

20. Denzinger, ibid., 1636, 1651; Clarkson, ibid., 719, 728.

21. Denzinger, ibid., 1637; Clarkson, ibid., 719.

art sometimes depicted Jesus at the last supper distributing communion wafers to kneeling apostles, the sacrament being referred to here is the sacramental reality (*sacramentum et res*), the invisible sacrament, if you will, rather than the visible one. In other words, the claim is not that Jesus designed the Latin mass but that he brought into being the sacramental reality that is brought into being by the saying of his words in the mass.

- "[B]y the consecration of the bread and wine a change takes place in which the whole substance of bread is changed into the whole substance of the body of Christ our Lord and the whole substance of the wine into the substance of his blood. This change the holy Catholic Church fittingly and properly names transubstantiation."[22] Again, "substance" (*substantia*) is a technical term in scholasticism meaning something that is real. The idea here is that something that was really bread and wine becomes something that is really different, namely, a divine person. Hence, it is most aptly (*aptissime*) called transubstantiation (*transubstantionem*). Note that transubstantiation is not declared to be a doctrine but a very apt way of naming the eucharistic change that takes place.[23] This was done out of deference to those scholastic theologians who, although totally orthodox in their doctrinal positions, held that the theory of consubstantiation was a better explanation of eucharistic change.

- Because Christ's humanity cannot be separated from his divinity, and because in his humanity his body cannot be separated from his blood, the whole Christ is truly present in both forms (under both *species*) of the sacrament.[24]

- Those who receive communion worthily receive Christ both sacramentally and spiritually.[25] In more precise scholastic terminology, they receive both the *sacramentum et res* (the Blessed Sacrament) and the *res sacramenti* (the grace of Christ's presence, as well as other spiritual gifts).

Trent's remaining chapters and canons on the Eucharist regard the reception of communion (under one or both forms, by children, etc.) and with the sacrifice of the mass (its explanation and practice), and so they do not pertain directly to the topic of this study.

The Council of Trent dealt extensively with the sacrament of penance, in part because of its association with the notion of indulgences for the remission of spiritual punishment in the afterlife. The crass selling of indulgences had been the spark that

22. Denzinger, ibid., 1642, 1652; Clarkson, ibid., 722, 729.

23. The early history of the mistaken belief that transubstantiation is a Catholic doctrine can be found in James McCue, "The Doctrine of Transubstantiation from Berengar through the Council of Trent," in Paul C. Empie and T. Austin Murphy, eds., *Lutherans and Catholics in Dialogue III: The Eucharist as Sacrifice* (Minneapolis, MN: Augsburg Publishing House, 1967) 89–124.

24. Denzinger, *Enchiridion Symbolorum*, 1639–41; Clarkson, *Church Teaches*, 721, 730, 731.

25. Denzinger, ibid., 1648, 1658; Clarkson, ibid., 726, 735.

ignited the Protestant reformation. Indulgences, however, were given separate treatment in the last session of the council.[26]

The council's canons on penance that are of interest to us may be summed up briefly.

- Penance is a sacrament instituted by Christ as a remedy for sins committed after baptism.[27]

- The sacramental ritual, popularly known as confession, is composed of matter and form, the form being the words of absolution spoken by the minister. The effect of receiving the sacrament is reconciliation with God and forgiveness of sin.[28]

Again, the institution by Christ (appealing to John 20:22–23) is the institution of the sacramental reality, not the externals (matter and form) of the sacrament. *Matter* and *form*, as already noted, are philosophical terms that were used by the scholastics to refer to the material elements in a sacramental ritual (e.g., bread and wine in the Eucharist) and to the meaning of the ritual as expressed in words. In the case of penance, there is no material element as such, and so the penitent's contrition, the confession of sins and performing works of repentance are called the "quasi-matter" of the sacrament.[29] Although the sacrament (i.e., the spiritual reality) is spoken of as something that is received (*suscipiatur*),[30] the reference to it is not very specific. In fact Catholic theologians were never very clear about the *sacramentum et res* of penance, even though before Vatican II it was common to speak about "receiving the sacrament of penance" when referring to the practice of going to confession.

The sacrament of extreme unction (today called anointing of the sick) may also be treated briefly.

- Extreme unction is a sacrament instituted by Christ which confers grace, which forgives sins, and which comforts the sick.[31]

- The matter of the sacrament is oil that has been blessed by a bishop, and the form is found in the words spoken by the priest while anointing the sick person.[32]

As in the case of penance, Catholics prior to Vatican II spoke about "receiving the sacrament of extreme unction," but neither the bishops at Trent nor subsequent theologians were clear about the *sacramentum et res* associated with this rite.

---

26. Denzinger, ibid., 1835; Clarkson, ibid., 828. Note that the translation in *The Church Teaches* does not contain the condemnation of abuses mentioned in the Latin original.

27. Denzinger, ibid., 1668–72, 911–12; Clarkson, ibid., 800–801.

28. Denzinger, ibid., 1673–78; Clarkson, ibid., 790–92.

29. Denzinger, ibid., 1704; Clarkson, ibid., 803.

30. Denzinger, ibid., 1677; Clarkson, ibid., 792.

31. Denzinger, ibid., 1716–17; Clarkson, ibid., 835–36.

32. Denzinger, ibid., 1695; Clarkson, ibid., 832.

The Council of Trent paid special attention to holy orders, not only because many of the reformers attacked the medieval understanding of priesthood but also because reforming the clergy was essential for stopping the clerical abuses that had led to widespread dissatisfaction with the medieval church order. The bishops were therefore careful to treat this sacrament in some detail.

- Ordination is a sacrament instituted by Christ, which imprints a character that can never be lost.[33]

- By virtue of their ordination, priests have the "power of consecrating and offering the body and blood of the Lord, and of remitting and retaining sins."[34]

- There are different grades or orders of ministry to this sacrament, which is also called the sacrament of order (*sacramentum ordinis*) or holy orders.[35]

- Bishops have the power and authority to ordain priests and administer confirmation.[36]

The priestly character, which is permanent, is the sacramental reality that is bestowed in the rite of ordination. The character, which is both *sacramentum* and *res*, is the reason why priests have the power to consecrate the Eucharist and to remit sins, although the precise relationship between the character and these powers is left undetermined. The character also gives bishops the power to confirm and ordain, although the reason why bishops can do things that priests cannot is also not determined.

Finally, the sacrament of matrimony is defined exclusively in terms of the marriage bond, which is understood to be a sacramental reality in the scholastic conceptual system.

- Matrimony is a sacrament which was instituted by Christ and which confers grace.[37]

- The marriage bond cannot be dissolved except in rare cases when the marriage has not been consummated.[38]

Again here, what was instituted by Christ is the invisible sacrament (*sacramentum et res*) for it is clear from the gospels that wedding ceremonies were already in existence when Jesus was alive. Thus, it is the sacramental reality which is said to confer grace.

---

33. Denzinger, ibid., 1773–74; Clarkson, ibid., 846–47.

34. Denzinger, ibid., 1764, 1771; Clarkson, ibid., 840, 844.

35. Denzinger, ibid., 1765, 1773; Clarkson, ibid., 841, 846.

36. Denzinger, ibid., 1768, 1777; Clarkson, ibid., 843, 850.

37. Denzinger, ibid., 1798–99, 1801; Clarkson, ibid., 855, 857.

38. Denzinger, ibid., 1805–7; Clarkson, ibid., 861–63.

The *sacramentum et res* of matrimony is not a character but a bond between two persons. Implicit in the council's teaching[39] is that a marriage bond is dissolved upon the death of one of the spouses, unlike a character, which can never be lost. Trent does not use the language of administering or receiving this sacrament.

In summary, Trent's doctrinal pronouncements use the word "sacrament" in two different senses without explaining the difference between them. Moreover, they formulate Catholic doctrine in concepts inherited from the Aristotelian-scholastic theory of sacramental effectiveness, for example, matter and form, substance and accidents, validity and invalidity, supernatural grace, and character as an indelible mark. Nonetheless, the doctrines are primarily concerned with received sacraments or sacramental realities, not with sacramental rites. The received sacraments are understood to be spiritual realities that account for various aspects of Christian society such as membership in the church, priestly powers, and the permanence of marriage.

b. The Catechism of the Council of Trent

The Roman Catechism (the official name of the catechism promulgated for the universal church after the Council of Trent) reiterates and expands on the doctrines proclaimed by the council, so there is no need here to summarize what it contains. Suffice it to say that proper indoctrination about the sacraments was a primary concern of the council fathers, because abuse of the sacramental system was largely responsible for the Protestant objections to Catholic beliefs and practices. As set forth in the council's call for a catechism,

> That the faithful may approach the Sacraments with greater reverence and devotion, the Holy Synod commands all Bishops not only to explain, in a manner accommodated to the capacity of the receivers, the nature and use of the Sacraments, when they are to be administered by themselves; but also to see that every Pastor piously and prudently do the same, in the vernacular language, should it be necessary and convenient. This exposition is to accord with a form to be prescribed by the Holy Synod for the administration of all the Sacraments, in a Catechism, which Bishops will take care to have faithfully translated into the vernacular language, and expounded to the people by all pastors.[40]

This catechism, first published in Latin in 1566, was intended to be used by bishops as a guide to what ought to be contained in local catechisms to be published in the languages spoken by Catholics around the world. Although an English translation of this catechism was available as early as 1816 in Great Britain, the American edition

---

39. See Denzinger, ibid., 1807; Clarkson, ibid., 863.

40. Cited in *Catechism of the Council of Trent*, p. 3. The reference is to Session XXIV, the Decree on Reformation (i.e., ecclesiastical reforms to be implemented after the council), 7.

commonly called the Baltimore Catechism did not appear until 1885.[41] Versions of this catechism, adapted for younger and older children, were used in the instruction of children in the United States until the 1960s. It is divided into four major parts: (1) The Twelve Articles of the Creed, (2) The Sacraments, (3) The Decalogue, and (4) Prayer (especially the Lord's Prayer), with the section on the sacraments comprising one third of the book—more than any other section. In that section, as in the decree cited above, sacraments are said to be administered and received, but nothing more is said about the nature of those sacramental realities beyond what was laid down by the council.

c. The 1917 Code of Canon Law

For centuries, the Roman Catholic Church's legal structure rested on a concatenation of conciliar, synodal and papal decrees, universal and local legislation, papal and episcopal rules enacted at various times and places during more than a millennium of institutional history. It was not until 1904 that Pope Pius X ordered a simplification and codification of all these laws and regulations, resulting in the first Code of Canon Law for the universal church in 1917 during the pontificate of Pope Benedict XV.[42]

The Code itself was not directly concerned with liturgy, whose proper performance was regulated by the rubrics and notes found in official missals and sacramentaries. It therefore contains scant reference to sacraments as ritual actions or liturgical acts, and almost all of its references both to sacraments in general and to particular sacraments regard sacraments that are confected, administered and received (c. 733 §1). The first part of Book Three, covering canons 731 to 1153, contained the legislation on the sacraments.

Since the Code's treatment of sacraments as spiritual realities is so pervasive, a textual analysis is prohibitive and a statistical analysis will have to suffice.

In the **introductory canons** 731–736, sacraments are said to be *administered* three times, *received* two times, *conferred* two times, and *effected* one time. The last reference is to the Eucharist, which was understood to be brought into existence by a validly ordained priest saying the words of consecration over bread and wine. Canon 732 also mentions the sacramental character of baptism, confirmation and orders, which is spoken of as being *conferred* or *imprinted*.

In canons 737–779, **baptism** is said to be *administered* four times and *conferred* fifteen times. It is never spoken of as being received, and the person being baptized is

---

41. See "Baltimore, Archdiocese of," *New Catholic Encyclopedia* (London:Thompson/Gale 2003) Vol. 2, 40–41.

42. The *Codex Juris Canonici* was available in a number of Latin editions, including ones published in the United States by The Newman Press of Westminster, Maryland, by special permission of the Holy See. It is available in English translation under the title, *The 1917 or Pio-Benedictine Code of Canon Law*, edited by Edward N. Peters (San Francisco: Ignatius Press, 2001).

not referred to as the recipient of the sacrament but as the subject of baptism (c. 745). There is no mention of a sacramental character in this section; it is baptism that is said to be conferred, not the character. In the section "On the rites and ceremonies of baptism," the baptismal ritual is not referred to as a sacrament, but only as a rite or ceremony. The emphasis is entirely on the sacrament as something that is conferred through the performance of the ecclesiastical ritual. As we shall see later, when we get to the scholastic theology of baptism, the received sacrament (in this case, baptism), the character, and the *sacramentum et res* are one and the same.

In canons 780–785, **confirmation** is said to be *administered* six times and *conferred* six times. Again, the character is not mentioned by name, but confirmation is said to be *received* in canons 974 (on ordination) and 1021 (on marriage), where the reference is undoubtedly to the sacramental character mentioned in canon 732.

Canons 801–869 are on the **Eucharist**, which in scholastic terminology was said to be confected by a priest through the prayers of consecration said at mass, but the word "confect" does not appear in this section. The Eucharist is said to be *administered* six times and *received* five times, but the reference is clearly to administration and reception of holy communion, or the Blessed Sacrament, and not merely to bread and wine. Thus implicitly these canons refer to the sacramental reality or the real presence of Christ under the appearances of bread and wine, else why the care to be taken in its administration and reception? The brief section "On the rites and ceremonies of Mass" speaks of the mass as a sacrifice, not as a sacrament, nor are the bread and wine referred to as sacraments. The Code's focus is on the *sacramentum et res*, not the *sacramentum tantum*.

Canons 870–910 are on **penance**, but the word "sacrament" hardly appears; instead, it is displaced by the word "confession" and its cognates. To some extent, then, the emphasis in this section is on the sacramental rite rather than on the sacramental reality, about which there was some theological uncertainty.[43] When canon 870 speaks of "the sacrament of penance" it is clearly speaking of the rite of confession. And the person who goes to confession is referred to as the subject of the sacrament, not the recipient of the sacrament, in the section on who should confess their sins (cc. 901–907).

Canons 911–936 are on indulgences and need not concern us here.

Canons 937–947 are on **extreme unction**, as the anointing of the sick was then called. The sacrament is spoken of as *administered* four times, as *conferred* three times, and as *received* one time. The reference is clearly to the *sacramentum et res*, although the nature of that sacramental reality is not identified, there being the same theological uncertainty here as with the sacrament of penance.

Canons 948–1011 are on the sacrament of **order** (*ordo* in Latin), although in English it is usually referred to as holy orders—a reference to the minor and major

---

43. There was no uncertainty that a sacramental reality was received, but the nature of that metaphysical entity was uncertain, since it was neither a character nor a divine presence.

orders or ecclesiastical ranks to which men were ordained in the Tridentine church.[44] The sacrament and various orders are spoken of as being *conferred* thirteen times, and as being *received* twice. The sacrament is never spoken of as being administered. More often, the canons speak of bishops *ordaining* and of subjects *being ordained*. When the term *ordination* is used, it does not refer primarily to the concrete liturgical ritual (which is never described) but to the activity of conferring various orders, that is, of bestowing the sacramental reality, considered in general, as in canons 964.1, 968 §1, 992, and 1003.

Canons 1012–1143 on **marriage** never mention the term "sacrament" except in canon 1012, which states that "Christ the Lord raised the marriage contract to the dignity of a sacrament among the baptized," and that for Christians "there can be no valid contract of marriage without its also being a sacrament." As can be seen from these opening sentences of the section on marriage, marriage is regarded as a contract between two persons. Thus, the Code speaks of the *contract*, or more simply, of *marriage*; but since marriage = contract = sacrament, whenever it talks of marriage or the marriage contract, it is speaking abut the sacrament of marriage, and "contracting a marriage" is equivalent to two people "receiving the sacrament." The priest who presides at a wedding is said to assist at a marriage (cc. 1095–1098), and the ceremony itself is called the celebration of marriage (cc. 1100, 1003). In the Code, there is no mention of the sacrament being administered or conferred; in scholastic theology it was understood to be conferred by the spouses on one another.

In summary, the 1917 Code of Canon Law continues the Tridentine practice of speaking about sacraments as invisible entities that are both administered and received. The reality of received sacraments is assumed without question.

2. Scholastic Sacramental Theology before Vatican II

If in general the task of theology is to make sense of the data of religion, and if in particular the task of Catholic sacramental theology is to explain the church's ecclesiastical rituals, the data on the sacraments has been understood to be found in the doctrinal pronouncements of the Roman Catholic Church, primarily those of the Council of Trent. The bishops at Trent, it should be noted, appealed to the scriptures, to writings of the church fathers, and to the decrees of earlier councils, so earlier doctrinal data were implicitly included in the official affirmations and anathemas of the Church in the sixteenth century. Neither the Roman Catechism nor the 1917 Code of Canon Law added to the body of doctrine, but they sometimes made explicit what was implicit in the conciliar documents. For example, the Catechism confirmed the

---

44. The Second Vatican Council redefined the major orders as deaconate, presbyterate and episcopate, and implicitly eliminated the minor orders that had existed in the church for many centuries. Information about this redefinition of orders can be found *passim* in the decrees on bishops, priests, priestly formation, and missions.

terminology of administering and receiving the sacraments. Also, the Code gave this terminology systematic expression, and it frequently made the notion of administering more exact through its use of the word, "conferring."

Moreover, Catholic bishops and canonists thought and wrote within a broad theological framework of medieval scholasticism, which itself was an adaptation of classical Aristotelianism. This interrelated set of philosophical terms (e.g., matter and form, substance and accidents, potency and act) provided an intellectual framework within which the doctrines could be stated, and from which logical implications could be drawn. For example, the Code equated the marriage contract with the marriage bond spoken of by Trent, and both the bond and the contract were equated with marriage. Since marriage was understood to be a sacrament instituted by Christ, then the contract entered into by the spouses and the bond created between them could be understood as a sacramental reality, a *sacramentum et res.*

Catholic theologians, operating within this framework and often writing in Latin even well into the twentieth century, developed a Catholic sacramental theology that was systematically Aristotelian and methodically scholastic, that is, they developed a systematic theology of the sacraments using a general method introduced by Anselm and Abelard, developed by Lombard and Aquinas, and refined by Scotus and Suarez.[45] By the Tridentine period, the method generally treated theological issues (not just sacramental ones) by stating Catholic doctrines, presenting proof texts from the scriptures, the fathers and councils, and refuting the errors of Protestants and other heretics. With regard to the less dogmatic issues (about which there could be legitimate disagreement among Catholic theologians), positions were taken, arguments for the position included ideas taken from earlier scholastics such as Aquinas or Suarez, and arguments against other positions were provided.

In the nineteenth century, the scholastic method had devolved into a somewhat mechanical and apologetic style labeled manualist theology by its critics, for it appeared in the form of Latin theology manuals used in seminaries, which presented Catholic teachings and acceptable theological positions in great detail, and which gave rather short shrift to the teachings of non-Catholic churches and the positions of non-Catholic theologians (the *adversarii*). This state of affairs was ameliorated somewhat by the immense amount of historical research done primarily by scholars during the first half of the twentieth century, resulting in critical editions of medieval works (primarily those of Thomas Aquinas) and numerous monographs by Catholic philosophers and theologians on the accurate interpretation of scholastic texts. Thus by the mid-twentieth century, scholastic theology had attained greater intellectual respectability, and it demonstrated its vitality by blossoming into self-styled neo-scholastic

---

45. See Martin Grabmann, *Die Geschichte der scholastischen Methode: Nach den gedruckten und ungedruckten Quellen* (Darmstadt, Germany: Wissenschaftliche Buchgesellschaft, 1956). Also Yves Congar, *A History of Theology* (Garden City, NY: Doubleday and Company, 1968).

and neo-Thomist schools of thought.[46] The best known figures in Catholic philosophy and theology just prior to Vatican II (e.g., Karl Rahner in Germany, Edward Schillebeeckx in Holland, Yves Congar in France, and Bernard Lonergan in Canada) were all steeped in scholastic and Thomistic thinking.

It can be argued that scholasticism and neo-scholasticism reached an apex in the 1950s and 1960s, when Catholic doctrines were still rather clear and Catholic theology was still rather apologetic in the sense that it explained the truths of faith and did not question them. Two works that appeared in those decades will be used here to demonstrate how Catholic thinkers at the height of scholasticism in the mid-twentieth century articulated and explained the Church's sacramental doctrines and practices. *Fundamentals of Catholic Dogma* by Ludwig Ott was first published in German by Verlag Herder in 1952; the first edition of the English translation appeared in 1955 published by The Mercier Press of Cork, Ireland and the B. Herder Book Company of St. Louis, Missouri. The 544-page volume is divided into five books, with Book Four covering the topics of grace, the church, and the sacraments; but this one book is as long as the other four combined, or about half of the total material, indicating the importance of ecclesiology and sacramentology in Tridentine Catholicism. *Principles of Sacramental Theology* by Bernard Leeming was published by The Newman Press of Westminster and Baltimore, Maryland, in 1956, but it was printed in England, where Leeming was on the faculty of Heythrop College in London. Over 600 pages long with numerous references to and quotations from earlier works, it too is a testimony to the centrality of sacraments in Catholic life and theology during the period when scholasticism thrived—from the Middle Ages to the mid-twentieth century.[47] Both men were priests and scholars who taught in Catholic institutions; Leeming was also a Jesuit.

a. Grace

Both Ott and Leeming open their discussion of sacraments with a treatment of grace.[48] The word in English can be used to speak about many things, from gracefulness in movement or form, to a favor or blessing, to a prayer of thanksgiving. But in Tridentine Catholicism, grace was often referred to "as a thing, an object, almost as if it were tangible or movable."[49] Trent had dogmatically affirmed that the sacraments "contain the grace which they signify and bestow it on those who do not hinder it."[50] The Bal-

46. See "Scholasticism," *New Catholic Encyclopedia*, (London: Thompson/Gale, 2003) Vol. 12, 757–78; "Thomism," *ibid.*, Vol. 14, 40–51; "Neoscholasticism and Neothomism," *ibid.*, Vol. 10, 244. Scholarly journals that supported these developments in Catholic philosophy and theology were *The New Scholasticism* (published from 1927 to 1989) and *The Thomist* (launched in 1939 and still being published).

47. See above, note 5.

48. Ott, *Fundamentals*, 219–69. Leeming, *Principles*, 3–125.

49. Leeming, ibid., 3.

50. Ott, *Fundamentals*, 328; See Denzinger, *Enchiridion Symbolorum*, 1606, Clarkson, *Church*

timore Catechism spoke of sanctifying grace, actual grace, and sacramental grace. Theologians wrote about created and uncreated grace, antecedent and consequent grace, external and internal grace, to name but a few of the categories into which grace was sorted.

The word "grace" is a transliteration of the Latin word *gratia*, a translation of the Greek word χάρις, which had as varied a usage as the English word noted above. In the context of sacramental theology, however, it might be helpful (even if somewhat of a simplification) to think of grace, *gratia* and χάρις in their basic meaning of *gift*. Thus sanctifying grace can be thought of as a gift from God that promotes sanctity, actual grace can be thought of as a gift of God in the doing of something (*in actu exercito*), sacramental grace can be thought of as a gift of God associated with a sacrament, and so on. Moreover, not all of the categories listed in the preceding paragraph were mutually exclusive; for example, actual graces associated with church rituals could also be called sacramental graces, such as the grace of remorse received by a sinner when going to confession, which might also be considered an internal grace and a consequent grace. What all "types" of grace had in common is that they were God's freely bestowed gifts.

It would seem that "grace" is a term that is first employed in hindsight. One narrowly escapes a car accident and attributes it to divine intervention—a grace or gift from God. One lands a job after a long unemployment and thanks God for the gift, or in Protestant terminology, for the blessing. One listens to a sermon and feels spiritually moved; Evangelicals might call this being blessed, but older Catholics would have called it an actual grace. In the history of Christianity, however, results that were originally named gifts in retrospect, such as membership in the Christian community, become anticipated and called grace, such as the grace of union with the Church. Although graces in the sense of God's gifts or blessings are always particular and concrete, Catholic preachers and theologians in the past tended to generalize them and talk about them rather abstractly as grace. Hence the tendency, noted above, to talk about grace as something tangible and almost quantifiable.

In talking about the sacraments and grace, therefore, it might be helpful to use the word "gift" rather than "grace" in certain places. The grace that got referred to in English as sanctifying grace (literally the grace that enables sanctity) was termed *gratia gratum faciens* (the gift making one gifted) by the young Thomas Aquinas in his commentary on Peter Lombard's *Sentences*.[51] Implicit in that more cumbersome name for the grace is the notion that God gives Christians the gifts they need in order to be good and ultimately to be holy. St. Augustine had argued successfully against Pelagius

---

Teaches, 670.

51. Book IV, d. 1, q. 1, a. 4, qc. 5. Aquinas does not refer to *gratia gratum faciens* or *gratia sanctificans* in the *Summa Theologica*, but speaks only more generally of *gratia*. The term came into more general use in later scholasticism. See Ott, *Fundamentals*, 221-22.

that human beings cannot lead lives of sustained goodness without God's help,[52] and so in the medieval perspective, baptism is necessary for salvation because in being baptized people receive the grace (the gifts) they need to follow Christ and ultimately to experience the beatific vision in heaven.

In one sense, all is grace. God owes us nothing, so all the beauty and goodness in the world—indeed, the entire universe and life itself—are God's gifts to us. But the scholastics did not refer to the gifts of nature (either the world around us or our human nature) as instances of grace. Instead, they reserved the term *gratia* for those gifts that were above and beyond God's natural gifts; hence these were called supernatural gifts or supernatural grace.

To the medieval mind, one example of a supernatural gift would have been the information God had given to human beings in the scriptures. It seemed that without God's revelation, we would have no knowledge of the creation of the world and the fall of Adam and Eve, we would not have the Ten Commandments and the Eight Beatitudes, and we would know nothing about the incarnation of Christ and redemption of the human race.[53] But the scholastics also reasoned that, in order to accept God's revelation in the Bible, and even to recognize the Judeo-Christian scriptures as God's word, supernatural help was needed; otherwise, it would not be perceived as coming from God but only as ancient literature.[54] Also, while Christian philosophy in the natural law tradition would have said it is possible for human beings to know right from wrong and to perform morally good acts without special help from God, Christian theology asserted that neither pagans nor the baptized could avoid sinning in the long run without God's grace.[55] Moreover, to perform acts that merit salvation, even the natural acts of Christians must be elevated by God (e.g., through an actual grace) to a supernatural level, since the simple performance of morally good acts are not in themselves capable of receiving a supernatural reward.[56]

But God can raise not only individual acts to a supernatural level; he can also give the baptized the ability to perform entire classes of action that are above the capability of human nature. Priests, for example, can confect the Eucharist and absolve sins, which are supernatural acts, and they do not need an actual grace every time they do it. But even ordinary Christians habitually believe in God, hope for salvation, and

---

52. See Ott, ibid., on the necessity of grace, 229–33. On the historical background, see Bernard Lonergan, *Grace and Freedom* (New York: Herder and Herder, 1971), ch. 1.

53. See Ott, ibid., on external grace, 221.

54. "Internal supernatural grace is absolutely necessary for the beginning of faith and of salvation. (*De fide.*)" Ott, 229.

55. "Without this gift, in the actual order of things in which we live, man is incapable of fulfilling his own nature; for he cannot overcome the forces of evil within and without himself unless he is sustained and uplifted by God's supernatural help." Leeming, *Principles*, 5. See also Ott, *Fundamentals*, 231–36.

56. "For every salutary act[, the] internal supernatural grace of God (*gratia sanans*) is absolutely necessary. (*De fide.*)" Ott, ibid., 229.

love others selflessly, so the ability to perform such elevated acts repeatedly is more economically explained as God's infusion of habitual grace into the soul. This is the gift that is commonly called sanctifying grace since it enables the performance of acts that demonstrate and even increase the holiness of the performer. This is also the gift that is sometimes referred to as *gratia gratum faciens*, the gift that makes one gifted by salvation and holiness, as mentioned above.[57]

Sacramental grace, as its name implies, is a gift that is received through the sacraments, and since there are different sacraments, the scholastics generally agreed that there are different sacramental graces. But is sacramental grace different from sanctifying grace? In answering this question, the scholastics were divided. According to some, "Sacramental grace is nothing else than sanctifying grace, together with a right or title to actual graces when they are needed in order to fulfill the purpose of the sacrament."[58] According to others, "Sacramental grace is something like an infused habit, which flows from sanctifying graces and is distinct from it as are the infused virtues."[59] In either view, however, it is a type of habitual grace or a God-given ability to perform on a consistent basis certain types of acts related to the different purposes of the different sacraments.[60]

b. Sacrament

As already noted, Catholic theologians tend to use the word "sacrament" in two senses without adverting to which sense they are intending in any given instance, and without alerting their readers to it. In his treatment of "The Doctrine of the Sacraments in General," for example, Ludwig Ott devotes 25 pages to talking about sacramental rituals as performed, and only occasionally speaks of them being administered or received—and then without noting that he is speaking about sacraments in a different sense.

After an initial page about the etymology of the word, Ott cites the Roman Catechism's definition of a sacrament as "a thing perceptible to the senses, which on the ground of Divine institution possesses the power both of effecting and signifying sanctity and righteousness."[61] He then speaks about "The Constituent Parts of the Sacramental Sign," mentioning briefly that, in addition to the visible rite and the invisible grace, there is also "an intermediary element," the *res et sacramentum*, but he does not explain what it is.[62] Writing next about the efficacy of the sacraments, their mode of operation and their effects, Ott continues to speak about sacraments as religious

---

57. See ibid., 221–22.

58. Leeming, *Principles*, 100.

59. Ibid.

60. On this point, see ibid., 96. For a fuller treatment, see 94–125.

61. Ott, *Fundamentals*, 326. The reference in the Catechism is to 2.1.8. In the translation by Donovan cited above, the definition is found on page 102, worded slightly differently.

62. Ibid., 327–28.

rituals. Three sacraments (baptism, confirmation and holy orders) are said to "imprint a character, that is, an indelible spiritual mark" on the soul, but he does not identify the character as a sacrament that is received.[63] Even when talking about the institution of the sacraments by Christ, it is not clear whether he is talking about the visible rites, the received sacraments, or both; and although he argues that "Christ fixed the substance of the Sacraments" and not necessarily the details of each ritual, he does not explain what he means by "the substance."[64] Could he mean the sacramental reality, the *sacramentum et res*?

This ambiguity remains as Ott goes on to discuss the necessity of the sacraments and the minister of the sacraments. It is only when he gets to "The Recipient of the Sacraments" that it is clear that he must be talking about the sacramental reality, even though he himself does not make this clarification.[65] In treating the sacrament of penance, he does not mention the sacramental reality, although when talking about the recipient of the sacrament, he is clearly not referring to the rite of confession.[66] The same can be said about the sacrament of extreme unction and its recipient.[67] Ott's failure to say much about the *sacramentum et res* (except in relation to the characters received in baptism, confirmation and ordination, the bond of matrimony, and the consecrated Eucharist) is probably due to his work's focus on basic dogmas rather than on theological explanations, but his book does illustrate how Catholics easily slide from talking about a religious ritual as a sacrament to talking about one of the effects of the ritual as a sacrament.

c. Sacramental Reality

At the basic level of Catholic doctrine, it is clear that something is received in a sacramental ritual—something that is called a sacrament.[68] Although Ott does not give a theological explanation for this received sacrament, he does refer to it as a character—a term introduced by Augustine and repeatedly used in doctrinal pronouncements—in the case of baptism, confirmation and holy orders. In the case of marriage, the sacrament is a contract or bond between the spouses.[69] In the cases of penance and extreme unction, the received sacrament is not specified. Eucharist is a special case, for the Blessed Sacrament is said to be effected or confected independently of its being administered or received as holy communion.

---

63. Ibid., 333–35. He does, however, refer to it as a "sacramental character."
64. Ibid., 336–39.
65. Ibid., 344–46.
66. Ibid., 440.
67. Ibid., 450.
68. We are bypassing here the question of validity; the discussion is only of sacraments that are validly administered and received.
69. Ibid., 465–468.

To understand the nature of the received sacrament (termed variously *sacramentum et res*, *res et sacramentum*, sacramental reality, and symbolic reality) in scholastic thought, it is necessary to move from doctrine to theology, which is, as said earlier, an attempt to make intellectual sense of religious beliefs. In traditional sacramental theology, for example, how does one make intellectual sense of the notion of a character that is impressed on a soul? The image is obviously a metaphor and cannot be taken literally, for the soul is not something material that can have something stamped on it. How then was the received sacrament understood in the context of Aristotelian-scholastic thought, the context within which these doctrines were formulated?

Leeming's *Principles of Sacramental Theology* was never the most widely used textbook on the sacraments, for it was published shortly before the Second Vatican Council, when the attention of seminarians and their professors suddenly turned from scholasticism to more contemporary approaches, such as that of Schillebeeckx.[70] But it was the last and best of the manuals of sacramental theology in English, replacing Pourrat's *Theology of the Sacraments*, which had been translated from the French in 1910.[71] Other comprehensive manuals were available in Latin, which were used even in American seminaries for years, the most well known being that of Lennerz.[72] Leeming's book contains references to these two predecessors as well as others, so to some extent it represents a summary of the recent manualist tradition.

Section II in its entirety is devoted to "The Sacraments and the Character." Chapter 4 on "The Sacramental Character" establishes the fact of the doctrine, examines it in greater detail than we have done here, and defends it against heretical positions that denied its reality. Chapter 5 on "The Seal of the Spirit" traces the notion of a mark or seal, σφράγις in Greek, that is received by the baptized from the New Testament to St. Augustine, who sometimes referred to it as a *character* in Latin, in the general sense of figure or symbol. Chapter 6 is on "The Perfecting of the Seal," for once it was agreed that both baptism and confirmation confer a seal or character, theologians were presented with having to explain the difference between the two characters. Chapter 7 is devoted to "The Nature of the Sacramental Character," which reviews attempts to understand the character within an Aristotelian-scholastic context. Chapter 8, on "The Symbolic Reality and the Validity of the Sacraments" shows how the theological concept of *sacramentum et res* can be used to explain the canonical concept of validity. Since our concern is to understand the character as explained by scholastic theology, our focus will be on chapter 7.

---

70. Edward Schillebeeckx, *Christ, the Sacrament of the Encounter with God* (New York: Sheed and Ward, 1963).

71. Pierre Pourrat, *Theology of the Sacraments: A Study in Positive Theology* (St. Louis: B. Herder, 1910).

72. Heinrich Lennerz, *De sacramentis novae legis in genere* (Roma: Universitas Gregoriana, 1928, 1930, 1950).

After presenting the state of the question (a common procedure in scholastic theology manuals), Leeming gathers scriptural and patristic texts that convey the idea that Christians are a priestly people (e.g., 1 Peter 2:4–10) and relates this to the fact that priests can do things that ordinary people cannot do.[73] Priests therefore have certain abilities or powers that the non-ordained do not possess. Priests in the Old Testament offered sacrifices to God on behalf of the people. Christ the high priest as described in the Epistle to the Hebrews offers an eternal sacrifice which brings true salvation to those who accept him in faith (Heb. 2:5 – 5:10). But if Christians share in the priesthood of Christ, they must somehow share in his priestly power.

Medieval Latin had a number of words that could be used to express the idea of power of one sort or another: *potentia*, *potestas*, *habitus*, and *virtus*.

Potentia (from which we get the words potent, potential, and potency) is the power or ability to come into being. Theoretically, anything imaginable can possibly exist (e.g., unicorns, warp drive), but if metaphysics is a science of the real rather than the imaginary, the notion of *potentia* should always be used in reference to things that exist. According to one scholastic maxim, *Ab esse ad posse valet illatio*: From the existence of something it is valid to infer that it is possible. In other words, if something is, it is able to be.

For example, all human beings are, by nature, able to walk and talk, see and hear. Aristotle would have said that these are powers of the human soul, or in plainer English, these are things that human beings can naturally do. But some people are physically handicapped, and so these individuals do not have the *potentia* or potential to actually do those things. Likewise, other people are talented and can run faster, think more quickly, and are more perceptive than others, and so those individuals can be said to have extraordinary powers or abilities.

Potestas is power to act or to do something that has an effect on another. Some animals are not only stronger (more natural strength potential) than others, but they are also predators who have the ability to attack and kill their prey. Human beings likewise have the physical ability to act on things in their environment, but they can also have social power over others. Parents have power over their children, rulers have power over their subjects, armies have military power, and so on.

Habitus is the power to act with ease or to do something consistently. Anyone can play sports or card games, but the ability to play well requires some skill. Hitting the ball is one thing; hitting it most of the time is another. Sending the ball to where you want it to go is an even higher level of skill. It takes skill to do something habitually well. One might regard a *habitus* as an advanced or developed *potentia*.

Virtus is the power to do good with ease or consistency. In the Aristotelian world view, habit is a neutral term (able to do good or ill), virtue is morally positive (an ability to do good consistently and with ease), and vice is morally negative (an ability to do evil consistently and with ease). But the word "virtue" has lost its original manly

73. Leeming, *Principles*, 230–36.

overtones (related to *vir* or man), so today it is better to think of *virtus* as strength in the sense of strength of character or personal strength. When applied to a sacrament, its *virtus* is an inherent ability to produce a good effect.

To sum up: *Virtus* is a *habitus* for right action, provided that the subject has the *potentia* to do it and the needed *potestas* in society. Or to say it in more contemporary language: Moral strength is the skill of consistently doing the right thing, provided that one is not prevented from doing it. Moreover, one can infer *potentia* from *actus*, or potential power from the exercise of power. So someone who consistently does the right thing obviously has the power to do so, and someone who actually exercises that power is clearly able to have that power.

The reasons for this brief excursus into the scholastic understanding of power is two-fold.

First, as was shown earlier, it is an axiom of faith that grace is necessary for salvation. This means in general that one needs God's help to get into heaven, but more specifically from Augustine onward it meant that even though human beings have the natural power to do good in single instances, natural habits alone cannot lead to the moral strength necessary to be saintly and merit the beatific vision.[74] Second, the scholastic solution to how to understand the metaphor of the character was to understand it as a power (*potentia*), and indeed as a God-given ability to receive supernatural habits (e.g., sanctifying grace) and virtues (e.g., faith, hope and charity).

In Aristotelian thinking, nothing happens unless it is able to happen. This may appear to be obvious and even tautologous, but translated into scholastic terminology, it provides a basis for saying that human beings cannot naturally receive supernatural gifts (graces) without being given the ability or power (*potentia*) to receive them. Thus when Aquinas says that "the character is a power," the word he uses is *potentia*.[75]

Aquinas and other scholastics, therefore, took a term inherited from their religious tradition, i.e., *character*, and interpreted it in a way that satisfied the data of faith (that some sacraments imprint a character on the soul) and that also satisfied the requirements of Aristotelian science (that the soul is a spiritual entity with active and passive powers). Aristotle had long ago identified various natural powers of the soul, such as the power of sensation, the power of intellect, the power of reason, and the power of will. How was ancient science able to identify these unseen powers? Through their effects: *Ab esse ad posse valet illatio*. If animals can see, hear and smell things, they have the powers of sensation. If human beings have the ability to understand and figure things out, they have the powers of intellect and reason. If they can make decisions, they have the power of free will. The mysterious "powers" in

74. See Denzinger, *Enchiridion Symbolorum*, 1551–53; Clarkson, *Church Teaches*, 575–77.

75. *Summa Theologica*, Bk. III, q. 63, art. 3, *Sed contra*. Thomas goes on to say in the *corpus* of the same article that the character is a passive power, i.e., an ability not to act but to receive divine gifts, and that it is also an instrumental power, i.e., capable of letting God work through it.

Aristotelian science are nothing more than the abilities we easily attribute to humans and other living beings.

For people to be able to do things that are beyond natural human ability, however, they must receive that ability as a gift (grace) from God. Ordinary people have no problem with this; characters in folk tales get endowed with special powers all the time. But according to classical scientific thinking, before the soul can receive supernatural gifts, it has to be made capable of receiving them; otherwise it would be like trying to fill a pot with thoughts: a material pot is simply incapable of holding immaterial thoughts. In order to hold what it is not naturally able to hold, the pot would have to be given that capability by a power greater than itself. Likewise, in order to receive supernatural gifts, people need to be first given that capability by God. The scholastics even gave names to this divine action: prevenient grace (*gratia preveniens*) and operative grace (*gratia operans*).[76]

Once the soul has been give the ability to receive supernatural gifts, then, how are we to conceive of those gifts? They could be one-time gifts, technically known as actual graces. Or they could be lasting gifts, usually called habitual graces. Such is sanctifying grace (also known as justifying grace and *gratia gratum faciens*) and various supernatural virtues such as faith, hope and charity.[77] In other words, God gives human beings the ability to perform works that merit salvation not once but repeatedly, habitually.

Nevertheless, these divine gifts still leave people free. For just as one can have the power of sight and not look, just as one can have the power of running and not move, and just as one can have the power of reasoning and not think, so also one can have the virtue of faith and still doubt, one can have the virtue of hope and still worry, and one can have the virtue of charity and still act selfishly. Having an ability is no guarantee that one will use it.

d. Received Sacraments

The character is another name for the sacrament that is received in baptism, confirmation and holy orders. But in the traditional Catholic manner of speaking, all sacraments are said to be received. What of the other sacraments?

We shall not treat the Eucharist here for two reasons. First, "receiving the Eucharist" is clearly not metaphorical language but is literally true when one is speaking about receiving communion, so there is no question of something being received here. Second, the scholastic understanding of the Blessed Sacrament as a sacramental

---

76. See Denzinger, *Enchiridion Symbolorum*, 1525, 1553; Clarkson, *Church Teaches*, 561, 577. Also Lonergan, 26–33: the book's subtitle is *Operative Grace in the Thought of St. Thomas Aquinas*.

77. See Ott, *Fundamentals*, 250–57; Lonergan, 22–25. Also, *Summa Theologica*, Bk. III, q. 68, art. 9, ad 3 (sanctifying grace is a habit); q. 69, art. 4, obj. 3 (virtue is a habit); q. 69, art. 6, *corpus* (virtues are habits).

reality is quite different from the way that the sacramental reality in the other six sacraments was understood—so different, in fact, that treating it with the other six would double the length of this study.

With regard to the other six, then, it will be convenient to begin with ordination or holy orders since the supernatural powers bestowed by this sacrament are clearly discernable. They are what make, in Catholic thinking and scholastic theology, a priest different from a layperson.

- **Holy Orders**

  The name of the sacrament is simply *ordo* (order) in Latin, and it is occasionally referred to as *ordinatio* (ordination) in church documents. The common view of the earlier scholastics is that this was one sacrament that was received in seven stages, as it were, through the ordinations to each of the four minor and three major orders (porter, lector, exorcist, acolyte, subdeacon, deacon, priest). The episcopacy was not regarded as a separate order but as the "fullness of the priesthood."[78] This began to change after the Council of Trent, however, which placed special emphasis on the hierarchy in rebuilding the organizational church, and the notion of an episcopal *ordo* was endorsed by Pope Pius XII in 1947. Modern scholastics regarded the minor ordination rites as separate sacramentals rather than as parts of the sacrament of order.[79]

  It is a moot (and probably pointless) question today whether the sacrament requires one character or three separate characters for the orders of deacon, priest, and bishop. The powers bestowed by God through ordination to those in the different grades of the sacrament are quite clear. Deacons are able to preach and to serve on the altar at the eucharistic liturgy. Priests are able to preside at the eucharistic sacrifice and consecrate the eucharistic elements; they can administer the sacraments of penance and extreme unction; and they are also able, with their bishop's permission, to administer the sacrament of confirmation. Bishops, in addition to the aforementioned powers, can also administer the sacrament of order, making men deacons, priests, and even bishops.[80] In doctrinal and liturgical documents, the Latin word *potestas* (the ability to do or act in such a way as to have an effect on others) is used when referring to these powers.

  Church doctrine teaches that this sacrament confers sanctifying grace as well as sacramental graces, but the number and nature of these gifts have never been spelled out in detail. Ott says simply, "The grace of Order has

---

78. See "Priest," *The Catholic Encyclopedia* (New York: Robert Appleton Co., 1911) Vol. 12, 406.

79. See Ott, *Fundamentals*, 452–52 The Second Vatican Council went further, eliminating the orders of porter through subdeacon and reinvesting the order of deacon with a permanence it had not enjoyed since the patristic era. See Dogmatic Constitution on the Church (*Lumen Gentium*), 56.

80. See Ott, ibid., 457.

the purpose of and is specially adapted to enabling the recipient worthily to perform the functions of his Order, and to lead a worthy life."[81]

- **Baptism**

  This sacrament derives its name from the Greek word βαπτίσμα, which means immersion, and from which the Latin *baptisma* and the English "baptism" are transliterations. Historically it was the first rite that was said to confer a character. St. Augustine borrowed the Greek word χαρακτήρ (meaning impression) in explaining why the rebaptism of repentant heretics and apostates was neither needed nor helpful. When they were first baptized, he said, their soul was permanently marked as belonging to Christ, and even though they had left the church, they had never lost this *character*. The existence of the character as an effect of baptism was generally accepted by theologians in the Middle Ages, but it was not affirmed as an article of faith until the Council of Trent in 1547.[82]

  Baptism confers the grace of justification, also called justifying grace and sanctifying grace. On the one hand, baptism remits all sins (both original sin and personal sins, if any) and on the other hand it infuses virtues and other gifts of the Holy Spirit that enable the recipient to lead a just and even holy life.[83] The infused virtues are identified as faith, hope and charity (understood as supernatural habits as discussed above), that give the baptized the power to believe what God has revealed, to hope for everlasting life, and to love others with the love of Christ. Thus Christians are justified by faith, not by believing that they are saved, but by receiving the supernatural virtue of faith.[84] In addition, the reception of baptism implicitly confers the ability to receive other sacraments.[85]

  Consequently, either baptism itself or the desire for baptism is necessary for salvation.[86]

- **Confirmation**

  In the early church, the blessing of the recently baptized by the bishop was referred to by a variety of names (e.g., blessing, signing, consignation, anointing, perfection, consummation), but by the Middle Ages it was commonly called confirmation. The fact that this sacrament, like baptism, was

---

81. Ibid, 456.

82. See Denzinger, *Enchiridion Symbolorum*, 1609; Clarkson, *Church Teaches*, 673.

83. See Trent's Decree on Original Sin, Denzinger, ibid., 1510–1516; Clarkson, ibid., 371–76. Also the Decree on Justification, Denzinger, ibid., 1524–31; Clarkson, ibid., 560–64.

84. See Denzinger, ibid., 1532; Clarkson, ibid., 565.

85. See canon 737 in the 1917 Code of Canon Law.

86. See Ott, *Fundamentals*, 356–57. Also, Denzinger, *Enchiridion Symbolorum*, 1618; Clarkson, *Church Teaches*, 691.

never repeated led to the theological conclusion that it too conferred an indelible character on the soul. This conclusion was affirmed as an article of faith by the Council of Trent.[87]

Like other sacraments, confirmation causes an increase in sanctifying grace and perfects the grace of baptism,[88] but it is unclear how it does this. According to some, confirmation confers the gifts of the Holy Spirit, but since these are said to be received through baptism, this opinion is not widely held, the words of the Rite of Confirmation notwithstanding.

- **Marriage**

Like the above three sacraments, marriage (in Latin, *matrimonia*) bestows a sacramental reality on the recipients, but it is not referred to as a character. Indeed, doctrinal pronouncements refer to it only as a marriage bond or contract, but in scholastic sacramental theology it is understood to be another *sacramentum et res*. Theologically, the sacramental bond raises a natural marriage to a supernatural level, giving it the ability (*potentia*) to sanctify the spouses and to be indissoluble, so its effects parallel that of the sacramental character.

In doctrinal pronouncements and in canon law, the sacramental reality can be referred to as the contract, the bond, or simply as the marriage. Theologically, it is also referred to as the sacrament, and a number of papal documents have declared that there can be no marriage between Christians that is not at the same time a sacrament.[89] Moreover, it is the Catholic understanding (although not a doctrine) that this sacrament is bestowed on the spouses not through any ministerial activity of the priest (who only witnesses the marriage on behalf of the Church) but through their exchange of vows and marital consent.[90]

The sacrament brings with it an increase in sanctifying grace, which "brings natural love in marriage to perfection, strengthens the indissoluble unity, and sanctifies the spouses." Furthermore, it gives the spouses "the right to ask for and receive the help of actual graces as often as they need it to fulfill the duties of their state."[91]

---

87. See Denzinger, ibid., 1609; Clarkson, ibid., 73.

88. See Ott, *Fundamentals*, 365–66. In 1439 the Council of Florence declared that "by confirmation we grow in grace and are strengthened in the faith (Denzinger, ibid., 1310; Clarkson, ibid., 663).

89. For example, Pope Pius IX, *Acerbissimum vobiscum* (1852); Pope Leo XIII, *Arcanum divinae sapientiae* (1880); Pope Pius XI, *Casti connubii* (1930). See relevant passages cited in Denzinger, ibid., 3145–46; Clarkson, ibid., 869–70; Denzinger, ibid., 3713–14; Clarkson, ibid., 877.

90. See Ott, *Fundamentals*, 468.

91. Pope Pius XI, *Casti connubii* (1930). Denzinger, *Enchiridion Symbolorum*, 3713; Clarkson, *Church Teaches*, 877.

- **Penance**

    What is commonly called the sacrament of reconciliation today was re-
    ferred to as penance before Vatican II, yet the name in Latin has remained
    sacramentum poenitentiae, literally the sacrament of repentance.

    As mentioned earlier, traditional Catholics speak of receiving the sac-
    rament of penance, but they probably think more about receiving God's for-
    giveness for the sins that they confess. Furthermore, the Aristotelian logic
    that governed the scholastics' analysis of the character ought to hold here as
    well: if all sacraments bestow grace, and if the human soul (especially a soul
    that has lost the state of grace through committing a mortal sin) is naturally
    incapable of receiving a supernatural gift, then it must first receive from
    God the ability (*potentia*) to receive the grace of forgiveness and any other
    graces that would flow from the reception of the sacrament.

    One difficulty faced by the scholastics in naming the *sacramentum
    et res* in this sacrament is that there was no terminology in the tradition
    that lent itself to the scholastic analysis. As noted above, church documents
    speak rarely of receiving the sacrament and they speak more commonly
    of confessing one's sins and receiving absolution. Such language led Duns
    Scotus to pronounce confidently, "Penance is absolution, that is, a defini-
    tive judgment absolving the guilty."[92] Others such as Aquinas, however,
    argued that the sacramental reality must be the repentance of the sinner,
    for it is that which mediates between the outward rite and the inward grace
    of forgiveness.[93] The inability to specify the *sacramentum et res* with exact-
    ness even led some scholastics to deny that the concept could be applied
    to this sacrament.[94]

    In the scholastic view, the gifts received through this sacrament are
    not only the forgiveness of sins but also the sanctifying grace needed to heal
    the soul and the actual graces needed to avoid sin in the future. The eternal
    punishment (in hell) that would have resulted from mortal sins is remitted,
    but not all of the temporal punishment (in purgatory) due for serious and
    lesser sins. But the spiritual merits that were lost though the commission of
    sin are restored.[95]

- **Extreme Unction**

    The name of this sacrament is a transliteration from the Latin, *extrema unc-
    tio*, meaning last anointing. This name accurately reflected the theology of
    the sacrament, which was intended to be administered to the dying.

---

92. *Oxford Commentary on the Four Books of the Sentences*, 4.4.4, cited in Leeming, *Principles*, 264.
93. *Summa Theologica*, Bk. III, q. 84, art. 1, ad 3.
94. See Leeming, *Principles*, 265.
95. See Ott, *Fundamentals*, 437.

What was said above about penance needs to be said about extreme unction as well, namely, that Aristotelian logic required the bestowal of a sacramental reality (a special *potentia* or receptive power) in order for supernatural grace to be received. But neither the words of the rite nor the theological tradition give a clear indication of what it might be. Leeming suggests that it is "a commitment of the sick [person] to the mercy of God, which makes an enduring sacrament of the condition of illness and its danger."[96] The commitment is something that is real and that makes the illness symbolic, but this does not satisfy the requirement that received sacrament must be a supernatural *potentia* in the soul of the recipient. Various candidates for the position were named by Aquinas, Scotus and other theologians, but the unavoidable lack of data on a sacrament received by the dying prevented any agreement among medieval and modern scholastics.

Even about the effects of the sacrament there was disagreement, although Catholic doctrine affirmed that every sacrament confers grace. Ott suggests that sanctifying grace in this case "has the power and purpose of curing the soul of the sick person, of raising it up and strengthening it, by awakening confidence in God's mercy and by giving strength to bear the hardships of the sickness and of the mortal agony, and to resist the temptations of the devil."[97] Traditional Catholics sometimes spoke of this as the grace of a happy death. Suggestions from other theologians included the remission of unconfessed sins, the washing away of the remnants of sin that still stained the soul, and in some cases the restoration of physical health. Although it was a popular Catholic belief that one's soul went straight to heaven after receiving extreme unction, the theological tradition did not support it.

e. Summary

Catholic theologians in the nineteenth and twentieth centuries took the sacramental doctrines of the Council of Trent and the canons of the 1917 Code as a framework on which to build a philosophical understanding of sacraments that was more detailed and nuanced than the bare bones of dogma. Fleshing out the analogy, we could say that textbook writers such as Pourrat, Lennerz and others constructed the body of work known as scholastic sacramental theology on the skeleton of Catholic doctrine and canon law. Then, compilers such as Leeming and Ott provided something like an X-ray of the system, revealing how the basic parts—doctrine and practice on the one hand and explanatory concepts on the other—were interconnected.

96. Leeming, *Principles*, 265.
97. Ott, *Fundamentals*, 448.

Needless to say, the doctrines were not questioned because they were the reason for the entire enterprise. The purpose of theology was to understand and explain the faith, and the faith was found in the church's doctrines. Not questioned as well were the explanations provided by Aristotelian scholasticism, for they were the only kinds of explanations that were acceptable at the time. Especially after the Protestant Reformation, all alternative explanations were regarded as heresy.

Thus the very language in which the doctrines were formulated and in which the explanations were expressed was assumed to be factual and objective by all the parties involved, from the illiterate peasant laity to the uppermost echelons of the hierarchy. The language of giving and receiving sacraments, of administrators and recipients, as well as the rest of the terminology introduced in this chapter was regarded as objective and accurate, revealing how God worked in human souls to bring about their salvation.

In the next chapter we shall see how Christian thinkers from the second to the twentieth century, reflecting somewhat naively on their ritual practices in light of texts inherited from the past, produced the construct set forth here in some detail. Then, in the third chapter, we shall review the same history, this time taking a critical look at the uncritical use of biblical and patristic texts by early and medieval writers.

Before concluding this chapter, however, we need to demonstrate that basic Catholic sacramental doctrine was not changed by the Second Vatican Council, nor was it altered in any official way after the council, even though a plethora of unofficial sacramental theologies were proposed by individual theologians during the decades following the council.

3. Scholastic Sacramental Theology after Vatican II

Most Catholic theologians in the sixties and seventies turned away from scholasticism and toward more contemporary approaches to doing theology. Sacramental theology left the scholastic method, based on Aristotelian metaphysics, and experimented with methods based on phenomenology, existentialism, personalism, process thought and liberation theology.[98] Indigenous thinkers in the increasingly Catholic populations of Africa and Asia were likewise envisioning new ways to interpret Christian beliefs in ways that were appropriate for non-European cultures. For a while, it seemed that scholasticism would fade in the same way that neo-platonism had faded during the rise of scholasticism.

The pontificate of Pope John Paul II, however, brought with it a renewed emphasis on traditional European Catholicism, and with it a reluctance to relinquish the certainties of faith, primarily those doctrines that were formulated in scholastic terminology. The revision of the Code of Canon Law, already begun in the 1970s, was amended to include more of the thinking that had gone into the 1917 code. Encouraged by the

98. For a summary, see Joseph Martos, *Doors to the Sacred: A Historical Introduction to Sacraments in the Catholic Church* (Liguori, MO: Liguori Publications, 2014), ch. 5.

Vatican's renewed traditionalism, some conservative bishops proposed a new edition of the Roman Catechism, the first systematic rewriting of Catholic beliefs since 1566, in the hope that a clear and comprehensive statement of doctrine would slow what they saw as a dilution of the faith by multicultural forces.

The 1983 Code and the 1994 Catechism did not live up to the restorationist hopes of the most ardent integralists, as those who wished to restore the integrity of the Catholic faith styled themselves, but they did to a large extent retain the scholastic expression of traditional doctrine.

a. The 1983 Code of Canon Law

With regard to legislation on the sacraments, the new code is somewhat simpler, with 20% fewer canons than in 1917 (325 vs. 412). To some extent, the language has evolved (Sacraments are now said to be celebrated as well as administered and received.), but not much. The following statistical analysis shows that the Church's legal framework for the sacraments remains overwhelmingly scholastic.[99]

The **introductory canons** 840–848 speak of sacraments being *administered* five times, being *conferred* two times, and being *received* four times. In one place, sacraments are said to be celebrated, but this is clearly in reference to liturgical rituals. Canon 845 refers to baptism, confirmation and order as *imprinting* a character.

In canons 849–878, **baptism** is said to be *administered* three times and *conferred* thirteen times, which is about the same distribution as in the older code. When speaking about adult baptism, the sacrament is said to be *received* twice, and when speaking once about the liturgical ritual, baptism is said to be *celebrated*. The character is mentioned, but it is not said to be imprinted or conferred.

In canons 879–896, **confirmation** is said to be *administered* eight times, *conferred* five times, and *received* two times, plus occurrences in canon 1033 on orders and canon 1065 on marriage. The ritual is described as being *celebrated*, and the character is spoken of once as being *conferred*.

There is a great change in the language and structure of the section on the **Eucharist**, covering canons 899–958. Overwhelmingly—25 times—reference is made to the *celebration* of the Eucharist, that is, to the eucharistic liturgy. In the three places that speak about the Eucharist being *administered*, and in the six places that speak about the Eucharist being *received*, the reference is clearly to holy communion.

Canons 951–991 on the sacrament of **penance** (*sacramentum poenitentiae*), speak once about the sacrament being *administered*, once about it being *received*, and once about it being *celebrated*. The phrase that occurs overwhelmingly is "hearing confessions," indicating that the law is primarily concerned with sacramental practice,

99. See *Code of Canon Law: Latin-English Edition* (Canon Law Society of America, Washington, DC, 1983).

just as in the past. Moreover, in the discussion of the first form of the liturgical celebration, absolution is said to be given and received three times.

Canons 992–997 are on indulgences, a fifth of the number that treated the topic in the older code.

In canons 998–1007 on **anointing of the sick**, the sacrament is said to be *administered* seven times, *conferred* one time, and *celebrated* two times. The sacrament is never referred to as being received.

Canons 1008–1054 are on **orders** (a different translation of *ordo*), which are said to be *conferred* four times and *received* seven times. The sacrament is not spoken of as administered, but the new code speaks repeatedly of the ordination ceremony, twice referring to it as being *celebrated*. Canon 1024 speaks of ordination (rather than orders) as being received.

Canons 1055–1165 are on **marriage**, and although the wording initially reflects the theology of Vatican II, speaking of marriage as a covenant and partnership, it quickly shifts back to the terminology of the older code, which spoke of marriage as a *contract*. Canon 1055 §2 repeats verbatim its counterpart in the 1917 Code, affirming that "a valid marriage contract cannot exist between baptized persons without its being by that very fact a sacrament." The new code speaks ten times of the wedding ritual as the *celebration* of marriage, and only once does it speak of marriage being *received*. Although the law does not speak of marriage being administered or conferred, Canon 1057 does say that "a marriage is brought into being" through the consent of the partners.

In summary, although there are changes between the two editions of the *Codex Juris Canonici*, there are no substantial differences in their legal approaches to the sacraments being administered or conferred on the one hand and being received on the other hand. Sacramental celebrations are mentioned more frequently, perhaps to regulate aspects of the rituals about which there had previously been more latitude, for example, the places where masses and weddings could take place. With regard to the received sacraments (the character, the bond, etc.), Catholic canon law still exists within a scholastic framework.

b. The 1994 Catechism of the Catholic Church

Part Two of the Catechism is on "The Celebration of the Christian Mystery," following Part One on the Nicene Creed, and followed by Part Three on morality and Part Four on prayer. As in the Roman Catechism, then, liturgy and sacraments are clearly central to Catholic faith, and the space devoted to them is about 25% of the total.

In general, the Catechism's treatment of Christian worship reflects the pastoral concerns of the Second Vatican Council, the liturgical changes that were implemented after the Council, and advances in scripture scholarship, at least to the extent that biblical quotations are less blatantly used as proof texts. But the Catechism also includes sacramental doctrines dating back to the Council of Trent, and it includes sacramental regulations found in the Code of Canon Law. The reader who is not aware of these various sources is liable to view the Church's catechetical teaching on liturgy and sacraments as well woven together, but to the careful eye it has more the appearance of a patchwork quilt—stunning, but nonetheless composed of separate pieces.

Our concern here must necessarily be limited to only some of those pieces, namely, the ones that have a bearing on sacraments that are administered and received, or more technically, the *sacramentum et res* of scholastic theology. For the same reasons mentioned above in the section on modern scholastic theology, we will not treat what the Catechism says about the Eucharist. The sacramental reality referred to in the eucharistic liturgy is of a different order from that of the character and the bond, and there can be no argument that it is received by the faithful.

Although Part Two on liturgical celebration opens with paragraph number 1066, the Catechism does not begin to treat the Church's sacraments until paragraph 1113. Citing the Council of Trent, the Catechism repeats the Catholic position that the sacraments were "all instituted by Jesus Christ our Lord" (1114). Research by Catholic scholars in the twentieth century demonstrated conclusively that many of these ecclesiastical rites cannot be traced back to the first century (except, *mutatis mutandis*, for baptism and Eucharist), so if the claim is true, it must refer to the sacramental reality. But the text gives the impression that it is talking about the Church's rituals.

This introductory article (as the sections of each chapter are called) notes that baptism, confirmation and holy orders confer a sacramental character or seal, besides conferring grace. The character is called a "configuration to Christ and to the Church" and, because it is indelible, "these sacraments can never be repeated" (1021). Again here the language is ambiguous. Is the reference here to liturgical sacraments or to received sacraments? Church law does not allow individuals to go through the rituals a second time, so in that sense the rites cannot be legally repeated. But scholastic theology explains that going through the ritual a second time would have no real effect on the soul because the effect had already been received the first time. Analogously, two people going through a second wedding ceremony do not become more married than they were after the first one.

Like the new Code, the Catechism speaks of sacraments being *celebrated* when it talks about performing and participating in sacramental rituals. But what is meant when the Catechism says that "the sacraments confer the grace that they signify" (1127)? Is it the sacramental ritual or the sacramental reality that is being referred to? Although the text is ambiguous here, the ambiguity is irrelevant, for the Catholic teaching is that God acts through the sacraments—both through the rituals and through the passive powers that are received.[100] Thus, even though church documents commonly speak of sacraments doing things and effecting things, it must be

---

100. See above, note 75.

remembered that this is simply a shorthand way of saying that God makes things happen through the sacraments.

Scholastic theology also speaks of sacraments acting *ex opere operato*, or being effective *ex opere operato*, but again here the phrase must be taken to mean that it is God who operates, not the sacrament that operates. The Latin phrase can be literally translated as "from the work worked" or more loosely rendered as "through the performance of the act," and it was introduced as a way of emphasizing that in the sacraments God acts through the ritual and not through the minister. Hence any unworthiness of the minister does not interfere with the effectiveness of the sacrament.[101] Over the course of time, grace and other effects got spoken of as though they came *from* the sacraments rather than *through* the sacraments, but theologically it was always understood that the sacraments were only instruments or channels of grace.[102]

With regard to the necessity of the sacraments for salvation, the Catholic Church seems to have moderated its position. The Council of Trent had condemned the ideas that "the sacraments of the New Law are not necessary for salvation," that people can be saved "without the sacraments or the desire for them," and that they can "obtain the grace of justification by faith alone."[103] But the Catechism teaches that "for believers the sacraments of the New Covenant are necessary for salvation."[104] Non-believers, it would appear, are now exempt from the rule that the sacraments are needed in order to be saved. No doubt, the Vatican II documents on ecumenism and on non-Christian religions had an influence here.

After a chapter on some practical matters related to liturgy (the when and how of liturgical celebrations), the Catechism treats each of the sacraments individually.

Baptism is spoken of as being both celebrated and administered (1226), and although it is hard to say what the Catechism means by this distinction (Could it mean that the sacramental ritual is celebrated and the sacramental reality is administered?), it is clear that baptism is also received (1259).[105] The traditional teaching about the sacramental seal or character is reaffirmed (1272–74), but the character is not identified with the sacrament that is received. The principal effects of baptism are spoken of as "purification from sins and new birth in the Holy Spirit." (1262). The former is clarified as the forgiveness of original sin and all personal sins, as well as any punishment they incur. The latter is explained as the reception of "sanctifying grace, the

---

101. See Ott, *Fundamentals*, 329–30; Leeming, *Principles*, 27–29; Denzinger, *Enchiridion Symbolorum*, 1608; Clarkson, *Church Teaches*, 672; *Catechism of the Catholic Church* (Città del Vaticano: Libreria Editrice Vaticana, 1994) 1128.

102. The fact that in Aristotelian science instruments were called instrumental causes no doubt created a certain amount of confusion, for the Catholic teaching that sacraments are causes of grace was criticized by the sixteenth century Protestant reformers.

103. Denzinger, *Enchiridion Symbolorum*, 1604. Clarkson, *Church Teaches*, 668.

104. *Catechism*, 1129, italics omitted.

105. Ibid., page 318.

grace of justification," (1265),[106] which enables the baptized "to believe in God, to hope in him, and to love him through the theological virtues." Baptism also gives "the power to live and act under the prompting of the Holy Spirit through the gifts of the Holy Spirit," and it allows Christians "to grow in goodness through the moral virtues. Thus the whole organism of the Christian's supernatural life has its roots in Baptism" (1266). Although the language has been updated, underlying the text are many ideas taken from of medieval scholasticism.

In the article on confirmation, the Catechism says that reception of the sacrament "is necessary for the completion of baptismal grace. For 'by the sacrament of Confirmation, [the baptized] are more perfectly bound to the Church and are enriched with a special strength of the Holy Spirit.'"[107] Clearly the effect is a supernatural gift, described as extra spiritual strength (a *virtus*?). The effects of the sacrament are more specifically described in paragraph number 1302: "the full outpouring of the Holy Spirit as once granted to the apostles on the day of Pentecost," and by its grace,

- it roots us more deeply in the divine filiation which makes us cry, "Abba! Father!"
- it unites us more firmly to Christ;
- it increases the gifts of the Holy Spirit in us;
- it renders our bond with the Church more perfect;
- it gives us a special strength of the Holy Spirit to spread and defend the faith by work and action as true witnesses of Christ, to confess the name of Christ boldly, and never to be ashamed of the Cross.[108]

Obviously these are not natural human powers, so they must be supernatural powers. Here as elsewhere, the Catholic Church continues to express itself in the language of scholastic theology, even when it does not adopt the entire conceptual lattice of medieval Aristotelianism. The Catechism also speaks of the sacramental character and seal of the Spirit as "an indelible spiritual mark" that is imprinted on the soul. Paragraphs 1295 and 1296 speak of the seal as an entity that marks a person as belonging to another; paragraphs 1304 and 1305 speak of it as a reception of power. Thus the reception of the sacrament, the character, grace, and power are all related, even though their relation to one another is not spelled out.

The article on the next sacrament calls it the sacrament of conversion, of penance, of confession, of forgiveness, and of reconciliation—obviously using the word "sacrament" in a variety of senses (1423–24). Nowhere in this article is the sacrament said to be received, but in paragraph 1457 absolution is said to be received through

---

106. Italics omitted.

107. *Catechism*, 1285. The quotation is from the Dogmatic Constitution on the Church (*Lumen Gentium*), 11. See also reference to the reception of the sacrament in the *Catechism*, 1306 and 1310, and to the administration or conferring of the sacrament in 1312–14.

108. Ibid., 1303.

the sacrament, and in 1458 "the gift of the Father's mercy" is said to be received, which is consonant with scholastic sacramental theology.[109] On the whole, however, the article is written from a pastoral perspective with scriptural references to repentance and forgiveness.

When the Catechism speaks about administering and receiving the anointing of the sick, it is unclear whether it is talking about the physical anointing (*sacramentum tantum*) or the sacrament (*sacramentum et res*); likewise, when it talks about repeating the sacrament (1515–16). The heading of Part II, however, clearly asks, "Who Receives and Who Administers This Sacrament?" and paragraph 1516 speaks twice about receiving the sacrament. This article waxes theological when it speaks about the effects of the sacrament, referring to it as a grace "of strengthening, peace, and courage to overcome the difficulties that go with the condition of serious illness or the frailty of old age," and as a gift of the Holy Spirit "who renews trust and faith in God and strengthens against the temptations of the evil one, the temptation to discouragement and anguish in the face of death (1520). "By the grace of this sacrament the sick person receives the strength and the gift of uniting himself more closely to Christ's Passion" (1521). "The sick who receive this sacrament, 'by freely uniting themselves to the passion and death of Christ,' 'contribute to the good of the People of God'" (1522).[110] When the sacrament is received by those "at the point of departing this life," it fortifies them "for the final struggles before entering the Father's house" (1523). All of this is consonant with scholastic theology's understanding of supernatural gifts that are bestowed through the sacraments.

With the articles on holy orders and matrimony, the Catechism displays a style that is somewhat reminiscent of Catholicism before the Second Vatican Council. In the Tridentine church, priesthood was conceived primarily in terms of sacerdotal power: the power to confect the Eucharist and to offer the Sacrifice of the Mass, the power to bestow absolution for confessed sins, and so on. At Vatican II, however, the world's Catholic bishops shifted the focus from power to service, and both the decree on priests and the decree on bishops emphasize above all the ministry and spirituality of the ordained. The revised Rite of Ordination, promulgated by Pope Paul VI in 1968, speaks mainly of the priestly office, the prebyteral order, consecration by God, the power of Christ, and celebration of the divine mysteries, mentioning only in one prayer "the grace and power of the priesthood."[111] Nonetheless, in the Catechism, the emphasis is on sacerdotal power, with many references to the scholastic theology of ordination. A similar return to pre-Vatican II thinking is evident with regard to marriage, as will be seen shortly.

---

109. Additional scholastic elements appear in the summary at the end of the article, especially 1495–98.

110. The reference is to the Dogmatic Constitution on the Church (*Lumen Gentium*), 11.2.

111. "Ordination of a Priest," *The Rites of the Catholic Church*, Vol. 2 (Collegeville, MN: The Liturgical Press, 1990), 43.

In one of its first paragraphs, the article on holy orders states that ordination "confers a gift of the Holy Spirit that permits the exercise of a 'sacred power' (*sacra potestas*)," and for this reason it is also called consecration (*consecratio*).[112] The gift of the Holy Spirit is, as we have seen, the priestly character, although the Catechism does not clearly identify the two as identical. Notice how carefully this wording follows the scholastic interpretation of the character as a passive power: ordination confers an ability (*potentia*) to exercise a supernatural power (*potestas*).

Following the teaching of the Second Vatican Council, the Catechism identifies episcopal consecration as a sacramental ordination that bestows a sacred character as well as the grace of the Holy Spirit (1557–58). The Catechism goes on to say that the order of priesthood is conferred on priests "by its own particular sacrament," which must refer to the *sacramentum tantum* or ordination ritual, and which is another clear usage of scholastic terminology. By being ordained, priests "are signed with a special character and so are configured to Christ in such a way that they are able to act in the person of Christ the head [of the church]."[113] In other words, priests receive a character that enables them to exercise supernatural power. Likewise, the order of deacons is conferred in yet another sacramental ritual, which imprints a character on the ordained and configures them to Christ the servant of all (1570–71).

When the Catechism asks, "Who Can Confer This Sacrament?" and "Who Can Receive This Sacrament?" it is speaking not of the *sacramentum tantum* but of the *sacramentum et res*.[114] But when it says, "This sacrament configures the recipient to Christ by a special grace of the Holy Spirit, so that he may serve as Christ's instrument for his Church" (1581), it must be speaking of the sacramental ritual, for the *sacramentum et res* is in fact the configuration referred to—also known as the character—which is an instrumental cause of grace. Remarkably, the connection between the configuration and the character is overlooked in paragraphs 1582 and 1583, which mention only that the character is indelible and thus can neither be lost nor received more than once. Nevertheless, the configuration to Christ is called a grace that is "proper to this sacrament" (1585), which is to say that the priestly character is an abiding supernatural gift (a habitual grace) bestowed for the sanctification of others (*gratia gratis data*) and for the increased holiness of the priest himself (*gratia gratum faciens*), whence it may also be called a sanctifying grace. The graces proper to each of the orders are listed in paragraphs numbered 1586 to 1588.

The article in the Catechism on "The Sacrament of Matrimony" talks repeatedly about the covenant of marriage, echoing the language of the Second Vatican Council. Nonetheless, most of what it says about marriage is rooted in medieval thinking and scholastic theology, and in many places the word "covenant" could easily be replaced

---

112. *Catechism*, 1538. The reason for the quotation marks around "sacred power" is not clear.

113. Ibid., 1563. The quotations are from Vatican II's Decree on the Ministry and Life of Priests (*Presbyterorum Ordinis*), 2.

114. See page 394 of the *Catechism*. See also paragraphs 1575–78.

by the word "contract" because the Catechism presents marriage as a contractual relationship, albeit a solemn one.

Apparently referring to the story of Adam and Eve as literal history, we are told that "the first sin had for its first consequences the rupture of the original communion between man and woman," resulting in disordered relationships marked by "discord, a spirit of domination, infidelity, jealousy, and conflicts that can escalate into hatred and separation" (1606–1607). Therefore, "To heal the wounds of sin, man and woman need the help of the grace that God in his infinite mercy never refuses them" (1608). Moreover, without this supernatural help, married people cannot achieve the intimate communion of life and love that was intended for them before the fall.[115]

Jesus confirmed the goodness of marriage by his presence at the wedding feast at Cana, and he taught that God had made marriage indissoluble.[116] This seems to place an impossible demand on men and women who marry—and it would be, were it not for the grace that God provides through the sacrament of marriage.[117]

As was noted earlier, canon law does not discuss the minister of the sacrament, but the Catechism mentions the commonly accepted view that "the spouses, as ministers of God's grace, mutually confer upon each other the sacrament of Matrimony by expressing their consent before the Church" (1623). Consent is a legal requirement for a valid contract, and so the long section on "Matrimonial Consent" (1625–37) lists the legalities that must be observed for a valid and licit marriage. Mutual consent results in the creation of the marital covenant, traditionally referred to as the marriage bond, which God established "in such a way that a marriage concluded and consummated between baptized persons can never be dissolved" (1640). The grace of the sacrament makes it possible to strengthen the indissolubility of marriage,[118] but the Catechism says little more about the sacramental graces that come with marriage.

4. Conclusion

There is a great consistency in Catholic sacramental teaching, both doctrinal and theological, since the Council of Trent. On the one hand, medieval Aristotelianism provided the conceptual structure that enabled the sacraments to be talked about in terms of being conferred and received, and in terms of causality and effectiveness. On the other hand, scholastic analysis showed the way to go beyond basic doctrine to explanations cast in terms of the best science of the day with concepts such as potency (*potentia*), power (*potestas*), habit (*habitus*), and strength (*virtus*). The scholastics systematized the biblical notion of grace, making it a technical term that could

---

115. See *Catechism*, 1608, 1603.

116. See ibid., 1612–13. The scripture references are to Matthew 19:3–8, but the exception clause in Matthew 19:9 is not mentioned.

117. See ibid., 1614–16.

118. See ibid., 1641–42.

expand to cover the giftedness of all creation and contract to identify subtleties such as habitual and actual grace, sanctifying grace and sacramental grace. In this theological synthesis, the terms and relations were woven together in a system that was both intellectually satisfying and experientially plausible.

This consistency, however, which is the scholastic system's greatest strength, would also prove to be its greatest weakness. To that analysis we must eventually turn, but before that, we must look carefully at how the synthesis came into being. Where did the ideas originate, not in some vague attribution to Aristotle or Augustine, but specifically in their concrete historical and theological contexts? What were the questions that patristic and medieval theologians were trying to answer? And how does one correlate the answers that they gave with the evidence that they found persuasive? For it is not sufficient to know what any theology says, nor is it enough to understand what it means, but it is necessary to determine what it is talking about.

Toward achieving that end, the next chapter will discuss the development of this theological construct from the first to the sixteenth centuries.

II

Construction

*The Naïve Development of Sacramental Theology**

THE FIRST CHAPTER DISCUSSED in some detail the end product of a lengthy intellectual development, namely, the Roman Catholic understanding of sacraments as presented in doctrinal pronouncements by the magisterium and as explained in the conceptual framework of scholastic sacramental theology. The two are necessarily intertwined because the bishops and popes who made the doctrinal pronouncements thought about sacraments within the conceptual framework provided by medieval scholasticism. Yet Christians and Catholics did not always think about the church and its sacraments in terms provided by Aristotelian metaphysics.

I have previously written about the historical development of Catholic sacramental thinking both in its broad scope and its detailed unfolding.[1] This chapter and the next will attempt to examine the history of early sacramental theology in some detail, or at least in sufficient detail to demonstrate both its intellectual soundness and its cultural relativity. The present chapter will focus on Christian rituals as described and explained by those who wrote the Christian scriptures, by patristic authors primarily in the Latin west (since eastern theology developed in a somewhat different direction), and by educated clergy in medieval Europe. It will show how each stage of the development built upon the previous stage, resulting in the intellectual synthesis of religious experience and philosophical understanding known as scholastic sacramental theology. The next chapter will focus on the same fifteen centuries, but it will show how the meanings of words changed, and how developments were sometimes based on a misunderstanding of what had gone before. It will therefore show that the

---

* For an abstract of this chapter, please read the summary of the argument that begins on page 283.

1. See Martos, *Doors to the Sacred*, esp. chapters 2 and 3 for the broad development from the New Testament to the Middle Ages. For convenience, I will refer to this work when additional information about the history of the sacraments might be helpful to the reader.

medieval synthesis overlooked much that today would be deemed relevant for understanding Christian rituals. It will also explain why scholastic sacramental theology is both culturally conditioned and intellectually inadequate for understanding sacraments in the twenty-first century.

1. Sacramental Theology in Historical Perspective

The New Testament makes reference to rituals such as baptism, the Lord's supper, and the laying on of hands, but it never calls them sacraments. The scriptures also talk about forgiveness, about healing, and about ministry, but they speak only indirectly about rituals that may have been connected with them. Nonetheless, Christian writers through the centuries have searched the scriptures for ways to understand the seven church rituals that came to be designated as sacraments. For if sacramental theology is the church's attempt to understand and explain its liturgical rituals, it stands to reason that the scriptures should be asked to contribute to that understanding.

Of course, the earliest Christians to write about the sacraments did not have the benefit of being able to search the scriptures to deepen their understanding, for these writers were the authors of the New Testament itself. The four evangelists and St. Paul, for example, had only oral tradition and their own experience on which to base their reflections on Christian practices. And even through the second century, apologists such as Justin Martyr and Ignatius of Antioch probably did not have access to the entire New Testament since the canon of Christian scriptures had not yet been defined. It was not until some time in the third century that most of today's 27 books were recognized as inspired.

Reflection on Christian rituals was, in effect, cumulative. New Testament writers such as St. Paul presented their own understanding of community practices, and this may have included elements of the earlier oral tradition.[2] Second and third century writers reflected on the practices of their day, they utilized the scriptural sources that were available, and they supplemented this with insights from their own pastoral and personal experience.[3] Fourth century writers did the same, utilizing the insights of previous generations, and from the fifth century onwards, theologians in the eastern part of the Roman Empire tended to rely more heavily on the writings of the Greek fathers of the church, while writers from Italy and westward (including north Africa)

---

2. Thus Paul in 1 Cor 11: 2 and 23 makes reference to the tradition he had received about the Lord's supper and other practices.

3. For example, Clement of Alexandria around the year 200 seems to draw on his experience when he writes, "We who are baptized wipe away the sins which, like a fog, clouded the divine spirit and blocked God's way. Our spiritual vision is now free, unrestrained and shining" (*The Instructor*, 1.6). Personal testimonies of this sort can be found today among evangelical Christians who talk about their experiences of being "saved" and being "baptized in the Spirit." English translation by William Wilson in *Ante-Nicene Fathers*, Vol. 2, edited by Alexander Roberts, James Donaldson, and A. Cleveland Coxe. (Peabody, MA: Hendrickson Publishers, 1994).

relied more heavily on the writings of their Latin speaking predecessors. After the fall of the Roman Empire in the west in the late fifth century, theological activity in Europe came to a virtual halt, and it was not widely resumed until the eleventh century with the gradual establishment of monastery schools and cathedral schools. When it did resume, the schoolmen or *scholastici* (as they came to be known) relied heavily on St. Augustine and other Latin fathers, although they also had translations of works and parts of works written originally in Greek.

The utilization of theological precedents during the patristic period was necessarily selective, not only because later thinkers could refer only to the earlier writings that they had on hand, but also because the fathers of the church were bishops who were also pastoral theologians. They directed sermons and similar works to the church-going populace, commentaries on the scripture and liturgy to the clergy, and works explaining doctrine and condemning heresies to their educated peers. Patristic theology therefore tends to be localized and diverse, although as time went on, the bishops tended to reach broad agreements with regard to doctrine and practice. The history of the first seven ecumenical councils offers ample testimony both to the diversity of patristic theologizing and to the gradual emergence of ecclesiastical consensus around matters of major concern.[4]

It was really not until the Middle Ages that theological reflection around church rituals evolved into a discipline that can be called sacramental theology. The schoolmen used *sacramentum* as a general term when referring to such rituals, and they focused specific attention on those *sacramenta* that were known to have ecclesial effects such as initiation and ordination, as well as the *sacramentum* produced by the words of consecration during the mass. By the thirteenth century, treatment of the sacraments was rather systematic, as can be seen in the *Summa Theologica* of St. Thomas and other works of the period.[5]

Sacramental theology gained particular importance after the Reformation because the Council of Trent (1545–1563) was largely devoted to combating Protestant heresies related to the sacraments. Until the mid-twentieth century Catholicism placed great emphasis on the mass and the sacraments in contrast to Protestantism, which placed great emphasis on the Bible. Around the time of the Second Vatican Council (1962–1965), sacramental theology witnessed a burst of creativity as contemporary theologians developed new theologies based on conceptual frameworks other than scholasticism, but the Church's magisterium continues to show a marked preference for traditional scholasticism.

---

4. See, e.g., Leo Donald Davis, *The First Seven Ecumenical Councils (325–787): Their History and Theology* (Collegeville, MN: Liturgical Press, 1990); Philip Schaff and Henry Wallace, eds., *The Seven Ecumenical Councils* (New York: Cosimo Books, 2007).

5. On the development of systematic theology by the medieval scholastics, see Congar, *History*, 69–114. See also Ulrich Gottfried Leinsle, *Introduction to Scholastic Theology* (Washington, DC: Catholic University of America Press, 2010), ch. 3.

2. Sacraments in a Literal Reading of the Scriptures

In this section, and elsewhere in this chapter, *scriptural and patristic texts will be given a deliberately naïve interpretation*, mirroring the practice of the patristic and medieval authors whose writings contributed to the development of Catholic sacramental doctrine and scholastic sacramental theology.

As already indicated, it is only in retrospect that we can find information about the sacraments in the New Testament, since the authors of those early documents did not speak about religious rituals in general but only about specific ritual practices. In the Middle Ages, sacraments were understood to be church rituals that had been instituted by Christ. This definition led Protestants to insist that only two of the Catholic sacraments had biblical support, namely, baptism and eucharist,[6] for which they preferred the more biblically grounded name of the Lord's supper.[7]

Christian baptism is often referred to in the Acts of the Apostles and also in a number of epistles,[8] and the repentance ritual performed by John the Baptist is mentioned in each of the four gospels.[9] The ritual is never described in detail, but since it was commonly performed in a river, it is assumed to have entailed full or partial immersion. The risen Christ commands his disciples to go forth into all nations, baptizing in the name of the Father and of the Son and of the Holy Spirit.[10] Thus baptism easily meets the two requirements for being called a true sacrament, namely, a religious ritual and institution by Christ.

The same can be said about the eucharist. The Christian meal is mentioned in Acts and also in the epistles,[11] and Jesus' last supper with his disciples, during which he gives the command to do this in his memory, is found in the three synoptic gospels.[12]

The other five sacraments fall short of the stringent double criterion imposed by the Reformers, but for over a thousand years both the Latin-speaking west and the Greek-speaking east had followed somewhat looser standards. Believing that the Holy Spirit would not lead the church into error, they assumed that the other ceremonies were rightly called sacraments (*sacramenta* in the west, μυστήρια in the east), so no proof was needed that they were legitimate church rituals. All that was needed, then, was evidence of divine approval.

---

6. In this work, when the word "eucharist" refers to the ritual meal, it is not capitalized, just as the names of the other sacramental rituals are not capitalized. However, when the word refers to the consecrated bread and wine, known by Catholics as the Blessed Sacrament, it is capitalized (as it was in chapter 1).

7. See 1 Cor 11:20.

8. See Acts 2:38–41; 8:12–16; 8:36–38; 10:47–48; 16:15; 16:33; 18:8; 19:5; 22:16. Also Rom 6:3–4; 1 Cor 1:14–17; Gal 3:27; Eph 4:5; Col 2:12; 1 Pt 3:21.

9. See Mt 3:1–16; Mk 1:1–9; Lk 3:1–22; Jn 1:19–34.

10. See Mt 28:19.

11. See Acts 2:42, 46; 1 Cor 11:23–26.

12. See Mt 26:20–29; Mk 14:17–25; Lk 22:14–20.

Reading the scriptures literally and taking them as supporting the Catholic tradition, we can see how the schoolmen and the scholastic tradition could say that there is no lack of New Testament evidence for Jesus' command to forgive sins, and in the Gospel According to John he explicitly gives his disciples the power to forgive and retain sins.[13] Likewise, Jesus clearly had the power of healing, and in his own lifetime he gave that power to the apostles, telling them to anoint the sick.[14] Evidence of this sacrament can even be found in the early church, for the apostle James apparently mentions it in his epistle.[15] Evidence for the sacrament of confirmation can be found in the laying on of hands after baptism, as described in Acts of the Apostles, and in John's Gospel Jesus explicitly bestows his spirit on the disciples at the last supper.[16] It was commonly understood that at the last supper, Jesus gave the apostles not only the command but also the power to consecrate bread and wine, turning them into his body and blood. In doing so, he implicitly made them priests, for the power of consecration is a priestly power. Further evidence of ordination in the early church can be found in the pastoral epistles, which speak of the laying on of hands when talking about bishops and deacons.[17] Jesus clearly approved of marriage in his condemnation of divorce, and the Epistle to the Ephesians teaches that the relationship between husband and wife is as permanent as the relationship between Christ and the church.[18]

Turning now to the theology of the sacraments, the synoptic gospels speak mostly of John's baptism, which was not a Christian sacrament, but the schoolmen easily found ingredients of what could become a more fully developed theology of baptism. Matthew 3:11 and Luke 3:16 speak of Christ as one who will baptize with the Holy Sprit and fire, and Mark 16:16 clearly connects baptism and salvation. The fourth gospel likewise talks mostly about John's baptism, but in a clear reference to Christian baptism Jesus says to Nicodemus, "no one can enter the kingdom of God without being born of water and the Spirit" (Jn 3:5).

Acts of the Apostles continues this theme, contrasting John's baptism for repentance with baptism with the Holy Spirit.[19] Indeed, in Acts baptism seems to be a prerequisite for receiving the Holy Spirit, for Peter promises the crowd on Pentecost that if they are baptized they will receive the gift of the Holy Spirit, and in other passages,

13. See Mt 6:14; 9:6; 12:31–32; Mk 2:10; 3:28–29; Lk 1:76–78; 5:24; 12:10; 17:3–4; Jn 20:23.

14. See Mk 6:7–13. Also Acts 3:1–10; 28:8.

15. See James 5:14.

16. See Acts 6:6; 8:17; 19:6; Jn 20:22.

17. See 1 Tim 4:14; 5:22; 2 Tim 1:6.

18. See Mt 5:31–32; Mk 10:5–12; Lk 16:18; Eph 5:21–33. The scholastics also found evidence for the sacrament of marriage in Eph 5:32, which the Vulgate translated as "*Hoc enim est sacramentum magnum*," and which can be understood as saying "For this is a great sacrament."

19. See Acts 1:5; 11:16.

those who are baptized receive the Holy Spirit.[20] Like John's baptism, Christian baptism also requires repentance, and it brings forgiveness of sins.[21]

Paul expands on this theology of repentance and forgiveness, speaking of baptism as baptism into Christ and into his death, and also as being clothed in Christ.[22] For Paul, however, receiving the Spirit is both a means of individual salvation and also a matter of becoming incorporated into the community of the saved, which he calls the body of Christ.[23] The first letter of Peter connects baptism with salvation through the power of Christ's resurrection, apparently connecting the death and resurrection of the Lord in what would later be called the paschal mystery.[24]

All of these scripture passages could easily be taken literally, which is to say that they could be read as if they meant what medieval Christians thought they meant.

With regard to the Eucharist, both the fathers and the schoolmen believed that their theology was solidly grounded in the gospel accounts themselves. In all three synoptics, Jesus at the last supper says over the bread, "This is my body." In Matthew and Mark, he says clearly, "This is my blood." Luke's version refers instead to "the new covenant in my blood," which is close enough to support the understanding that Jesus, by divine power, changed the bread and wine into his body and blood.[25] Like later Catholic thinkers, they assumed that John's eucharistic theology is found not in his account of the last supper but in the bread of life discourse of chapter 6, where Jesus says, "I am the bread of life," "This bread is my flesh, which I will give for the life of the world," and "Whoever eats my flesh and drinks my blood has eternal life, and I will raise him up at the last day."[26] It appeared to them that St. Paul knew of this theological tradition, for in writing to the Corinthians he echoes the synoptic accounts, adding that "whoever eats the bread or drinks the cup of the Lord unworthily is guilty of the body and blood of the Lord."[27]

Although the New Testament nowhere refers to the eucharistic meal as a sacrifice, the scriptures contain the seed of this theological interpretation which will bear fruit in later centuries. In the synoptic gospels, Jesus at the last supper refers to the contents of the cup as the blood of the new covenant that is about to be poured out,[28] which calls to mind the Israelite practice of pouring the blood of sacrificed animals on or around the altar.[29] Romans 3:25 speaks of Christ as a sacrifice of atonement, and

20. See Acts 2:38, 8:14–17; 19:5–6.

21. See Acts 2:38; 22:16.

22. See Rom 6:3–4; Col 2:11–14; Gal 3:27.

23. See 1 Cor 12:13; Eph 2:1–10.

24. See 1 Pt 3:20–22.

25. See Mt 26:26–28; Mk 14:22–24; Lk 22:19–20.

26. See Jn 6:35–59.

27. See 1 Cor 11:23–32.

28. See Mt 26:28; Mk 14:24; Lk 22:20.

29. See, e.g., Ex 24:6–8; Lv 1:5–15, 4:13–35; Dt 12:27.

this interpretation is echoed in Ephesians 5:2. Likewise the first letter of John speaks of Christ's death as an atoning sacrifice for sins.[30] Finally, the Epistle to the Hebrews develops the theme of Christ the high priest who offers himself in sacrifice, especially in chapter 10.

The New Testament theology of forgiveness is sprinkled throughout the synoptic gospels, both in aphorisms and in parables. Jesus plainly tells his followers to forgive others every time they repent, no matter how often they sin,[31] and in the Lord's prayer they are to ask to be forgiven just as they forgive others. God's willingness to forgive the repentant is taught in the parable of the prodigal son, and God's love for sinners is illustrated in the parables of the lost sheep and the lost coin.[32] The gospels agree that any sin can be forgiven except for sinning against the Holy Spirit, and they teach that Jesus himself claimed the power to forgive sins.[33] Both in the synoptics and in John's gospel, Jesus gives the apostles the power to forgive sins.[34] Catholic intellectuals from the second century onward interpreted many of these passages as being directed to the successors of the apostles, namely the bishops.

God's willingness and power to heal is exemplified in the many healing miracles of Jesus, and the transmission of that power to the apostles is attested to in the gospels.[35] Incidents at the beginning and end of the book of Acts show that both Peter and Paul had this power.[36] St. James told Christians in Jerusalem to go to the clergy when they were in ill health, so it appeared to later generations that priests had been given the power to anoint the sick.[37]

That spiritual power can be bestowed through the laying on of hands could be inferred from a number of passages in the Acts of the Apostles, where the recently baptized display spiritual gifts such as praising God in foreign languages.[38] Such displays of spiritual power may have been given to the early church as a sign of divine presence and approval, later Christians reasoned, but the book of Acts also makes reference to the gift of the Spirit.[39] Two lists of gifts that come from the Holy Spirit can be found in the epistles,[40] and this list can be amplified with the help of revelation from the prophets. Seven of these gifts of the Holy Spirit (wisdom, understanding,

---

30. See 1 Jn 2:2, 4:10.

31. See Mt 18:21–22; Mk 11:25; Luke 6:37; 17:3.

32. See Lk 15:1–31.

33. See Mt 9:1–8; 12:31–32; Mk 2:1–12; 3:28–29; Lk 5:17–26; 12:10.

34. See Mt 16:19; Jn 20:23.

35. See Mt 10:8; Mk 3:14–15; 6:12–13; Lk 9:1–2; 10:17.

36. See Acts 3:1–10; 28:7–9.

37. See Jas 5:14–15.

38. See Acts 6:6; 8:17; 19:6.

39. See Acts 2:38; 10:45.

40. See Rom 12:6–8; 1 Cor 12:7–10; Is 11:2.

counsel, fortitude, knowledge, piety, and fear of the Lord) later found their way into the traditional theology of confirmation.[41]

In the New Testament, hands are laid not only on the recently baptized but also on deacons, apostles, presbyters and bishops.[42] Although the scriptures do not recount Jesus laying hands on the original twelve apostles, it was clear to later generations that he gave them the power to baptize, to impart the Holy Spirit, to change bread and wine into his body and blood, to forgive sins, and to heal. What he did by divine command was believed to have been ritualized by the early church in the laying on of hands so that these priestly powers would be passed on to future generations in an unbroken apostolic succession.

Christian thinkers discovered elements of the theology of marriage in both the gospels and the epistles. Each of the synoptics records Jesus' teaching about the sacredness of marriage and the prohibition of divorce.[43] The Epistle to the Ephesians teaches that the relationship between husband and wife reflects the relationship between Christ and the church, and if the latter is indissoluble, then the former must likewise be indissoluble. Moreover, a husband is to love his wife as Christ loves the church, and a woman is to obey her husband even as the church obeys Christ.[44]

The fathers of the church built on these scriptural foundations, sometimes finding additional texts that illuminated the ones that are mentioned here, but these are sufficient to show that they, the medieval scholastics, and modern Catholic theologians built on what apparently was there to be found in the Bible.

3. Sacraments in the Writings of the Church Fathers

Some documents dating to the patristic period are anonymous. These were often written by unknown Christians for catechetical or liturgical reasons, and they often summarize the state of things in a particular church at a certain time. Thus the *Didache* gives us a fuzzy snapshot of moral teachings and ritual practices in the second half of the first century, written apparently for a community with strong Jewish roots.[45] The *Didascalia Apostolorum* captures images of church life in the mid-third century in the eastern Mediterranean, probably in present-day Syria.[46] The *Apostolic Tradition* gives us a more detailed picture of Christian ceremonies, but its authorship and provenance are uncertain. If written by Hippolytus of Rome as traditionally ascribed, it dates from

---

41. See Is 11:2.

42. See Acts 2:26; 6:6; 13:2–3; 1 Tim 4:13–14; 5:22; 2 Tim 1:6.

43. See Mt 5:31f; Mk 10:5–12; Lk 16:18.

44. See Eph 5:21–33.

45. See Aaron Milavec, *The Didache: Faith, Hope, and Life of the Earliest Christian Communities, 50–70 C.E.* (Mahwah, NJ: Paulist Press, 2003).

46. See Paul F. Bradshaw, *The Search for the Origins of Christian Worship.* (New York: Oxford University Press, 2002).

Rome in the early third century; if written in Egypt as recent scholars suggest, it describes eastern church practices in the fourth century.[47] The *Apostolic Constitutions* is a late fourth century work that selects from and adds to the aforementioned works to present a rather thorough picture of what was going on in the Antiochene church at that time. All of the documents claim apostolic authority, but none actually date from the first century. They describe baptismal, eucharistic, ordination and other ceremonies, but none of them refer to all such ceremonies as sacraments (i.e., μυστήρια, since these quasi-ecclesiastical documents were all originally written in Greek).

The first Christian writer known to have used the Latin word *sacramentum* is Tertullian, a north African whose works are dated from around 197 to around 213 AD. In his treatment of baptism, he speaks about the *sacramentum* of the water, referring to the water as a symbol, but it may also mean the mystery that it symbolized.[48] For *sacramentum* at this point could be used to translate both senses of the Greek μυστήριον, which could refer either to a symbolic ritual or to the hidden reality behind it. A ritual *sacramentum* known to Tertullian was the military oath by which Roman soldiers swore their allegiance to the emperor, and in which Tertullian saw a parallel to Christian baptism.[49] All things considered, for Tertullian the sacrament of baptism was probably the water of baptism or the baptismal ceremony, which referred to a hidden mystery.[50]

A generation later, Cyprian of Carthage uses *sacramentum* quite often, but it almost always refers to a mystery, not a sacred ritual. In his *Letter to Quirinus*, he speaks of the mystery of Christ (*sacramentum Christi*) as well as the mysteries of his incarnation, passion, chalice, altar, and apostles.[51] He talks about the unity of the church as a mystery (*unitatis sacramentum*) and he refers to the paschal mystery (*sacramentum paschae*).[52] He speaks of the mysteries of the Lord's Prayer (*orationis dominicae sacramenta*),[53] and at times he appears to contrast *signum* and *sacramentum* as one might contrast a sign with the mystery to which it points.[54] In many of his letters, Cyprian's use is ambiguous, with the result that *sacramentum* could be translated as mystery or as sacrament (i.e., a sacred sign) and both translations would make sense.[55]

---

47. See Paul Bradshaw, Maxwell E. Johnson, and L. Edwards Philips, *The Apostolic Tradition: A Commentary* (Minneapolis: Fortress Press, 2002).

48. See Tertullian, *Baptism*, 1 (*sacramento aquae nostrae*); 12 (*aquae sacramentum*).

49. See Tertullian, *The Crown*, 11–12.

50. *Baptism*, 13 makes reference to Mt 28:19 and Jn 3:5.

51. See Cyprian, *Letter to Quirinus*, 1, Pref.; 2.2.

52. See Cyprian, *The Unity of the Church*, 7–8.

53. See Cyprian, *The Lord's Prayer*, 9.

54. See Cyprian, *Exhortation to Martyrdom, Addressed to Fortunatus*, 8; *An Address to Demetrianus*, 25.

55. See Cyprian, *Letters*, e.g., Letter 63, 13 (*sacramentum spiritale et caeleste*); Letter 69, 4 (*de sacramento paschae et agni*); Letter 73, 5 (*Insinuat trinitatem, cuius sacramento gentes tinguerentur.*); Letter 74, 4 (*ad celebranda sacramenta*); Letter 74, 11 (*sacramentum divinae traditionis*).

Tertullian articulated a theology of baptism that was based on the scriptures but that also embellished what can be found there. For him, the waters of baptism cleanse the soul and wash away past sins, thus admitting the newly baptized to eternal life.[56] The physical element performs this spiritual action not of its own power but through the power of the Holy Spirit, acting through an angel.[57] The anointing with oil and the imposition of hands after the bath invite the Holy Spirit to enter the soul.[58] Moreover, baptism is necessary for salvation because Jesus himself said that one cannot have life without being born of water and the spirit.[59]

Other early Christian writers record similar ways of understanding baptism. Justin Martyr around the year 150 spoke of baptism as a spiritual regeneration that is necessary for salvation.[60] Clement of Alexandria, writing in the latter half of the second century, said that baptism is for the remission of sins, that it is a spiritual purification, and that through it Christians become adopted children of God who inherit eternal life.[61] Cyprian of Carthage, writing in the next century, likewise maintained that baptism brought forgiveness of sins and bestowed the Holy Spirit, but he also contended that those who had been baptized by heretics were not truly baptized since heretics could not give what they did not have.[62]

The meaning and validity of baptism were topics of discussion among church leaders in the early centuries, not only because of apostasy but also because of heresy and schism. What was the status of baptisms performed by those outside the true church? And what happened to the baptism of those who left the church? Did it have to be repeated if they returned to the fold? Eventually questions of this sort were raised about ordination as well. Did priests and bishops who left the church lose their ordination? Were those ordained by heretical bishops truly ordained? And would they need to be reordained (i.e., properly ordained) if they were reconciled with the church?

Many of these issues came to a head when a north African cleric named Donatus became bishop of Carthage (present-day Tunis) in 313, not long after a period of Christian persecution by Roman emperors that ended only with Constantine's edict of toleration. Like his predecessor Cyprian, Donatus took the position that baptisms performed by apostates and heretics were of no spiritual merit and therefore had to be repeated. Moreover, he held that priests who had given up the faith had to be both rebaptized and reordained if they wanted to resume their priestly ministry. Donatus and his followers accepted Cyprian's logic that those who had left the church had lost

---

56. Ibid., 1, 4, 7.

57. Ibid., 4, 6.

58. Ibid., 7, 8.

59. Ibid., 12. The scripture reference is to Jn 3:5.

60. Justin Martyr, *First Apology*, 61.

61. Clement of Alexandria, *The Instructor*, 1.6.

62. Cyprian of Carthage, *Letters*, 73.

the Holy Spirit, so they could not give to others what they themselves no longer had.[63] This theology did not match the practice of the rest of the church, but it took the genius of another north African to provide Christianity with a more satisfactory theology.

Augustine of Hippo was born in present-day Algeria not far from the city to which he would eventually return as bishop. As a young man, he had sought his fortune in Italy, where he was awarded a position as a teacher of language arts at the imperial court in Milan. While there he came under the influence of the bishop, Ambrose, whose persuasive preaching led him to ponder the possibility of becoming a Christian, which he eventually did in his early thirties. Returning to his homeland, he was ordained a priest and led a monastic lifestyle, but his popularity as a preacher led to his being selected to succeed the bishop of Hippo about ten years later, in 395.

Donatus was long gone from the scene. However, during his lifetime there had arisen a schismatic church in competition with the rest of the western church, so that in many north African cities there were both Donatist and Catholic churches. Augustine tried to persuade the Donatists to return to orthodoxy, and in the process of demonstrating the reasonableness of Catholic practice he contributed much to the development of sacramental theology.

First, he advanced beyond Tertullian's identification of the baptismal rite as a sacrament by capitalizing on the Latin word *sacramentum*'s ability to translate both senses of the Greek word μυστήριον, which could be used to mean both visible signs and the invisible realities that they signify. Since the time of Cyprian, Latin churchmen had spoken of the gift of baptism as something that was received in the baptismal ceremony, and as something that either could be lost (the Donatist position) or not lost (the Catholic position).[64] At the same time, however, Catholic bishops insisted on reconciling those who had left the church even though they did not rebaptize them. Catholic practice therefore suggested that heretics and apostates had sinned but they were still baptized.

Augustine argued that those who receive the sacrament of baptism receive not just the water but an invisible reality that could also be rightly called a sacrament: "the sacrament of baptism is what a baptized person has" (*sacramentum enim baptismi est quod habet qui baptizatur*).[65] By the same token, those who are ordained also receive an invisible reality, which Augustine sometimes calls the sacrament of ordination or, since theological terminology was still fluid, "the sacrament of giving baptism."[66] In a single stroke, then, Augustine addressed both the question of rebaptism and the question of reordination by identifying what is received when a sacrament is received. It is not something material like water or oil but something spiritual, and something

---

63. For a slightly fuller account, see Martos, 43–44. See also D. Faul, "Donatism," *New Catholic Encyclopedia*, Second Edition (Farmington Hills, MI: Gale, 2003) Vol. 4, 861–864.

64. See Cyprian, *Letters*, 69.11; 70.1–3.

65. Augustine, *Baptism, Against the Donatists*, 1.1.

66. *Sacramentum dandi baptismi*, ibid.

that cannot be lost. Augustine likened it to a military tattoo (*nota militaris*) that is permanent, for it cannot be lost by deserters and it is not reapplied if they come back to their ranks.[67]

Yet clearly something was lost by those who became heretics or schismatics. Augustine identified it as unity with the church, for Catholic practice required such people to go through the process of reconciliation in order to regain that unity. Thus heretical and schismatic groups could rightly confer the sacraments of baptism and ordination, Augustine reasoned, but they could not confer unity with the church since they did not possess it.[68]

Augustine accepted the baptism of infants as a practice of the universal church which had the authority of a long tradition behind it, and he argued for its appropriateness by comparing it with the divinely instituted practice of circumcision among the Jews. In Augustine's mind, baptism was something that is given to infants even before they are capable of active faith, and they receive the invisible sacrament just as surely as Jewish infants receive the visible sign of the covenant.[69] Moreover, infants are in need of baptism because it bestows not only the sacrament but also the remission of original sin and an infusion of the Holy Spirit, which can also be called the grace of Christ.[70] Without forgiveness and without this grace, infants carry the sin of Adam that has been transmitted from generation to generation, and thus they are not able to enter the kingdom of God. Nonetheless, Augustine surmised that the punishment of unbaptized infants is very mild since the sin that keeps them out of heaven is not theirs but that of their first parents.[71]

Of all the Latin fathers, Augustine was the first to speak clearly about the sacrament of marriage. His mentor, Ambrose, had spoken of the marriage bond and the sacredness of marriage,[72] but none before Augustine had written extensively about it. Citing the gospel prohibitions of divorce,[73] Christian church leaders had consistently argued for the permanence of marriage, but Augustine was the first to proffer a theological explanation for this permanence. Writing early in his episcopal career, he spoke of the sacramental nature of the marriage bond and the permanence of the sacrament.[74] Some 20 years later he spoke of the marital relationship as a sacrament of the relationship between Christ and the church, citing Ephesians 5:32.[75] Just as

67. Ibid., 4. See also *Treatises on the Gospel of John*, Treatise 6, 15–16; *Commentaries on the Psalms*, Psalm 39.1; *Sermon to the People of the Church of Carthage*, 2.

68. Ibid., 2–3, 8–12.

69. Ibid., 4.24.

70. *Merit and the Forgiveness of Sins, and the Baptism of Infants*, 1.9, 15.

71. Ibid., 19–21. See also *The Proceedings of Pelagius*, 23–24.

72. See Ambrose, *Letters*, 63.10, 22, 32.

73. See Mt 5:31–32; Mk 10:11–12; Lk 16:18.

74. See *The Good of Marriage*, 6, 17, 21. In chapter 32 he compares the permanence of the sacrament of marriage with the permanence of the sacrament of ordination.

75. See *Marriage and Concupiscence*, 2.12.

the divine-human relationship is permanent, so also the husband-wife relationship is permanent; and just as baptism cannot be lost through apostasy or schism, the bond of marriage cannot be lost through adultery or divorce.[76]

In one of his earliest writings as a bishop, Augustine referred broadly to sacraments as visible signs of invisible things, and thus church ceremonies, religious symbols, and even scriptural narratives could be regarded as sacramental.[77] About ten years later, sharing his ideas about baptism with a fellow bishop, Augustine developed his ideas further, suggesting that

> if sacraments did not bear some resemblance (*quamdam similitudinem*) to the things of which they are the sacraments, they would not be sacraments at all. Moreover, this resemblance to those things is most often why they are called sacraments.[78]

From the examples he gives in this letter, it is clear that he is thinking that baptism is a sacrament because it washes away sin, that the consecrated elements are a sacrament because they bear some resemblance to flesh and blood, and that the Easter liturgy is a sacrament because it is celebrated at the time of the resurrection, i.e., in the morning. Augustine's writings were used by later Christian thinkers to develop what became known as sacramental theology, but his creative usage of the term lacked the specificity and precision that would eventually be needed for a systematic treatment of church rituals.

In this respect, Augustine was not unlike other writers in the patristic era who wrote about Christian practices but did not refer to them collectively as *sacramenta*. As already noted, *sacramentum* could be used to translate the Greek μυστήριον, which referred both to hidden mysteries and to the rites that celebrated them. Indeed, a close examination of Tertullian's usage discloses that in many instance *sacramenta* refer to spiritual realities rather than to symbolic rituals.[79] It is primarily when writing about baptism that Tertullian uses *sacramentum* consistently in reference to the initiation ritual or to elements within it.[80] Nonetheless, many times Tertullian's usage remains

---

76. See ibid., 1.12, 19, 23.

77. See *Catechizing the Uninstructed*, 26.

78. Augustine, *Letters*, 98.

79. For example, *de Dei verbo et Christi sacramento*: concerning the word of God and the mystery of Christ (*Prescription Against Heretics*, 26); *ob nominis sui futuri sacramentum*: because of the mystery of [Jesus'] future name (*Against Marcion*, 3.7); *Ipse si esset, latere non posset, nedum aliqua eius sacramenta*: If [God] exists, he cannot be concealed, nor any of his mysteries (ibid., 5.6); *in sacramento voluntatis suae*: in the mystery of [God's] will (ibid., 5.17); *dispensatio sacramenti occulti*: the dispensation of the hidden mystery (ibid., 5.18); *magno nominis sacramento*: the great mystery of [God's] name (*Against the Valentinians*, 39); *sine fidei sacramento*: without the mystery of faith (*The Soul*, 1); *haereticarum idearum sacramenta*: the mysteries found in heretical ideas (ibid., 18); *Sit nunc et potior sensu intellectus et potior cognitor sacramentorum*: the intellect is better than the senses for understanding mysteries (ibid.).

80. For example, *Deus disposuit etiam in sacramentis propriis parere fecit*: God caused to appear in

ambiguous, and *sacramentum* could be justifiably translated either as mystery or as ritual, reflecting the ambiguity of the Greek μυστήριον.[81]

About a generation after Tertullian, but still in the third century, the works of Cyprian of Carthage manifest this same ambiguity. *Sacramentum* is best translated as mystery in most of the places where Cyprian uses the word,[82] And in his letters, the following are all referred to as *sacramenta*: Noah's drinking of wine, the offering of Melchizedek, Jesus turning water into wine, the mingling of water and wine in Christian worship, the joining of many grains in one loaf of bread, Jewish circumcision, and the manna in the desert. Of course, baptism and the eucharistic bread and wine are also called *sacramenta*.[83]

By the latter half of the fourth century, *sacramentum* was most often used to refer to religious rituals such as baptism and eucharist, but it was still sometimes used as a synonym for *mysterium*. Ambrose of Milan, for example, consistently refers to the mystery of the incarnation as *sacramentum incarnationis*,[84] and Latin versions of the New Testament sometimes translated the Greek μυστήριον as *sacramentum*.[85]

Like the ritual of baptism, the eucharistic meal in early patristic literature was most often referred to by its proper name, although the bread and wine (or cup) were occasionally called *sacramenta*.[86] The theological understanding of the eucharistic elements remained consistent throughout the patristic period: they are the body and

---

special sacraments (*Baptism*, 3); *Igitur omnes aquae . . . sacramentum sanctificationis consecuntur*: All waters, therefore, . . . become a sacrament of sanctification (ibid., 4); *sacramento obsignatio baptismi*: the sealing ritual of baptism (ibid., 13); *sacramento infanticidii*: the ritual of infanticide (*Apology*, 17); *Judaici sacramenti et inde iam et nostri*: Jewish rituals and our rituals (ibid., 19); *ipsum fidei eius sacramentum*: [baptism is] the very sacrament of his faith (*Against Marcion*, 1, 38); *ecclesiarum sacramenta*: the religious rites of church (ibid., 22); *dilectio, summum fidei sacramentum*: love, the greatest sign of faith (*Patience*, 12).

81. For example, *de sacramentis nostrae religionis*: about the sacraments/mysteries of our religion (*To the Nations*, 1.16); *panis et calicis sacramento*: the sacrament/mystery of the bread and cup (*Against Marcion*, 5.8); *meditandum atque celebrandum semper sacramentum*: thinking about and celebrating the mystery/sacrament (*Against the Valentinians*, 30); *eucharistiae sacramentum*: the sacrament/mystery of the eucharist (*The Crown*, 3); *De sacramento aquae nostrae*: About the sacrament/mystery of our water (*Baptism*, 1).

82. See for example *The Unity of the Church* and *The Lord's Prayer*, where almost all the *sacramenta* referred to are Christian mysteries, such as the mystery of unity and the mystery of Easter.

83. Found in *Ante-Nicene Fathers*, Vol. 5, Edited by Alexander Roberts, James Donaldson, and A. Cleveland Coxe (Peabody, MA: Hendrickson Publishers, 1994), esp. Letters 63, 64, 68, 72 and 73.

84. See *Commentary on Psalm 118*, 3.8, 24; 5.34; 11.21; also *The Mystery of the Lord's Incarnation*, passim.

85. This is especially true of Ephesians 5:32, which speaks about the relationship between Christ and the church. Ambrose cites this verse in *An Explanation of the Prophet David to the Emperor Theodosius*, 5.23; *Commentary on Psalm 37*, 27.2; *Commentary on Luke's Gospel*, 4.826; *Widows*, 15.89. Tertullian and Cyprian also cite this text, which indicates that this verse read *sacramentum hoc magnum est* in Latin versions of the NT even before Jerome's translation. See also Eph 1:9 and 3:3, and Col 1:27, where *mysterion* is translated as *sacramentum* in the Vulgate.

86. See, e.g., Tertullian, *Against Marcion*, 5.8. Cyprian, *The Lapsed*, 25; *Letter 62*, 2. Ambrose, *The Mysteries*, 9.55, 58; *Commentary on Luke's Gospel*, 2.144.

blood of Christ. But how bread and wine become the body and blood of Christ is a theological question that had not yet arisen.

The patristic period also saw the development of the concept of sacrifice as applied to the early church's eucharistic practices. The earliest mention is in the *Didache*, which in chapter 14 refers to the Lord's day meal as a sacrifice (θυσία in Greek) and sees it as the pure sacrifice predicted in Malachi 1:11. In the second century, both Justin Martyr and Irenaeus of Lyon cited the prophet Malachi's θυσία καθαρά as a way to understand eucharistic worship.[87] Writing somewhat later and in Latin, Tertullian spoke about the sacrificial prayers (*orationes sacrificiorum*) that are offered before the reception of the Lord's body.[88] But it is Cyprian in the mid-third century who first elaborated on this concept, saying that the priest "offers a true and full sacrifice in the church to God the Father, when he proceeds to offer it according to what he sees Christ Himself to have offered."[89]

After the Council of Nicaea, bishops in both the east and west spoke of eucharistic worship as sacrificial in nature. Preaching on the Epistle to the Hebrews, John Chrysostom argued that the sacrifice of the church is the same as the sacrifice of Christ.[90] Augustine defined sacrifice as a "visible sacrament, that is a sacred sign, of an invisible sacrifice," which is the church offering herself to God.[91]

By the end of the patristic period, then, baptism and eucharist were understood as sacraments, that is, as visible rituals that signified invisible realities. With regard to eucharistic worship, however, there was a tendency to call the consecrated elements sacraments and to interpret the ritual surrounding the elements as a sacrifice. Augustine also referred to marriage and ordination as sacraments. When the bishop's baptismal blessing was separated from the rite of baptism in the west, it was not originally thought of as a separate *sacramentum*, nor did it have a developed theology. The public reconciliation of heretics and apostates had flourished prior to Constantine's edict of toleration in 313, but this practice all but disappeared in subsequent decades, and it was not referred to as a *sacramentum*. Anointing of the sick was still a predominantly lay practice, although the oil used was often blessed by a monk or cleric.[92]

87. See Justin, *Dialogue with Trypho*, 41; Irenaeus, *Against Heresies*, 4.17–18.; 5.2.

88. See Tertullian, *Prayer*, 19.

89. Cyprian of Carthage, Letter 63, 4, translation by Robert Ernest Wallis in *Ante-Nicene Fathers*, Vol. 5, cited above. Editors of Cyprian's works have given this letter the title, *The Sacrament of the Cup of the Lord*, because of its extensive treatment of the eucharist. See esp. chapters 4, 9, and 14–17.

90. See John Chrysostom, *Homilies on Hebrews*, 11.3; 14.1; 17.3; excerpted in Paul F. Palmer, ed., *Sources of Christian Theology: Sacraments and Worship* (Westminster, MD: Newman Press, 1957), 188–189

91. See Augustine, *The City of God*, 10.5, 6, 20; excerpted in Palmer, *Sacraments and Worship*, 190–91.

92. See Martos, *Doors to the Sacred*, chapters on confirmation, reconciliation, and anointing of the sick, especially the second section in each of those chapters.

4. Sacraments in Medieval Theology

There are some notable differences between the way theology was done in the patristic period and the way it was done in the Middle Ages. Patristic theology, as the name implies, was done by fathers of the church, that is, by church leaders who were, for the most part, bishops. Their work was largely *ad hoc*, for they usually had practical reasons for sitting down and writing out their reflections not only on church practices but also on fundamental beliefs about God, Jesus, revelation, prayer, the church, and so on. In this respect their theologizing was non-systematic, although any father who wrote over an extended period of time tended to develop an internal coherence of thought and to build on what he had said in earlier writings. Augustine's extension of the term *sacramentum* to marriage and ordination, in the same way that he had previously applied it to baptism, is a good example of this.

After the collapse of the Roman Empire in the west, church life continued, albeit in much different cultural and liturgical forms. Bishops were no longer cosmopolitan intellectuals but pragmatic administrators functioning in a feudal system of tribal loyalties. The laity were no longer mostly urban dwellers but rather subsistence farmers scattered over the countryside. The boundaries of the Catholic world no longer hugged the Mediterranean coast but stretched into northern Europe, and especially after the loss of north Africa to the Muslims, its geographical center shifted to present-day France and Germany in what was sometimes called the Holy Roman Empire.

During the patristic period, five major cities had dominated the Christian landscape: Jerusalem, where the faith had originated; Antioch, a hub of commerce and travel; Alexandria, an intellectual and cultural center; Constantinople, the seat of imperial power; and Rome, the founding city of the empire. By the eighth century, Muslim caliphates had swallowed Jerusalem, Antioch and Alexandria, and the Roman Empire in the east was shrinking to Greece and Asia Minor with Constantinople at its center. For almost a thousand years after the fall of Rome, the Byzantine Empire (as it became known) was able to retain its cultural continuity, including its richly elaborate liturgical forms. Today they can still be seen in Orthodox churches and in the Byzantine rite of the Catholic Church.

But the church in the west, now Latin-speaking rather than Greek-speaking, evolved new liturgical forms to meet the needs of the times. Baptism became a shortened ceremony for children born into Christian families, and when it was used for adult converts (as when Charlemagne converted entire tribes in expanding his empire[93]), this abbreviated rite was used with the expectation that instruction in the faith would follow afterward. Confirmation became an episcopal ceremony performed on children some time after baptism according to a variety of local customs, but often neglected due to episcopal or parental negligence. The eucharistic liturgy became the

---

93. See Richard Fletcher, *The Conversion of Europe: From Paganism to Christianity 371–1386 AD* (London: Harper Collins, 1977), 210–15.

sacrifice of the mass, offered by a single priest on behalf of the faithful who attended in silence. By the ninth century, the monastic practice of private confession had evolved into a priestly absolution of sins. In the same century, the anointing of the sick became a priestly prerogative that was administered shortly before death. By the twelfth century, a fully developed wedding ceremony was in place so that all marriages could be witnessed and duly recorded by the clergy. Men entered the holy orders of the church through a sequence of seven rituals, each of which was called an ordination.[94]

While the church's rituals were evolving, theology was also evolving. No longer the province of bishops, it gradually became a profession for those who had the leisure (σχολή in Greek) to study the scriptures and the writings of the fathers. The first schools were opened in monasteries which had been copying and preserving ancient manuscripts for centuries. Cathedral schools quickly followed, bringing seculars as well as regulars into the project that Anselm of Canterbury called faith seeking understanding. By the high Middle Ages, schools were coalescing into universities, so called because they attempted to embrace the whole universe of knowledge that was then available.[95]

In a world without printed books, some method was needed to enable students of theology to find and read the relevant texts on a wide variety of topics from the creation of the world to the second coming of Christ. At the cathedral school in Paris, Peter Abelard posed over a hundred questions related to faith and reason and lined up quotations on both sides of each issue, calling his work *Sic et non* and encouraging his students to arrive at logical conclusions. At what became the University of Paris in the mid-twelfth century, various collections of *sententiae* or theological opinions were compiled by professors who, unlike Abelard, offered their own opinions after citing texts for and against a series of theological questions. The most popular of these was the *Sentences* of Peter Lombard, which by the early thirteenth century had become the standard text book for theology students at the university, including Thomas Aquinas. The final stage in this evolution was the *summa*, of which Aquinas produced two, and within which the pro and con format of the scholastic method is still visible.[96]

Whereas the theology of the fathers had been occasional and pastoral, the theology of the schoolmen was systematic and scientific, but the *scientia* of the day was that of Aristotle, which sought to understand things both in themselves and through what caused them.[97] In themselves, for example, things were both experienceable and

94. See Martos, *Doors to the Sacred*, chapters 6–12 on the historical development of the individual sacraments. More detailed information can be found in the historical works cited at the end of each chapter.

95. On the rise of medieval universities, see Justo L. Gonzalez, *A History of Christian Thought*, Vol. 2 (Nashville: Abingdon Press, 1971) 225–29; also Richard E. Rubenstein, *Aristotle's Children* (New York: Harcourt, 2003), 160–63.

96. For more details, see Congar, *History*, 50–114.

97. "We suppose ourselves to possess unqualified scientific knowledge of a thing . . . when we think that we know the cause on which that fact depends, as the cause of that fact and of no other,

intelligible; in scholastic terminology, they had both matter and form. Any particular thing or substance had something in common with similar things (its essence) as well as attributes that made it uniquely itself (its individual qualities or accidents). And the causes of any reality, whether material or spiritual, could be understood by discerning that on which it depended, whether for its immediate existence or its ultimate existence.[98]

Medieval life presented the schoolmen with a variety of Christian practices that could be investigated systematically and understood scientifically, most notably the seven church rituals that Peter Lombard had identified as having spiritual effects. These ceremonies were experienceable in that they could be seen and heard and they involved the use of material elements, but they were also intelligible because Christians understood what they were doing when they performed or participated in the ceremonies. By the thirteenth century, the name *sacramenta* came to be restricted to just these seven, other church rituals and religious symbols being referred to as *sacramentalia* or sacrament-like.[99]

Moreover, many aspects of Christian life could be traced back to sacraments as their causes. Priests were priests because they were ordained. Married people were spouses because they had been joined in matrimony. The Eucharist was the body and blood of Christ because it had been consecrated in the mass. The repentant were forgiven because they had confessed their sins and had been given absolution. Most fundamentally, people were not pagans because they had been baptized, and because they had been baptized, they were saved by God's grace.

But there was a problem with this simple schema. The consecrated eucharistic elements were called a sacrament. However, since the eleventh century, when Berengar of Tours had been condemned for holding that the Eucharist was only a sacrament, it was a matter of faith that the Eucharist is a reality, namely the body and blood of Christ.[100] Moreover, St. Augustine had contended that the sacrament of baptism is something that is received by the baptized and can never be lost. How could these elements of tradition be incorporated into a systematic understanding of sacraments?

The solution was to distinguish between sacraments that are experienceable and intelligible church rituals on the one hand, and sacraments that are not sensible but only intelligible, that is, known by the mind. Thus the rite of baptism could be called a sacrament in the first sense, and the baptism that was administered and received

---

and, further, that the fact could not be other than it is." Aristotle, *Posterior Analytics*, 1.2, translated by G.R.G. Mure, in Richard McKeon, *The Basic Works of Aristotle* (New York: Random House, 1941) 111. See also Patrick H. Byrne, *Analysis and Science in Aristotle* (Albany, NY: State University of New York Press, 1997) 82–85.

98. See Aristotle, *Physics*, 2.3; also his *Metaphysics*, 5.2.

99. See Martos, *Doors to the Sacred*, 54–56. Also Elizabeth Frances Rogers, *Peter Lombard and the Sacramental System* (Merrick, NY: Richwood, 1976) 25–29.

100. See Gary Macy, *The Banquet's Wisdom: A Short History of the Theologies of the Lord's Supper* (Mahwah, NJ: Paulist Press, 1992), 77.

through the rite could be called a sacrament in the second sense. Likewise, the consecration of bread and wine during mass could be called a sacrament in the first sense,
and the consecrated Eucharist could be called a sacrament—indeed, it was called the
Blessed Sacrament—in the second sense. Similarly, the wedding rite could be called
a sacrament in the first sense, and the bond of marriage could be called a sacrament
in the second sense. Finally, the ordination ceremony could be called a sacrament in
the first sense, and each of the holy orders administered and received through such
rites could be considered parts or degrees of the sacrament in the second sense. The
Latin term given to sacraments in the first sense was *sacramentum tantum*, meaning
it is a sign and only a sign. The term given to sacraments in the second sense was
sacramentum et res, meaning that it is a sign that is also a reality.[101]

Using Aristotelian analysis on these two, sacraments in the first sense (i.e., the
external rituals) could be understood as being composed of matter and form. But
what might be the metaphysical status of sacraments in the second sense? Logically
they had to be causes of some sort, for they are what made the difference between the
unbaptized and the baptized, the unordained and the ordained, the unmarried and
the married. The scholastic axiom was *Ab esse ad posse valet illatio*, "From existence to
possibility is a valid inference," or more loosely translated, "That something is possible
can be inferred from the fact that it is." On the surface, this may appear to be a truism,
but in the hands of the scholastics it became a powerful analytical tool.

How this tool worked can be seen most clearly in the case of ordination. An
obvious fact of medieval Christian life was that priests could do things that lay people
could not do: priests could absolve sins, they could offer the eucharistic sacrifice, and
they could (in the terminology of the day) confect the Eucharist, that is, they could
turn ordinary bread and wine into the body and blood of Christ. They had abilities
or powers that the unordained did not have, and it was clear they must have received
these powers through ordination. In other words, when they went through the rite of
ordination (*sacramentum tantum*) they received the powers of the priesthood (*sacramentum et res*) that enabled them to perform their priestly functions.[102]

Powers of this sort were conceived to be analogous to what were regarded as
natural powers in Aristotelian philosophy, which was based on ordinary observation
and simple logic. Plants can do things that sand and rocks cannot do, namely, they are
able to live and they are able to reproduce; in Aristotelian terms, they have the power
of life and the power of reproduction. Animals too have these vital powers, but they
also can do things that plants cannot do, namely they are able to see, hear and smell,
and they are also able to move about; in Aristotelian terms, they have the power of
sensation and the power of local motion. Human beings clearly have all of the powers

---

101. In some scholastic textbooks, the sacrament in the second sense is called the *res et sacramentum*, which emphasizes that it is a reality that is also a sign of something other than itself, in contrast
with a reality that is not also a sign. See Leeming, *Principles*, 251–255.

102. For a slightly fuller account, see Martos, *Doors to the Sacred*, 502–503.

that plants and animals have, for they can reproduce, they can experience sensations, and they can move about. But human beings can also think and reason, and so they must have additional powers as well; in Aristotelian terms, they are rational animals.[103]

All of the aforementioned powers are clearly natural powers; these activities are found in the natural world, and so their underlying powers must be regarded as natural. Priests, however, can do things that other human beings cannot do, and so priestly powers must be more than natural powers, that is, they must be supernatural powers.[104] Yet priests obviously had these powers because they did things that could only be explained, in the Aristotelian scheme of things, by the possession of the power to do them.[105]

Behind the English word "power" in translations of scholastic texts lie one of three Latin words. *Potestas* is a power to do or act, especially the ability to effect change; it is the power of monarchs to rule and of administrators to perform their functions. *Potentia* is power in a more general sense; it can be an active *potestas* but it can also be a passive ability such as the ability to see or to think. Most plant, animal and human powers are potencies or abilities of this sort. *Virtus* is a power to do something well, repeatedly or readily. Thus the ability to move about might be regarded as a potency or *potentia*, but the ability to run swiftly and win races could be considered a virtue or *virtus*. Likewise, the ability to eat might be regarded as a *potentia*, but the ability to select and prepare foods in such a way as to eat healthily would be regarded as a *virtus*. In Aquinas's treatment: sacramental power is sometimes called a *postestas*, such as the priest's ability to offer the mass; it is sometimes called a *potentia*, such as the baptized person's ability to receive the other sacraments; and it is sometimes called a *virtus*, such as spiritual gifts that are given to the baptized.[106]

The *sacramentum et res* or sacramental reality of the Eucharist was regarded as analogous to these powers, for the Blessed Sacrament made it possible for Christians to adore Christ in the Eucharist and to receive Christ in communion. Historically, the scholastic discussion of the consecrated elements as a sacramental reality preceded the application of the term *sacramentum et res* to most of the other sacraments. In fact, the realization that the body and blood of Christ were neither just a material

103. See Aristotle, *The Soul*, 2.2–3 on the souls of vegetables and animals; also *Nicomachean Ethics*, 1.13 on the rational soul in human beings.

104 For Aquinas' understanding of supernatural powers as habits, see Lonergan, *Grace and Freedom*, 42–45.

105. See the more detailed treatment of the different types of power above, pages 23–24.

106. Question 63, article 2 in Part III of the *Summa Theologica* asks "Whether a character is a spiritual power?" The Latin text distinguishes between *potestas* and *potentia*, and it points out that a *virtus* is a *habitus* for doing good. See also Q. 62, a. 4–5, where the sacraments' ability to cause grace is called a *virtus*; Q. 63, a. 5, where the character is called a *potentia*; Q. 64, a. 3–4, where the power of Christ and the power of the sacraments is called either *potestas* or *virtus* depending on the context; Q. 69, a. 4–6, which discuss the effects of baptism; Q. 72, a. 5, where the character is called a *potestas* when it is an ability to do something; Q. 82, a. 1 and 8, where the priestly power to consecrate the eucharist is called a *potestas*.

sign (*sacramentum tantum*) nor just a spiritual reality (*res tantum*) led early on to the conclusion that the consecrated elements had to be a *tertium quid*, a third something that was neither simply a sign nor simply a reality but somehow both. Augustine's affirmation that the received sacrament of baptism was likewise a *tertium quid* that did not fit into either into the category of sign nor into the category of a spiritual reality (grace) provided the clue that the concept of *sacramentum et res* might be able to be generalized and applied to additional sacramental rituals. Rather quickly, what was received through ordination, confirmation and marriage was categorized as a sacramental reality, yielding a schema such as the following.[107]

Sacramentum tantum Liturgical ceremony	*Sacramentum et res* Sacramental reality	*Res tantum* Grace
Rite of Baptism	Baptismal Character	Justification
Rite of Confirmation	Seal of the Spirit	Spiritual strengthening
Rite of Consecration	Body and Blood of Christ	Union with Christ
Rite of Ordination	Priestly Character	Grace of Orders
Rite of Matrimony	Bond of Matrimony	Grace of Marriage
Rite of Penance	Contrition? Absolution?	Forgiveness of sins
Rite of Extreme Unction	(Difficult to determine)	(Preparation for heaven)

The items in the column on the left were known through experience: they were Christian rituals that could be seen and heard in medieval Europe. The items in the right column were known by the mind through faith, for they were the communal beliefs of the church, based on the teachings of the fathers and supported by proof texts from the scriptures. The items in the middle column were known by the mind through logical inference, for they answered the problem as to how a physical action could bring about a spiritual result, or to phrase it somewhat differently, how a natural action could produce a supernatural effect. The scholastics' answer was that, when a sacramental rite was performed, God gave the recipient a supernatural ability (power) to receive supernatural gifts or graces. Thus, when the scholastics spoke about receiving a sacrament, they were not talking about water, oil or a blessing, but

107. See Martos, *Doors to the Sacred*, 60–64, 276. This schema, or at least the terminology on which it is based, was in existence prior to the time when Thomas Aquinas was a student at the University of Paris. See Radulphus Ardens, *The Questions on the Sacraments* (Toronto: Pontifical Institute of Medieval Studies, 2010), esp. chapters 44–47, where he distinguishes between the *sacramentum* (=sacramental reality) and the *res* (=grace) of baptism. In chapter 63 he applies the triple distinction to the Eucharist. Ardens completed this work in the late twelfth century.

they were talking about a spiritual reality (*res*) that was both a gift (*gratia*) and a sign (*sacramentum*) of something further, namely, the pure grace of the sacrament.

This conceptual schema provided solutions to other theological problems as well. First, it made sense of the way that the Latin fathers had spoken about the giving and receiving of sacraments. Second, it justified the traditional contention that sacraments worked *ex opere operato*, for it showed that the operative factor in the administration of any sacrament was not the worthiness of the minister but the proper performance of the rite. Third, it explained why baptism was necessary for salvation, for the beatific vision is not a natural human ability, and so the very ability to see God would have to be a supernatural *potentia* bestowed by God on individual persons. Fourth, it explained delayed effects of the sacraments as a sort of reviviscence, showing that a sacrament could be received at one time without much visible effect (e.g., infant baptism) and later have the proper effect (e.g., a morally upright life).

While this schema was very satisfactory, it was nonetheless not perfect. Since baptism, confirmation and holy orders could be received only once, it was easy to identify the *sacramentum et res* of those rites as an indelible character. Since a person could be married to only one person at a time, it was easy to identify the *sacramentum et res* of matrimony as a spiritual bond that was indissoluble until death. But a person could receive the sacrament of penance more than once, and scholastics speculated about the operative factor. (The two most often proposed were contrition and absolution.) And it was extremely difficult to get information about the effects of extreme unction since almost all recipients died shortly after being anointed.

The sacramental reality of the Eucharist was regarded as different from all the others in that it was not a power received into the soul but a change in substance (*substantia*) without a change in appearances (*accidentalia*). But it did fit the general pattern of being a cause (*causa*) or condition for the possibility of adoring Christ in the consecrated elements, for if Christ were truly present then he could be truly perceived. Likewise, Christ's presence in the consecrated elements explained the spiritual benefits experienced after a devout reception of communion, such as growth in holiness.

As already noted, the liturgical action surrounding the Eucharist was not thought of as a sacrament but as a sacrifice—the sacrifice of the mass. During the Dark Ages, Christian thinkers such as Amalarius of Metz (later bishop of Trier) had proposed allegorical interpretations of the different parts of the mass, for example, the Gloria symbolizing the song of the angels announcing Christ's birth and the separate consecrations of bread and wine representing his death.[108] But when patristic writings referring to the Eucharist as a sacrifice were discovered, scripture references to the sacrificial character of the last supper and crucifixion helped the early scholastics develop an understanding of the mass as a mystical re-enactment of Christ's death on the

---

108. For an outline of Amalarius' full interpretation, see Josef Jungmann, *The Mass of the Roman Rite: Its Origins and Development (Missarum Solemnia)* (New York: Benziger Brothers, 1950), Vol. 1, 89–90.

cross. The words of consecration produced the sacramental reality of Christ present under the appearances of bread and wine, which the priest offered *in persona Christi* to God the Father in atonement for sins.[109]

Thus in the Middle Ages, the *sacramentum et res* as conceived by the schoolmen at once tied together many disparate elements of Catholic sacramental teaching and experience (theological language, liturgical practice, religious experience), and it also provided a framework for the juridical governance of sacramental activity. Canon law could clearly prescribe who could and could not administer holy communion and the other sacraments, when the sacraments should and should not be received, and what the juridical effects of receiving the sacraments would be. But this conceptual clarity came at a price, for over time it tended to promote a rather legalistic attitude about the administration of sacraments and a rather mechanistic perception about the effects of sacraments.

5. Sacraments in Modern Theology

Late medieval scholastic theology was not the high point of Catholic thinking about the sacraments. Instead of building on what had been achieved in the high Middle Ages, theologians of the fourteenth and fifteenth centuries tended to exploit the flaws in the scholastic system which, as has already been noted, was never perfect to begin with. Canonists, for their part, turned legalism into minimalism through casuistry, that is, though the process of considering various cases in order to determine the minimum that needed to be done in order to produce sacramental effects. In due time it was determined that uttering the words, "I baptize you in the name of the Father and of the Son and of the Holy Spirit," while pouring or sprinkling a tiny bit of water, could satisfactorily confer the sacramental character and eternal salvation. Likewise with regard to the other sacraments: even when reduced to their minimal matter and form, their effectiveness was guaranteed.

Parallel to the exaggerated confidence in the power of the sacraments was the power of the keys, as it came to be known. Just as priests had powers that lay people did not have, bishops had powers that were reserved to them, namely the power to administer confirmation and the power to bestow holy orders. Theologically, bishops received their powers as successors of the apostles when they were consecrated as bishops, and ultimately this power derived from Christ, who had given Peter and the Twelve the authority to rule the church when he said, "I will give you the keys to the kingdom of heaven. Whatever you bind on earth will be bound in heaven, and whatever you loose on earth will be loosed in heaven."[110] Bishops had exercised this power since patristic times, when they would restrict public sinners from eucharistic participation and later loosen those restrictions after the offenders had done penance

109. See Leeming, *Principles*, 255–56.

110. Mt 16:19

for their sins. The bishops also exercised clemency or *indulgentia*, granting early release from the penitential process in the event that a sinner was seriously ill and might die before being reconciled with the church.

During the early Middle Ages, episcopal indulgence was extended first to knights who volunteered to fight in the Crusades, and then to those who spent money to outfit and supply one or more crusaders. With the passage of time and the development of the doctrine of purgatory, the forgiveness of earthly penances was logically extended to include the punishment for sins that might have to be suffered in the afterlife.[111] By the late Middle Ages, the power of the keys was said to be so great that indulgences could be applied to any soul designated by someone who donated even a small amount of money. But since the amount of punishment due for sins was impossible to determine, people were encouraged to keep buying additional indulgences for their dearly departed.

Much the same could be said about the spiritual benefits of the mass. In each mass, Christ offered himself in sacrifice to God the Father,[112] and since Christ is divine, this offering was considered to be of infinite merit. Such merits could be applied, by the intention of the priest who said the mass, to any soul in purgatory, but since it was impossible to determine how much any individual soul actually benefited from this, people were encouraged to have as many masses as possible said for their loved ones. The length of masses was shortened to what was absolutely needed for validity, priests got into the habit of saying multiple masses every day, and churches had to build additional altars along the sides of the nave in order to accommodate them.

Clearly this legalism and minimalism had gotten out of hand. Reformers called for an end to such superstition and abuse beginning with Martin Luther's Ninety-Five Theses in 1517. But the bishops and pope (the ones who benefited the most from the sale of indulgences) were loathe to change the system, and it was not until 1545 that the reform-minded Pope Paul III was able to convene a general council of similarly minded bishops at Trent. The council met on and off for twenty-five sessions until 1563, dealing extensively with the doctrine and discipline of the sacraments.

The Catholic teaching on the sacraments as set forth by the Council of Trent was summarized in the first article of this series, and it need not be repeated here. Here it is sufficient to note that the council fathers and the magisterium thereafter utilized the conceptual structure of Aristotelian scholasticism to formulate doctrine and

---

111. On the historical development of indulgences, P.F. Palmer and A. Tavard, "Indulgences" in *New Catholic Encyclopedia*, Second Edition (Detroit: Thomson Gale, 2003), Vol. 7, 437.

112. As indicated above, the mass was regarded as a re-presentation of Christ's death on the cross, an unbloody sacrifice that re-enacted the bloody sacrifice on Calvary. The priest, regarded as *alter Christus*, acted *in persona Christi* when offering the Body and Blood of Christ to God the Father after the eucharistic elements were consecrated. Thus the mass repeated in a mystical way the self-offering of the Son to the Father to atone for the sins of humankind, thus effecting the salvation of the world. For the Doctrine Concerning the Sacrifice of the Mass as promulgated by the Council of Trent, see H. J. Schroeder, ed., *Canons and Decrees of the Council of Trent* (St. Louis: B. Herder Book Co., 1941), 144–45.

condemn heresy. From this point onward, leaders and scholars of the Catholic Church accepted the three-fold structure of the sacramental system (as presented above) as factual and unquestionable, and they implicitly used these concepts whenever talking about Christian rituals and their effects.[113]

Scholastic thinking about the church and its sacraments also facilitated the structural reforms mandated by the council and implemented by the pope and the curia. The power (*potestas*) of the Roman pontiff was expanded to include total control of the texts and rubrics of the mass and the other sacraments. This power had earlier been held by bishops and regional synods, which previously could make local adjustments in the rites as they saw fit. Moreover, by making explicit the requirements for sacramental performance (the matter and form of each rite), the Church could clearly determine which Christian rituals, both Catholic and Protestant, conferred the sacramental reality, and which ones did not.

Almost all of Trent's twenty-five sessions promulgated reforms directly related to the lives of the clergy in addition to doctrinal decrees that corrected the errors of the reformers. Perhaps based on what happened during the council's first session, the second session in January 1546 issued a Decree Concerning the Manner of Living and Other Matters to Be Observed During the Council, which exhorted bishops to be blameless, sober and chaste, citing 1 Timothy 3:2–3 in support of this directive.[114] More to the point of this chapter, the fourth session later that year issued a Decree Concerning the Canonical Scriptures, declaring the Latin Vulgate to be regarded as the only one having the approval of the Church.[115] Although the main intention of the decree was to counter Protestant claims that the Old Testament books originally written in Greek rather than Hebrew (the so-called Apocrypha) should not be included in the canon of the Bible, this decision also had the effect of enshrining *sacramentum* as the appropriate translation of μυστήριον in Ephesians 5:32 and other places.

The first doctrinal decree was issued in the fifth session on June 17, 1546. The Decree Concerning Original Sin summarized the Catholic understanding of human origins, and in doing so it explicitly adopted Augustine's interpretation of the sin of Adam and its transmission to all other human beings. The grace of Jesus Christ is necessary for salvation, the council declared, and this grace is conferred in the sacrament of baptism.[116]

---

113. The terms *sacramentum tantum*, *sacramentum et res* and *res tantum* do not necessarily appear in Church documents of the modern era, but the concepts behind them do. As we have seen in the first chapter, both ecclesiastical rituals and sacramental realities are referred to simply as sacraments; it is necessary to examine the context of any usage to determine whether the word *sacramentum* refers to the *sacramentum tantum* or to the *sacramentum et res*. In official documents, the *res tantum* is referred to simply as grace.

114. See Schroeder, *Canons and Decrees*, 13.

115. See ibid., 18.

116. See ibid., 21–23.

Closely related was the Decree Concerning Justification issued on January 13, 1547, at the conclusion of the sixth session. It described justification, mentioned in the letters to the Romans and the Corinthians, in very scholastic terms as "not only a remission of sins but also a sanctification and renewal of the inward man through the voluntary reception of the grace and gifts whereby an unjust man becomes just."[117] It set forth the causes of justification in terms of its final, efficient and formal causes, and designated the sacrament of baptism as its instrumental cause.[118] Through baptism, the council declared, the virtues of faith, hope and charity are infused in the soul, making the recipient of baptism truly just and not simply regarded by God as just, as Luther had taught.[119] Nonetheless, the grace of justification could be lost through sinning, but if it were lost it could be restored through repentance, sacramental confession and spiritual exercises.[120]

The seventh session in March of that year issued no general doctrine on the sacraments, but it did issue short canons on the sacraments in general, on baptism, and on confirmation. The ones pertinent to this study have already been discussed in the first chapter. One reason for this brief treatment of the sacraments may have been the deteriorating political situation in northern Italy, which necessitated a transfer of the council to Bologna shortly thereafter.[121] Not much was accomplished during the three sessions held in that city during the spring of 1447.

The topic of the sacraments did not come before the council again until the thirteenth session in October of 1551, after the bishops had again taken up residence in the city of Trent. Church teachings promulgated in the Decree Concerning the Most Holy Sacrament of the Eucharist and its attendant canons can be found in the preceding chapter. Here it can be observed that the medieval practice of reserving the sacramental bread was both endorsed and expanded to include a celebration of the Real Presence of Christ on a special feast day (*Corpus Christi*) with "processions through the streets and public places."[122] Moreover, the Blessed Sacrament was to be worshiped in the manner "which is due to the true God,"[123] implicitly affirming the presence of the sacramental reality under the sensible species.

The fourteenth session in November 1551, the twenty-first session in July 1562 (after another long hiatus due to political instability in Europe) and the twenty-second session in September of the same year dealt with doctrinal matters already sufficiently treated in the first chapter: the sacraments of penance and extreme unction, the

117. Decree Concerning Justification, 7, ibid., 33.

118. See ibid.

119. See Decree, 7–9, ibid., 34–35.

120. See Decree, 14, ibid., 39–40.

121. See B. J. Kidd, *The Counter-Reformation 1550–1600* (London: SPCK, 1933), 67–69.

122. Decree Concerning the Most Holy Sacrament of the Eucharist, 5, in Schroeder, *Canons and Decrees*, 76.

123. Ibid.

distribution of communion under one or both species, and the teaching on the mass as a sacrifice.

The twenty-third session in July 1563 promulgated its decree on the sacrament of order, in which priesthood was defined in terms of the supernatural powers discussed earlier. Thus, when the council affirmed that "the order of priesthood is truly a sacrament,"[124] it was referring to the *sacramentum et res*. But when it said that "grace is conferred by sacred ordination"[125] it was also referring to the *sacramentum tantum*, for priestly powers and divine assistance to use them well were both regarded as instances of grace that resulted from the valid performance of the ordination rite.[126]

The Doctrine of the Sacrament of Matrimony was promulgated at the conclusion of the twenty-fourth session, in November 1563. That the sacrament being defined was the sacramental reality and not the liturgical rite has already been discussed. In addition, the council issued its Decree Concerning the Reform of Matrimony, which declared that henceforth marriages must be entered into in the presence of a priest and at least two witnesses. While such a declaration might be regarded as a simple rule change for the social regulation of marriage,[127] bishops and theologians at the council believed that this prescription regarding the liturgical form had ontological ramifications. Since Trent, the Church has taught that if a wedding does not conform to this requirement, the marriage is invalid, that is, the marital bond does not come into existence and the relationship is not a true marriage.[128]

The twenty-fifth and final session of the council resulted in the issuance of two decrees on December 4, 1563, indirectly related to our topic. The Decree Concerning Purgatory affirmed the existence of a place or state of purgation for souls in need of purification before being admitted to heaven, and it declared that souls detained there

---

124. The True and Catholic Doctrine Concerning the Sacrament of Order, 2, in ibid., 161.

125. Ibid.

126. One of the canonical requirements for validity is proper intention, that is, the minister of the sacrament must intend to do what the Church wants while performing the ceremony. Thus a couple who pronounce the wedding vows when practicing for the next day's wedding are not yet married since they do not intend to marry during the rehearsal. Following the same logic, a bishop does not validly ordain if he does not intend to confer the power to change bread and wine into the body and blood of Christ, e.g., during a rehearsal. This is why ordinations in the Anglican Church have been regarded as invalid, for many ordaining bishops do not believe in the real presence of Christ in the Eucharist. They do not intend to bestow on ordinands the power to change bread and wine into the body and blood of Christ, and thus they do not intend to do what the Catholic Church does when ordaining.

127. The problem was so-called clandestine marriage, which according to Roman law could be initiated by a couple secretly and without any witnesses. The Council sought to put an end to this practice, which often enough had given rise to questions about propriety (Were the couple living in the state of marriage or in the state of sin?), paternity and inheritance. See the Decree Concerning the Reform of Matrimony, 1, in Schroeder, *Canons and Decrees*, 183; also Martos, *Doors to the Sacred*, 428–430, 440.

128. Initially, this implied that Christians who married in a civil ceremony or in front of a Protestant minister were not validly married, but this position was later modified.

could be aided by the offering of prayers and masses on their behalf.[129] The Decree Concerning Indulgences acknowledged that the selling of indulgences had become "a most prolific source of abuses"[130] and commanded that any such sale of spiritual goods would henceforth be abolished. Nevertheless, the council and the Church retained the practice of granting indulgences for the performance of spiritual works provided that they were not motivated by "superstition, ignorance, [or] irreverence."[131] Thus Trent dealt at last with the practice that had sparked the Protestant Reformation, but it did so by again speaking about metaphysical realities that could be effected by earthly activity.

The work that the Council of Trent had initiated continued long into the sixteenth century, in what is sometimes called the Catholic counter-reformation. Some of these reforms had been commanded in conciliar decrees; others were mandated by popes and the Roman curia in subsequent decades. Bishops were forbidden to hold multiple sees as benefices from which to draw income, they were required to actually live in the diocese over which they presided, they were told to visit each parish at least once a year, and they were enjoined to ordain only worthy men as priests. Seminaries were established to train priests in theology, morality, spirituality, and priestly duties. Uniform standards were adopted for religious orders regarding qualifications for membership, the regulation of finances, and the election of superiors. Against the innovations of the reformers, the Church maintained the rule of celibacy for the clergy and the use of Latin in the liturgy. The Roman Catechism, based on the decrees and canons of the council, was published in 1566; the Roman Breviary of prayers and psalms to be recited daily by priests was published in 1568; and the Roman Missal, now made uniform for the Church and imposed on all dioceses with few exceptions, was published in 1570. And, perhaps symbolic of Catholicism's acceptance of scholasticism as the only correct conceptual framework for understanding the sacraments and other doctrines, St. Thomas Aquinas was proclaimed a doctor of the church in 1567, and his *Summa Theologica* was declared to be a preferred source of theological reasoning.[132]

6. Conclusion

Our investigation into the development of Catholic sacramental theology from the first to the sixteenth centuries is thus concluded. We have seen how scriptural references to Christian practices and mysteries were taken up by the fathers of the church and used to understand patristic practices and beliefs. We have seen how the writings of the fathers were in turn taken up by the scholastics and used to explain medieval practices and beliefs. And we have seen how scholastic theology was used first by the

129. See Decree Concerning Purgatory, in Schroeder, *Canons and Decrees*, 214.

130. Decree Concerning Indulgences, in ibid., 254.

131. Ibid.

132. See Henri Daniel-Rops, *The Catholic Reformation* (New York: E. P. Dutton & Co., 1962), 104–108.

bishops at the Council of Trent to define Catholic orthodoxy, and then by the pope and curia to implement liturgical orthopraxis. From the sixteenth to the twentieth century, Catholic teaching and sacramental practice remained virtually unchanged.

In the mid-twentieth century, the bishops at the Second Vatican Council heeded the advice of historical and liturgical scholars by recommending that the mass and the sacraments be reformed in ways that reflected their historical origins and that made them more accessible to the laity.[133] While not rejecting scholastic sacramental theology, the council for the most part avoided speaking of Catholic worship in scholastic terms, preferring instead to speak of it in biblical and pastoral terms.[134] This lack of an ecclesiastical endorsement for scholastic thinking, combined with a contemporary exploration of new philosophical systems, gave Catholic thinkers implicit permission to reflect on the Church's liturgical practices in the light of new intellectual frames of reference such as phenomenology, existentialism and process thought.[135]

In the late twentieth century, however, the pope and the curia re-endorsed scholastic thinking in the 1983 Code of Canon Law and the 1994 Catechism of the Catholic Church. In addition, traditional beliefs and attitudes toward the sacraments gave rise to what is sometimes called a "reform of the reform," an attempt to curb what are labeled as exaggerations and excesses that were tolerated in the years immediately following Vatican II. They have also inspired a return to devotional practices such as Benediction of the Blessed Sacrament, which focuses on the presence of Christ in the Eucharist outside the context of liturgical worship.

Implicit in this return to the past is a belief that the fathers of the church, the scholastic theologians, and the bishops at Trent achieved an understanding of sacraments which is solid and immutable, and which therefore must be upheld against cultural and philosophical relativism. An operative assumption of this position is that Catholic doctrine was built step by step, truth adding to truth, until the fullness of truth was reached in a scholastic synthesis of dogmatic certainty.

In the next chapter, this assumption will be deconstructed.

---

133. See *Sacrosanctum concilium*, the Constitution on the Sacred Litury, in *The Documents of Vatican II*, edited by Walter M. Abbott (London: Geoffrey Chapman, 1966).

134. See "The Approach of Vatican II" in Joseph Martos, *The Sacraments: An Interdisciplinary and Interactive Study*, (Collegeville, MN: Liturgical Press, 2009), 134–137.

135. See Martos, *Doors to the Sacred*, 120–138.

III

Deconstruction

A Critical Analysis of the
Theological Development*

THE FIRST TWO CHAPTERS were necessary preliminaries to the task that is now at hand.

The first chapter presented a summary of Catholic sacramental theology found in the Church's official teachings, as expressed primarily in its doctrinal statements and its canon law. That chapter took pains to show that the word "sacrament" in Catholic theology is used in two different senses. On the one hand, the word refers to a religious ritual or liturgical ceremony; on the other hand, it refers to a spiritual reality that is administered and received through that performance. Catholic doctrine also makes extensive use of the term "grace," and that chapter explained how the term is used in the traditional understanding of the sacraments.

The second chapter took the doctrinal and canonical expressions of Catholic teachings about the sacraments as the terminus of a historical development, and it traced that development from the New Testament to the Council of Trent. Although contemporary theologians have proposed alternatives to scholasticism as a framework for understanding the sacraments, the Church's official teaching continue to be couched in scholastic terminology, which reached its fullest doctrinal expression in the sixteenth century.

The historical development described in the second chapter was based on information that was available in the mid-twentieth century. The New Testament does make reference to religious rituals and theological ideas, patristic authors wrote what was reported about the sacraments, and the scholastic synthesis was accurately presented. However, the presentation was uncritical in two ways. First, the development described was itself uncritical. Patristic and medieval thinkers took their sources literally; that is, they interpreted older texts as meaning what they seemed to mean, and they made no attempt to understand what those texts meant to the original authors or audiences. Moreover, as we shall see, patristic and medieval thinkers had no

---

* For an abstract of this chapter, please read the summary of the argument that begins on page 284.

inhibitions about proof texting; that is, they were not reluctant to use older texts to prove positions that were taken long after the older texts were written, and that the earlier authors could not have had in mind. But the account of historical development was also uncritical in a second way, namely, it did not critically examine the ways that patristic and medieval authors used older texts to support their positions; instead, it simply reported what they wrote. Thus scripture texts were interpreted to mean what Catholic theology for the most part has taken them to mean, patristic developments were described the way they are described in Catholic histories of the sacraments, and the presentation of medieval theology showed how the schoolmen made sense of the data they had to deal with.

One could say that the first chapter was reportive, for it reported the basic tenets of Catholic sacramental doctrine with as little theological elaboration as possible while admitting that official Church teaching is often expressed in scholastic terminology. Similarly, one could say that the second chapter was apologetic, for it explained how Catholic sacramental theology developed in ways that were intellectually defensible at the times when crucial developments took place. It also showed how the scholastic synthesis was both sophisticated and realistic: sophisticated because it was relatively complex and able to address all of the major issues it had to deal with, yet realistic because it was solidly grounded in the social and cultural reality of medieval and modern Catholicism.

This third chapter will attempt to undo that apologetic, not by attacking it from without, but by critically examining its components and its construction. First, it will take a close look at some of the scripture texts that were used to develop Catholic sacramental theology. Second, it will look at developments during the patristic era that created the language patterns that were uncritically adopted by the schoolmen of the Middle Ages. Third, it will show that the scholastic apologetic for the sacraments was deeply flawed in that it misinterpreted biblical and patristic texts that it inherited. Moreover, it generalized medieval Catholic experience and belief into an abstract theology that claimed to be universal for all places and times. Lastly, it will point out how traditional sacramental theology is no longer universally applicable to Catholic life and worship.

1. Sacraments in the Christian Scriptures

There is no word for sacrament in the Greek New Testament, although centuries later the Latin *sacramentum* did get introduced as a translation of the Greek word μυστήριον in some scripture passages. The earliest canonical writings, the letters of the apostle Paul, nonetheless mention some ritual practices of the first followers of Jesus—most notably the immersion of converts in water and the sharing of a commemorative meal—that later Christian writers referred to as sacraments.[1] The synoptic gospels describe Jesus' last supper with his disciples, during which Jesus instructs them to continue the practice in his memory, and which ostensibly was the model on which the early Christian Lord's supper was based.[2] The synoptics also mention the ritual immersion practiced by John the Baptist in which Jesus himself participated. Matthew 29:18–20 also portrays the risen Lord as commanding his disciples to baptize using a Trinitarian formula that is more likely a reflection of early church practice than a precedent for it. John's gospel describes Jesus' baptism, and John 4:1–2 also suggest that Jesus' disciples practiced a form of immersion analogous to the Baptist's. The Acts of the Apostles enlarges the scriptural picture of the early church with some references to the Lord's supper[3] and a number of stories about baptisms.[4] Acts also mentions another ritual action, the laying on of hands, which in this context usually results in charismatic activities such as speaking in tongues, but which is sometimes described rather vaguely as "receiving the Holy Spirit."[5] The deutero-Pauline letters give brief theological interpretations of baptism,[6] but they say nothing about the other two rituals. Likewise, the pastoral epistles do not mention baptism or the Lord's supper, and references to the laying on of hands are still in a charismatic context.[7] James 5:14–16 mentions anointing and praying over the sick, as well as a mutual confession of sins, as ritual actions familiar to the letter's intended recipients.

Looking at the New Testament chronologically, therefore, we find references to baptism and the Lord's supper in the earlier decades of Christianity (c. 50–65), and references to these two rituals and the laying on of hands in the next two decades (c. 65–85). Not much is said about rituals after that, except for rituals practiced perhaps in Jerusalem and possibly in the closing decades of the first century.

This situation—Christian authors writing about particular religious rituals without any collective designation for them—persisted all through the second century and well into the third. As we begin this review of early developments, therefore, it is necessary to speak separately of the different rituals.

1 Regarding baptism, see Rom 6:34, 1 Cor 1:13–17, and Gal 3:27. Regarding the Lord's supper, see 1 Cor 11:17–34.

2. See Lk 22:14–19. Mk 14:17–24 and Mt 26:20–29 provide accounts of the Jesus' last meal but not the words of instruction.

3. Acts mentions Christians getting together for "the breaking of bread." Some are quite possibly eucharistic gatherings (e.g., on the first day of the week) but others are probably just community meals. See Acts 2:42; 2:46; 20:7; 20:11; 27:35.

4. See Acts 2:38–41; 8:12–16; 8:36–39; 9:18; 10:47–48; 16:14–15; 16:33; 18:8; 19:5.

5. See Acts 8:17–19; 9:17; 19:6 (a clear reference to speaking in tongues and prophesying). Sometimes laying hands on a person being prayed for resulted in healing, as in Acts 9:12 and 19:11.

6. See Eph 4:4–6; Col 2:9–14. See also the theology of baptism in 1 Pt 3:21–22.

7. See 1 Tim 4:14; 5:22; 2 Tim 1:6.

a. Baptism in the New Testament

Volumes have been written about the ritual of immersion in water as it appears in early Christian writings, sometimes from confessional or apologetic perspectives and sometimes in a purely exegetical fashion. The exposition here will be more modest. It will simply review most of the New Testament texts that refer to this practice and look for clues in the documents themselves about the meaning and importance that the authors ascribed to the practice.

The word "baptism" derives from the Latin *baptisma* and in turn from the Greek βαπτίσμα; in other words it is a transliteration of a transliteration rather than a true translation of the Greek word. βαπτίσμα does not appear in classical Greek but only in Koine Greek, the language of commerce and culture in the ancient world since the time of Alexander the Great, the second language of those who knew more than their mother tongue in the ancient world, and the language in which the New Testament was written. The verb form βαπτίζειν means to immerse or to plunge, and so the noun refers to an immersion, whether full or partial, and usually in water. A related verb is βάπτειν, meaning simply to dip or to dunk, as when dying cloth. Derivatives of this word are found in three accounts of the last supper, where Jesus announces that his betrayer will be someone who has dipped into the bowl during that meal.[8]

That a ritual immersion in water was important in the earliest decades of the Jesus movement is clear from the many references to it in the letters of the apostle Paul (d. 66), in Mark's gospel (c. 65–70), in the other two synoptic gospels (c. 85–90), and in the book of Acts (c. 85–95). The genuinely Pauline letters mention baptism 11 times. Jesus' baptism in the Jordan is described by Mark, and this event was considered significant enough by Matthew and Luke to be included in their gospels written about two decades later. Words referring to baptism appear 27 times in Acts of the Apostles, almost an average of once per chapter.

Why did ritual immersion become the definitive act of initiation into the Christian community? Writing more than 50 years after the death of Jesus, Matthew puts these words into the mouth of the risen Lord: "Go and make disciples of all nations, baptizing them in the name of the Father and the Son and the Holy Spirit," witnessing to the evangelist's belief that Christians were doing what Christ had commanded, even if the account is not historical by modern standards.[9] The end of Mark's gospel has Jesus saying, "Whoever believes and is baptized will be saved," but this is part of the so-called longer ending of the gospel, which was probably not in the original and which may have been added under the influence of resurrection scenes in Matthew

---

8. See Mk 14:20, Mt 26:23, and Jn 13:26. In John's account, Jesus dips bread into the bowl and hands it to Judas as a sign that he knows who his betrayer will be.

9. Mt 28:19. See Raymond Brown, Joseph Fitzmyer and Roland Murphy, eds., *The Jerome Biblical Commentary* (Englewood Cliffs, NJ: Prentice-Hall, 1968), Vol. 2, 113, n. 206.

and Luke.[10] The risen Christ in Luke's gospel says nothing about baptism, perhaps because baptism is treated so thoroughly in Luke's sequel, the Acts of the Apostles.

Although the gospels testify to the early Christian belief that they were doing what Jesus wanted, the actual origins of this practice are hidden from view. Historical precedents include Essene purification rituals, the immersion of Jewish converts to symbolize their crossing of the River Jordan with the chosen people, and John's baptism for repentance. Thus this type of ritual was not unknown in the first century.[11] Moreover, it can be argued that symbolically such a ceremony is quite apt for ritualizing an immersion into a new community and a new way of living—the way of life, as the *Didache* called it, in contrast to the way of death.[12] Add to this the feelings of rejuvenation aroused by bathing, and a ritual bath for washing away the sinful habits of the past seems an almost obvious choice. Little wonder that, once baptism was adopted, Christians came to understand that it had the approval of the risen Lord.

What did this water ceremony mean to those who underwent it and to those who performed it? Their ideas and feelings are lost forever in unrecorded history, but Paul the apostle began recording his thoughts about many things in letters to various Christian communities. His first letter to the Corinthians, written around 55–57 AD, addressed some disagreements in the community, including disagreements about baptism. In 1 Cor 1:10–17, he frames some of the dissent in terms of who baptized whom and who is loyal to whom, apparently because of an idea that whoever is immersed is a follower of the person who performs the immersion. But the meaning of βαπτίζειν is not entirely clear, for Paul speaks in one place of their ancestors in the desert being "baptized into Moses in the cloud and in the sea" (1 Cor 10:2). He also speaks of "baptism for the dead" as something that was done so that those who had not been immersed would be raised when Christ returns (1 Cor 15:29).

When Paul speaks of being "immersed in one spirit" and "into one body," however, it appears that he talking about the ritual's marking an entrance into the community and sharing a communal spirit (1 Cor 12:13). In other words, here he is speaking metaphorically about something that they have experienced. But for Paul, the body into which they have been immersed is not just a group or social body; it is also the body of Christ, for it is united and animated by the spirit of the risen Lord (1 Cor 12:12–27). In his letter to the Galatians, possibly written around the same time, Paul extends the metaphor, saying that the baptized have been plunged into Christ, but he also adds a new image, saying that they have put on Christ (Gal 3:27).

10. Mk 16:16. See ibid., 60, n. 96–97.

11. For a summary of Jewish precedents, see Ben Witherington III, *Troubled Waters: The Real New Testament Theology of Baptism* (Waco, TX: Baylor University Press, 2007) 16–24. For a more detailed treatment, see Everett Ferguson, *Baptism in the Early Church: History, Theology, and Liturgy in the First Five Centuries* (Grand Rapids, MI: William B. Eerdmans, , 2009), ch. 4.

12. *Didache*, 1.

How are we to interpret this language? Later Christian thinkers took claims such as these in a metaphysical sense. They took Paul at his word and interpreted his words literally, as though they were describing something that was happening beyond the physical realm, perhaps caused by the ritual that was occurring in the world of space and time. However, it seems equally possible that Paul was speaking to his converts in much the same way that parents often speak to young children, reminding them that they are good and so they should not misbehave, or telling them that they are big and so they should act their age and not behave like babies. Taken in this latter sense, Paul's language is hortatory rather than descriptive. He is reminding the recently baptized that they have been immersed in their local Christian community, a social body that is distinct from others in that it is animated by the spirit of Jesus, and so they should behave accordingly. It is analogous to a scout master telling the tenderfeet that they are now in the Boy Scouts and so they ought to behave like scouts. Paul is not necessarily making any claims about supposedly metaphysical effects of ritual immersion.

In Second Corinthians, also written in the late fifties, we find another metaphor that would later be taken literally. Paul writes in 1:22 that God "seals us and gives us the pledge of the spirit in our hearts." What is Paul talking about here? The participle σφραγισάμενος means to stamp with a seal or to put a seal on something, as with sealing wax, by having an image impressed on it. Likewise, αρραβῶνα refers to a down payment given in advance. A likely explanation of the meaning of τὸν αρραβῶνα τοῦ πνεύματος (literally, the down-payment of the spirit) is that Paul is speaking metaphorically about the inner transformation that his readers have experienced, including the spirit of fellowship among them, and perhaps also the spiritual charisms that they have received, with the suggestion that this is but a down payment of more to come. What then is the seal or σφράγις? It would probably be the outward manifestation of that inner spirit, the way that they behave toward one another and perhaps even to those outside the community. There is no reason to believe that Paul was referring to a metaphysical stamp or seal on the souls of Christians.

In his letter to the Christians in Rome, probably written around 60–61 before his visit to that city, Paul again refers to the Christian community as the body of Christ, saying that those who are baptized are plunged into Jesus the anointed one. But again he extends the metaphor by adding that they are also plunged into his death so that they can rise with Christ from the dead and walk in a new way of life (Rom 6:3–4), an idea very similar to one found in the Jewish practice of proselyte baptism.[13] This image is found again in the letter to the Colossians which, although probably written after Paul's death, reiterates his understanding of baptism (Col 2:11–13). The images of a body, of immersion or plunging, and of dying and rising can all be plausibly interpreted as referring to changes in group membership, in attitudes and in behaviors that were experienced by Paul and other early members of the Jesus movement.

13. See David Daube, *The New Testament and Rabbinic Judaism* (New York: Arno Press, 1973) 111–113.

To summarize, Paul does not develop an elaborate theology of baptism but, reflecting on the rite and its aftermath, and perhaps borrowing Jewish ideas with which he was familiar, he sees it as a symbolic immersion not only into the community of believers but also into the way of life that Jesus himself had lived. Whether or not his readers fully realized it at the time, he tells them that their baptism was a commitment to a new set of relationships and values, and as well, an initiation to a new set of experiences, especially the experience of spiritual gifts.

The community in Corinth was apparently what today would be called charismatic or pentecostal, for besides disagreeing about baptism, the Corinthians also disagreed about religious charisms or spiritual gifts. Paul clearly understood what these were, and he did not hesitate to set the record straight. In discussing the gifts (χαρίσματα), he refers to the ability to give good advice (λόγος σοφίας), to give instruction (λόγος γνώσεως), the gift of faith (πίστις), that of healings (ιάματα), the ability to perform works of power (ενεργήματα δύναμεων), the gift of prophecy (προφητεία), the ability to make judgments about spirits (διακρίσεις πνευμάτων), the gift of speaking diverse languages (γένη γλώσσων), and the ability to interpret what is said in those languages (ἑρμηνεία γλώσσων) (1 Cor 12:8–10).[14] Addressing the question as to which is the greatest charism, Paul announces that it is none of these, for they are all gifts of the spirit that come from God (1 Cor 4–7). Moreover, the charisms are given not for the benefit of the individuals who have them but for the entire community, the body of Christ (1 Cor 12:12–14). Yet if there is any charism that is to be considered the greatest, it is none of the above, but love (αγάπη) in the sense of caring about and caring for others (1 Cor 13:1–13).

If Christians exhibited these gifts after joining the community, ritualized by immersion in water, it would appear that in Paul's mind the rite of immersion was both a prerequisite for receiving the gifts and also a sign that a change had taken place in those who had made the decision to throw in their lot with the followers of Jesus. They had changed their mind about how to live, and they had undergone a change of heart, letting go of their previous spirit and accepting the spirit of Christ. They had also changed their behavior, demonstrating the charismata described above and also leading more upright lives. Having died to sin and risen with Christ to a new way of life, they were no longer bound by the strict requirements of the Law, for the spirit within them enabled them to do more than what was required and to live without written rules, guided primarily by the direction and energy of God's spirit within them.[15]

Paul is the main character in Acts of the Apostles, written perhaps twenty years after his death. Although not a literal history in the modern sense, it can provide an

14. In addressing the believers in Rome, writing in hope for a future visit, Paul assumed that they also were familiar with these gifts (Rom 12:3–8), which is not to suggest that all early Christians were charismatics. To understand what Paul is talking about, participating in charismatic worship or pentecostal services is indispensable.

15. See Paul's discourse on the moral life of the Christian in Rom 5–8. Reading all four chapters at one sitting is the best way to get a picture of the behavioral changes to which Paul is referring.

accurate picture of the types of things that were publicly said and done during the first decades of the religious movement that eventually became known as Christianity. By the time this book was written, immersion in water had become the standard ritual for joining those who followed the teachings of Jesus. The second chapter describes the conversion of a large group of people, and even though this may not recount a historical event, the description would not have been credible to first century Christians if it had been radically different from their own experience in the Jesus movement. The same can be said of other activities such as baptisms and communal meals in the book of Acts: they may be stylized, even idealized, but they are probably not untypical.

This being said, Acts 2:14–41 portrays Peter speaking to a large crowd in Jerusalem on the Jewish feast of Pentecost. After being persuaded that Jesus of Nazareth, recently put to death despite his good deeds, was indeed the long-awaited messiah, they ask Peter what they should do. "Turn your lives around (μετανοήσατε) and be immersed (βαπτισθήτω) in the name of Jesus the messiah to be freed from your sinful ways (εἰς ἄφεσιν τῶν ἁμαρτιῶν) and to receive the gift (λήμψεσθε τὴν δωρεὰν) of the Holy Spirit," he replies. "Be rescued from this corrupt age!" (Acts 2:38, 40) Whereupon a large number agree to ritual immersion and join the community of those who are faithful (πιστεύοντες) to the teachings of Jesus. Immersion in water ritualizes immersion into the community and into Jesus' way of life.

Chapters 8 and 9 reinforce this picture of immersion following a profession of faith as a way of initiating people into the community of believers. They present vignettes of three different converts: a magician of sorts named Simon, an unnamed Ethiopian eunuch, and Saul, who until then had been persecuting Jews who recognized Jesus as the messiah. In each case, baptismal immersion is taken for granted as a symbolic action that is needed in order to join the community, but it is all rather informal and performed on the spot. Moreover, receiving the gift (δώρεα) of the Holy Spirit seems to be equated with receiving the spiritual gifts (χαρίσματα) enumerated above, for in one story, converts who had been previously baptized in the name of Jesus do not receive the spirit until they are prayed over.[16] The reception of the spirit must have been manifested in some sort of unusual behavior because the aforementioned Simon asks, in effect, how to perform that magic, only to be rebuked for his effrontery.[17] This inference is reinforced by a story in a later chapter, in which a group of gentiles respond to Peter's preaching by praising God in strange languages, which is one of the charismatic gifts mentioned in 1 Corinthians. This behavior leads Peter to conclude that, since even non-Jews can receive the spirit, they should not be refused the rite of immersion and its implicit membership in the community.[18] Stories of spontaneous baptisms such as these are found throughout the remainder of the book.[19]

16. See Acts 8:14–17.

17. See Acts 8:18–24.

18. See Acts 10:44–48; 11:1–18.

19. See Acts 16:11–15; 16:25–34; 18:5–8; 18:34 – 19:7.

It is noteworthy that the noun βαπτίσμα is used in reference to the Christian rite of immersion very infrequently in the New Testament, and then only in pseudepigraphal letters written late in the first century.[20] This suggests that what Christians thought they were doing when they immersed new members in water was not so much baptism as it was baptizing. They did not think that they were performing a rite with a name, but rather they thought of themselves as doing something symbolic. By allowing themselves to be immersed in water in the name of Jesus (actually, into—εἰς—the name of Jesus), converts signified that they were willing to be immersed in Jesus' way of life. Both Paul and Acts consistently use forms of the verb βαπτίζειν when talking about symbolic immersion. The noun βαπτίσμα does not appear in Acts except in reference to the practice of John the Baptist, when it is commonly referred to as "John's baptism."[21] In the gospels too, the noun is literally applied only to John's ritual, although it is used twice in the metaphorical sense of immersion in suffering.[22] It would appear, therefore, that this early Christian practice did not have a proper name until some time after the Acts of the Apostles was written around 85–90 AD.[23]

To summarize, baptism is a common occurrence in the book of Acts, indicating that it had become commonplace by the mid-80s (if the book was written then) and probably by the mid-50s (when Paul was converted), even though it describes baptisms taking place within weeks after Jesus' resurrection and ascension into heaven. Moreover, the emphasis is always on initiation rather than on the ceremony, which is never described (For example, was it a full or partial immersion?) and which is never formally called βαπτίσμα but is always referred to using the verb form, βαπτίζειν. In Acts, ritual immersion is always performed after a profession of faith in Jesus as the messiah, and its immediate effect is introduction into the community of believers. But since charismatic behavior (especially praising God in strange languages) often followed the immersion, the ritual was also perceived as resulting in the reception of spiritual gifts (χαρίσματα) or in the reception of the gift (δώρεα) of the Holy Spirit.

b. Eucharist in the New Testament

The noun ευχαρίστια appears nowhere in the New Testament as the name of a Christian ritual. Instead, forms of the verb ευχαρίστειν are used to express the giving of thanks, especially over food.[24] The synoptics refer to Jesus' last meal with his disciples

20. See Eph 4:5; Col 2:12; Heb 6:2, 9:10; 1 Pt 3:21.

21. See Acts 10:37; 13:24; 19:3.

22. With reference to John's baptism, see Mt 21:25; Mk 11:30 and Lk 3:3. With reference to immersion in a period of suffering, see Mk 10:38–39 and Lk 12:50.

23. Some scholars have dated Acts as late as the early second century, which, if true would suggest that the practice of immersing new members was not regarded as a ritual with a proper name until much later than 85. See Richard I. Pervo, *Dating Acts: Between the Evangelists and the Apologists* (Santa Rosa, CA: Polebridge Press, 2006).

24. See Mt 15:36; 26:27; Mk 8:6; 14:23; Lk 17:16; 22:17–19; Jn 6:11, 23; Acts 27:35; 28:15. The verb

as a Passover supper, and in John's gospel it is not given any special name. In the Acts of the Apostles, the communal meal of the Christians is called the breaking of bread, and in 1 Corinthians it is called the Lord's supper.[25] In 11:20–34, Paul writes,

> When you gather together, it is not the Lord's supper that you eat, for there are those who eat their food before the others can eat, so that some go hungry while others are drunk. Don't you have your own houses to eat and drink in? In God's assembly, is it right to belittle and shame the poor? What can I say to you? Should I praise you? Certainly not!
>
> What I passed on to you is what I received from the Lord, namely, that on the night he was betrayed, the Lord Jesus took bread, gave thanks, broke it, and said, "Take and eat. This is my body that is broken for you. Do this and remember me." Likewise, he took the cup after supper and said, "This cup is the new covenant in my blood. As often as you drink from it, remember me."
>
> As often as you eat this bread and drink this cup, you are proclaiming the death of the Lord until he comes. Therefore, anyone who eats this bread or drinks the cup unworthily will be accountable for the body and blood of the Lord.
>
> People should ask themselves, when they eat the bread and drink the cup, whether they are eating and drinking unworthily, so that no one can say that they are not recognizing the body of the Lord.
>
> This is why many of you are sick and weak, and many have fallen asleep. If we were more mindful, we would not suffer such judgment. But when the Lord does pass such judgment on us, it is to correct us and to keep us from being condemned with the world.
>
> Brothers and sisters, when you gather together for a meal, wait for one another before eating. If you are really hungry at the time, eat something at home before coming. This way, you will do nothing wrong. With regard to any other matters, I will address them the next time I come.

Observations that can be made about this situation include the following:

- The gathering is for a meal to which the participants bring food.

- The Corinthians call it the Lord's supper, but Paul argues that some participants' inconsiderateness for others shows that it is not really the Lord's supper, that is, what they are doing is not what Jesus intended.

- Paul quotes what will later come to be called the words of institution (i.e., Jesus' institution of the eucharist), but there is no indication that the words were quoted during the meal.

- Paul does not explain how he received these words "from the Lord." Was it a personal revelation, an utterance spoken by a charismatic prophet, a tradition of the Jerusalem church, or what?

- Paul quotes "This is my body" (τοῦτό μού ἐστιν τὸ σῶμα), but his interpretation of those words is not clear. As a Pharisee, Paul was familiar with the use of symbolic

---

is also used with some frequency in the epistles.

25. See Acts 2:42; 2:46; 20:7, 11; 1 Cor 11:20.

foods at the Passover seder, so it is not immediately evident that he took these words literally. Moreover, as a Jew, he believed that eating human flesh was morally repugnant.

- Paul's reference to the content of the cup as "the new covenant in my blood" (τοῦτο τὸ ποτήριον ἡ καινὴ διαθήκη ἐστὶν ἐν τῷ ἐμῷ αἵματι) increases the likelihood that he is thinking symbolically, for the wine is not literally a covenant, and drinking together is a symbolic way of sealing an agreement.[26]

- Although he warns that those who eat and drink unworthily will be held accountable for (other translations say guilty of) the body and blood of the Lord, there is little to determine whether Paul meant those words to be taken literally (e.g., they will be condemned for disrespecting the body and blood that they have eaten) or metaphorically (e.g., they will be responsible for what happens to the community and its life).

- Likewise, when Paul argues that some in the community do not recognize the body of the Lord (τὸ σῶμα τοῦ κυρίου), it is possible that he is referring metaphorically to the community as the body of Christ rather than literally to the bread as the body of Christ.

- Paul addresses the whole community, indicating that there is no single person or small group in leadership that is accountable for what happens during the meals.

Mark's account of the last supper was written about ten years after Paul's, and it is likely the source from which Matthew and Luke drew in creating their accounts. Mark indicates that it is a Passover meal, but the narrative (14:17–26) makes no mention of anything that would be unique to a seder. There is some dialogue about Jesus' imminent betrayal, and this is followed by some words of instruction.

> While they were eating, Jesus took bread, blessed it, broke it, and gave it to them saying, "Take and eat. This is my body."
> And taking the cup, he gave thanks and passed it to them, and they all drank of it. And he said to them, "This is my blood of the new covenant, which is being poured out for many. Truly I tell you that I will not drink again of the fruit of the vine until the day when I drink wine anew in the kingdom of God."[27]

In later centuries, Christian writers insisted that the words, "This is my body, this is my blood," be taken literally, but neither Jesus nor the evangelists necessarily meant them to be taken that way. Indeed, a few factors argue against a literal interpretation:

---

26. Paul's source is evidently in the Lukan tradition, which does not say plainly, "This is my blood," as do the gospels of Mark and Matthew. Moreover, blood in the ancient world was a symbol for life, so Paul and his source could be thinking that the reference is to a covenant in Jesus' way of life. Drinking the cup could therefore signify sealing the agreement.

27. Mark 15:23–25. See parallels in Mt 26:26–29 and Lk 22:14–20. Luke's retelling changes the sequence and the wording of sentences more than Matthew's does, but these are incidental for our purposes.

- Jesus and his disciples were Jewish, and there is a prohibition in the Torah against the drinking of blood (Lv 17:10).

- It is generally agreed that Matthew wrote his gospel for Jewish Christians, and he could have changed the wording to make drinking the cup sound less offensive. Since he did not do this, it is unlikely that he or his audience took the words about the blood literally. If this is the case, it is equally unlikely that they took the words about the body literally.

- At a Passover meal, a number of foods are given symbolic meaning (salt water, bitter herbs, etc.), so it is probable that the words of Jesus were understood symbolically or metaphorically by first-century Jewish Christians.

- Although the words of institution in Greek and Latin say "This *is* my body, this *is* my blood," Jesus spoke Aramaic, and that language leaves out the copula in short sentences. In Aramaic, Jesus would have said, "This my body, this my blood." Thus it is impossible to argue from his words that Jesus meant to equate the bread with his body and the wine with his blood quite literally.

- As Protestants from Zwingli onward have noted, Jesus often speaks metaphorically in the gospels (e.g., "You are the salt of the earth," "I am the light of the world"), yet no one insists that those passages be taken literally.

The Gospel of John has a last supper narrative, but it does not contain the words of institution. Catholic scholars have suggested that John's understanding of the Eucharist is found in the bread of life discourse found in John 6:32–58. Toward the end of this passage, Jesus seems to speak very plainly:

> Truly I tell you that if you do not eat the flesh of the Son of Man and drink his blood, you will have no life in you. Those who eat my flesh and drink my blood have everlasting life, and I will raise them up on the last day. For my flesh is truly food and my blood is truly drink. Those who eat my flesh and drink my blood remain in me, and I remain in them. (vv. 53–56)

Nonetheless, there are some factors that argue against taking this passage literally:

- The Gospel of John is acknowledged to be the most symbolic of the four canonical gospels. Since the gospel uses symbolism and metaphorical language throughout, this passage should be interpreted in that light.

- The Gospel of John is the furthest removed from the early oral tradition. Both Catholic and Protestant scholars acknowledge that the historical Jesus probably did not say most of the things that this gospel puts in the mouth of the Johannine Jesus.

- It is quite possible to interpret the bread of life discourse as having the same spiritual meaning as the passages in John's last supper discourse in which Jesus says, "I am the vine and you are the branches" (Jn 15:1–8). Both passages appear to be about the spirituality of discipleship.

Certainly the presence of the synoptic narratives in Greek and the appearance of the Johannine gospel late in the first century could have contributed to the early Christian identification of bread and wine, when used in the context of the Lord's supper, with the body and blood of Christ in a rather literal sense. But it seems questionable to attribute a literal reading of the above passages to either their authors or the audiences for whom they were written.

c. Other Sacraments in the New Testament

As noted in the previous chapter, Protestants in the early days of the Reformation examined the New Testament in light of the commonly accepted understanding of sacraments, with which they had grown up as Catholics. Since sacraments were understood to be symbolic rituals that had been instituted by Christ, the reformers found all but baptism and the Lord's supper wanting when measured against this double criterion. The Catholic Counter-Reformation rejected this stringent criterion and accepted all scriptural references to symbolic rituals and their meaning as pertaining to the sacraments. They did this because Christian theology since the time of the church fathers had given broad (and we would now say, uncritical) acceptance to anything in the New Testament that seemed related to the seven sacraments. Thus, Christ's breathing on the disciples at the last supper and saying, "Receive the Holy Spirit. Whose sins you forgive, they are forgiven, and whose sins you retain, they are retained" (Jn 20:22–23) has been variously taken as referring to confirmation, ordination and penance.[28]

Our examination of biblical texts that are potentially related to the remaining sacraments will be neither as dismissive as the Protestants' nor as uncritical as the Catholics' treatment of them. We will find that the reformers were generally right to conclude that the New Testament says little about the remaining five liturgical sacraments, and that the Church has often been right to claim that the New Testament speaks clearly about the mysteries that the sacraments celebrate and ritualize.

Our treatment of each of the sacraments will begin with a brief review of the historical data about the first appearance of the liturgical rite. It will then list the scripture texts that have been used in reference to the rite. Next it will discuss what the authors were probably referring to when they wrote the texts. Lastly, it will point out the mystery or spiritual reality that is both mentioned in the scriptures and celebrated in the sacraments.

---

28. See, e.g., Brown et al., *Jerome Biblical Commentary*, 464, n. 177.

(1) Confirmation

Overview

Confirmation emerged from baptism as a separate ritual in the fourth century, after Christianity was made a legal religion in the Roman Empire, leading to a sharp increase in the number of people wanting to join the church. Prior to that time, Christian communities were relatively small and their supervisors or overseers (later known as bishops) had presided over baptisms once a year during the Easter Vigil (or in some places, on the feast of Pentecost). Christians were able to move out of house churches and build their own places of worship, but it became physically impossible for the bishop of each city to preside over all the baptisms and receive all the newly baptized into the community. In the east, the problem was solved by authorizing the pastors of parishes to preside over baptisms and anoint the neophytes with oil that the bishop had blessed, symbolizing his presence and extending his blessing to them. In the west, the problem was solved (in most places, for there were exceptions) by allowing priests to perform baptisms and postponing the ritual in which the neophytes would receive the bishop's blessing with either an anointing or a laying on of hands (or in some places, both). The episcopal rite was called simply a blessing or anointing, and in various places it was given the names consignation, consummation and perfection. It was called confirmation in fifth century France, and this name eventually gained wide acceptance in the west. In the east, the anointing with chrism was called chrismation, and it came to be regarded as a separate sacrament in the fifteenth century, motivated by an ecumenical desire to align the sacramental practices of the Greek and Latin churches.[29]

In the New Testament, a symbolic gesture often connected to baptism was the laying on of hands, which is most often, even today, a placing of both hands on the head of someone while praying or blessing, either silently or out loud. In Acts, the apostles lay hands on people for the reception of the Holy Spirit and also to bestow a blessing.[30] The gesture does not appear in the Pauline epistles, but in the pastoral epistles it refers to some kind of blessing.[31] Thus the ritual does have some support in the scriptures, but the laying on of hands in Acts 8 appears to have been for the bestowal of charismatic gifts, the hand-laying in Act 9 precedes Paul's baptism and is not performed by an apostle, and the incident in Acts 13 is clearly a blessing bestowed before a journey. The paradigmatic narrative about the reception of the Holy Spirit is

29. See Martos, *Doors to the Sacred*, 218–219, 229; Austin Milner, *The Theology of Confirmation* (Notre Dame, IN: Fides Publishers, 1971); Kenan Osborne, *The Christian Sacraments of Initiation* (Mahwah, NJ: Paulist Press, 1987).

30. See Acts 8:17–19; 9:17; 13:3.

31. See 1 Tm 4:14; 5:22; 2 Tm 1:6.

in Acts 2:1–13, but this is a spontaneous occurrence and not a religious ceremony. In John 20:22, Jesus breathes on those gathered in the upper room and says "Receive the Holy Spirit" (a word play based on the fact that *ruah* in Hebrew means both breath and spirit), but this scene was never developed into a Christian ritual.

In the above paragraph and earlier in this chapter, we capitalized the words, "Holy Spirit," as do all translations of the New Testament, but it must be remembered that the epistles and gospels were written some 200 years before the development of Trinitarian doctrine. In the minds of the authors and original readers, the words probably did not refer to a distinct divine entity. Unlike English, the Greek language has no indefinite article such as "a" or "an" to speak in general about something, such as a table or an idea, but it does have a definite article to speak about a particular or individual something. In Greek, then, when the article is not used, what is being referred to is not a definite individual. It is interesting, therefore, that when the genuine Pauline epistles speak about πνεῦμα ἅγιον, in almost half the cases it is not preceded by a definite article.[32] In these places, it would probably be better to translate the phrase as "a holy spirit" or "a divine spirit" rather that as "the Holy Spirit." In the other places, it is quite easy to translate the phrase without personifying the spirit.[33]

In Hellenistic Judaism, a spirit (πνεῦμα) was the energy or force within a person that resulted in a certain kind of behavior. In the synoptic gospels, references to spirit appear in a number of contexts: a person's spirit is the energy of life, so when that spirit departs, the person dies;[34] the spirit is also the locus of awareness, feeling and thought;[35] an eager person is a person with a willing spirit (πνεῦμα πρόθυμον);[36] unclean spirits (πνευμάτα ακαθάρτα) are the cause of disease and illness, whether physical or mental.[37] The language in John's gospel is similar but also different. Jesus is troubled in spirit, and when he dies he gives up the spirit.[38] There are no Johannine references to unclean or evil spirits, but those who believe and have faith in Christ have a spirit of truth that is born of the spirit of God.[39]

32. See I Thes 1:5, 6; 1 Cor 2:13; 12:3; 2 Cor 6:6; Rom 5:5; 9:1; 14:17; 15:13, 16.

33. For example, 1 Thes 4:8 τὸ πνεῦμα αὐτοῦ τὸ ἅγιον = his holy spirit (i.e., God's spirit of holiness, or the spirit of God's holiness); 1 Cor 6:19 τοῦ ἐν ὑμῖν ἁγίου πνεύματός = the divine spirit in you; 2 Cor 13:13 ἡ κοινωνία τοῦ ἁγίου πνεύματος = the fellowship of the holy spirit (i.e., sharing the same divine spirit, or even the divine feeling of togetherness).

34. See Mt 27:50 = Mk 15:37, 39; Lk 1:80; 2:40; 8:55; 24:37–39 (a disembodied spirit or ghost).

35. See Mk 2:8; 8:12; Lk 1:17, 47; 9:55; 10:21.

36. See Mt 26:41 = Mk 14:38 = Lk 23:46.

37. See Mt 8:16; 10:1; 12:43–45; Mk 1:23–27; 3:11, 30; 5:2–13; 6:7; 9:17; 9:25 (a dumb or speechless spirit: πνεῦμα ἄλαλον); 9:20–25; Lk 4:33–36; 6:18; 7:21and 8:2 (from evil spirits: πνευμάτων πονηρῶν); 8:29; 9:39–42; 11:24–26; 13:11 (a spirit of illness: πνεῦμα ασθενείας).

38. See Jn 11:33; 13:21; 19:30.

39. See Jn 3:5–8; 4:23–24; 6:63. In the last supper discourse, the spirit of truth is identified with the spirit of God, the Holy Spirit: Jn 14:17, 26; 15:26; 16:13.

With regard to the synoptics, English translations often speak of the Holy Spirit, but in almost half of these instances the Greek lacks the definite article, suggesting that Christians did not have a clear concept of God's spirit as a separate entity in the latter part of the first century.[40] Even John's gospel, which speaks often of the spirit (τὸ πνεῦμα), sometimes speaks more indefinitely of a holy spirit (πνεῦμα ἅγιον).[41] The same pattern is found in the pastoral epistles, with the definite article more absent than present.[42] The Epistle to the Hebrews speaks of the holy spirit when it refers to God's spirit, but it speaks of a holy spirit in people.[43]

What, then, were these authors talking about, when they wrote about a holy or divine spirit? Lacking a Trinitarian theology, they were most likely talking about a force or energy within people that leads them to behave in a certain way. It is clearly the opposite of an unclean or evil spirit, for it enables people to behave in an upright and godly way. In some places, it is plausibly an ecstatic spirit enabling its recipients to demonstrate charismatic gifts such as speaking in tongues, but a closer textual analysis would be needed to clarify the referents with such precision. Nonetheless, it is highly probable that they were writing about something that they had experienced, some positive behavioral change in themselves and others, so they could write about it from their own experience and their readers would recognize what they were talking about.

In very general terms, these scripture texts often refer to a group spirit, a feeling of togetherness or fellowship, and very likely a sense of empowerment to live according to the teachings of Christ rather than according to the spirit of the world. Together they could live the way they felt God wanted them to live, and not in the way they had lived before. They were empowered, they were energized, they were enthusiastic.

This is not a strange phenomenon. We have all been in groups that had a certain spirit, a certain dedication to goals or ideals, or a certain contagious energy that enabled their members to do more than they would have done or could have done on their own. When we reflect on our own experiences in clubs, on teams, in musical or dramatic productions, on service projects, and so on, we can see that this happens all the time. Today we might describe the phenomenon in psychological or sociological terms, but those vocabularies did not exist in the ancient world. People in the Hellenistic world of first century Judaism would have spoken in terms of spirit, of receiving a new spirit. If it was an energy that enabled them to do good, they would have called it a divine spirit or even the spirit of God.

---

40. The definite article is lacking in Mt 1:18, 20; 3:11; Mk 1:8; Lk 1:15, 35, 41; 67; 2:25; 3:16; 4:1; 11:13. Although the article is found in Mt 12:32; 28:19; Mk 3:29; 12:36; 13:11; Lk 2:25; 3:22; 12:10, 12, the holy spirit is not necessarily personified.

41. See Jn 1:33; 3:6, 8, 34; 6:63; 7:39; 14:17, 26; 15:26; 16:13 for reference to the spirit, and Jn 1:33; 7:39; 20:22 for reference to a holy spirit.

42. The article is not used in 2 Tm 1:14; Ti 3:5; 1 Pt 1:2, 12; 2 Pt 1:21; Jd 1:19–20; but only in 1 Tm 4:1.

43. See Heb 2:4; 3:7; 6:4; 9:8; 10:15.

At the same time, however, psychological transformation is a mysterious phenomenon. It is something that we do not fully understand or fully control. We cannot make it happen, although if we are group leaders we can try to set the conditions so that things will click, so that the group will come together, so that they will share the vision and energy that perhaps only a few have at the outset. Scout masters, retreat directors, coaches of sports teams, band leaders and play directors do it all the time. Yet that spirit, that energy, is never fully under control. It is always elusive, surprising, and sometimes disappointing when it is lost. In that most fundamental sense, it is a mystery.

But such transformation is something real. It is undeniably real. It is experientially real. You the reader have memories of it, and you also remember times when it has been absent. It is something that really happens within and among people. Yet it is not a physical reality, it is not something material; it is not something that you can experience with your five senses. From that perspective, then, it is a spiritual reality. It is something real that you can experience and have experienced, but not with your eyes, ears, nose, tongue or hands. It is something real in your conscious experience, something that you are actually aware of. But it is not a material reality, and in that plain and basic sense, it is a spiritual reality.

From our brief study of scripture texts related to the spirit experienced by first-century Christians, we can say that we have identified a spiritual reality that can be recognized and celebrated, that can be fostered and communicated, and that can be defined by the way people behave when they are under its influence. Christians today might call it the spirit of Christ, for it is easily perceived in the figure of Jesus as portrayed in the gospels. His actions are motivated by fidelity to God and compassion for people; his words speak of being faithful to God and caring for others. Whether or not the sacrament of confirmation has always celebrated that spirit or communicated that spirit is another matter. But it is clearly a spiritual reality, albeit a complex and multifaceted reality, that can be and ought to be celebrated in the Christian community. As we have seen from the few mundane examples given above, it is a spiritual reality that can be communicated.

(2) Penance or Reconciliation

Overview

If *sacramentum penitentiae* can be translated literally as "the sacred ritual of repentance," then we would have to say that in the New Testament there is no description of a ritual or ceremony associated with repentance, conversion, or the forgiveness of sins. In the Pauline epistles, however, there is mention of a process or procedure for dealing with malefactors who offended the Christian community by violating its moral norms. Such a procedure is also mentioned in *The Shepherd* of Hermas around the turn of the second century for dealing with those who have either left or been ejected from the community. Although the documentary evidence of its development is sketchy, it is clear that by the third century the churches in many parts of the Roman Empire had developed ecclesiastical procedures for mending relationships with members who had once cut their ties with the church by renouncing their faith in Christ or by joining heretical groups. These procedures always involved rituals that were presided over by the local bishop, but there is no evidence that these were scripted liturgies since no written rites from this era have come down to us. With the legalization of Christianity in the fourth century, the public reconciliation of apostates and heretics gradually fell into disuse. Contributing to the decline of public repentance for adultery and other public sins was the fact that a person could be reconciled with the church only once, and so those in need of reconciliation often postponed it until late in life. Meanwhile, missionary monks were allowing those outside the monastery to confess their sins in privacy when seeking spiritual direction, and gradually the hearing of confessions became a standard practice of the secular clergy as well. At first condemned by bishops for being contrary to church laws pertaining to public repentance, private confession became a widespread ecclesiastical practice by the high Middle Ages.[44]

Even a cursory reading of the gospels shows that Jesus was concerned with the forgiveness of sins and the reconciling of sinners to God. He himself forgave sins,[45] he told his followers to forgive sins,[46] and he taught them to seek reconciliation with one another.[47] He also taught that God is a loving father who will always forgive those who repent by renouncing their wrongful behavior and resolving to reform their lives.[48] Indeed, this type of moral conversion is referred to as salvation in Luke's gospel.[49] Jesus even asks God to forgive those who are putting him to death on a cross.[50]

In John's gospel, the risen Lord says, "If you forgive anyone's sins, their sins are forgiven; if you withhold forgiveness, forgiveness is withheld from them."[51] Although the Catholic tradition has used this text to prove that Christ gave the apostles the

---

44. See Martos, *Doors to the Sacred*, 320–341; Bernhard Poschmann, *Penance and the Anointing of the Sick* (New York: Herder and Herder, 1964); Ladislas Orsy, *The Evolving Church and the Sacrament of Penance* (Denville, NJ: Dimension Books, 1978); James Dallen, *The Reconciling Community: The Rite of Penance* (New York: Pueblo Books, 1986).

45. See Mt 9:1–7 = Mk 2:1–12 = Lk 5:17–26; Lk 7:48–49.

46. See Mt 6:12–15 = Lk 11:14; 18:21–25; Mk 11:25f; Lk 17:3–4.

47. See Mt 5:23–24; 18:15–17; Mk 11:25.

48. See Mt 18:12–14; Lk 15:4–32; 18:9–14.

49. See Lk 19:1–10; 24:47.

50. See Lk 23:34.

51. Jn 20:23. Support for the interpretation given here can be found in 2 Cor 2:10.

power to forgive sins in the sacrament of penance, an examination of the context shows that Jesus is speaking to a group of disciples or followers, not specifically to the twelve apostles. Moreover, the meaning of this text is more likely something practical, such as this: if you forgive people in your community, others should not be treating them as though they were still guilty of their offense, and if you do not forgive offenders, others should not be treating them as though they had done nothing wrong. In other words, reconciliation or the lack of it between the offended and the offender is primary. This is perhaps an echo of something in Matthew's gospel, written some decades before, where Jesus says to his followers, "I tell you truly that whatever you bind on earth will be bound in heaven, and whatever you loosen on earth will be loosened in heaven."[52] What we have here is is most likely a reference to the ancient practice of binding and loosing, that is, restricting those who violate the social order from normal interaction with the community, and then loosening those restrictions after a certain length of time or after a sufficient demonstration of remorse.[53] Again here, Jesus is speaking to a wider group than the twelve, and Matthew is directing this teaching to the community for whom his gospel was written and not just the community leaders. The community is being assured that the moral sanctions they employ are respected in heaven, that is, by God.

The letters to the Corinthians show that Paul was quite aware of this procedure. In 1 Corinthians 5 he tells the community that they should have nothing to do with a member who has seriously violated sexual mores, adding, "Do not associate with any community member who is known to be impure, greedy, an idolater, foul-mouthed, a drunkard or a thief. Do not eat with someone like that."[54] Then in 2 Corinthians 2 he tells them what to do when someone who has been ostracized in this manner is clearly repentant: "It is time now to do the opposite, offering forgiveness and comfort, lest he be overwhelmed by remorse. And so I ask you now to confirm that you care about him."[55] Although it is not obvious that Paul is referring to the same person in both letters, there is little doubt that he is writing about two stages in the same type of process.

Knowing the history of ritual repentance in Christianity, one can see how this simple cultural practice could have evolved in a couple of centuries into the more elaborate practice of ecclesiastical repentance. This practice came to be known as canonical penance because it was governed by canons or rules concerning the types of sins to be covered, the works of repentance to be performed, and the lengths of time involved. During the patristic period, bishops enjoyed a great deal of autonomy and so the rules were not uniform, but one can suppose that there was a degree of similarity among them since there are no recorded disputes about the practice.[56]

52. Mt 18:18. See verses 15–17 for the context.

53. See, e.g., Brown, *Jerome Biblical Commentary*, Vol. 2, 95, n. 128.

54. 1 Cor 5:11.

55. 2 Cor 2:7–8.

56. The Donatist dispute was not about the procedure as such but about those who ought to be

Reflecting on the scriptural texts related to forgiveness and reconciliation, what are the spiritual realities to which they refer? As above, it is important to remember that for our purposes, spiritual realities are neither metaphysical entities nor immaterial beings, but they are quite simply things (in the broadest sense of that word) that are real but not physical. Thus many things that are frequently thought of as abstractions are, in the experience of them, spiritual realities.[57] Justice, compassion, honesty and other virtues are real both as motivating different types of individual behavior and as characterizing different types of social relationships. Family, community, and other forms of association are real, and they can even be protected by law, but relationships are fundamentally non-material in the sense that they cannot be weighed or measured. Ideas and beliefs, values and ideals are not physical even though they can be thought and felt and known by the mind. Were such things not real, then there would be no real justice in the world, there would be no such thing as a real family, and no one could ever really have an idea.

At the same time, realities such as these are mysterious in an ordinary and familiar way, for even though they are experienced, they are never fully understood. We know quite well the relationships we are in, but questions always remain: Why do they like me? Why did I fall in love with that person and not another? What obligations do I have as a friend? I am aware of my ideas, but how good are they? How well do they correspond to reality? Would I be better off with a different set of ideas? I know that I am honest because I am aware that sometimes I am dishonest. So is honesty just a feeling, is it a matter of social conditioning, or is there something more to it? These realities are mysterious, not because we don't understand what is said about them (although this can also happen) but because we don't fully understand our experience of them. A mystery, as said earlier, is something that is experienced as real but not fully understood.

This having been said, being forgiven is a spiritual reality and a mystery. When someone tells us they forgive us for something we have done, we can accept the announcement dispassionately, or with relief, or gladly, or with a number of other emotions. If the person is someone we love or respect or look up to, being told that we are forgiven can lift a burden of guilt and remorse. Being forgiven can unblock a blocked relationship, and thus reconciliation makes possible a renewal of the relationship. Being forgiven by someone else makes it easier for us to forgive ourselves for what we have done, once we realize the harm and the hurt we have caused. Being told that we are forgiven by God can make it possible for us to put the past behind

---

required to undergo ecclesiastical repentance.

57. Technically, it would be more exact to say that they are experienced as instances of spiritual realities, but we do not speak of physical realities that way. That is, we do not say, "I see an instance of a chair," but rather, "I see a chair." Nor do we say, "I felt an instance of respect," but rather, "I felt respect." The same can be said of any spiritual reality that is felt, sensed, intuited, or otherwise experienced.

us and start afresh, for if the One who knows all forgives us, what we did in the past must be forgivable.

Forgiving others entails a different but equally healing dynamic. Forgiving those who have wronged us frees us from the emotional bonds that constrict our dealings with them and others. Forgiving them enables us to let go of the pain and anguish we have suffered since being harmed. Forgiving them dissolves the anger and vengeance that we have felt toward them since being hurt. Forgiving them makes it possible to re-establish a positive relationship with them and those who love them. For no one is an isolated individual; there is always a network of kinship and friendship that is affected by our attitude and behavior toward anyone. If there is to be anything like community or fellowship, then, there must be a willingness to forgive and an ability to accept the forgiveness of others. Without both of these, there is no possibility of reconciliation.

Reconciliation requires not only forgiveness and the acceptance of forgiveness, but many other elements such as acknowledging guilt, taking responsibility, and community involvement in the restoration of positive social relations. Each of these is spiritual and they are all mysterious for they are all risky and no one fully understands their dynamics. Yet the result of passing through the process of reconciliation is palpably positive, it is a benefit to individuals that also benefits those who are connected to them. Reconciliation untangles the emotional knot created by wrongdoing and straightens out social relationships. It is clearly a spiritual reality that is worthy of being fostered and celebrated.

(3) Anointing of the Sick

Overview

Vatican II suggested that extreme unction is more fittingly called anointing of the sick because by the 1960s it had become clear that the purpose of the sacrament had originally been for the sick and not for the dying, as when it first appeared as a clerical ritual in the ninth century. Before then, anointing the sick with blessed oil, sprinkling the sick with blessed water, and laying hands on the sick when praying for them had been an informal ritual or broadly sacramental practice for centuries. The practice is alluded to in James 5:14–15:

> Are there any of you who are sick? If so, let them call for the elders
> of the church, and let them be prayed over and rubbed with oil in
> the name of the Lord. Praying in faith will relieve those who are
> beaten down and the Lord will raise them up, and any sins they
> have committed will be forgiven.

The ninth century liturgical ritual was adapted from a monastic practice of praying over and anointing a sick monk in chapel. As it was supposed to be done in a church by a number of priests, it was often postponed until all other remedies had been tried. As a result, those who received the anointing often died, so the prayers changed from petitions for the healing of the body to petitions for mercy on the soul, and the rite became known in Latin as *extrema unctio* or final anointing. This is the form of the sacrament that was known to the scholastics, and it is the form that was affirmed by the Council of Trent. After Vatican II the rite was redesigned so that it could be performed for the seriously sick, the chronically ill, and the aged.[58]

In the New Testament, healing the sick is one of the outstanding features of Jesus' ministry. The Gospel According to Matthew records fourteen instances of healing by Jesus,[59] the much shorter Gospel According to Mark records six such instances,[60] and the Gospel According to Luke, traditionally reputed to have been a physician, recounts the most individual encounters in his thirteen instances of healing.[61] Moreover, Jesus expects his disciples to heal others the same way he did.[62] And Jesus is sometimes depicted as physically touching people in his ministry of healing.[63] Acts of the Apostles contains some stories of healings by Jesus' followers, but it is not a central element in their ministry.[64] Stories of healing are not prominent in the epistles, but 1 Corinthians makes reference to the charismatic gift of healing.[65]

Sickness has an obviously physical dimension that argues against its being considered a spiritual reality. Still, in the experience of it, sickness contains elements of mystery. Why am I sick? How did this illness come upon me? Why did it happen now? When will I get better? These and other questions show that illness and injury are experienced realities that are not fully understood. In addition, sickness is never purely physical, for there is always a mental and emotional dimension to it. We can be in pain. We can be discouraged and even depressed. We can be worrying about the things we are prevented from doing because we are in hospital or homebound. If the

---

58. See Martos, *Doors to the Sacred*, 383–386; James Empereur, *Prophetic Anointing: God's Call to the Sick, the Elderly, and the Dying* (Wilmington, DE: Michael Glazier, 1982); Charles W. Gusmer, *And You Visited Me: Sacramental Ministry to the Sick and the Dying* (New York: Pueblo Books, 1984); John J. Ziegler, *Let Them Anoint the Sick* (Collegeville, MN: Liturgical Press, 1987).

59. See Mt 4:23f; 8:5–13; 8:15; 8:16; 9:35; 12:9–14; 12:15; 12:22; 14:14; 15:22–28; 15:30; 17:18; 19:2; 21:14.

60. See Mk 1:34; 3:10; 5:24–34; 5:40–43; 6:5; 6:13.

61. See Lk 4:40; 5:15; 5:17; 6:17–19; 7:2–10; 8:43–48; 8:51–55; 9:6; 9:42; 13:10–13; 14:1–4; 17:11–14; 22:50–51.

62. See Mt 10:1–8; 17:15–21; Mk 3:14f; 6:12–13.

63. See Mk 1:41; 8:22–25; Mt 8:3; 8:15; Lk 4:40; 5:13; 13:13. Jn 9:6–7. See also Acts 9:12 for healing through the laying on of hands.

64. See Acts 3:1–16; 5:12–16; 8:7; 9:32–35; 9:36–41; 14:8–10.

65. See 1 Cor 12:9; 12:28–30.

illness is very serious, we can be anxious about the future. All of these are spiritual realities—negative ones, to be sure, but nonetheless spiritual realities.

Health is likewise a spiritual reality, or at least it has a spiritual dimension. Health is more than the sum of the readings which report that our body is functioning within normal parameters for organs, blood chemistry, muscle tissue, and so on. In many respects, health is as much a mystery as sickness, for we do not really know what health is even though we normally experience it more than we do illness. Why should we be blessed with health while others suffer from diseases and injuries? Yet we usually do not ponder the mystery of health until we lose it.

Healing is likewise mysterious. Again, we can be subjected to tests that tell us and our physician that the bodily dimensions of our health are improving. But how and why do medicines work, whether they be simple remedies such as aspirin or a complex regimen of antiretroviral drugs? Most of us do not know and, frankly, we usually do not care. Nevertheless, the experience of regaining health, just like the experience of falling ill, is something we do not fully understand and so it is somewhat mysterious.

Medical research tells us that there is a connection between our mental state and our physical condition.[66] A positive outlook can speed up healing, and a seriously negative mentality (depression, anguish, resentment) can be a factor in the onset of illness. The placebo effect is quite well known, but how it works is still not understood. Why does taking something that we believe will make us well sometimes work, even though all of its ingredients are inert? When we are sick, why do we feel better when someone hugs us, or touches us, or changes the dressing on our wound, or even simply asks how we feel? How do touch and attention improve our spiritual state? It is rather mysterious.

People who receive the anointing of the sick often report that it had a positive spiritual effect on them. It calmed their nervousness before an impending surgery, or it helped them to put their condition into perspective, or it just made them feel better. Occasionally there are even physically inexplicable (Should we say miraculous?) cures, such as those that are reported by practitioners of charismatic healing or faith healing.[67] The modest claim, therefore, that healing can be facilitated by religious ritual, is quite reasonable. The spiritual power behind such healing, ultimately attributable to the power and love of God, is something that deserves to be celebrated.

---

66. See, e.g., Donald A. Bekal, *Psycyhology and Health* (New York: Springer Publishing, 1992); also many of the articles in Bill Moyers, ed., *Healing and the Mind* (New York: Doubleday, 1993).

67. The literature, especially from the height of the charismatic renewal in the twentieth century, is quite ample. See, for example, Francis MacNutt, *The Power to Heal* (Notre Dame, IN: 1977); Dennis Linn, Matthew Linn and Sheila Fabricant Linn, *Praying with Another for Healing* (New York: Paulist Press, 1984); Joseph Champlin, *Healing in the Catholic Church* (Huntington, IN: Our Sunday Visitor, 1985).

(4) Ordination

Overview

One of the earliest records of an ordination ceremony is a Greek text that has been given the name *The Apostolic Tradition* from words that are found at the beginning and end of the document. Long attributed to Hippolytus of Rome, a presbyter who died a martyr's death in the early third century, it is now thought by some scholars to be an anonymous work written in Syria or Egypt in the late fourth century.[68] Among other things, the work gives instructions for the ordination of a bishop by other bishops, of an elder or presbyter by a bishop and other presbyters, and of a deacon by a bishop alone.[69] During the patristic period, the duties and powers of those ordained to these ministries varied somewhat from place to place, and since the church offices to which they were appointed were local, they were not regarded as powers that could be exercised elsewhere. During the Dark Ages of the sixth to tenth centuries, however, the need for missionary priests led to the understanding that priestly powers were not necessarily limited by geography. By the high Middle Ages it was assumed that the powers were permanent even though their licit exercise required the permission of the local bishop. Priestly training was a sort of apprenticeship, with clerics rising through a series of ranks or orders as they learned their liturgical duties. The scholastic theology of holy orders reflected the state of the priesthood in the thirteenth century.[70]

In the section on confirmation, above, we reviewed the New Testament passages having to do with the laying on of hands, and none of them can be easily equated with ordination to a ministerial rank. The pastoral epistles refer to a hand laying that could arguably be a gesture of ordination, but it could also refer more broadly to a commissioning for ministry or even to a blessing given to one who has been selected for a certain task or mission.[71] In any event, the letters to Timothy and Titus were probably written in the latter part of the first century and at best reflect a practice that had already evolved, not a practice in place during the first decades of Christianity. Perhaps

---

68. See Paul Bradshaw, *Search for the Origins*, 78–80. Also his *Reconstructing Early Christian Worship* (London: SPCK, 2009), 47–51.

69. See the translation by Kevin P. Edgecomb available on line at http://www.bombaxo.com/hippolytus.html.

70. See Martos, *Doors to the Sacred,* 472–99; Bernard Cooke, *Ministry to Word and Sacraments: History and Theology* (Philadelphia: Fortress Press, 1976); Kenan Osborne, *Priesthood: A History of Ordained Ministry in the Roman Catholic Church* (Mahwah, NJ: Paulist Press, 1988); Edward Schillebeeckx, *Ministry: Leadership in the Community of Jesus Christ* (New York: Crossroad, 1981).

71. See 1 Tm 4:14; 5:22; 2 Tm 1:6. See also Acts 6:6 regarding distributors of food.

more to the point for the theology of holy orders is the fact that in the New Testament no Christian minister is referred to as a priest (ἱερεύς in Greek, *sacerdos* in Latin).

The four gospels mention disciples and apostles, but they most frequently refer to the group closest to Jesus as "the twelve." In a few places, Matthew and Luke refer to the twelve as either disciples or apostles,[72] but Mark, written earlier, and John, written later, do not do so. In terms of early Christian history, the twelve last appear at the beginning of the book of Acts, and apart from the replacement of Judas by Matthias, they as a group were never replaced. Although local legends attribute the founding of far-flung churches to one or other of the twelve, these legends are not supported by documentary or archeological evidence.[73] There is evidence that Peter reached the city of Rome, but he was most likely there more as a distinguished guest than as the head of that church because the community in that city was governed by a council of presbyters at least until the end of the first century.[74]

The word "disciple" comes from the Latin *discipulus*, which means a student, as does the Greek word that it translated, μαθητὴς. So the disciples mentioned in the gospels are those who listened to the teachings of Jesus, which is why they are referred to in some translations as followers. The Greek ἀπόστολος means one who is sent out, and in the gospels the twelve are occasionally sent out to preach and heal.[75] Although not numbered among the twelve, Paul and other early missionaries were regarded as apostles.[76]

Elders or presbyters (πρεσβύτεροι) are mentioned in Acts and in the pastoral epistles, all of which were written after the genuinely Pauline letters.[77] Although the English "priest" is descended from this Greek word, no scholarly versions of the New Testament translate πρεσβύτεροι as priests, so the presbyters referred to are the elders in the community. They were not necessarily the oldest but they were older and more respected members of the community who have been given some responsibility for the well-being of the local church. Since Jewish synagogues were organized along this model, it is quite plausible that Christian house churches followed this model as well.

72. See Mt 10:1; 10:2; 11:1; 20:17; Lk 6:13; 9:1. Also Acts 1:26, written by Luke.

73. For example, James is reported to be buried in Spain, and Thomas is said to have reached India.

74. In Clement of Rome's first letter to the Corinthians (written around the end of the first century), the churches in both cities appear to be governed by a group of presbyters or elders. The apostles are referred to as ἐπίσκοποι and διάκονοι, probably meaning that they supervised and served the church, not that they were bishops and deacons in the later sense of those terms (1 Clement 42, 4–5). Likewise, the strife over the office of ἐπίσκοπος in Corinth mentioned in 44, 1–3, which is the occasion for the letter, most likely concerns a supervising elder rather than a monarchial bishop.

75. See Mt 10:1–15 = Mk 6:7–13 = Lk 9:1–6; also Mk 3:14.

76. See, e.g., Rom 1:1; 16:7; 1 Cor 1:1; 9:5; 12:28–29. In the opening sentence of all of his letters, Paul identifies himself as an apostle. In 1 Cor 3 Paul speaks about someone named Apollos, who seems to be a missionary although he is not referred to as an apostle.

77. See Acts 11:30; 14:23; 15:1–6; 15:22–23; 16:4; 20:17–18; 1 Tm 4:14; 5:17–19; Ti 1:5.

The pastoral epistles also mention ἐπίσκοποι,[78] but again these are not bishops, even though "episcopal" is derived from this Greek word. The term means literally supervisor or overseer, which is the way that it is translated in some recent Bibles. In the first century, the ἐπίσκοπος would have been the supervising elder, a first among equals, something like a committee chair. Likewise, διάκονοι in the New Testament are not deacons in the ecclesiastical sense but servants or helpers in a general sense, even though in a Christian context they might be thought of as ministers appointed to a variety of functions and tasks.[79]

The letters of Paul mention a variety of charismatic gifts (χαρίσματα) which can be thought of as ministries benefiting the local church ("the building up of the body") even though the ministers were not appointed or ordained.[80] Some in the community give good practical advice, others have a wealth of knowledge, and still others have strong faith. Some are able to heal physical ailments, and some have other powerful abilities. Some are able to tell the community what God wants them to hear, and others are good at discerning what is going on inside of people. Some can pray in strange languages, but there are also some who can interpret what they say. Some are gifted teachers, others are good at encouraging and persuading. Leading, organizing and showing compassion are also gifts that contribute to the well-being of the community. These gifts are understood to come from God and they are regarded as manifestations of a holy spirit that is given for the common good.

This holy spirit can be called the spirit of God because it inspires and enables people to do what God wants, namely, to care for and take care of others. And since this is the same spirit that motivated and empowered Jesus, it can also be called the spirit of Christ and the spirit of the risen Lord.[81] It is a spirit of obedience to God and service to others, or to say it in other words, it is a spirit of fidelity to God and of ministering to others. The spiritual reality to which ordination points is therefore none other than the spirit that is manifested by Jesus in the gospels, that is displayed by Peter and others in Acts of the Apostles, and about which Paul and John write in their letters. In a word, it is αγάπη, which is usually translated as love in the New Testament, but which is better thought of as caring about and caring for others. Ministry is a matter of putting other people's needs ahead of one's own wants, of placing their well-being above self-centered desires. This is precisely what Paul is talking about in First Corinthians when he explains to his audience the meaning of αγάπη.

78. See Acts 20:28; Phil 1:1; 1 Tm 3:2; Ti 1:7; also 1 Pt 2:25, where the reference is to Christ.

79. So, for example, the seven who are chosen to help distribute food to the poor in Acts 6:1–6. Their selection is followed by a laying on of hands, which at this early date is unlikely to have been an ordination in the liturgical sense of the term. See also the mention of διάκονοι in Phil 1:1; 1 Tm 3:8–13.

80. See 1 Cor 12:4–11; Rom 12:4–8.

81. See Rom 8:9; 2 Cor 3:17–18; Phil 1:19; 1 Pt 1:11.

> To be caring is to be patient with others and kind to others. Caring about others does not mean envying them, and it certainly excludes having an inflated sense of self-worth and bragging about yourself. Caring for others means not doing anything that is improper or selfish. If you are truly caring you are not short-tempered and you do not blame others. You do not gloat over other people's misfortunes, but you do appreciate knowing the truth. To be caring means putting up with a lot of things, believing what others tell you, hoping for the best, and sticking with it. Caring never gives up. (1 Cor 13:4–8a)

Those who are filled with this spirit are doing what God wants, and so they do not have to worry about obeying written rules such as those codified in the Torah, for they are already fulfilling the purpose for which the law was given.[82] In a sense, everything they do is lawful, for they always do the right thing, but this does not mean that they can do whatever they please. Doing the right thing means doing what is good for others.[83]

If αγάπη or caring is the focal point of following Christ and central to the Christian community, it deserves to be celebrated in many ways. Indeed, one could argue that all Christian feast days that commemorate the life of Christ and the lives of the saints display many facets of the caring life. But when Christians decide to lead lives of service to the community and to join the ranks of those whose lives revolve around ministering to others, it is a cause for special celebration. Ordination has been and can be a special celebration of this spiritual reality.

(5) Marriage

Overview

The followers of Christ have married ever since the beginnings of Christianity. The gospels indirectly reveal that the apostle Peter was married, and others among the twelve may well have been married. Paul never married, but he wrote about marriage to people who were married or thinking about it.[84] The Epistle to the Ephesians contains a passage on the proper behavior of husbands and wives.[85] The pastoral epistles list marital fidelity as an important quality to look for when selecting community leaders and ministers.[86] But Christians married according to local customs and Roman law for as long as the Empire lasted. A Christian wedding ceremony developed

---

82. See Rom 2:13; 3:27–28; 8:1–11; Gal 5:13–23.

83. See 1 Cor 10:23–24.

84. See, e.g., Rom 7:2–3; 1 Cor 7:1–15; 7:25–40.

85. See Eph 5:22–33.

86. See 1 Tm 3:2; 3:12; Ti 1:6. Since the patristic era, the phrase ανήρ μίας γυναικός has been taken to mean a man who is married only once, but in the context of these passages it is better understood as a man who is faithful to his wife—literally, a one-woman man.

in the Byzantine east around the seventh century, but Christians in western Europe continued to marry according to Mediterranean and Germanic customs throughout the Dark Ages. The need for a public record of marriages led bishops to insist that such records be kept in every parish. Over the course of time, priests not only witnessed marriages, but they also blessed them, and they came to preside over them, displacing the parents who had presided over weddings in earlier times. By the twelfth century, a church ceremony had replaced the traditional family ceremony for the joining of couples in marriage, and in the thirteenth century matrimony came to be listed as one of the sacraments by scholastic theologians who were interested in explaining how church rites produced their effects.[87]

In the gospels, Jesus speaks of marriage only indirectly, when addressing the question of divorce.[88] Jesus' condemnation of divorce and remarriage has been interpreted in many ways, most recently as a protest against the injustice of Jewish men being able to dismiss their wives for trivial reasons.[89] The prohibition of divorce in Matthew 5:32 and 19:9 allows for an exception in the case of πορνεία, which has often been translated as adultery, but the Greek word can refer to any type of immoral or inappropriate behavior. During the patristic period, this text was used to justify men divorcing adulterous wives, but since there is no text granting similar permission to wives, women were not allowed to divorce philandering husbands. That said, unjust divorce was regarded as a sin that called for public repentance and marriage was not considered indissoluble. The only other New Testament text that speaks about divorce is 1 Corinthians 7:10–16, where Paul prohibits divorce and remarriage for Christians but gives permission for Christians to divorce pagan spouses who strongly object to their partner's religious conversion.[90]

One argument against using Jesus' condemnation of divorce as proof for the indissolubility of marriage (besides the historical facts just mentioned) is that it is an apodictic statement similar to others in the gospels, and since no one takes other apodictic statements literally, the condemnation of divorce should not be taken literally.

---

87. See Martos, *Doors to the Sacred*, 412–431; Edward Schillebeeckx, *Marriage: Human Reality and Saving Mystery* (New York: Sheed and Ward, 1965); Theodore Mackin, *What is Marriage?* (New York: Paulist Press, 1982); Philip Lyndon Reynolds, *Marriage in the Western Church* (Leiden: E. J. Brill, 1994).

88. See Mt 5:31–32; 19:1–10; Mk 10:2–11; Lk 16:18.

89. See Pierre Hegy, "Disputed Biblical Interpretations about Marriage and Divorce" in Pierre Hegy and Joseph Martos, eds., *Catholic Divorce: The Deception of Annulments* (New York: Continuum, 2000).

90. What Paul is saying here is that Christians should not divorce, and if they divorce, they should not remarry. In other words, Paul regards divorce as wrong, but he does not say it is impossible. The passage was taken as a moral prohibition during the patristic era, especially as a prohibition against divorcing a spouse unfairly or for trivial reasons. Only much later was marriage regarded as indissoluble.

For example, in the Sermon on the Mount, anger is condemned as being as bad as murder, lustful looks are regarded as sinful as adultery, a hand that commits a sin it to be cut off, no one should ever swear an oath, people should always turn the other cheek, they should always give in to those who sue them, and they should love their enemies.[91] If the other commands and prohibitions are not taken literally, the prohibition of divorce should not be taken literally.

The only New Testament text that directly addresses the marital relationship is Ephesians 5:22–33:

> Wives should submit to their husbands as to the Lord, for the husband is the head of the wife just as Christ is the head of church and is the savior of the body. Thus, just as the church is subject to Christ, so also wives should be subject to their husbands in all things. Husbands, take care of your wives just as Christ takes care of the church and gives of himself for her, making her pure by cleansing her in the bath of water and word, so that she might be presented to him as a glorious church without any spot or wrinkle or other defect, but pure and flawless. Likewise, husbands should take care of their wives just as they take care of their own bodies. In caring for his wife, a husband cares for himself as well. After all, no man detests his own body; rather, he values and feeds it just as the Lord values and feeds the church, we being members of his body, his flesh and bones, as it were. "For this reason, a man shall leave his father and mother, and shall be joined to his wife, becoming two in one body." This is a great mystery, but I am speaking of it in reference to Christ and the church. To sum up, each one of you should take care of his wife as he takes care of himself, and the wife should show deference toward her husband.

This text obviously refers to a patriarchal marriage in which husband and wife are not equal. In ancient times, when the two became one body, that body was the man's and the woman's identity disappeared into that of her husband. Her duty was to attend to her husband and take care of his needs, and perhaps for that reason her obligation to care is not mentioned here. The husband, though, was lord of his wife and everything about her, and so he could treat her as his slave or property if he wanted to. Possibly playing on that relationship, Ephesians tells wives to submit to the lord of their household the same way that they submit to Christ the Lord. But the author (whether Paul or someone else) tells Christian husbands that they are not to lord over their wives but to love them with the love that the New Testament consistently calls ἀγάπη or caring. He drives the point home by telling men to take care of their wives with the same diligence with which they take care of their own bodies. Thus the relationship is to be one of mutual caring, even if it is not egalitarian. Adding theological reinforcement to this argument, he reminds his readers that Christ the Lord cares for

---

91. See Mt 5: 21–48.

and takes care of the church, and since ἐκκλησία is a feminine noun, the masculine-feminine parallel is easy to draw.

The spiritual reality of Christian marriage, then, is the same as the one at the heart of ministry, namely, ἀγάπη, but here the caring goes both ways: the wife takes care of her husband and the husband takes care of his wife. In a culture such as our own that prizes egalitarian marriage, gospel texts that speak of ἀγάπη can be taken as referring to the quality of love that ought to be found on both sides of the equation. For example, John 15:13 says,

> No one has greater love than this: laying down one's life for one's friends.

This is obviously a type of love that is more than just a feeling, for it entails giving the needs of others priority over one's own wants. And if mutual friendship is the hallmark of egalitarian marriage, then mutual ἀγάπη is the hallmark of Christian marriage. Another helpful text is John 13:34:

> I give you a new commandment: Love one another. Indeed, love one another as I have loved you.

Translating ἀγάπη as care and its cognates, this can be rendered,

> Take care of one another. In fact, care for one another the way that I have taken care of you.

This interpretation takes the husband-wife relationship out of the realm of romance and puts it squarely in the practical sphere of attending to the needs of another. It does not deny that romantic love can lead to self-giving love, nor that romance and sexuality can energize mutual caring. But the love between spouses that makes a marriage solid and lasting is essentially the same as the love of parents for children: it is not a matter of feeling but a matter of caring about and caring for. Caring is a spiritual reality that is important for human living and it deserves to be celebrated.

d. Summary and Conclusion

The early followers of Jesus celebrated their faith in him and their new life together in a weekly meal. They initiated new members of the community by immersing them in water and blessing them with a laying on of hands. In some places this hand-laying resulted in charismatic manifestations such as glossolalia or speaking in tongues, but in all cases the initiation rituals symbolized a passage from a former way of life to a new way of life, from living according to the spirit of the age to being animated by the spirit of Christ, from being caught in moral shortcomings to being freed or saved from those undesirable habits. By living according to the way proclaimed by Jesus, members of the community cared about and cared for one another, forgiving faults and being forgiven, healing and being healed, serving and being served. Marital relationships, service relationships and mutual relationships were all to be guided by the principle of ἀγάπη. Luke sketches an idyllic picture of community life at the beginning of Acts, and this sketch is both fleshed out and corrected by information from the epistles. The beliefs and norms, values and ideals that Christians found in their new way of life were spiritual realities that they experienced and attempted to write about using the vocabulary that was available to them.

2. Sacraments in the Second and Third Centuries

As the faith was spreading throughout the Roman Empire, Christian intellectuals had occasion to write about their beliefs and practices for a number of reasons. Those called apologists wrote explanations for non-believers. Disagreements among Christians led some to argue for their own positions and against the positions of others. Lastly, Christian teachers wrote catechetical works for converts and bishops wrote sermons and other works for the faithful in their pastoral care.

Just as in the first century when the scriptures were being written, Christian rituals were not spoken of collectively as *sacramenta* in Latin although the Greek words μυστήριον and μυστήρια were used when talking about baptism and the eucharistic meal. It could be said that these ceremonies were spoken of as mysteries, meaning that they were recognized as religious rites that celebrated sacred realities, but there was no general discussion of Christian μυστήρια or *sacramenta*.

Moreover, as already noted, μυστήριον could refer either to a symbolic ritual or to the hidden reality that it symbolized. The word retained this referential ambiguity among the Greek-speaking fathers of the church, and it has both meanings even today in Greek Orthodox theology. When *sacramentum* was used to translate μυστήριον, the Latin word likewise had a dual meaning, and its sense or referent therefore has to be determined from the context in which it is used. Even in Augustine's writings at the end of the patristic period in the west, *sacramentum* sometimes refers to a sacred mystery, sometimes it refers to a sacred ritual, and sometimes the referent is ambiguous.[92]

The second and third centuries of the Christian era are sometimes referred to as the pre-Nicene period or the ante-Nicene period in Christian history because Constantine's edict of toleration in A.D. 313 and his convocation of a council of bishops at Nicaea in 325 introduced a period of development that was markedly different from what had gone on before. During the two hundred or so years prior to that, the Christian religion was not recognized by the Roman government, so the followers of Christ were sometimes regarded with suspicion by civil authorities and they were occasionally persecuted for being different from other subjects of the empire. In fact, discussions among Christians about those who had given up their faith during

92. See chapter 2, section 3, above, pages 48–55.

persecutions led to key developments in their understanding of baptism, particularly about the effects of baptism and the question of rebaptism.

a. Baptismal Metaphors of the Conversion Experience

The *Didache*, whose full title translates as "Teaching of the Lord to the Nations by the Twelve Apostles," was written in Greek before the end of the first century and was included in some early lists of inspired writings. Like many books in the New Testament, its author or authors are unknown, and it is concerned more with Christian moral standards and ritual practices than with doctrinal matters. Thus it describes how baptisms are to be performed, but it does not offer a theology of baptism other than indicating that it is to be done in the name of the Father and of the Son and of the Holy Spirit. Its short chapter on baptism says that the preferred method is immersion in cold running water, but warm or standing water may be used, and in case of necessity, water may be poured on the head of the initiate.[93] The preference for running water in early Christianity may have derived from a literal interpretation of the story in John's gospel in which Jesus tells the woman at the well that she should have asked him for living water, in Greek, ὕδωρ ζῶν, which also means running water.[94]

The next early witness to Christian practices is Ignatius of Antioch, whose seven authentic letters written in the early second century mention Christian baptism only twice. Concerned with the role of church leaders in maintaining Christian unity, Ignatius insists that no baptizing should be done without the approval of the ἐπίσκοπος.[95] He does not mention the Trinitarian formula found in the *Didache* and at the end of Matthew's gospel, but this ecclesiastical ritual is evidently a far cry from the spontaneous baptisms described in Acts. Whether Ignatius has in mind full immersion or another form of the ritual is not clear from the text, but it is clear that he is talking about a rite of initiation into the community of which the ἐπίσκοπος is the head, and who functions more like a bishop than like a presiding elder. Ignatius also speaks metaphorically of baptism as a kind of spiritual armament, drawing his imagery from the Pauline corpus, but he does not explain how baptism affords this protection.[96]

A Palestinian philosopher named Justin lived in Rome for about 25 years before being martyred for the faith in 165. Among his extant works are two apologies, one of which offers an explanation of baptism for pagan readers. Justin describes the process of "being made new through Christ," which entails the remission of sins (τῶν προημαρτημένων ἄφεσιν) with the support of those who already live according to the teachings of the gospels. Then they are brought to the place of regeneration (τρόπον ἀναγεννήσεως) where they are washed with water (εν τῷ ὕδατι τότε λουτρὸν

93. *Didache*, 7.
94. See Jn 4:10–11 and 7:38; also Jer 2:13.
95. *Letter to the Smyrnaeans*, 8.
96. *Letter to Polycarp*, 6. See 1 Thes 5:8 and Eph 6:17.

ποιοῦνται) in the name of the Father, Son and Holy Spirit. The purpose of this washing is to change from being a person of necessity and ignorance (ανάγκης, αγνοίας) to being a person of decision and knowledge (προαιρέσεως, επιστήμης), which may be understood as changing from acting out of habit because of not knowing any better to choosing a way of life that is known to be better. The process is therefore one of being morally regenerated or born again (αναγεννηθῆναι) and those who go through it are illuminated (φωτιζομένων) in their understanding of how to live.[97]

Of note in Justin Martyr's description is the fact that the word βάπτισμα is not used, nor is the action described as βαπτίζειν, which suggests that the ritual may not have been a full immersion in water. As in the *Didache*, the emphasis is on the Christian way of life rather than on religious doctrines, which appear to be summed up in the acceptance of "God the Father and Lord of the universe," Jesus Christ, the savior who was "crucified under Pontius Pilate," and the Holy Spirit, who "through the prophets foretold all things about Jesus." The remission of sins, then, likely refers to getting rid of sinful habits and not simply to the forgiveness of sins committed in the past.

Irenaeus was bishop of Lyon in Gaul during the latter half of the second century, a church leader who is a good example of the monarchial episcopate advocated by Ignatius of Antioch at a time when Christian communities needed strong leadership against persecutions and heresies. Indeed, his best known work is *Against Heresies*, often cited by its Latin title, *Adversus haereses*, even though it was originally composed in Greek. Unlike earlier Christian writings that focused on lifestyle and practices, this work amply explains and defends doctrinal beliefs against those of the heretical Gnostics. Except for references to the New Testament, this work does not discuss Christian baptism, but in passing it does refer to baptism as a means of receiving the truth, as a spiritual rebirth, and as something that is done for the remission of sins, for redemption, for perfection, and for eternal life.[98] How baptism accomplishes these things, however, is not amplified.

The textual evidence from the first two centuries indicates that βάπτισμα in Greek and *baptisma* in Latin were becoming special terms in the Christian vocabulary. As mentioned above, the *Didache* says that baptism can be performed by pouring if there is not enough water for immersion, indicating that the Greek word even at that time meant something more than immersion in water. Gradually it came to mean the rite of Christian initiation and indeed a church ritual presided over by a bishop, in contrast to the spontaneous baptisms described in Acts. When the Greek was transliterated into Latin, its linguistic connection to immersion was completely

97. The Greek words in this paragraph and the phrases translated in the next paragraph are from the *First Apology* of Justin Martyr, 61.

98. See Irenaeus of Lyon, *Against Heresies*, 1.9.4; 1.21.1–2; 1.23.5. It should be remembered that baptizing and baptism during this early period could refer to the entire process of immersion in the Christian community and way of life, and not simply to the culminating water ritual.

lost. *Baptisma* thereafter refers exclusively to a religious ritual. *Immersio* is not a noun in classical Latin, and the idea of plunging or immersing is rendered by the verbs *immergere* and *summergere*.

With Tertullian, who was writing around the end of the second century, we come to the first Christian intellectual who wrote in Latin. His spare theology of baptism was summarized in the second chapter,[99] but the following may be added here. As noted previously, *baptisma* for Tertullian is the name of a Christian ritual and it does not necessarily refer to a rite of immersion. Indeed, Tertullian nowhere describes the rite, but since he speaks of giving and receiving baptism (*dandi et accipiendi baptismi*) he quite possibly has in mind a ritual in which water is poured on the head of a candidate who is standing in water, a scene found in frescoes and mosaics from the patristic era, even in depictions of John's baptism of Jesus. Tertullian agrees that baptism is a physical act that has spiritual effects, which he identifies as sanctification and the remission of sins.[100] Another gift or *gratia* of baptism is spiritual strengthening.[101] Through the physical washing, the soul is made clean by the action of an angel so that it can receive the Holy Spirit.[102] In *De baptismo*, Tertullian does not reveal the source of this theological information, but he does cite the authority of Christ in claiming that it is necessary for salvation.[103] Moreover, throughout this work, Tertullian prefers arguments from authority, primarily from scripture, giving the impression that he is not so much drawing his insights from experience as he is from reading and reasoning.[104]

Of particular interest for this study is the language of giving and receiving. As already noted, Tertullian speaks of giving and receiving baptism, but he also says that baptism gives (*daret*) the Holy Spirit and the remission of sins, he speaks of Peter being able to confer (*conferre posset*) the profitable result of baptism, and he argues that baptism is able to be performed (*exerceri potest*) by all Christians, not just by bishops and priests.[105] With Tertullian, then, we find not only the first use of *sacramentum* to talk about Christian rituals and their mysteries,[106] but also the first mention of giving and receiving sacraments.[107]

99. See above, pages 49–50.

100. See Tertullian, *Baptism*, 4, 7 and 10.

101. See ibid., 9.

102. See ibid., 6 and 10.

103. See ibid., 12. The scripture reference is to Jn 3:5.

104. Tertullian appealed to experience in other works, however. For example, in chapter 6 of *Repentance* he wrote, "We are not washed in order to stop sinning, but because we have stopped, since in our heart we have already been cleansed. For the first baptism of a learner is perfect fear. After that, if you know the Lord, your faith is sound, for your conscience has embraced repentance once and for all."

105. See ibid., 10, 12 and 17.

106. See chapter 2, around footnote 47–49, above.

107. In other works, Tertullian more clearly says that the sacraments of Christ (i.e., baptism and eucharist) are administered, and that John the Baptist administered a sacrament when he baptized. See *The Prescription of Heretics*, 40 (*sacramenta christi administrantur*), and *Against Marcion*, 4.38

The Apostolic Tradition, whether written by Hippolytus early in the third century or by an anonymous liturgist in the fourth century, was originally composed in Greek, but only fragments of the Greek text remain. The best preserved texts are Coptic translations from which the original Greek can be tentatively reconstructed. Nevertheless, the general outline and basic meaning of this work are clear, and some things can be learned from it even in translation.[108] It is primarily a liturgical document that prescribes how various church ceremonies are to be performed. The section on initiation says little about the theology of baptism or indeed about Christian doctrine apart from a profession of faith which is quite similar to what later became known as the Apostles' Creed. It prescribes that catechumens should be instructed for three years, but the time may be shorter if their conduct is exemplary. If they were to be martyred for the faith during their preparation period, it assures them that they should not worry because they will have been baptized in their own blood.[109] Before being admitted to baptism, the candidates' lives should be examined to ascertain if they perform works of mercy, and witnesses should attest to whether they are living according to the demands of the gospel. If they are found to have shortcomings, they should receive additional instruction until their spirits are purified.[110] The immediate preparation (during Holy Week) and the baptismal ceremony itself is very similar to the current Rite of Christian Initiation of Adults; indeed, the RCIA was modeled after *The Apostolic Tradition* and other patristic liturgical records. In brief, *The Apostolic Tradition* displays an emphasis on moral conversion that is similar to what is found in the *Didache*, but the doctrinal content of the baptismal ceremony has been expanded from a Trinitarian formula to a short creed.

From the third century onward, the terminology surrounding baptism remains relatively stable in the eastern, Greek speaking part of the Roman Empire. In the west, however, the language begins to change. We have already seen the start of this evolution in Tertullian's introduction of *dare* (to give), *conferre* (to confer) and *administrare* (to administer) when speaking about the performance of the baptismal rite, and in his use of *accipere* (to accept or receive) in reference to the effect of the rite. It is primarily in north Africa, the birthplace of Tertullian and later of Augustine, that theological reflection on the church's rituals becomes a major undertaking.

The first empire-wide persecution of the Christian religion was ordered by Emperor Decius in the year 250 in an attempt to shore up public morality by insisting that everyone subscribe to the religion of the state. All residents of the empire were required to demonstrate their loyalty by burning incense to an image of the emperor, who was regarded as a god. Many Christians regarded this as idolatry and refused,

---

(*sacramentum iohannes administrabat*).

108. See Gregory Dix, ed., *The Treatise on the Apostolic Tradition of St. Hippolytus of Rome, Bishop and Martyr* (London: SPCK, 1968), originally published in 1937.

109. See *The Apostolic Tradition*, 17.1; 19.2.

110. See ibid., 20.1–4.

but some acquiesced or paid for documents certifying that they had done so. Those who gave in under pressure were regarded as apostates by the faithful, and those who pretended to give in were regarded with suspicion.

What was to be done about those who had fallen from the faith? Rigorists such as Novatian in Rome opposed the church's policy of reconciling sinners, but they were in the minority. Not only was the practice of rebaptism virtually unknown in the west, but the rule of baptizing only once seemed to have scriptural support. Ephesians 4:5–6 says there is "one Lord, one faith, one baptism; one God and Father of all, who is over all and through all and in all." In context, the Pauline author is concerned about discord among factions in the community and he is exhorting his readers to unity, reminding them that they all believe and practice the same things. But in the context of the rebaptism controversy two centuries later, the text was used to prove that people could be baptized only once.[111]

More important for this study is the way western churchmen from Cyprian onward began to speak about baptism and its effects. Cyprian's Latin is not as sophisticated as Tertullian's; his vocabulary is rather basic and his sentence structure is comparatively simple. He often constructs sentences with *dare*, *habere* and *accipere* to speak of what is given and received in baptism. Most commonly he speaks of giving and receiving the Holy Spirit, grace, and the remission of sins. Perhaps this manner of speaking was caused by the need to discuss complex issues with a limited vocabulary. Very likely, a contributory factor was the way the issues had been framed by Novatian and others who claimed that those who had apostatized during the Decian persecution of 250–251 had lost the Holy Spirit that they had once received in baptism and, since there is only one baptism, they could never be readmitted to the communion table.

Cyprian held what at the time was a middle position between those who, like Novatian, argued that those who lost the Holy Spirit had to remain outside the church forever, and those who, like the majority of western bishops, held that apostates and heretics could be readmitted to communion after they had gone through a process of public repentance. Cyprian allowed that those who had been baptized in the church could eventually be reconciled , but he believed that those who had been baptized by heretics did not truly receive the Holy Spirit, and therefore they would have to undergo baptism in order to join the one true church. Since heretics were outside the church, they did not have the Holy Spirit, and so they could not give what they did not have.

Posing the question and debating it in this manner indicate that Christian thinking about the Holy Spirit was becoming less metaphorical and more metaphysical. Christians in the first two centuries perceived that God's holy spirit was present when people behaved in ways that were different—by speaking in tongues, by transforming

---

111. See, e.g., Cyprian of Carthage, *The Unity of the Church*, 4 (*unum corpus et unus Spiritus, una spes vocationis vestrae, unus Dominus, una fides, unum baptisma, unus Deus*); 11 (*aliud baptisma praeter unum esse non possit*).

their lives, by attending to the needs of others, and so on.[112] Being filled with God's spirit or the spirit of Christ was a metaphor for such behavior, a way of naming what they saw by relating it to Jesus and the Father. By the third century, however, Christians were thinking of the Holy Spirit as a spiritual entity that is received through baptism and the laying on of hands, or as something that Christians possess and non-believers do not. In other words, thinking about the Spirit was becoming more tied to ritual than to lifestyle.

The connection with lifestyle was not entirely lost, however, since if people renounced their faith they were clearly behaving in a way that was not holy. But theological thinking about this behavior was rather simplistic: either one had the Spirit or one did not, so if one offered incense before an image of the emperor, one had evidently lost it. The thinking was also somewhat mechanical: by going through a ritual such as public reconciliation with the church, one could get the Spirit back. Cyprian's attitude toward those baptized by heretics was similarly simple and mechanical. If one was baptized in the true church, one automatically received the Spirit, but if one was baptized outside the true church, the ritual was not a real baptism, and one did not receive the Spirit. Evidence of being filled with the Spirit was no longer behavior such as glossolalia or caring for the welfare of others, but the evidence was instead having been baptized in the Catholic Church.

According to Cyprian,

- Baptism is something that the church, and only the church, has (*habet*). Whatever water ritual heretics and schismatics have, it is not baptism.[113]

- Only ecclesiastical baptism has grace (*habet gratiam*) which is given (*datur*) to the baptized.[114]

- Through baptism the Holy Spirit is received (*spiritus sanctus accipitur*).[115]

- Heretics and schismatics cannot give (*dare non possint*) the Holy Spirit because they do not have it.[116]

- The remission of sins is given (*remissio peccatorum datur*) in baptism, but only if the one baptizing has the Holy Spirit.[117]

In sum, the church has baptism and baptism has grace which can be given to others. In Cyprian's mind, however, grace and the Holy Spirit are given to the baptized

---

112. See Acts 8:14–19; 10:44–47; 11:28; 19:1–6.

113. See Cyprian of Carthage, *Letters*: Letter 71, 1; Letter 72, 1; Letter 73, 25; Letter 74, 7. An English translation by Sister Rose Bernard Donna, CSJ, can be found in *The Fathers of the Church: A New Translation*, Vol. 51 (Washington, DC: Catholic University of America Press, 1964).

114. See ibid., Letter 64, 3; Letter 69, 5; Letter 70, 2; Letter 73, 9 and 16; Letter 74, 7.

115. See ibid., Letter 63, 8; Letter 72, 1; Letter 73, 6, 9 and 17; Letter 74, 5.

116. See ibid., Letter 69, 10f; Latter 70, 3.

117. See ibid., Letter 64, 5; Letter 69, 11; Letter 70, 1; Letter 73, 5, 7 and 9.

from someone in the true church, that is, by someone who has the grace to give and who can bestow the Holy Spirit on others. The same is true of the remission of sins.

Two developments can be noted here. First, according to Cyprian's theology of baptism, it is the minister and not the ritual through whom God acts in bestowing grace and remitting sins. This interpretation of the ritual will later be rejected by Augustine and the Catholic tradition, but at this point in history it is an open question. Second, and of more immediate interest, Cyprian develops his theology of baptism using simple verbs such as have, give, and receive, making it possible to talk about who has and who does not have baptism, who has and who does not have the Holy Spirit, who can give grace and forgiveness and who cannot. This pattern of language will continue to be found in Latin theology and to influence the way questions are posed and problems are solved.

b. Eucharist

(1) A Methodological Preface

Our primary concern is with the development of the concept of *sacramentum et res* and with the way that speaking about sacraments being given and received may have promoted that development. In the case of baptism, for example, the practice of pouring water over candidates rather than immersing them fully could easily have led Christians to speak about giving and receiving the water, as Tertullian seems to have done. In the case of eucharist, however, there was no question that the language of giving and receiving was appropriate because an important part of the meal was the sharing of bread and wine, eventually referred to as communion. So important was the symbolism of this sharing that the consecrated bread and wine were not offered to those who had serious moral lapses, which is to say they were excommunicated. Since the language of giving and receiving was present from the beginning, therefore, it does not offer any clues to the development of beliefs about the eucharist.

Nevertheless, considering the *terminus ad quem* of eucharistic theology in the Middle Ages, two ideas in particular stand out: (1) that during the mass the bread and wine become the body and blood of Christ, and (2) that the ritual surrounding the use of bread and wine is a sacrifice. Much can be learned by asking where these ideas came from and how they developed over the course of time.

Changing our focus in this manner does not deflect us from our stated goal of understanding the function of the *sacramentum et res* in scholastic theology, for the consecrated bread and wine were themselves regarded as a sacramental reality. To be sure, this reality was thought to be something quite different from the baptismal character, but it had one important feature in common with it, namely, it was the condition of the possibility of a change in perceived reality. Just as the baptismal ritual changed the way one looked at the baptized (they were seen as members of the church, cleansed of sin, and filled with the Holy Spirit), so the consecration ritual in the mass changed the way one looked at the consecrated elements (they were seen as the body and blood of Christ). In the same manner, being ordained changed the way those in holy orders were perceived in the church, and being married changed the way that a man and woman were regarded in society. If one assumes, as most ancients and medievals did, that in order to be perceived as real an object had to be really present, then one could easily conclude that if one sees something it must be really there.[118]

The contention that there was an evolution in the language that Christian authors used to talk about their rituals is fairly straightforward and easy to document. Contending that those who have left written records of their ideas were thinking in a certain way is a more difficult claim and harder to demonstrate. Most people, including theologians, are more aware of their thoughts than they are of their thinking, that is to say, that they are more aware of cognitional contents than they are of cognitional processes. Ask anyone what they are looking at, and they can quite easily tell you what it is. But ask them to describe the process of going from the sense data that their eyes are collecting to a judgment about what is in front of them, and they may be hard pressed even to understand your question. Yet we are never so focused on the objects of our attention that we have no awareness of our conscious mental processes. If someone were to ask you, the reader, what you are doing right now, you would reply without hesitation that you are reading. When you read these sentences, you are not thinking about the activity of reading, but you are nonetheless aware of what you are doing. This peripheral self-awareness is what makes it possible for us to say what we are doing even though we are consciously focused on something else.[119]

This having been said, please notice that there are times when our perception of things changes. You bump into someone you do not know, but after she tells you her name, you recognize her as a high school classmate. You are at a naturalization ceremony, and after the immigrants have sworn allegiance to the government, you regard them as citizens of your country. You are at a wedding, and after the couple pronounce their vows, you perceive them as married to each other. In none of these cases did what you were looking at change; the people looked pretty much the same throughout. What changed was how you interpreted what you were looking at. What changed was your understanding of what you were seeing. What changed was something in the

118. This epistemological assumption is common today and even throughout human history. People spontaneously believe that if they see something, it is there to be seen, and if they know something, it is a fact that is objectively true, i.e., independent of whether they personally know it or not. Bernard Lonergan calls this naïve realism, and he refers to what is perceived as the already-out-there-now real in *Insight: A Study of Human Understanding* (London: Longmans, 1958) 250–254, 381–384.

119. This is not a claim that peripheral self-awareness is a logical condition of the possibility of talking about what we are doing. Rather, this vague awareness of what we are doing even when we are intensely concentrating on something else is an existential or empirical condition of the possibility of doing that. Indeed, it is a condition that can be empirically verified by noticing that we are seeing whenever we are looking at something, that we are hearing whenever we are listening to something, that we are thinking whenever we are thinking about something, and so on.

realm of thought or meaning rather than something in the realm of images or sense impressions. Change of this sort is not uncommon; indeed, it happens all the time. But unless we are psychologists or philosophers, we do not pay attention to it, and it remains in our peripheral awareness until we advert to it.

Even today, cognitive psychologists and philosophers of knowledge have various theories or explanations for the process we have just been thinking about. People in the ancient world, like people today, did not try to explain how their perceptions changed, but if their physiology and mental processes were essentially the same as that of *homo sapiens* today, we can assume that they perceived changes such as the ones described above, just as people do today. The Greek philosopher Plato theorized that, just as our eyes see physical objects in the physical world, our mind sees spiritual objects in a realm of ideas or intellectual forms. His student Aristotle offered a different explanation for the same phenomenon, suggesting that just as our eyes perceive physical data, our mind perceives the intelligibility in those sense impressions. Some early Christian writers may have been familiar with neo-platonic philosophy, and some even brought it into their theological reflections. But regardless of their philosophical leanings, if their minds worked basically the way our minds do, they would have been familiar with the phenomenon of changing and changed perceptions, about which we have been talking.

Thus Christian writers looked at people before they went through a ritual of washing, and they perceived them as in need of salvation. After the ritual bath, they perceived the same individuals as having received the salvation of Christ. Thus too they looked at the food to be used in their ritual meal and regarded them as bread and wine. But during the meal, they looked at the same objects and regarded them as the body and blood of Christ. How do we know this? From their writings.

While it is true that we cannot get inside the minds of people in the past (any more than we can read the minds of people today), it is equally true that we have access to what they thought through what they wrote. When we understand what they wrote, we can get a sense of what they were talking about. If we can assume that what they perceived is similar to what we perceive (which is not a great leap, since we do this all the time when talking with people around us and when reading contemporary authors), then we can distinguish between what they wrote and what they were writing about. What they wrote helps us to infer what they were writing about.

With regard to the eucharistic elements, we know that apologists and later writers referred to them as the body and blood of Christ, but what did they perceive that led them to say so? Likewise with regard to the eucharistic meal, we know that apologists and later writers referred to it as a sacrifice, but what did they perceive that led them to say so? We can naïvely claim that they called the ritual foods the body and blood of Christ because they *were* the body and blood of Christ. And we can naïvely claim that they called the ritual meal a sacrifice because it *was* a sacrifice. But this begs the question, and it springs from the same naïve realism that assumes that knowing is the same as looking, or at least that knowing is analogous to looking. Don't we say, "I see what you mean"? And don't we say, "Look at what I'm telling you"? Ordinary language often uses metaphors of sight when what we are talking about is not seeing but understanding, not looking but knowing. To comprehend the development of eucharistic theology, it is necessary to move beyond ordinary language to a more precise distinction between physical data and the interpretation of those data, between what is experienced and what is understood.

What was believed by past writers can be determined by translating the words that they wrote. But to get at what they were writing about—what they were experiencing or remembering when they wrote—requires some reasoning and imagination. Very often, however, taking this step is not a great leap. When considering baptism in the New Testament, for example, we noticed that βαπτίζειν means to immerse, and from this we inferred that initially the water ritual was very likely a full immersion. Likewise, when discussing what Paul wrote in 1 Corinthians 11 about the communal meal, we saw that Paul scolded some in that local church for eating before everyone had arrived, with the result that others went hungry, and from this we inferred that the meal was supposed to be one in which food was shared. Paul nowhere says that the κυριακὸν δεῖπνον was what today is called a potluck or covered-dish supper, but from what he says we can infer with some probability that he was talking about a meal of that sort. Making the distinction between what is said and what is being referred to is often helpful for understanding why authors wrote what they did.

(2) From Lord's Supper to Eucharistic Meal

After Paul's letter to the Corinthians and the book of Acts, the earliest reference to the Lord's supper is in the *Didache*, composed in the second half of the first century. This document contains three references to eating together, and it is not clear whether or not the references are to separate meals or to different aspects of the same meal.[120] In any event, none of the three descriptions corresponds exactly to what would later be called a eucharistic liturgy.

The first description, in chapter 9, contains a thanksgiving (ευχαριστία) to be said over bread and wine, but it does not contain any reference to the last supper nor to what are called the words of institution. Prayers are addressed to God as Father, and Jesus is referred to as God's child or servant (παῖς), but also as Lord (κύριος). There is an admonition not to share the food of thanksgiving with anyone who is not baptized.

Chapter 10 contains words to be said at the end of a meal, presumably not just a symbolic meal of bread and wine, for the words are to be said when the participants

---

120. The text is based on a manuscript discovered in 1873, which may be a composite based on earlier oral traditions, making it unclear whether the passages about meals refer to one, two or three types of gatherings. It is also possible that the communal meals did not have a well defined format, and so the author of this document is proposing acceptable forms for the prayers.

"have had their fill," but there is no specific reference to bread and wine. In this chapter, the action is not called a thanksgiving but the prayers give thanks (εὐχαριστέιν) for the holy name that dwells in our hearts (κατεσκήνωσας εν ταῖς καρδίαις ἡμῶν), for knowledge, faith and immortality (γνώσεως καὶ πίστεως καὶ αθανασίας), for food and drink that give enjoyment (εις απόλαυσιν), for spiritual food and drink (πνευματικὴν τροφὴν καὶ ποτὸν), and for eternal life (ζωὴν αιώνιον).[121] Moreover, this is only a suggested pattern of prayer, for the chapter instructs that prophets (προφήταις) should give thanks however they want.[122]

Chapter 14 instructs Christians to gather on the Lord's day (i.e., Sunday, the day of the resurrection), to break bread and give thanks (εὐχαριστέιν). They are to first confess their faults (προεξομολογησάμενοι τὰ παραπτώματα ὑμῶν) so that their sacrifice may be pure (καθαρὰ ἡ θυσία), and they are to be reconciled (διαλλαγῶσιν) with one another so that their sacrifice will not be defiled (μὴ κοινωθὴ).[123] Note that sacrifice (θυσία) "in the ancient world was commonly associated with a fellowship meal. Thus, both Jews and gentiles would have been disposed to regard the eucharistic meal as a kind of 'sacrifice.'"[124] Moreover the purity of the sacrifice regards the ritual readiness of the participants, not the quality of the offering. From this perspective, "a pure sacrifice can be offered only by one who is holy."[125] The confession of faults and reconciliation with one another ensures that the participants are ritually pure.

The *Didache* was regarded as a sacred writing by some early church fathers, but ultimately it was not included in the canon of the New Testament. It gives us three snapshots of early Christian worship, from which the following may be inferred:

- The custom of the community meal mentioned in Acts and 1 Corinthians continued for some decades, at least in the region where the *Didache* was written.

- Prayers of thanks were said over bread and wine, as well as after eating, preparing the way for the name "Lord's supper" to be replaced by the name "eucharist" when the full meal was replaced by a symbolic meal.

- Although these prayers were religiously formal, they apparently allowed for variation and did not have a fixed wording.

- If at least one of the gatherings was what would later be termed a eucharistic meal, repeating the words of Jesus at the last supper does not seem to have been

---

121. Although the food and drink that give enjoyment undoubtedly refer to things that are actually edible and drinkable, it is difficult to determine whether the spiritual food and drink refer to the eucharistic bread and wine or to inspiring prayers and edifying stories.

122. The prophets referred to here appear to be itinerant preachers with the charism of speaking on behalf of God. They are described in chapters 11–13.

123. The reference is to Mt 5:23–24. There is also a reference in this chapter to Mal 1:11, which will be treated below.

124. Aaron Milavec, *Didache*, 535.

125. Ibid., 537.

regarded as essential.[126]

- The giving of thanks on the first day of the week was referred to as a sacrifice (θυσία). Why it was called a sacrifice, however, is not explained. The Matthian verses to which the writer appeals use the word δῶρον or votive gift rather than θυσία or sacrifice.

The first three centuries are sometimes called the age of martyrs, and although Christians were not widely persecuted before 250, they did experience persecution and martyrdom from time to time. In the early second century, Ignatius of Antioch was arrested in Syria and sentenced to death in Rome. While en route to the empire's capital, Ignatius wrote a series of letters that sometimes give us a picture of early Christianity and sometimes show us what Ignatius wanted Christianity to look like. Some of his theological concern was with those who regarded Christ as so divine that they denied his humanity. In one of his letters, Ignatius describes these heretics as refraining from the Christian thanksgivings (ευχαριστίας) because they do not believe that the food of thanksgiving (ευχαριστίαν) is "the flesh (σάρκα) of our savior Jesus Christ, which suffered for our sins, and which the Father in his goodness raised up again."[127] Ignatius is the first clear witness that Christians regarded the eucharistic bread and wine as the body and blood of Christ.[128]

About a half century later, Justin Martyr wrote in defense of Christianity against its detractors, some of whom claimed that the followers of Jesus performed immoral acts during their μυστήρια or secret rituals. After describing the new religion's initiation rites, his *First Apology* describes its ritual meal as one in which bread and wine (mixed with water) are brought to the one presiding, who then offers praise to the Father of all through the Son and the Holy Spirit. The presider then prays, offering thanks (ευχαριστίαν) on behalf of all, after which they say, "Amen." Those in attendance partake of the thanked-for bread and wine and water (τοῦ ευχαριστηθέντος ἄρτου καὶ οἴνου καὶ ὕδατος), and some is carried to those who are absent.[129]

Justin explains that this food is called thanksgiving (ευχαριστία), and only those who believe (πιστεύοντι), who have been washed in the bath (λουτρόν), and who live (βιοῦντι) according to the teachings of Christ may partake of it. Christians believe that, just as Jesus Christ was made flesh by the word of God, and just as food nourishes our bodies by being changed (κατὰ μεταβολὴν), the food that is blessed (ευχαριστθείσαν τροφήν) by the prayer of his word is made the flesh and blood (σάρκα καὶ αἷμα) of that

126. The lack of the so-called words of institution has traditionally been one of the Catholic arguments against calling the meals in chapters 9 and 10 eucharistic. By the same token, since the mass in later centuries was regarded as a sacrifice, the thanksgiving ritual in chapter 14 was regarded by Catholic interpreters as eucharistic.

127. Ignatius of Antoch, *Letter to the Smyrnaeans*, 7.

128. It must be remembered that the body referred to in 1 Cor 11:27 is ambiguous. above, pages 79–80.

129. See the *First Apology* of Justin Martyr, 65.

same Jesus. The apostles remembered (ἀπομνημονεύμασιν) that Jesus had said over the bread and cup, "This is my body," "This is my blood," and "Do this in memory of me." Furthermore, Justin charges, the followers of the god Mithras have wickedly imitated this in their own ceremonies.[130]

There follows a brief description of the Christian practice of gathering on the day of the sun, which is the day on which Christ was raised from the dead, to praise the maker of all (τὸν ποιητὴν τῶν πάντων), and to listen to readings from the memoirs (ἀπομνημονεύματα) of the apostles and the writings (συγγράμματα) of the prophets. The presider (προεστώς) then instructs and encourages the imitation of these good things, after which more prayers are said, and then bread and wine and water are brought in. He offers prayers and thanks (εὐχὰς καὶ εὐχαριστίας) according to his ability, and the people assent by saying Amen. That for which thanks has been given (εὐχαριστηθέντων) is shared with those present, and some is sent to those who are absent. A collection is then taken for those in need, and this is distributed to widows, orphans, the sick, the imprisoned and visiting strangers.[131]

With regard to the First Apology, the following may be noted:

- As in the *Didache*, there is a moral requirement for participating in this weekly ritual, for besides being baptized and accepting Christian beliefs, participants must live according to the teachings of Christ.

- In chapter 66 Justin says that the bread and wine become the body and blood of Christ, but in chapter 67 they are not specifically called this; instead, they are spoken of indirectly as that for which thanks has been given. This suggests that the bread and wine are thought of and perceived as the body and blood of Christ, but there is no claim that the food at the meal is identical with them.

- On the other hand, in chapter 67 Justin may have refrained from identifying what is shared as the body and blood of Christ out of consideration for his pagan audience, who might have misinterpreted his words. One of the charges leveled against Christians during this period was that they ate human flesh and drank human blood.

- The presider is said to give thanks over the bread and wine, but there is no insistence that the words of thanks include the words of institution. This omission in the description may or may not reflect an omission in the practice to which Justin is referring. In any event, the *First Apology* cannot be used as evidence that the words of institution were included in the prayers that were said at these gatherings.

In his *Dialogue with Trypho*, a fictional rabbi, Justin argues that Christianity has supplanted Judaism and is now the true religion for all. Until the destruction of the

130. Ibid., 66.
131. Ibid., 67.

Jerusalem temple in 70 AD, sacrifices were an important part of the Jewish religion, and references to sacrifices abound in the Hebrew scriptures. Inevitably the discussion turns to sacrifices, and Justin invokes Malachi 1:10–11 as a prediction that Christian worship will supplant Jewish worship:

> I am not pleased with you, says the Lord almighty, and I will not receive a sacrifice from your hand. From east to west, my name is great among the nations. Everywhere a pure sacrifice (θυσία καθαρά) is offered to my name because my name is great among the nations, says the Lord almighty.[132]

Justin identifies the offering of bread and wine in the rite of thanksgiving (εὐχαριστία) as the predicted sacrifice, for by this time there are Christians living throughout the Roman world. Moreover, temple sacrifices in the ancient world almost always entailed a meal. The food brought for the ceremony was offered to the god, some of it was symbolically given to the god by being burned or poured out, some of it was a gift for the priests, and the rest of the food was shared by the participants in a sacred meal.[133] Thus, any sacrifice included a meal shared in the presence of a god, so Justin had no difficulty in identifying the Christian thanksgiving meal as a sacrifice, for it was shared in the presence of the risen Lord who could be perceived in their midst through his body and blood.[134] Such a presence could be experienced as no less real than the presence of any other human being, perceived through his or her being there in the flesh.[135]

132. See Justin, *Dialogue with Trypho*, 28.

133. In the Jewish religion, one exception to this rule was a holocaust or whole burnt offering, which was entirely consumed in flames on the altar. This type of sacrifice signified total dedication and loyalty to God, a complete offering of a victim symbolizing self-giving without reserve. A holocaust could be an atonement ritual in expiation of sins, but it could also be an act of supplication or thanksgiving. See John L. McKenzie, "Sacrifice," *Dictionary of the Bible* (London: Geoffrey Chapman, 1965) 754–756. Also, Robert J. Daly, *The Origins of the Christian Doctrine of Sacrifice* (Philadelphia: Fortress Press, 1978), 1–6.

134. The experience of communion with the deity was an important dimension of sacrifices in the ancient world, which were modeled on the offering of gifts to a king, local lord, tribal leader, family head, etc. Depending on the context, the offering could symbolize thankfulness, subservience, repentance, a request for a favor, or just about anything that gifts today might symbolize in society, business or politics. The meal or banquet symbolized the acceptance of the gift and of the giver through the sharing of food and drink. See McKenzie, "Sacrifice," 755–757.

135. In pagan temples and shrines, the god's presence was usually represented by a statue or another type of image. The Jewish religion forbade making images of God, but the presence of Adonai was represented by the Ark of the Covenant and other symbolic objects. The presence that is experienced by the devout in such circumstances would be analogous to the experience of the Blessed Virgin when praying before an image of her. Phenomenologically, one can say that personal presence is perceived *through* sense data. Ordinarily these data are the skin, clothing, voice and movement of a nearby human being. Similarly, the presence of a deity or spiritual being is perceived *through* phenomena (e.g., an image or symbolic objects) that are seen and heard. Certainly such perception is liable to error, and so it is subject to critical evaluation, but religious people do not ordinarily question their perceptions of divine presence, just as no one ordinarily questions their perception of the presence of a person nearby.

The next witness is Irenaeus, bishop of Lyon during the closing decades of the second century. In Book IV of *Against Heresies*, he points out that God does not need offerings from human beings, and in fact the Israelites were told that God prefers justice and mercy to sacrifices and burnt offerings.[136] Therefore it was not for God's benefit but for the benefit of humankind that Jesus commanded his followers to offer God bread and wine, which are confessed to be the body and blood of Christ. This is a new gift in a new covenant, now offered in the church throughout the world, just as the prophet Malachi had predicted.[137]

The text from Malachi 1:10–11 is referenced in three of the earliest witnesses (*Didache*, Justin and Irenaeus) to the practice of calling the Christian thanksgiving meal a sacrifice. As has already been argued, however, this could be done because sacrificial meals in the ancient world were a common religious practice, and so the audiences addressed by these three writings would readily have understood the analogy. The Christian ritual could be called a sacrifice because it was a meal with food that had been made sacred (*sacrum factum*) by remembering Jesus and perhaps recalling the last supper, while they shared it in the presence of their Lord and Savior. At some point in the meal (probably before it was shared by the participants), some of the sacred food would have been offered in thanks to God the Father.

By the mid-third century, the sacrificial meal—by now a symbolic meal of bread and wine, and not a full meal—could also be shared in the morning, as mentioned by Cyprian of Carthage in one of his letters. He gives no reason for this practice, but it is possible that the danger of Roman persecution sometimes led Christians to assemble quietly at a time when their pagan neighbors were still asleep.[138]

Cyprian gives us the first evidence of magical thinking beginning to creep into beliefs about the bread and wine. We have already noticed how in the third and fourth centuries, thinking about baptism began to become more ritualistic, emphasizing the proper performance of the ritual rather than the transformation of behavior that baptism was supposed to initiate. In Letter 63, Cyprian discusses what might be regarded as a liturgical question, namely whether bread and water can be used in the sacrificial meal rather than bread and wine. Apparently there were some who believed that water was more appropriate for morning sacrifices, but Cyprian strenuously disagreed, arguing that since Jesus used wine at the last supper, Christians must likewise use wine:

> In offering the cup, the teaching of the Lord must be observed, and we should not do anything except what the Lord first did for us, so the cup which is offered in commemoration of him must contain wine. . . . It is not possible for

---

136. In *Against Heresies* 4.17, Irenaeus makes reference to 1 Kgs 15:22; Jer 7:21–23; Isa 43:23–24 and 46:2; Zech 7:9–10 and 8:16–17; Hos 6:6; Mt 12:7.

137. See ibid., 4.17.5. The verses from Malachi are cited above.

138. See Cyprian of Carthage, Letter 63, 15–16. A religious justification of the morning ritual given by Cyprian is that it took place at the time of the resurrection of Christ, which occurred on a Sunday morning. (Note that this letter is numbered 62 in some English translations of Cyprian's works.)

his blood, by which we are redeemed and enlivened, to be in the cup if there is no wine in the cup, for wine shows forth the blood of Christ, as predicted by sacred sign (*sacramento*) and testimony all through the scriptures.[139]

Unlike Paul, who argued that the ritual meal of the Corinthians was not the Lord's supper (regardless of the food they used) because they were not caring about one another, Cyprian's emphasis is on the proper food and on repeating exactly what Christ had done. After discussing various scripture texts that mention wine and water, Cyprian concludes,

> It is clear that the blood of Christ is not offered unless there is wine in the cup, and that the sacrifice of the Lord (*sacrificium domenicum*) is not celebrated with a proper holiness (*legitima sanctificatione*) unless the offering and our sacred sharing (*oblatio et sacrificium nostrum*) correspond to [the account of] the passion.[140]

Again, Cyprian's criteria are ritualistic and reveal a kind of magical thinking, according to which an effect does not occur unless the proper formula is followed.[141]

Later in the same letter, Cyprian borrows imagery from the Epistle to the Hebrews in speaking about Christ's self-offering and the offering of Christians that takes place in their ritual meal. Here the word *sacrificium* is better translated as offering than as sacrifice. At a sacrificial meal, the food offered (to a deity) symbolized the self-offering of the participants and, depending on the context, either the shared meal or the offered food could be called a *sacrificium*. The same ambiguity is found in the use of the Greek word, θυσία.

> For if Jesus Christ our Lord and God is himself the high priest of God the Father, and he first gave himself as an offering (*sacrificium*) to the Father, and then commanded this to be done in his memory, certainly the priest (*sacerdos*) who imitates what Christ did truly serves in the place of Christ, and he makes in the church a true and complete offering (*sacrificium*) to God the Father when he proceeds to offer what he sees Christ himself offered.[142]

---

139. Ibid., 2.

140. Ibid., 9.

141. Religion is not the only sphere in which magical thinking occurs. Legalistic arguments are similar to ritualistic ones when they contend that the letter of the law must be observed and that contracts can be voided if they do not contain the proper wording. This type of thinking led to Barak Obama's taking the oath of office a second time (in private) because Chief Justice Roberts misplaced an adverb when he administered the presidential oath during the public ceremony. See Susan Davis, "So Nice He Did It Twice: Obama Retakes Oath" in the Washington Wire blog of the *Wall Street Journal* on January 21, 2009 (http://blogs.wsj.com/washwire/2009/01/21/so-nice-he-did-it-twice-obama-re-takes-oath).

142. Ibid., 14. Notice that the person who was called the presider by Justin a hundred years earlier is here called a priest, probably because priests presided at temple sacrifices in the ancient world and the Christian ritual meal was increasingly being perceived as a sacrifice. We will discuss the evolution of ministerial nomenclature in our treatment of ordination.

By the close of the third century, then, Christians were perceiving the bread and wine at their ritual meal as the body and blood of Christ, and they were thinking about that meal as a θυσία in Greek and a *sacrificium* in Latin. Moreover, Christians in the Latin-speaking western half of the Roman Empire (if Cyprian of Carthage can be taken as representative) were beginning to identify the words spoken by Jesus at the last supper as essential to effecting the change from bread and wine into the body and blood of Christ. As we shall see, eucharistic theology in the Greek-speaking eastern half of the Empire did not take this same turn.

c. Other Sacraments During the Era of Persecution

(1) Confirmation

During this period, initiation into the Christian community moved from being a somewhat informal immersion in water, with a laying on of hands for imparting a holy spirit, to a more formalized ritual performed under the supervision of community leaders. The more extended ritual began to include an action symbolizing the imparting of the spirit, either the traditional laying of hands on the head or an anointing with oil on the head of the candidate, performed by the supervising elder and done either before or after the water rite. This was not a separate ritual, however, and so it could not be said to have a separate theology. Rather, the general understanding was that people who went through the entire ritual were fully members of the community by the time of its completion, and this was dramatized by the neophytes' first participation in a eucharistic meal.

(2) Penance

From what Paul wrote in his earliest preserved letters,[143] it is clear that the first devotees of the risen Lord fully expected him to return in glory relatively soon. As the followers of the Way coalesced into a distinct group, first as a sect of Judaism and later as a confederation of Jews and Gentiles, they would have continued the rabbinic practice of binding and loosing, described above,[144] to deal with individuals who violated the community's moral norms. But when the Second Coming did not happen as quickly as had been hoped, community leaders increasingly had another behavioral problem to deal with: the question of what to do with those who quit the community and later wanted to return to it. Quitting the community could happen when people (for whatever reasons) stopped participating in community life or when they did something offensive and then failed to comply with the expectations surrounding binding and loosing.

143. See 1 Thes 5:1–3 and 2 Thes 1:7 – 2:3.
144. See above, page 88.

By the second century, initiation into the Christian community was developing into a more formal process, as already mentioned. In the absence of information to the contrary, we can reasonably assume that those who left the community and wanted to return were faced with two options: either submit once again to the process of immersion in the way of life taught by Jesus, which concluded in a ceremony of immersion in water, or remain outside the community forever. For the process of binding and loosing was for members of the community who had misbehaved, not for people who had given up membership in the community.[145]

As alluded to earlier, the first known Christian writing to address this pastoral problem was *The Shepherd* of Hermas, who appears to have been a Christian living in Rome (though not a church leader) at the beginning of the second century. The problem may have been aggravated by the fact that by this time, disagreements within local communities sometimes led to splits or schisms, and as yet there was no process for reconciling differences between groups or for reintegrating those who repented and wanted to return to the larger community.[146] *The Shepherd* pictures the church as a tower that is in the process of being built, and it says that those who have left the tower ought to be readmitted after doing penance, so that they might once again help with building it. At the same time, however, this should be allowed only once, lest people get the notion that they can leave and return to the church as often as they like.[147]

Neither this work nor others from the second and third centuries that speak about the process that became known as public repentance or canonical penance cite any liturgical texts. This suggests that those who presided over the process knew what needed to be said and prayed appropriately when they welcomed people into the penitential process, when they encouraged them during their period of penitence, and when they readmitted them back into full communion with the church. However, early writers do mention confession of sins, repentance of heart, weeping, and works of penance.[148]

Only occasionally does the language of giving and receiving appear in works on this topic during this period. Speaking of "the second repentance" around the year 200, Clement of Alexandria notes that anyone who has received the forgiveness of sins (τὴν ἄφεσιν τῶν ἁμαρτιῶν) in baptism should sin no more, but the merciful God has

---

145. Since the focus of this study is on the language used in religious rituals and in theological reflection on those rituals, this is not the place to describe the evolution of the process of Christian initiation later referred to as the catechumenate. For that development, please see Paul Turner, *Hallelujah Highway: A History of the Catechumenate* (Chicago: Liturgy Training Publications, 2000).

146. See the letter of Clement of Rome to the Corinthians, par. 57, and the letter of Ignatius of Antioch to the Philadelphians, par. 3, quoted in Paul F. Palmer, *Sources of Christian Theology: Sacraments and Forgiveness* (Westminster, MD: Newman Press, 1959), 10–11. Both letters allude to schisms and were written around the year 100.

147. See selections from *The Shepherd* of Hermas (Vision 3.3; Commandment 4.1, 3; Similitude 9.26) quoted in ibid., 12–15.

148. See ibid., 16–20.

granted the chance for a second repentance (μετάνοιον δεύτερον) but only one time.[149] Thus, about a century after the idea was introduced by Hermas in Italy, Clement in Egypt is regarding the practice of public repentance to be of divine origin. However, Tertullian, writing in Latin around the same time, does not use the terminology of administering and receiving in his treatise on the practice of public repentance (*De paenitentia*), nor in his critique of lax penitential practices (*De pudicitia*). Even Origen, Clement's successor in the school of Alexandria, speaks of pardon or forgiveness being given by God in only two of his many works.[150]

The empire-wide persecution under Decius in 250–251 brought increased attention to the practice of public repentance. Many Christians either renounced their faith or paid for certificates saying that they had done so, and this led to questions about how they should be treated after the persecution had passed. Since there was no uniform church law at the time, different churches adopted different policies. Some church leaders argued that apostates could never be readmitted to the church; others argued that they would have to be rebaptized; still others (and this turned out to be the majority position) argued that the lapsed should go through the process of public repentance and then be readmitted to communion. In his collection of excerpts relating to the Decian persecution and its aftermath, Paul Palmer cites only a few texts that use the language of giving and receiving. The phrases in which the word "receive" is used refer to receiving a penitent's confession, receiving pardon from God, receiving communion or the right to receive communion, and granting and receiving peace (i.e., peace of mind or inner peace).[151] There are no texts that speak of administering or receiving a sacrament or that talk about forgiveness being given by the church or being received from anyone but God. The process of public repentance was long and arduous, whether undertaken for apostasy or other serious sin, and the understanding behind it at this point in time was that God forgives the sin when the sinner has demonstrated repentance.[152]

---

149. See Clement of Alexandria, *Miscellanies* (*Stromata*), 2.13. Interestingly, the first phrase was translated into Latin as *Eum . . . qui accepit remissionem peccatorum*, which could be understood as he who received the remission of sins. Likewise the second phrase was translated as *Dedit . . . secundum poenitententiam*, which could be understood as he (God) gives a second penance. The language of giving penance and receiving the remission of sins could have come, in cases such as these, from the Latin translations on which the scholastics depended even if such language was not to be found in the original texts, written in Greek.

150. See Palmer's translations of Origen's second homily on Leviticus (par. 4) and his treatise on prayer (ch. 28, par. 9) in *Sacraments and Forgiveness*, 35–36.

151. Speaking of penitential practices during the ante-Nicene period, Bernhard Poschmann in *Penance* notes on page 87, "The expressions *paenitentiam petere, dare, accipere* are everywhere established as technical terms," but *paenitentia* at this point in time refers only to an assigned penance such as fasting or wearing sackcloth.

152. See Palmer, *Sacraments and Forgiveness*, 40–59. Since there are so few references to giving and receiving, and since none of the references require special interpretation, I have not checked the translations against the original Greek and Latin texts. Older Catholic scholars often translated patristic texts using phrases that were congruent with modern scholastic sacramental theology, e.g.,

(3) Anointing

Despite the reference in the Epistle of James to elders anointing the sick, there is no evidence that this ever became a widespread clerical practice in the early church.[153] There is a prayer for the blessing of oil for strengthening and healing in *The Apostolic Tradition*, which may be from the third or fourth century, but there is no indication that this oil was used exclusively by the clergy.[154] Tertullian accuses heretical groups of allowing ordinary people (even women!) to perform exorcisms and cures, but he does not suggest that in the church some are ordained to do such things.[155] Given the state of medicine in the ancient world, it is likely that people attended the sick by themselves, sometimes using water, oil and herbal remedies, and sometimes calling in individuals who were reputed to have a gift for healing. In tribal cultures even today, shamans pray silently or out loud while applying healing remedies, so it is not unlikely that early Christians did the same.

(4) Ordination

The name "holy orders" derives from the Latin word *ordo*, which basically meant a series or row, but which by extension came to mean a rank or class. The Roman army had its *ordines militares* or military ranks, people in the government had various administrative orders, and Roman society was divided into different social classes. Early Christian communities were relatively classless and egalitarian, or at least they were supposed to be.[156] Even though the New Testament speaks of people in the early church with various duties or functions, we should not therefore think about them as having ministerial ranks or orders. For this reason as well, we should not think of the hand-laying mentioned in Acts and the pastorals as ordinations, that is, the conferral of ecclesiastical orders.[157] As we have already seen, πρεσβύτεροι were community elders, ἐπίσκοποι had some oversight of community affairs, and διάκονοι were community members entrusted with being of help in one way or another.

The Pauline epistles mention other ministries performed by those who had the talent or means. Those who could teach taught; those who were good organizers administered community affairs; those who had the gift of tongues or interpreting

---

"receiving baptism" when the original might have referred to being baptized. Here neither Palmer nor his sources use the language of giving and receiving in any way that seems to be influenced by scholastic thinking.

153. The scant information that is available is summarized in Martos, *Doors to the Sacred*, 380–382.

154. See *The Apostolic Tradition*, 5.1–2.

155. See Tertullian, *The Prescription of Heretics*, 41.

156. Paul's complaint in 1 Cor 11 that some were eating without waiting for others possibly indicates that the those who arrived early were members of a leisure class who could afford to buy food for the community meal, while those who came late were laborers who could only come after work.

157. See, e.g., Acts 6:6 and 13:3; 1 Tim 4:14 and 5:22.

what was spoken in tongues could inspire others; those who had the gift of prophesy could tell the community what God wanted them to hear.[158] Paul does not mention them, but presumably those who lived in houses large enough for community gatherings performed a ministry of hospitality. Some of these services (διακονίαι) were undoubtedly performed by women, who may even have presided at the Lord's supper since it was customary for heads of households to host gatherings in their homes.[159] That many of these ministries continued into the second century is attested to by the *Didache*, which mentions itinerant prophets, teachers and missionaries (ἀπόστολοι), and Justin Martyr, who speaks of the presider at the community meal of thanksgiving without indicating that it had to be a πρεσβύτερος or ἐπίσκοπος.[160]

In Antioch, however, Christian community organization was more structured. In one of his letters written around the same time as the *Didache*, Ignatius promotes the idea of the ἐπίσκοπος as someone who is the leader and spokesman for the local community. This person or his representative should preside over all baptisms and thanksgiving meals, and nothing pertaining to the community should be done without his permission.[161] This is the first indication that the role of the ἐπίσκοπος is evolving into an episcopal office, but Ignatius' letters provide no clues about how people got into that office.

The Apostolic Tradition has often been cited in Catholic literature as evidence of ordination in the early third century. Despite a reference in section 19 to the possible arrest and martyrdom of catechumens, which would place this work firmly in the age of persecution, its highly articulated system of ecclesiastical ranks and ceremonial ordinations makes it more likely that the present document dates from the post-Constantinian period even if parts of it were written earlier.[162] If this is indeed the case, then we would have to conclude that we have no direct evidence of ordinations during the first three centuries of Christianity, although the role described by Ignatius gives indirect evidence that the episcopacy was becoming an order, at least in some places.

158. See 1 Cor 12:4–11; Rom 12:4–8.

159. See Ron Saunders, *Outrageous Women, Outrageous God: Women in the First Two Generations of Christianity* (Alexandria NSW: E. J. Dwyer, 1996), 118–19. Also Karen Jo Torjesin, *When Women Were Priests: Women's Leadership in the Early Church and the Scandal of Their Subordination in the Rise of Christianity* (San Francisco: Harper Collins, 1993), 76–82.

160. See *Didache*, 10–13; Justin Martyr, *First Apology*, 67. Although the *Didache* in chapter 15 refers to πρεσβύτεροι and ἐπίσκοποι, their function seems very similar to what is found in the pastoral epistles written perhaps a few decades earlier or later, and they were apparently elected by the community (χειροτονήσατε ἑαυτοῖς means choose for yourselves).

161. Ignatius of Antioch, *Letter to the Smyrnaeans*, 8.

162. See Bradshaw, *Search for the Origins*, 81–83.

(5) Marriage

Like anointing the sick, marriage in the first three centuries was something that lay people did for themselves. Although Roman law regarded marriage as being contracted when a man and woman gave their consent to the relationship, most marriages between young people were still arranged by their parents, as they had been for centuries. The wedding was a festive occasion, as it is in every culture, and it was sacred only in the sense that it was an important occasion and a significant moment in the lives of the young people and their families. Among Christians, it was not a religious ceremony, and it was ordinarily presided over by the fathers of the bride and groom.[163]

The apostle Paul had recommended that Christians marry "in the Lord," that is, within the Christian community.[164] Ignatius of Antioch wanted Christians to seek their bishop's approval before marrying, but there is no contemporary evidence that his recommendation was heeded.[165] Written records suggest that families sometimes sought to have a new marriage blessed by a bishop or presbyter, but there is no evidence that their blessing was needed for the marriage to take place. Catholic scholars in the past interpreted a passage in one of Tertullian's writings as early evidence for a nuptial mass, but more recent scholarship points out that Tertullian was only arguing that Christians ought to marry other Christians so that both spouses could be blessed by participation in the eucharistic sacrifice.[166]

d. Summary and Conclusion

Despite its lack of standing as a recognized religion in the Roman Empire, Christianity in the ante-Nicene period underwent some noticeable developments in ritual practice. Baptism became more formalized into a period of preparation and a ceremony of transition into the Christian community, and it began to be spoken of in the Latin west as something that can be given and received. Confirmation as a separate rite had not yet appeared. The Lord's supper became simplified as a symbolic meal of bread and wine, but it was still described in Greek as a θυσία or sacred banquet, and in Latin as a *sacrificium* or a sacred sharing or offering; and although the bread and wine were referred to as the body and blood of Christ, there was no attempt to explain how or when they ceased being ordinary food. The disciplinary practice of binding

163. Edward Schillebeeckx makes the point that among pagans in ancient Europe, the wedding had had a religious dimension because by changing households, the bride was leaving the protection of her family's gods and entering the service of the household gods of her new husband. By the time of the Roman Empire, however, weddings were becoming increasingly secular in meaning and practice. See *Marriage: Human Reality and Saving Mystery* (New York: Sheed and Ward, 1965) 234–244.

164. See 1 Cor 7, esp. v. 39; also 1 Cor 11:11 and Col 3:18.

165. See his *Letter to Polycarp*, 5; also Schillebeeckx, *Marriage*, 244–250.

166. See Schillebeeckx, *Marriage*, 252–255; also, Theodore Mackin, *The Marital Sacrament* (Mahwah, NJ: Paulist Press, 1989) 126–129.

and loosing evolved into a penitential discipline for public sins, and although it was becoming ritualized it allowed for significant variation from one pastoral situation to another. Marriage and care for the sick were secular matters that did not call for intervention of the clergy except perhaps when a blessing was desired. Christian ministry was evolving from part-time service into a full-time role in the community, and although ministers were undoubtedly commissioned and blessed in some way, there is from that time no written record of an ordination ceremony as such.

3. Sacraments in the Christian Roman Empire

Constantine's Edict of Toleration in 313 AD marked a turning point in the history of Christianity. The new religion went from being suspect to being permitted, and within a few years it was being supported by the emperor who declared Sunday to be a legal holiday and allowed Christians to use public buildings (βασίλιχαι, or basilicas) for their weekly worship. More people joined the church, now that it was officially favored by the government, and what had started out as a ritual meal shared in homes became a public service, a λειτουργία (literally a people work), a liturgy. The ceremony expanded to fill the space and time available, and its style began to resemble the ceremonies that until then had filled pagan temples and shrines—rituals replete with candles and processions, sacred vestments and sacred vessels, incense and chanting. Ultimately the Christian liturgy developed an ornate style that can still be appreciated in the eucharistic liturgies of the Greek and other Orthodox churches.

From the fourth century onward, we have many more documents related to Christian worship, both liturgical texts and episcopal writings related to worship. The great bulk of these continue to be about the baptism ritual and the eucharistic liturgy, but we now also see more texts about public repentance and ordination. During this period, the episcopal confirmation of baptism became a separate rite in the west, whereas in the east the bishop's blessing was symbolized by an anointing with oil that he had blessed. Anointing the sick, when practiced, remained something performed by the laity for family and acquaintances. Marriage remained a family affair, with the wedding presided over by the fathers of the bride and groom.

Again here, our intention is not to present a thorough history of these ceremonies, but only to look at the language of liturgical texts and theological writings for indications of how the terminology surrounding them was evolving. For most of the sacraments, we will be looking for how they came to be spoken of as given and received. For the eucharist, we will be looking at the evolution of the concept of sacrifice as well as the notion that the bread and wine are the body and blood of Christ.

a. Baptism: From Metaphorical Description to Metaphysical Explanation

As mentioned in the previous chapter, when Donatus became bishop of Carthage after the Diocletian persecution, he adopted a policy toward apostates that was virtually identical to that of his predecessor Cyprian, insisting that they be rebaptized and, if they were clerics, reordained. This policy differed from that of the rest of the western church, which was to reconcile apostates after they had sufficiently demonstrated that they were repentant for having denied Christ. His episcopate lasted for four decades, during which time he ordained priests and helped ordain bishops in north Africa who shared his theology. The result was that during the fourth century, many cities there had two bishops, one who agreed with Donatus and one who sided with the rest of the Catholic Church. Thus, when Augustine was elected bishop of Hippo toward the end of the fourth century, the schism caused by rival theologies of baptism and ordination was still a major issue.

Prior to Augustine's arrival on the scene, both theologies were plausible and neither side could prove the other wrong. Indeed, the Donatist theory of sacramental effectiveness had much to recommend it, for the notion that the minister was the effective agent was based on the obvious principle, *Nemo dat quod non habet,* No one gives what one does not have. As already suggested, this way of posing the problem—giving and receiving baptism and ordination—eventually suggested an elegant solution to Augustine, but before looking at Augustine's theology we need to examine how his mentor, Ambrose of Milan, spoke about sacraments in general and about baptism in particular.

Two works devoted to sacraments in general are attributed to Ambrose, *The Mysteries* (*De mysteriis*), an authentic work written around 387, and *The Sacraments* (*De sacramentis*), possibly a pseudepigraphical work dating from the fifth or sixth century. The earlier work dates from the years when Augustine was in Milan, and parts of it may even have been read by him. If the latter work is not authentic, it nonetheless shows that Ambrose's way of talking about sacraments was entering into the western theological vocabulary on the continent during the decades following his death.

The Mysteries is a one-volume work in which Ambrose often uses the words *mysterium* and *sacramentum* in two different senses, with *mysteria* referring to hidden mysteries and *sacramenta* referring to signs or symbols of mysteries. Thus the earlier dual usage of *sacramentum*, paralleling the dual usage of μυστήριον, is here being replaced by the use of *mysterium* to refer to inner or spiritual realities and *sacramentum* to refer to outer realities or visible signs. Nonetheless, there are places in other works of Ambrose where he appears to use *sacramentum* in reference to a mystery.[167]

Ambrose begins this work of mystagogy, delivered to neophytes shortly after their baptism, by noting that he is going to speak of the mysteries (*de mysteriis dicere*)

---

167. For example, in *The Mystery of the Lord's Incarnation* (*De incarnationis dominicae sacramento*), the word *sacramentum* almost always means mystery.

and explain the meaning of the sacraments (*sacramentorum rationem edere*). The sacraments that he has in mind, however, are the various components of the Easter Vigil and baptismal ceremony that his listeners have recently experienced, so usage of the word has not yet been restricted to just a few church ceremonies. For example, one of the sacraments in Ambrose's instruction is the saying of the words, *"Epheta, quod est adaperire,"* a quotation from Mark 7:34, which refers to the mysterious opening of ears and minds.[168] According to Ambrose, baptism is a sacrament, but it is not just the water, for according to 1 John 5:6–9, spirit and blood are also needed for salvation, so "if you take away one of these, there is no sacrament of baptism."[169] Ambrose does speak of receiving sacraments in this work, but primarily in reference to the eucharistic elements.[170]

In his writings about the Old Testament, Ambrose often uses *sacramentum* in the sense of a sign of something hidden, a symbol of something sacred, or an image of something to come in the Christian dispensation. Occasionally the word refers to a Christian ritual such as baptism. Thus, God's word is a sacrament[171] and the marriage of Adam and Eve was a sacrament.[172] Old Testament persons and events are often viewed as sacramental prefigurements of New Testament revelations, especially baptism. Taking a cue from the Pauline letters, Ambrose says that the Israelites were baptized in a cloud and in the sea when they were fleeing from Egypt,[173] and that David foresaw the sacrament of baptism.[174] More often, however, Ambrose uses the Old Testament to teach New Testament lessons, for example, that baptism is necessary for salvation.[175] The sacrament of baptism is mentioned often enough,[176] but in at least some places Ambrose speaks of the sacraments (plural) of baptism.[177]

This same pattern appears in his commentaries on the psalms. At times, Ambrose distinguishes clearly between sacrament and mystery.[178] At other times, he

168. See Ambrose, *The Mysteries*, 1.2–3.

169. Ibid., 4.20: *si in unum horum detrahas, non stat baptismatis sacramentum.*

170. See ibid., 8.47 and 9.52.

171. See *Cain and Abel*, 1.10.43: *Deus autem et cum loquitur fidelis est, cuius sermo sacramentum est.*

172. See *Paradise*, 4.25; also Eph 5:32.

173. See *The Six Days of Creation*, 1.4.14; also 1 Cor 10:1–2.

174. See *An Explanation of the Prophet David to the Emperor Theodosius*, 12.58: *praevidit baptismatis sacramentum.*

175. See *Abraham*, 2.11.79: *nemo ascendit in regnum caelorum nisi per sacramentum baptismatis.* Also *The Six Days of Creation*, 6.6.38: *Qui crediderit et baptizatus fuerit hic salvus erit.*

176. See *A Dialogue between Job and David*, 4.10.36; *An Explanation of the Prophet David to the Emperor Theodosius*, 8.44; *Paradise*, 9.45; *Abraham*, 1.9.87.

177. See *Cain and Abel*, 2.6.19: *qui per baptismatis sacramenta renovantur.*

178. See, for example, his *Commentary on Twelve Psalms*, Psalm 38, 25.2: *sacrosancti huius mysterii sacramentum*; also ibid., Psalm 39, 6.2. In his lengthy *Commentary on Psalm 118*, Ambrose twice makes this distinction, first between inner mysteries (*interiora mysteria*) and sacraments in 1.16, then between mystery and sacraments (*si mysterium nescias, si sacramenta non noveris*) in 13.6.

uses *sacramentum* where one would expect to see *mysterium*.[179] Even before Jerome's Vulgate, Latin translations of the Bible used *sacramentum* for μυστήριον in Ephesians 5:32, and so he views the relation between husband and wife as a sacrament of the relation between Christ and the church, but he also calls the Christ-church relation a sacrament.[180] As already mentioned, Ambrose sometimes refers to sacraments in the plural when speaking about baptism.[181] What he has in mind are the various symbolic elements within the ceremony.

When Ambrose speaks about receiving sacraments, he is most commonly referring to the eucharistic elements. In a few places, he talks about baptism as being received,[182] but he never talks about it as being administered or given. In this respect, then, his manner of speaking differs markedly from that of north Africans who wrote about baptism in the aftermath of defections from the faith. However, by the time *De Sacramentis* was written, this language was apparently becoming more common.[183]

Ambrose's theology of baptism repeats what was said earlier, both in the scriptures and in the writings of his episcopal predecessors, but not in any way that suggests that he is talking about things that he or the baptized have experienced. Rather, his language suggests that he is talking about spiritual facts and metaphysical realities that need to be believed because they cannot be experienced. Ambrose frequently refers to Romans 6:3–4, where Paul says that those who are baptized are baptized into Christ's death and buried with him so that they may rise with him.[184] But Ambrose gives no indication that these scriptural images are metaphors for what the baptized have experienced; instead, he seems to take them as descriptions of metaphysical events that happen in parallel with the performance of the baptismal ritual. Thus when he invokes Mark 16:16 to the effect that anyone who believes and is baptized will be saved, but anyone who does not believe will be damned, he appears to be thinking somewhat

179. For example, Ambrose often refers to the *sacramentum incarnationis* in his *Commentary on Psalm 118* (3.8 and 24; 5.24; 11.21) and in his exposition of *The Faith* (2.5; 3.2–3) whereas later usage would more commonly refer to the mystery of the incarnation.

180. See *Commentary on Twelve Psalms*, Psalm 36, 7.3 (*Christi et ecclesiae nuptialis copulae sacramentis*); ibid., Psalm 37, 2.2 (*Christi autem et ecclesiae sacramentum non carnale, sed spirituale esse quis dubitet*).

181. See *Commentary on Psalm 118*, 18.25–26.; also *The Death of Valentinian*, 51 and 75.

182. See *Commentary on Psalm 118*, 16.19; also *The Holy Spirit*, 1.3.41. The reference in both places is to receiving the baptism of John the Baptist.

183. See *The Sacraments*, 1.1.1 (*De sacramentis, quae accepistis, sermonem adorior . . . . Ergo accepistis baptismum, credidistis.*); 2.4.13 (*acceperit caeleste sacramentum*); 2.7.23 (*accipis sacramentum*).

184. See *Jacob and the Blessed Life*, 1.5.17 (*Denique in morte ipsius baptizati sumus*; ibid., 2.7.34 (*quia omnes qui baptizantur in Christo consepeliuntur cum eo*); *Commentary on Psalm 37*, 10.1 (*descendit enim in mortem Christi qui baptizatur in Christo et in resurrectionem eius ascendit*); *Commentary on Psalm 61*, 3.2 (*homo renuntians mundo et consepultus Christo per baptismatis sacramentum*); *Repentance*, 2.2 (*quicumque baptizati sumus in Christo Iesu, in morte ipsius baptizati sumus*).

mechanically, as though confessing faith in Christ and going through the rite of baptism automatically results in salvation, with the opposite also being true.[185]

As mentioned, *The Mysteries* is a mystagogical instruction given to those who have recently undergone ritual initiation into the church. One of the unspoken assumptions of such catechesis is that initiates have participated in sacred rites which they do not understand, and which therefore must be explained to them. In other words, they have to be told that they have died to sin because they have had no experience of dying to sin, they have to be told that they have risen with Christ because they have had no experience of being born again, and they have to be told that they have been saved because they have had no experience of salvation. Mystagogy is the pedagogical interpretation of a ritual, not the unpacking of a spiritual experience. During the first decades, when converts were baptized and started speaking in tongues, they did not have to be told that they had received a holy spirit because they experienced receiving that spirit. And during the first centuries, when converts were initiated only after they demonstrated that they had died to sin and had put on Christ Jesus, they were not told that the water ritual did this because in fact it had been accomplished before their liturgical admission into the body of Christ. By the late fourth century in the Christianized Roman Empire, however, moral conversion prior to baptism had disappeared and had been replaced with the expectation of moral and doctrinal conversion after baptism. Hence the need for mystagogical catechesis.[186]

Other samples from Ambrose's writings strongly suggest that he is engaging in mechanical thinking, encouraging his listeners or readers to think as he does. On the basis of his reading of the scriptures, he firmly believes that certain ritual actions produce certain metaphysical results. His audience, however, is innocent of Christian theology, having recently consented to join the church by undergoing baptism and participating in the eucharistic liturgy. None of these rites were explained in advance because, ever since the era of persecution, the uninitiated were not allowed to attend Christian religious ceremonies, much less be taught about them.[187] Therefore his listeners were presumably baptized without much explanation of what would happen to them, they received an anointing and a laying on of hands without hearing any more than the words of the rite, and they received communion at the first eucharistic liturgy they had ever attended.[188] Now, after it was all over, their bishop was telling them what

---

185. See *The Holy Spirit*, 2.13.151 (*Et qui crediderit et qui baptizatus fuerit, hic salvus erit; qui vero non crediderit, damnabitur.*)

186. Ambrose states clearly at the beginning of his mystagogy that the candidates had been given the examples of the patriarchs and the teachings of the proverbs so that "renewed through baptism you might hold to a way of life that becomes the baptized." *The Mysteries*, 1.1. In other words, they were not expected to fully live the Christian way of life prior to their baptism. Also note that the morality in question is not that of the Sermon on the Mount but that of the Torah and the book of Proverbs.

187. In Ambrose's words, "If we had considered giving such instruction to the uninitiated before baptism, we would be regarded as traitors rather than as teachers." *The Mysteries*, 1.2.

188. Again, Ambrose has a reason for this approach: "The light of the mysteries penetrates more

it all meant, persuading them that his understanding of the ceremonies ought to be their understanding of the ceremonies, based on the testimony of sacred scripture.

Ambrose addresses them with a series of rhetorical questions:

> What did you see? Water, to be sure, but not just water. You saw levites ministering, and you saw the high priest questioning and consecrating. First of all, the Apostle tells you not to look at "the things that are seen but at the things that are not seen; for the things that are seen are transient, but the things that are not seen are eternal." For you read elsewhere, "Since the creation of the world, the invisible things of God are comprehended through things that are made; also, his eternal power and divinity can be determined from his works." For which reason the Lord himself says, "If you do not believe me, believe my works." Believe therefore that divinity is there. Do you believe in the action but not in the presence? How can the action follow unless the presence is already there?[189]

According to these proof texts as understood by Ambrose, mystagogical catechesis is a matter of being taught what is invisibly going on behind the visible rites. It is a matter of discerning the metaphysical beyond the physical with the help of someone in authority to reveal it to others.[190]

In Ambrose's mind, then, what is the result of the ceremony known as baptism? The physical washing produces a spiritual washing,[191] sin and shame are removed,[192] and grace is given,[193] although the nature and function of this grace are not explained. The bishop of Milan's mystagogical theology also proposes that there is one other result: the seal of the spirit, given as a pledge in the hearts of the baptized.[194] This notion,

---

deeply when it is unexpected than when it has been explained beforehand." Ibid.

189. Ambrose, *The Mysteries*, 3.8. The references are to 2 Cor 4:18, Rom 1:20, and Jn 10:38.

190. Not all patristic authors were guilty of such mechanical thinking. For example, both Cyril of Jerusalem (*Catechetical Lectures*, Prologue, 2–4) and Gregory of Nyssa (*Great Catechism*, 40) argued that baptism does not automatically bestow grace or wash away sin. See Aaron Milavec, *To Empower as Jesus Did: Acquiring Spiritual Power Through Apprenticeship* (New York: Edwin Mellen Press, 1982) 164–166.

191. See *Commentary on Psalm 118*, 16.9 (*spiritali abluta baptismate*). Also, *Commentary on Luke's Gospel*, 8.549 (*altera exterioris est hominis, qui corrumpitur, altera interioris, qui per sacramenta renovator*).

192. See *Commentary on Psalm 118*, Letter 5, 43 (*dilutum est omne peccatum et cum peccato obprobrium*); also *Repentance*, 1.8 (*Cur baptizatis si per hominem peccata dimitti non licet? In baptismo utique remissio peccatorum omnium est.*) Note that here, remission of sins no longer seems to mean getting rid of sinful habits by immersion in the Christian life but getting rid of sins themselves by going through the ritual of baptism. Also, *Commentary on Luke's Gospel*, 7.2632 (*omnem autem enormitatem sceleris baptismi sacramenta dimittunt*), where the baptismal rites (*sacramenta*) seem to be the operative factor.

193. See *Elijah and Fasting*, 10.36 (*ut tibi sua patefaceret sacramenta, daret gratiam spiritalem*); ibid., 22.84 (*Christus baptizat in spiritu, Christus gratiam dispensat*); *The Holy Spirit*, 1.14.148 (*Neque vero potest esse gratia sacramentorum*); ibid., 3.4.28 (*unum est baptisma et una est gratia sacramenti*).

194. See *The Mysteries*, 7.42 (*Unde repete quia accepisti signaculum spiritale, . . . et serva quod*

along with awareness that a soldier's tattoo is called a *sacramentum*, will eventually reappear in the writings of Augustine.

Augustine was baptized by Ambrose in Milan during the Easter Vigil of 387. About a year later he returned to his home in north Africa, where he founded a quasi-monastic community of men devoted to spirituality and study. His exposure to Ambrose's theology was therefore rather brief, but it arguably provided him with a theological foundation for his later thinking since he had had no formal instruction in the Christian faith prior to that time. Because Augustine could not read Greek, he was dependent on translations of the Bible, either the Old Latin version or the new translation begun by Jerome in the 380s. And being a north African, the writings of Cyprian of Carthage were readily available to him. He was ordained a priest in 391 and a bishop in 395. Almost all of his works that deal with *sacramenta* were written during the two decades from 400 to 420. He lived during the decline of the Roman Empire, which was accelerated by the sack of Rome by the Visigoths in 410, and he died in 430 during the siege of Hippo by the Vandals.

As already noted, the Christians in north Africa had been divided for some decades over the question of readmission to the church. Those who followed the strict discipline of Donatus held that apostates and heretics had to be rebaptized (and, if they were priests, reordained) when they renounced their erroneous beliefs and wanted to rejoin the church. The practice in the rest of western Christianity was to readmit such sinners to communion after they had demonstrated sufficient remorse and had performed public penance. This was hardly a lenient practice, considering the length and severity of the penitential discipline. However, it was erroneous from the Donatist perspective, according to which grace could be received only in baptism and only from someone who had the Holy Spirit. This was similar to the position of Cyprian, who had been regarded as an orthodox defender of the faith. But when Augustine returned to north Africa after living in Italy, he found not one church but two churches in Hippo and every other city: a Donatist church and a Catholic church. It is not surprising, therefore, that he expended quite a bit of energy on the theological reasoning behind this schism.

If Ambrose's works show that Catholic thinking in Italy about baptism was becoming somewhat mechanical and ritualistic, the same must be said of Donatist thinking. The determining factor for having the Holy Spirit was having been baptized by someone who was able to give the Holy Spirit because he had the Holy Spirit. If one received the Holy Spirit rather automatically, one also lost the Spirit rather automatically, that is, by renouncing one's faith or by adopting heretical beliefs. Extenuating circumstances such as being threatened or tortured or deceived were not taken into account. Interior factors such as personal intention or mental reservation were not taken into account. Neither the strength of one's faith in Christ nor the quality of

accepisti. Signavit te Deus Pater, confirmavit te Christus Dominus; et dedit pignus Spiritus in cordibus tuis.) The reference is to 2 Cor 5:5.

one's moral behavior were taken into account. Nothing demonstrated possessing the spirit of Christ except having been properly baptized and not having done anything worthy of excommunication. By the end of the fourth century, therefore, questions about baptism and other church rituals were being posed in terms that were rather mechanistic, and the language of giving and receiving sacraments both framed the problem and suggested an eventual solution.

Augustine wrote his only major work on baptism (*De Baptismo contra Donatistas libri septem*) around the year 400, and as the full title indicates, its purpose was to counter the teachings of the Donatists. As anyone familiar with the history of Christian doctrine knows, Augustine justified the Catholic practice of not rebaptizing by developing an ingenious theory about the effects of baptism. At the time, it was assumed by most that baptism had a fundamental effect, namely, reception of the Holy Spirit. This effect had multiple implications, however. One was the remission of sins, for a sinful soul could not possess the Holy Spirit. Another was membership in the church, for the church was the body of Christ, i.e., the community animated by the spirit of Christ. This in turn implied that one could receive communion and that one was eligible for ministry in the church. It took a genius such as Augustine to cut through the dilemma posed by thinking that having the Spirit was a prerequisite for giving the Spirit.

We do not know the precise thought process that led to Augustine's insight, but we can say in general that it resulted from a reflection on the practice of not rebaptizing apostates, heretics and schismatics. If the Holy Spirit dwelled in the body of Christ, Augustine might have reasoned, then the Spirit would certainly protect the church from serious error. But if it were not erroneous to reconcile public sinners, then it must be the case that they had not completely lost membership in the church even though they were excommunicated. There must be some tie that binds them to the church and makes them subject to the church's authority, which could impose a penitential discipline on them and eventually invite them back to the communion table. What was that spiritual connection? Searching through the scriptures, Augustine concluded that it must be a spiritual seal, a mark or character, an image of Christ imposed on the soul of each of the baptized and identifying that soul as belonging to Christ.[195] Thus those who committed serious sins such as murder or adultery lost the Holy Spirit, but remained in the church during the time that they endured the discipline of canonical penance. Likewise, then, those who committed the sin of leaving the church were in fact still members of the church, although not members in good standing. Something therefore happened at baptism which marked them forever as Christ's. Augustine sometimes used the word *character*, a transliteration of the Greek χαρακτήρ, which could mean a mark or a stamp, but also a likeness or representation, to name what was received whenever a person was baptized.[196]

195. See 2 Cor 1:22; also 5:5.

196. For a fuller account, see Martos, *Doors to the Sacred*, 34–45; also 180. Augustine used the

This is not the place to review in detail the development of Augustine's thinking or his complete theology of baptism. Our interest is in the language that was used to pose and resolve the Donatist dilemma, that is to say, the terminology of giving and receiving baptism that had been introduced by Tertullian and amplified by Cyprian, and in the terminological distinction between sacrament and mystery that, if not invented by Ambrose, found its most authoritative proponent in him. For if baptism could be spoken of as given and received, and if baptism could be called a sacrament, then sacraments in general could be spoken of as given and received. This is what we shall look for in Augustine, for this is what was later found by the medieval schoolmen and developed into the concept of the sacramental reality, the *sacramentum et res*.

Although Augustine's broad definition of sacrament was widely cited in the Middle Ages, [197] he nowhere treats sacraments in any systematic fashion. Nor does he speak of sacraments in the plural except when comparing sacraments of the old dispensation and sacraments of the new, and when making general comments about Christian symbols and rituals. In his works there are scattered references to marriage and ordination as sacraments (which will be treated later), but he most frequently refers to baptism as a sacrament. Unlike Ambrose, however, he does not talk about the sacraments (i.e., the various symbolic objects and gestures) of baptism.

Right from the outset of his treatise on baptism, Augustine refers to the *sacramentum baptismi* no less than five times.[198] In the very first chapter, baptism is said to be given (e.g., *dari, datur, datum est*) nine times; it is said to be received (e.g., *acceptatur*) five times; and it is said to be had (e.g., *haberi, habet*) nine times. Moreover, Augustine says that baptism cannot be lost (e.g., *non amittit*) seven times, and that it remains (*permanet*) two times. Since this is a work written to combat Donatist ideas, Augustine also speaks here about ordination, which he refers to here as the *sacramentum dandi baptismi*, for the *ordinati* are those who give the sacrament. Put succinctly, "The sacrament of baptism is that which is had by one who is baptized, and the sacrament of giving baptism is that which is had by one who is ordained."[199] Thus it is clear that by the year 400, when this work was written, Augustine is thinking of baptism as something that is given, received, and had, and it is something that cannot be lost.

Unlike his north African predecessor, Augustine does not argue that heretics and schismatics do not have baptism because they are outside the church. Rather, he argues from the fact that, since they are not rebaptized when they rejoin the church, they do indeed have the sacrament of baptism, and they can give it to others. Only members

word only in minor works, but the schoolmen equated it with the seal mentioned by Augustine and other patristic writers, and made it a central concept in the theology of baptism.

197. In Letter 138, 7, Augustine says that signs pertaining to divine or sacred things are called sacraments (*Nimis autem longum est, convenienter disputare de varietate signorum, quae cum ad res divinas pertinent, sacramenta appellantur.*), whether they be found in the Old or New Testaments.

198. See Augustine, *Baptism*, 1.1. The second paragraph of the passage contains much of what was suggested above about Augustine's thought process on this topic.

199. Ibid.

of the Catholic church can rightly (*recte*) give baptism; those outside the church can give baptism, but not rightly (or as canonists would later term it, illicitly).[200] Arguing for the permanence of baptism, Augustine likens it to a military tattoo (*similitudinem notae militaris*) which is permanent and is not reapplied when a deserter returns to the army. He regards baptizing outside the church as a sin, but still, what is received is "Christ's baptism."[201] What heretics and schismatics cannot give, however, is membership in the church of Christ, that is, unity with the true church.[202]

In the remainder of this work, Augustine continues to speak of baptism as something that is able to be given, received and had. In Book IV he argues that baptism is not able to be corrupted or polluted, for it is always the church's baptism, and the church itself is uncorrupt and pure.[203] In Book 7 he argues that there is only one baptism, whether given rightly or wrongly, yet his reasoning is not based on Ephesians 4:5 but on his own theology of the sacrament.[204]

Augustine speaks of baptism in similar way in other works such as *Against Cresconius, a Donatist Teacher*, written around 405, *A Summary of the Three-Day Conference with the Donatists*, whose year of composition is unknown, and *To the Donatists after the Conference*, also undated. It is clear that, just as the language of giving and receiving baptism was introduced by Cyprian in the context of the Donatist controversy, it later appears in Augustine primarily in the same context.

Although found only once in the above works, the word most often associated with Augustine's teaching on the permanence of baptism is character, spelled either *character* or *caracter* in Latin. This transliteration from the Greek χαρακτήρ is found rather infrequently in the post-Nicene fathers, where the word is sometimes used in anti-Arian writings to describe the likeness of the Son to the Father.[205] It is also used to speak about letters in non-Latin alphabets (e.g., Hebrew and Greek), personality or morality (e.g., a person's character), and also as a synonym for nature or type (e.g., the character of an argument or doctrine). Augustine is the only person to use the word as a name for what is received in baptism, putting emphasis on its permanence, but he developed this idea in other places than in his anti-Donatist writings. Thus heretics retain baptism in the same way that a deserter from the army retains his military stamp or tattoo,[206] baptism is compared to the imperial stamp on a soldier,[207] the stamp of a

200. Ibid., 1.2–3.

201. Ibid., 1.4.

202. Ibid., 1.5.

203. Ibid., 4.2.

204. Ibid., 7.14.

205. See, e.g., Ambrose, *The Faith*, 1.7 (*Alibi quoque apostolus adservit, quod ipsum posuit heredem omnium, per quem et fecit saecula, qui est splendor gloriae et character substantiae eius.*)

206. See Augustine, *Sermon to Catechumens on the Creed*, 8 ([*Heretici*] *habent baptismum, quomodo desertor habet caracterem: ita et isti habent baptismum; habent, sed unde damnentur, non unde coronentur.*).

207. See Augustine, *Treatises on the Gospel of John*, 6.15 (*Puta te esse militarem: si characterem*

king on a soldier,[208] a sure sign of a deserter,[209] and one that cannot be obliterated.[210] Augustine also likens it to a brand that is stamped on sheep,[211] marking Christians as members of the Lord's flock,[212] so if they stray from the fold, they still have their master's brand on them.[213]

Augustine developed this aspect of his theology of baptism by reflecting on the practice of the church and looking at it through the lens of certain scripture passages as he interpreted them. In other words, Augustine offered a theory to explain the practice of not rebaptizing those who have left the church, drawing on scriptural interpretations that made sense at the time (even though today they would not stand up to critical examination), and arguing in images and similes for what he believed to be a metaphysical entity, namely, a baptismal reality that is received when a person is properly baptized.

Thus Augustine continued the Christian intellectual tradition of the early fathers of the church, who explained what baptism is about by reflecting on their liturgical practices in light of the scriptures. During the patristic period generally, the *explicandum* (as the scholastics would later term it) was current church practice, whether local (during the pre-Constantinian era) or universal (in the Christianized Roman Empire), and the *explicatio* was developed by bringing what appear to be relevant biblical passages to bear on that practice. In other words, that which is to be explained was something that is given in experience, which is always a matter of ecclesial and ritual practice and sometimes a matter of personal and spiritual experience on the part of the writer. The explanation, then, took the form of ideas and images drawn from the scriptures and connected by the writer to experiential data that are to be explained. The explanation, in other words, was the meaning given to the experienced ritual, that is, a liturgical ritual that was part of Christians' social experience at the time.

This theological method, as it might be termed, can also be found in the development of the explanation termed original sin. Whereas Augustine developed the theory of the baptismal character in the context of the Donatist controversy, he developed the theory of original sin in the context of his debate with the Pelagians of his day.

---

imperatoris tui intus habeas, securus militas; si extra habeas, non solum tibi ad militiam non prodest character ille, sed etiam pro desertore punieris.); also Letter 185, 10.

208. See *Treatises on the Gospel of John*, 6.16 (*character est regis mei, non ero sacrilegus; corrigo desertorem, non immuto characterem.*); also Letter 185, 6.

209. See Augustine, *Commentaries on the Psalms*, Psalm 39, 1 (*Baptismus ille tamquam character infixus est, ornabat militem, convincit desertorem.*).

210. See Augustine, *Against the Letters of Petilianus*, 2.108, (*destruimus enim perfidiam desertoris, non destruimus characterem imperatoris.*).

211. See Augustine, *Sermons*, Sermon 229 O, 3 (*Nescitis cuius oves estis? Caracterem legite, in quo signati estis.*)

212. See ibid, Sermon 295, 5 (*Pasce oves meas: numquid dixit, tuas? Pasce, bone serve, oves dominicas, habentes dominicum characterem.*); also Letter 98, 5.

213. See Letter 173, 3 (*Et vos oves christi estis, characterem dominicum portatis in sacramento, quod accepistis, sed errastis et peristis.*); also Letter 105, 1.

Pelagius was an educated layman and ascetic teacher who was living in Rome around the same time that Augustine was living in Milan. Later branded as a heretic for doing so, Pelagius held that human beings are born in a natural state of grace and that God holds them accountable only for their personal sins. To Augustine, this seemed contrary to the Pauline teaching that sin and death entered the world through Adam, that all human beings died as a result of his sin, and that Christ is the only way to life.[214]

Augustine's attack on Pelagius might be theologically justifiable if one takes the Bible literally and assumes the existence of a first human pair some thousands of years ago, but not if one takes the Pauline images as attempts to articulate the spiritual experience of conversion. Today we must admit that, hidden within Augustine's theological method was a biblical fundamentalism that is inadmissible in contemporary scripture scholarship and biblical exegesis. Nor was fundamentalism limited to the patristic period, for it was the accepted mode of biblical interpretation until the twentieth century. We can also see it at work in the scholastic theology of the Middle Ages and the dogmatic theology of both the Protestant Reformation and the Catholic Counter-Reformation. Critical thinkers in the twenty-first century, however, need to question any theological edifice that was built on a literal and unscientific reading of the scriptures.

In the fourth century, the average age of those being baptized was declining. From the beginning, not only individuals but also households could be ritually initiated into the community,[215] but as generations passed, the age at which the children of Christian parents should be baptized remained an open question. The relation between baptism and salvation, however, was becoming understood more ritualistically and mechanically. If "Baptism is necessary for salvation" had originally meant something like "Immersion in Jesus' way of life is needed to be rescued from sinful habits," by the fourth century (as we see from the writings of Ambrose) it had come to mean something like "Going through this ritual is required to live a holy life and go to heaven." During the third century, catechumens had worried that they might be martyred before being baptized, thus losing their chance to enter heaven, but they had been reassured that if they died for Christ they would be baptized in their own blood.[216] Now in the fourth century, parents worried that their children might die before being baptized and lose the chance for eternal blessedness, so youngsters were being urged to be baptized as soon as they felt ready. At the same time, since baptism was said to remit sins, it was sometimes suggested that boys wait until they were no longer prone to the sins of youth before asking for baptism. Again here, then, we find evidence that baptism is being thought of as an automatically effective ritual than as a process of conversion.

214. Augustine makes this argument in *Merit and the Forgiveness of Sins, and the Baptism of Children*, 1.8, citing Rom 5:12 and 1 Cor 15:21–22.

215. See Acts 16:33–34 and 18:8.

216. See above, page 104. Also *The Apostolic Tradition*, 19.

With ideas such as these in the air, it is no wonder that by the fifth century, parents were bringing younger and younger children for baptism, which was still done only once a year at Easter (or, in some places, at Pentecost). It may even be the case that childhood baptism was being encouraged by some bishops and priests.[217] In the long run, however, this change in baptismal practice raised a new theological issue, for if baptism was for the remission of sins, why were children being baptized before they were old enough to sin?

Augustine might not have been drawn into a discussion of this pastoral practice if Pelagius and his followers had not been arguing that God's grace is available even to the unbaptized. Augustine saw clearly that this teaching ran contrary to the tradition (as he understood it) that baptism is necessary for salvation, the implication being that Catholic teaching and practice were mistaken if Pelagius was correct. Making the assumption as he had before, that the Holy Spirit would not lead the church to err in doctrine or practice, Augustine set about to defend the practice of childhood and, indeed, infant baptism. Using multiple texts from the Bible, Augustine proved that the sin of Adam affected all human beings born after the Fall, making it impossible for them to avoid sin (*non posse non peccare*, as the medieval schoolmen would put it) without the grace of Christ that is given only to the baptized. Adam's original sin, then, made salvation necessary, and Christ's baptism made salvation possible. But if salvation were possible only to the baptized, then the church was correct in allowing the baptism of children and even of infants. For if they died before being baptized, they would not be saved.[218]

Even though Augustine's positing of an original sin was not directly related to his practice of speaking of baptism (or the baptismal character) as something that is given and received, the theory fit comfortably into this way of talking. For if the sin of Adam led to Paradise being lost, it also led to the loss of righteousness and the loss of grace for the whole of humankind. The only compensation for such a loss, then, would have to be a gain. It would have to be something received from God to make up for the loss: it would have to be a gift, it would have to be grace.[219]

With Augustine we come to the end of the development of the theology of baptism in the Latin church during the patristic period. Since this has been a long and complex development, let us summarize what we have discovered along the way.

- Around the turn of the first century, the *Didache*'s emphasis is on the moral

---

217. See Ferguson, *Baptism in the Early Church*, 627–630.

218. See Augustine, *Merit and the Forgiveness of Sins, and the Baptism of Children*, 1.16.21; 1.22.33. The reason why some are saved and some are not, according to Augustine, is a mystery. See 3.4.7 for an argument for original sin from church practice.

219. In the same work, Augustine occasionally speaks of grace and the remission of sins being given and received, using various verbs such as *dare*, *accipere*, *percipere*, and *suscipere*. However, he speaks of baptizing and being baptized (*baptizare* and *baptizari*) rather than of giving and receiving baptism.

conversion that took place prior to ritual immersion. There is little concern about religious doctrine.

- This same emphasis is found in the writings of Justin Martyr, although the faith content has become a little more explicit.

- Early texts talk about βαπτίζειν or immersing rather than about βάπτισμα or baptism, suggesting that there was not yet a set name for this ritual action, which is also called a λουτρόν or bath.

- Around the turn of the third century, Tertullian is the first one to speak of giving and receiving baptism, but he seems to be referring to the water, which he calls the sacrament of baptism.

- In discussing baptism, Cyprian of Carthage uses the language of giving and receiving in reference to the Holy Spirit and the remission of sins. In his mind, only the true church has baptism; heretics and schismatics do not.

- Christian writers during this period always used phrases taken from the New Testament to discuss the effects of baptism. These phrases were originally metaphors that referred to spiritual realities that were experienced.

- By the fourth century, however, these phrases were taken to refer to metaphysical realities that were to be believed rather than experienced.

- Ambrose uses the word *sacramentum* to talk about any type of religious symbol. He does not speak of giving or receiving sacraments except in reference to the eucharistic elements. The north African manner of speaking about sacraments has apparently not yet reached northern Italy.

- By Ambrose's day, moral conversion prior to baptism was not expected (although presumably only the well behaved would be admitted into the church). Doctrinal instruction in the form of an explanation of the sacred rites was given afterwards.

- Augustine used the language of giving and receiving baptism when he formulated a theology according to which baptism is a metaphysical reality that is received whenever the baptismal ritual is rightly performed.

- Augustine's ritualistic thinking about baptism and its metaphysical effects led him to the theory of an original sin that was inherited due to the Fall and that was remitted when infants and others were baptized.

- All of the fathers developed their theologies of baptism by thinking about the liturgical practice as something to be explained, and by drawing on scriptural phrases in formulating their explanations.

b. Eucharist: From Eucharistic Meal to Eucharistic Liturgy

Until the end of the fifth century, when the western half of the Roman Empire fell to barbarian invaders and was severely impoverished, Latin liturgies in the west would have been similar to the eastern liturgies in cultural and religious style. Whether *The Apostolic Tradition* is from third century Rome or from fourth century Egypt, its liturgical prayers are similar to others that have been preserved from that period. In particular, there is one feature of the early liturgies that ought to be noted, namely, they invoke the Holy Spirit upon the offerings of bread and wine after the memorial of the last supper.

In *The Apostolic Tradition,* neither the prayer surrounding the words of institution nor the epiclesis or prayer of invocation give a clear indication of the point at which (if any) the bread and wine were thought to be changed into the body and blood of Christ.[220] The precise moment of transformation would later become an important question in western theology, but at this time no one raised the issue—nor had it been an issue in earlier times, as we have seen. Interestingly, all but one of the eastern liturgies from the fourth century onward clearly indicate that the bread and wine were believed to be changed after the remembrance of the last supper.[221]

- In the fourth century liturgy from Serapion of Egypt, this epiclesis is said after the words of institution are recalled: "O God of Truth, let Thy Holy Word come upon this bread, that the bread may become Body of the Word, and upon this cup, that the cup may become Blood of the Truth . . . ".[222]

- The liturgy of St. Cyril of Jerusalem is not a scripted prayer text but a description of eucharistic worship in mid-fourth century Palestine. It contains no words of institution, but it does contain an epiclesis in which God is called upon "to send His Holy Spirit upon the gifts that are set forth, that He may make the bread indeed the body of Christ, and the wine the blood of Christ; for whatsoever the Holy spirit shall touch, is sanctified and changed."[223]

- *The Apostolic Constitutions* dates from the late fourth century and contains rubrics and prayers for a eucharistic liturgy. It contains a memorial of the last supper similar to that found in 1 Corinthians 11, followed by a lengthy epiclesis that

---

220. See *The Apostolic Tradition,* 4.9–13 in Palmer, *Sacraments and Worship,* 41–42. For the sake of convenience, this collection of texts will be used for this discussion of the eucharistic memorial and epiclesis.

221. The one exception is the Papyrus of Der Balzeh, discovered in Egypt in 1907, in which the epiclesis is placed before the words of institution. See Palmer, ibid., 46–47. Before the fourth century, eucharistic prayers were apparently unscripted, although local churches most likely followed a general format that varied from region to region.

222. Translation from L. Duchesne, *Christian Worship: Its Origins and Evolution* (London, 1927) p. 76–77 , cited in Palmer, ibid., 43–44.

223. Cyril of Jerusalem, *The Mysteries,* 5.7 in ibid., 49.

asks God to "send Thy Holy Spirit upon this sacrifice" and "make this bread the body of Thy Christ."[224]

- Texts of the Antiochene liturgy ascribed to St. James and dating from the early fifth century are found in both Greek and Syriac. After lengthy remembrance of the last supper, the celebrant asks God to send the Holy Spirit to come down upon the gifts to "hallow and make this bread the holy Body of Christ, and this cup the precious Blood of Christ."[225]

The Orthodox liturgies of today, based on liturgies attributed to fourth century fathers, St. John Chrysostom and St. Basil the Great, likewise place the epiclesis after the memorial of the last supper, and although Orthodox theology is not as concerned as Catholic theology with the precise moment of change, it generally regards the transformation of the elements to coincide with the epiclesis rather than with the words of institution.[226]

When we read the Greek fathers testifying to the change from bread and wine into the body and blood of Christ, therefore, we see they believed and perceived that the change was effected by the Holy Spirit who was called down upon the gifts after the memorial of the last supper. Thus, Cyril of Jerusalem, reflecting on the epiclesis cited above, says, "Before the invocation of the adorable Trinity, the bread and wine of the eucharist were ordinary bread and wine, but after the invocation the bread becomes the body of Christ and the wine becomes the blood of Christ."[227] Cyril also urges the newly baptized not to believe their senses, but instead believe that the power of Christ can truly transform the eucharistic elements: "Do not judge the matter by taste, but by faith be fully assured that the body and blood of Christ have been granted to you."[228] From the age of the great fathers of the church and forward, it becomes common for Christians to be exhorted to look upon the consecrated elements as the body and blood of Christ, that is, to perceive a divine reality rather than an earthly one when their senses see what looks like bread and wine, whether the transformation is believed to take place during the epiclesis, as in the east, or during the memorial of the last supper, as in the west. Given the strength of the language that is used, it is easy to conclude that the fathers themselves perceived the presence of Christ in and through the consecrated elements. And given the persuasive power of the bishops, not to mention the

224. *The Apostolic Constitutions*, 8.12, in ibid., 54.

225. Translation from Gregory Dix, *The Shape of the Liturgy* (Westminster, 1945) 187–89, cited in Palmer, ibid., 58.

226. See Alexander Schmemann, *Sacraments and Orthodoxy* (New York: Herder and Herder, 1965) 52; also Hugh Wybrew, *The Orthodox Liturgy: The Development of the Eucharistic Liturgy in the Byzantine Rite* (Crestwood, NY: St. Vladimir's Seminary Press, 1990) 35–36.

227. Cyril of Jerusalem, Catechetical Lecture 19 (First Lecture on the Mysteries), 7. See also Catechetical Lecture 23 (Fifth Lecture on the Mysteries), 7, cited in Palmer, *Sacraments and Worship*, 50.

228. Catechetical Lecture 22 (Fourth Lecture on the Mysteries), 6. See also 9. Cited in Palmer, ibid., p. 50.

persuasive power of the faith of everyone around them, it is easy to infer that many if not most Christians in the ancient world not only believed in the presence of Christ but also perceived it, even though their senses saw something different.[229]

Later in the fourth century, eastern fathers in sermons and lectures repeatedly impressed upon their listeners that what looked like bread and wine was truly the body and blood of Christ. Ephrem the Syrian amplified the gospel accounts of the last supper with assurances that Christians who ate the sanctified bread and wine were partaking of food that was filled with Christ and the Holy Spirit.[230] Gregory of Nyssa explained, "In the dispensation of grace [Christ] plants Himself in all the faithful by means of that flesh fashioned from wine and bread, blending Himself with the bodies of the faithful."[231] John Chrysostom, archbishop of Constantinople, says in one place that in the liturgy, the words of the priest who stands in the role of Christ are filled with the power and grace of God, and so they transform the elements set forth. But in another place he says, "When the priest stands before the table holding up his hands to heaven and invoking the Holy Spirit to come and touch the elements, there is a great quiet, a great silence."[232] Chrysostom's words could be used to support both the western tradition, which understands the words of institution as effecting the consecration, and the eastern tradition, which takes the epiclesis to be the transforming moment.

The eastern fathers understood growth in holiness, which in the west was called sanctification, as divinization or becoming more like God. The notion of taking God's body into one's human body supported this concept, as witnessed by Cyril of Alexandria, who argued that the Holy Spirit could enter into our bodies if we were given the actual flesh and blood of Christ to eat. But he goes on to say, "For lest we be stunned with horror on seeing flesh and blood set out on the holy tables of the churches, God condescends to our weakness and sends the power of life into the elements and transforms them into the power of his own flesh, that we may have and partake of them as a means of life, and that the body of life may become in us a life-giving seed."[233]

In the Latin-speaking west, the two main witnesses are Ambrose of Milan and Augustine of Hippo. For both of these fathers, the words of Christ, recalled and repeated during the liturgy, provide the strongest argument in favor of eucharistic change. Ambrose in *The Mysteries* writes:

229. Again, phenomenologically, this is no different from looking at someone differently after being told who they are, or from perceiving something differently after being told that it is rare and valuable. Also, many Catholics and Orthodox are quite aware of this phenomenon from their own experience, although not all believers can attest to it. People in many faith traditions can identify with having had an experience of God's presence, but in ancient and medieval Christianity this experience became strongly linked to the eucharistic elements.

230. See Ephrem the Syrian, Fourth Sermon in Holy Week, 4 and 6, cited in Palmer, ibid., 138.

231. Gregory of Nyssa, Catechetical Oration 37, cited in ibid.

232. John Chrysostom, *Homilies on Cemeteries*, 2.474, cited in ibid., 139. See also his Homily on the Betrayal of Judas, 1.6, cited in ibid.

233. Cyril of Alexandria, Commentary on Luke 22:19, cited in ibid., 140. This notion is also found in the quotation from Gregory of Nyssa, cited above.

The Lord Jesus himself proclaims, "This is my body." Before the blessing of the heavenly words, something of a different nature is spoken of, but after the consecration, a body is referred to. He himself speaks of his blood. Before the consecration it is called something else, but after it is referred to as blood. And you say, "Amen," that is, "It is true." Let the mind within confess what the mouth utters, and let the affections feel what the voice speaks.[234]

In this last sentence, Ambrose urges his listeners to perceive what they believe and to feel what they hear themselves saying. Arguably, Ambrose would not invite the faithful to experience something that he himself had not experienced. Clues such as this suggest that devout church leaders were talking not only about received doctrines but also about religious experiences when they spoke of the real presence of Christ in the Eucharist. Ambrose is engaged in persuading his listeners to feel something that they say they believe in, which is quite different from what Paul and other early writers did when they attempted to articulate their experiences in religious language. In other words, here the movement is from theological belief to religious experience, whereas earlier the movement had been from personal experience to the religious interpretation of that experience.

No one who has read *The Confessions of St. Augustine* would conclude that the author was an emotionless intellectual. A north African by birth, a restless seeker after philosophical and religious truth, and dramatically converted to Christianity while living in Italy, Augustine of Hippo is a prime example of a theologian who felt what he thought and thought what he felt. His writings about the eucharist are peppered with hints that he was talking about what he both believed and experienced. For example, he refers to the eucharistic bread as the flesh of Christ, adding that "no one eats that flesh unless he has first adored it,"[235] something he probably would not have said unless he were familiar with the practice of eucharistic adoration. Still, he refers to the eucharist as a sort of sacrament (*sacramentum aliquod*), for it is celebrated visibly (*visibiliter*) but understood invisibly (*invisibiliter*).[236] With regard to the eucharist, Augustine does not seem to have insisted on the sacramental realism that eventually became part of the Latin theological tradition, but he did speak of the bread as a sign of an invisible presence.

Augustine never devoted an entire work to the eucharist, as he did to baptism and marriage, because it was not a matter of controversy during his day. Even in his lecture on John 6:41–59, called by later commentators the bread of life discourse, Augustine's focus is not on the real presence of Christ but on the importance of spiritual

---

234. Ambrose of Milan, *The Mysteries*, 9.54. Earlier, in 52, he argued, "If the word of Elijah had the strength to bring down fire from heaven, will not the words of Christ have the strength to change the nature of the [eucharistic] elements?" Ambrose also refers to the sacrament as the body of Christ in 8.47 and in 9.52–53, 58.

235. Augustine, Commentary on Psalm 98, 9.

236. Ibid.

nourishment for the Christian.[237] It is clear that Augustine thought of the bread and wine as the body and blood of Christ, who spoke of his body and blood as food and drink (*corpus dixit escam, sanguinem potum*).[238] But it is equally clear that for Augustine the body and blood are spiritual nourishment that is received when the bread and wine are received. Speaking to catechumens, he says, "Thus it will happen that the body and blood of Christ will be life for each of you, when that which is taken visibly in the sacrament is in very truth spiritually eaten and spiritually drunk."[239] Since this is an interpretation that is unique to Augustine, namely that Christ's nourishment is invisible and spiritual, there is reason to believe that he was talking out of his own personal experience and not as a result of a teaching he had received. Indeed, as we have just seen, his mentor Ambrose did not say much about the eucharist in his writings.

As was mentioned at the beginning of this section, Sunday worship in the fourth century began to take on the appearance and trappings of pagan temple worship. It can be reasonably assumed that devout pagans, once they became convinced that they ought to worship the God of the Christians, would have been comfortable with participating in the style of liturgy that was culturally appropriate for honoring a deity. It can even be imagined that many of the neophytes would have felt that their new God deserved no less than the honor that they had bestowed on their old gods. In any event, within a generation or two Christian liturgies were both imitating and displacing the older pagan liturgies, ancient temples and shrines were falling into disuse, and they were being replaced by Christian basilicas.

At this point, then, it became even more appropriate to refer to the eucharistic liturgy as a θυσία or *sacrificium*, for in structure and style Christian worship now closely resembled polytheistic sacrifices, the main difference being that the foods were limited to bread and wine which were offered and received in a symbolic meal rather than in an actual meal.

The prayers of fourth and fifth century eastern liturgies take for granted that the public services are sacrifices or contain elements of sacrifice.

- The liturgy of Bishop Serapion of Thmuis in Egypt asks God to "fill also this sacrifice with Thy power and Thy participation: for to Thee we offered this living sacrifice, this bloodless oblation. To Thee we have offered this bread, the likeness of the Body of the Only-begotten."[240]

- The anaphora or eucharistic prayer attributed to St. Mark compares "this reasonable sacrifice, this bloodless worship" to the pure sacrifice prophesied in Malachi

237. See Augustine, *Tractates on the Gospel of John*, 26.

238. Augustine, Sermon 131, 1.

239. Ibid.

240. Translation by Duchesne, quoted in Palmer, ibid., 43. Note that the first time it appears, "sacrifice" refers to the ritual, and in the second instance it refers to the food that is offered. Note also that the service is called a bloodless sacrifice, but whether this is in contrast with animal sacrifices or with the self-offering of Jesus is not specified.

1:10–11.[241]

- In a number of epicleses, the Holy Spirit is asked to come down upon the gifts or offerings on the altar, also sometimes referred to as the sacrifice being offered.[242]

In 380, Theodosius I declared Christianity to be the official religion of the Roman Empire, and Christians' familiarity with pagan sacrifices quickly became a thing of the past. The Greek word θυσία is probably best translated into English as "festive banquet," for a pagan θυσία was most often a sharing of food with a deity to whom one was thankful or from whom one was requesting a favor. The word was translated into Latin as *sacrificium*, literally a sacred making (*sacrum facere*), for the event and the food were made sacred by the presence of the god, the solemnity of the affair, and the devotion of the participants. Instead of being translated into English, however, *sacrificium* was transliterated into the word "sacrifice" at a time when it had lost all its festive connotations and instead meant a loss or a giving up. Quite possibly, the change in meaning of *sacrificium* occurred because the only sacrifices known to Christians from the fifth century onward were those about which they could read in the Old Testament, the descriptions of which often focus on the slaying of an animal. Also, in the Bible there is in places an emphasis on the burnt offering or holocaust, in which the animal is totally destroyed, often in propitiation for sins.[243]

By the fifth century, both θυσία and *sacrificium* were beginning to be understood more as an offering than as a meal, more as a sin offering than as a thank offering, and more as a unbloody offering in contrast to the bloody ones of the Old Testament. In his sermons on the Epistle to the Hebrews, John Chrysostom says,

> We have our victim in heaven, our priest in heaven, our sacrifice in heaven. Let us then present such sacrifices as can be offered on that altar, no longer sheep and oxen, no longer blood and steaming fat. All these things have been done away, and in their place the reasonable service has been brought in. [244]

> What then? Do we not offer every day? Certainly we offer, making a memorial of His death. And his death is one and not many. How is it one and not many? Inasmuch as it was offered once, just as that which was carried into the holy of holies. This [our offering] is a symbol of that [His offering]; this [our sacrifice] a symbol of that. For we ever offer the same person, not today one sheep and tomorrow another, but ever the same offering. Therefore, the sacrifice is one.[245]

241. Cited in ibid., 45.

242. See Palmer for the epiclesis of Cyril of Jerusalem (49), prayers in the liturgy of *The Apostolic Constitutions* (54–55), and the epiclesis in the Liturgy of St. James (58).

243. In Leviticus, Numbers and Deuteronomy there are multiple references to burnt offerings and sin offerings, indeed too many to cite here.

244. 11.3. Quoted in Palmer, ibid., 188.

245. 17.3. Quoted in ibid.

Chrysostom is clearly deriving his information about sacrifice from the Bible: from the Epistle to the Hebrews and from the descriptions of sacrifice in the Jewish scriptures. Writing in Greek, he is aware that there are two senses of the word θυσία, one being the food that is offered, but for him the other sense of the word is not a festive banquet but the ritual of making the offering. And his focus is on killing, for he speaks about the victim in the first passage above, and he refers to the death of Christ in the other.[246]

In one of his longest and most comprehensive works, Augustine reflects on the nature of sacrifice and its importance in worship. *The City of God* was written after the sack of Rome by the Visigoths in 410, which shocked the empire as much as the attack on the World Trade Center shocked the United States in 2001. Before the burning and looting of the city, Latin Christians had regarded Rome as the city of God because it was the center of western Christianity and the final resting place of St. Peter and St. Paul. Its vulnerability caused Augustine to rethink the matter, and the result was a lengthy treatise on the church as the true city of God and the universal means of spiritual salvation.

In Book X, Augustine discusses sacrifice as a unique act of worship dating from the days of Cain and Abel. After assuring the reader that God does not need the food that is offered to him, he draws attention to the spiritual dynamic of the ritual, which is the inner offering of the self to God: "A sacrifice, therefore, is the visible sacrament or sacred sign of an invisible sacrifice."[247] From this perspective, a sacrifice does not have to be an offering of food to God; rather, it can be anything that is done in order to be spiritually closer to God. Augustine offers an etymology of the Latin word, suggesting that *sacrum facere* implies that the one who sacrifices becomes holy or sacred when performing this religious ritual. "Thus man (*homo*) himself, consecrated in the name of God and devoted to God, is a sacrifice in so far as he dies to the world that he may live to God."[248] Augustine invokes the Epistle to the Romans to support this interpretation of sacrifice: "Therefore, brethren, I implore you by the mercy of God to present your bodies as a living sacrificial victim (*hostia*) holy and pleasing to God—your reasonable submission (*rationabile obsequium*)."[249]

Having established self-offering as the essence of sacrifice, Augustine expands on this idea to include the self-offering of the church, which is the redeemed city populated by the communion of saints. But the church, according to Paul, is the body of Christ, so ultimately the self-offering of the church is the self-offering of Christ. This self-offering was made once and for all on the cross by the One who was both priest and victim, so ultimately the redemptive self-offering of Christ is the sacrifice

---

246. In ancient sacrifices, the killing of animals was not a focal point but simply something had had to be done before the meat could be cooked and eaten.

247. Augustine, *The City of God*, 10.5.

248. Ibid., 6.

249. Rom 12:1.

in which all Christians participate whenever they make a spiritual sacrifice, especially by engaging in eucharistic worship:

> Hence, the true Mediator, inasmuch as he was made the mediator between God and humankind by taking the form of a servant, the man Christ Jesus— although in the form of God he receives sacrifice along with the Father, with whom he is one God—yet, in the form of a servant he preferred to be a sacrifice rather than to receive a sacrifice. Nor should anyone think on account of this that sacrifice is to be offered to some creature. In this way he is also priest (*sacerdos*), the very one who offers, as well as the offering (*oblatio*) itself. And he willed that the daily sacrifice of the church should be the sacrament of this. Since she is the body of this head, through him she is taught to offer herself.[250]

In the theology of Augustine, sacrifice becomes completely spiritualized, and the link between Christ's sacrifice on the cross and eucharistic worship is forged. Because he wrote in Latin, and because he wrote extensively on almost every issue related to the practice of Christianity, Augustine's works became a major source of theological ideas in the Middle Ages, second only to the Bible (in Latin translation, of course). The stage was set for the interpretation of the liturgy as the sacrifice of the mass.

c. Other Sacraments in the Christian Roman Empire

Between 312 and 476 (the symbolic date of the fall of the Roman Empire in the west),[251] Catholic rituals developed further in the direction that they would assume in the Middle Ages. The episcopal blessing, given at the end of the baptismal rite, became a separate rite in the Latin church. Penitential practices came increasingly under the jurisdiction of canonical regulations. Ordination expanded to include minor as well as major orders, and marriage began to fall under ecclesiastical influence, at least in the eastern part of the empire. Anointing and ministering to the sick, however, remained primarily a lay practices.

(1) Confirmation

Our treatment of baptism above focused on the language used to talk about the ritual and its effects, and in doing so, it omitted mention of an important pastoral and ceremonial development that resulted from the exponential increase in the number of converts in the years and decades following the Edict of Toleration. Christian

---

250. Augustine, ibid., 10.20.

251. The western part of the empire had been contracting under successive waves of invasions by barbarians (Germanic and Asiatic) all during the fifth century, when much of Italy was under the control of the Huns and other tribes. In 476, however, the Ostrogoth leader decided to end the pretense of an empire in the west by sending young Romulus Augustus from Ravenna, the western capital at that time, to Constantinople.

initiation during the second and third centuries had been a lengthy process of learning the good news of salvation and converting to a lifestyle in keeping with the gospel, which culminated in a symbolic immersion and a communal sharing of the body and blood of Christ. To accommodate the rush of new converts in the fourth century, bishops shortened the catechumenate and expanded their mystagogical efforts in the months after the neophytes joined the church. One thing they were not able to do was be present at the baptism of all the new converts, who soon were too numerous to fit into the local basilica. The solution was to create parishes around the city and countryside, and to appoint presbyters who would pastor the local congregations and oversee the initiation of new members.

All solutions create their own problems, and this time was no different. For centuries, bishops had been present at the baptisms of all the new Christians in their local community, but the burgeoning number of converts was now making this impossible. Since there was no central authority among the churches, each locality had to work out its own solution, and over the course of time, regional solutions emerged. By the fifth century, churches in the eastern part of the empire allowed presbyters to preside over the initiation ceremonies, but after the baptismal washing, neophytes were anointed with an oil that had been blessed by the bishop, thus symbolizing his presence and approval. Churches in the western part of the empire had somewhat more diverse practices, but in general the bishops there reserved the final blessing of the newly baptized to themselves, so converts were baptized by their local pastors and then went to the bishop to have their baptisms confirmed.

Baptismal rituals in the west included an immersion or pouring of water, to be sure, but in various places they may have included an anointing before or after the water rite, and some included both. Others called for a laying on of hands instead of an anointing by the bishop after the washing. The pre-baptismal anointing (with the oil of catechumens) symbolized strengthening, like gladiators preparing for combat. Both the post-baptismal anointing (with chrism) and the hand-laying symbolized the Holy Spirit's coming down into the soul of the new believer, so either one or the other was chosen, and never both. Thus when it became customary to postpone the bishop's blessing until after baptism, in some places that blessing was done with an anointing and in others it was done with a laying on of hands.

Complicating the picture was the custom in the west of reconciling people born into heretical and schismatic groups with a hand-laying administered by the bishop. Was this an acknowledgement of public repentance or a ceremony of welcoming into the church? The ritual arose out of pastoral sensitivity and practical necessity, so the theological justification of it came after the fact. In any event, receiving the anointing or laying on of hands was associated with receiving the Holy Spirit. As can be readily seen, discussion of receiving the anointing, receiving the hand-laying and receiving the Holy Spirit, as well as discussion about giving the oil and administering the blessing, increased the inclination to talk about these rites in terms of giving and receiving.

The separated western ceremony was referred to by a number of different names: blessing, perfection or consummation (of baptism), signing or consignation (with oil), and confirmation (of baptism). The integrated eastern practice was simply called chrismation after the name of the scented oil that was used.[252]

(2) Penance

In the post-Nicene period, ritual repentance can properly be called canonical penance because it was regulated by a great number of canons that were passed by local and regional councils. In theory, works of repentance were assigned so that virtuous habits might replace sinful ones.

> Accordingly, obduracy will be atoned for by kindness, insults and abuse by reparation, sadness by cheerfulness, harshness by mildness, glumness by light-heartedness, crookedness by straightforwardness, and whatever else can find a remedy by their contraries.[253]

In time, however, sins began to be equated with transgressions of the moral law, incurring penalties either in this life or the next. Accordingly, private as well as public sins became subject to the penitential process, and penances were increased in harshness and length, with the result that fewer people sought public reconciliation with the church and God until they were close to dying.[254]

As in the pre-Nicene period, there was little talk of giving and receiving, except where it would seem natural to do so, as in receiving (i.e., listening to) a person's confession, giving (i.e., assigning) works of penance, and receiving (i.e., being assured of) God's forgiveness. Nonetheless, there were some developments in the language used by church fathers in these centuries to speak about repentance, penitential practices and forgiveness.

For example, we have already noted that the phrase, "binding and loosing," is a technical term that originally referred to a process analogous to shunning in the Amish community. There, a person who has violated a group's norms is restricted (bound) from normal intercourse with the other members,[255] but when the person has changed his or her behavior (repented), the restrictions on interaction with community mem-

252. See Martos, *Doors to the Sacred*, 219; also Milner, *Theology of Confirmation*, 15–49.

253. Pacian of Barcelona, *Exhortation to Penance* (PL 13, 1083–84), quoted in Palmer, ibid., 95. Pacian was a bishop from 365 to 391 AD.

254. For example, sexual sins might incur a penance of chastity, not only during the penitential period but afterwards as well, even for married people. And since public reconciliation could be offered only once, it made sense to seek it only when one could be reasonably sure of not committing the same sin again. Other perpetual penances included abstinence from business or military service, and prohibitions against holding civil or ecclesiastical offices. See Poschmann, *Penance*, 89–98 and 105–109.

255. The Amish practice is called *Meidung* or avoidance, and it requires not speaking to the person who has been declared to be shunned.

bers are relaxed (loosed). There are two references to the practice in Matthew's gospel (16:19 and 18:18), which was written for an audience familiar with Judaism. There also appear to be two references to the practice in Paul's letters (1 Cor 5:1–13 and 2 Cor 2:5–11), although the process is not referred to as binding and loosing.

By the fourth century, however, Christians were no longer familiar with this Jewish practice, and so the Matthean passages began to be understood differently. John Chrysostom claimed that whereas earthly rulers have the authority to bind bodies, priests have the authority to bind souls.[256] Ambrose argued against those who said that some sins are unforgivable, and he maintained that the church is obedient to Christ when it both binds and looses sins (*peccatum et alliget et relaxet*).[257] And in the fifth century, Leo the Great applied the notion of binding and loosing to the guilt (*reatus*) of sins, which he said could be loosed by priestly supplication.[258]

Closely related, and perhaps influential on the patristic interpretation of binding and loosing, is the gospel text on forgiving and retaining sins (Jn 20:21–23). In its original context, the risen Lord says to a gathering of his frightened followers (μαθήται),

> "Peace be with you! As the Father has sent me, I am sending you." Then he breathed on them and said, "Receive a holy spirit.[259] The sins of those whom you forgive are forgiven, and the sins of those you refrain from forgiving are not forgiven."

Although John's gospel clearly distinguishes between Jesus' followers (who are many) and the twelve, and although these words are addressed to an indefinite number of followers, Christian writers in later centuries took them as being addressed to the twelve apostles, and through them to their successors, the bishops. Not infrequently, this text was interpreted in light of the binding and loosing mentioned in Matthew 16:19, which is clearly addressed to Peter, and which is preceded by the words, "I will give you the keys of the kingdom of heaven," even though the parallel saying in Matthew 18:18 is addressed to a larger group of followers. Together, the text from John and the two texts from Matthew were used in developing a theological rationale for the practice of public reconciliation, which was overseen by bishops and subject to ecclesiastical regulation.

Very quickly, then, the command to forgive becomes a power to forgive that is exercised by the successors of the apostles. Writing in the mid-fourth century, the hymnologist and theologian Ephrem the Syrian interprets John 20:22 as Christ speaking to bishops, saying, "Receive a power which will neither leave you nor fail, because

---

256. See John Chrysostom, *The Priesthood*, 3.5.

257. See Ambrose, *Repentance*, 1.2.7. Ambrose also uses the words *ligare* and *solvere*.

258. See Leo the Great, Letter 108, 3.

259. The Greek text does not precede πνευμα 'αγιον with the definite article.

your word is guaranteed."[260] This interpretation is amplified not long after by John Chrysostom in Constantinople, again referring to John 20:23: "What power (εξουσίαν) could be greater than this? The Father has given all judgment to the Son. But now I see that this same power in its entirety has been entrusted to priests (ἱερεῖς) by the Son."[261] By the fifth century, Cyril of Alexandria could write about the apostles that

> . . . those who even then possessed in themselves the divine and ruling Spirit should have authority (κατεξουσίαν) both to forgive the sins of any and to retain the sins of whomsoever they willed, since it would be the Holy Spirit dwelling in them who would both forgive and retain according to His own personal will, even though the actual operation should take place through men.[262]

In the west, Ambrose of Milan similarly understood that the power to forgive was the power of God, although it was exercised through human beings (*per hominem*).[263] Commenting on John 20:22–23, he says,

> Understand that sins are forgiven through the Holy Spirit. Human beings use their ministry for the forgiveness of sins, but they do not exercise the right of their own power. For they forgive sins not in their own name but in the name of the Father, Son and Holy Spirit. They ask, and the Godhead gives. The ministry is human, but the gift comes from a power that is above.[264]

Augustine of Hippo was undoubtedly influenced by Ambrose's theology, but he wrote much more than his mentor and his works became a major source of patristic thinking for the scholastics almost a thousand years later. His interpretation of John 20:22–23 is that the risen Christ is speaking to the church, giving it the power to forgive and withhold forgiveness.[265] By the church, however, Augustine does not mean the faithful but the hierarchy.

In Augustine, we also find evidence of another evolution in theological language. As we saw earlier,[266] the phrase "remission of sins" was first applied to the baptismal

---

260. See Ephrem the Syrian, *Sermon for the Nocturn of the Lord's Resurrection*, 6, apparently translated by Palmer in *Sacraments and Forgiveness*, 82, from a Latin collection of Ephrem's works. Importantly, Palmer notes in his introduction to this text that the bishop "does not grant divine pardon—only God can grant such; his action, if just and fair, is the sign and infallible pledge of divine forgiveness." Ephrem's understanding of what the bishop does is therefore close to that of his early patristic predecessors.

261. John Chrysostom, *The Priesthood*, 3.5. For more on Chrysostom's appreciation of priestly powers to forgive sins, see 3.6. Note that the Greek εξουσία means power in the sense of authority, but it was often translated as *potestas* in Latin, meaning the power or ability to do something.

262. Cyril of Alexandria, *Commentary on John 20:23*, 12.1, quoted in Palmer, ibid., 88–89. Cyril has in mind the authority to forgive both in baptism and in canonical penance.

263. See Ambrose, *Repentance*, 1.8.36.

264. See Ambrose, *The Holy Spirit*, 3.18.137.

265. See Augustine, *Baptism*, 3.18.23.

266. See above, pages 101–102.

process (later called the catechumenate), and evidence suggests that it meant getting rid of sinful habits. Thus, when Christian apologists said that sins were remitted through baptism, they would have been saying that sinful ways are gotten rid of by being immersed in Jesus' way of life. By Augustine's day, however, the baptismal process had evolved from a process of moral conversion that culminated in a ritual washing, anointing and food sharing to a process of ritual washing, anointing and worshipping that was followed by a theological debriefing known as mystagogy, or an explanation of the mysteries. Since there was no longer a period of moral conversion prior to the baptismal ritual, what had once been said of the baptismal process (i.e., immersion in the Christian community and their way of life), now got attributed to the baptismal ritual itself. And by extension, what had once been said about the remission of sins through baptism now got applied to the ritual of public repentance.

Augustine mentions the remission of sins (*remissio peccatorum*) in a brief work on faith, hope and charity written in response to questions from a layman named Laurence, first with reference to baptism and then with reference to penance. From the outset, it is clear that Augustine is engaged in a sort of magical thinking to which we have already alluded,[267] according to which invisible effects are affirmed to occur because certain rituals have been performed, for Augustine's first reference to the remission of sins regards the baptism of infants, who are developmentally incapable of conversion.[268] In Augustine's mind, then, it is the ritual of baptism and the ritual of penance that bring about the remission of sins.

Part of the reasoning behind this equation of the effects of both rituals is that remission had come to mean the same as pardon or forgiveness.[269] Furthermore, baptism was said to wash away sins,[270] a metaphor that also suggests getting rid of them in some way. And twenty years prior to the writing of this work, Augustine in his treatise on baptism had thought through the matter quite thoroughly, so that he could say with confidence there that the grace of baptism takes away all the actual sins found to have been committed in thought, word, and deed.[271] Moreover, if baptism takes away sins, then it also takes away the guilt of having committed them, whether it be inherited or added after birth.[272] Finally, it is only in the church that sins can be remitted in a way that leads to eternal life, for it is only to the church that the Holy Spirit has been promised.[273] Augustine saw where the logic of his reasoning was leading, but he

267. See above, pages 115–16.

268. See Augustine, *Handbook on Faith, Hope and Charity* (also called the *Enchiridion*) 13.44.

269. In Latin, *remittere* meant primarily to send away or send again, but it could also mean forgive in the sense of remitting a penalty. *Dimittere* originally meant send forth or send out, but by Augustine's time it had come to mean forgive or pardon, as in the Lord's prayer: *dimitte nobis debita nostra*.

270. See Augustine, *Baptism*, 4.3.5, 4.1.15, and 6.25.46. Also, Tertullian, *Baptism*, 5.6 and 15.

271. Augustine, *Enchiridion*, 17.64 (*activa quoque peccata, quaecumque corde ore opere commissa invenerit, tollit*).

272. Ibid. (*solvitur omnis reatus et ingeneratus et additus*).

273. Ibid., 65 (*Extra eam [ecclesiam] quippe non remittuntur: ipsa namque proprie Spiritum*

did not hesitate to conclude that those who leave this life spiritually unborn or bound (*non regenerati exeunt vel ligati*) will be in great danger if at that moment there are no ministers to save them from destruction (*exitium*).[274] In other words, just as surely as participating in the ritual effects the remission of sins, failing to participate in it means dying with sins on one's soul. Clearly Augustine is imagining the ritual, whether of baptism or penance, to be automatically effective.

Not everyone in the fifth century shared this view, however. Augustine's contemporary, Jerome, interpreted the role of the bishop in public reconciliation, not as effecting the remission of sins, but rather as declaring that a person's sins were forgiven when he saw evidence of remorse and repentance.[275] In addition, Augustine was writing in an African outpost of an empire under siege, and there is no evidence that his works were widely circulated in his own day. But they did get widely circulated centuries later, when the first schools were being founded after the long illiteracy of the Dark Ages.

(3) Anointing

Even though other symbolic practices became increasingly ritualized in the Christian Roman Empire, this did not happen to the use of oil for healing the sick. There are scattered references to anointing, but these are mostly connected to penitential practices. Even the passage in the Letter of James, later used to prove that the priestly anointing of the sick dated back to the time of the apostles, was applied primarily to the practice of public repentance.[276] Nonetheless, by the fifth century, James 5:14–15 was being cited in conjunction with ministering to people with physical illness.[277] As late as 416 Bishop Decent of Gubbio wrote to Innocent I in Rome, asking about the proper interpretation of that passage. Innocent replied that it refers to an anointing of the sick, adding that chrism blessed by a bishop can be used not only by priests but also by the faithful who may be attending to the sick in their own families.[278] The pope cautioned, however, that the oil should not be poured on penitents since it is a kind

---

Sanctum pignus accepit, sine quo non remittuntur ulla peccata ita ut quibus remittuntur vitam consequantur aeternam.)

274. See Augustine, Letter 228, 8.

275. See Jerome, *Commentary on Matthew*, 16:19 (PL 26, 122) quoted in Palmer, *Sacraments and Forgivenes*, 110.

276. See John Chrysostom, *The Priesthood*, 3.6; also in the third century, see Origen's second homily on Leviticus, 2. Interestingly, Chrysostom by this time is speaking of the ministry to the repentant in terms of a priestly power to forgive.

277. See Cyril of Alexandria, *Adoration in Spirit and in Truth* (PG 68, 472) and Victor of Antioch, *Commentary on Mark 6:13*, quoted in Palmer, ibid., 281–82.

278. See Innocent I, Letter 25, 8. (Denzinger, *Enchiridion Symbolorum*, 216; Clarkson, *Church Teaches*, 829)

of sacrament (*genus sacramenti*), but this is as close as the practice of anointing got to being called a sacrament during the patristic period.

(4) Ordination

Innocent I is usually referred to as a pope, but during the first centuries of Christianity the bishop of every local church was regarded as the *papa* or spiritual father of that community. Over the course of time, however, this term of endearment was no longer given to other bishops, and in the west only the bishop of Rome was called *papa* or pope.[279] One should not attribute to the early Roman popes the position that they later came to enjoy in the western church, but they did have authority in central Italy.

When discussing church leadership in earlier centuries, it is tempting but mistaken to refer to ἐπίσκοποι as bishops, πρεσβύτεροι as presbyters or priests, and διάκονοι as deacons in the sense that these terms came to have in later centuries. Beginning in the fourth century however, these titles did in fact begin to designate offices in the church rather than roles in the community, and those who held these offices were regarded as members of ecclesiastical *ordines* or orders. For the sake of simplicity, therefore, from here forward we will talk of bishops, presbyters and deacons rather than of supervisors, elders and helpers, as was more appropriate in earlier sections when we discussed various types of ministers in the church. It will not be possible to avoid all ambiguity, however, because at the beginning of the fourth century πρεσβύτερος still meant a presbyter, whereas by the end of the fifth century the Greek word and its Latin cognate, *presbyter*, for all practical purposes meant a priest. (The English word "priest" actually derives from the Latin *presbyter*.)

If *The Apostolic Tradition* attributed to the presbyter Hippolytus of Rome was composed in the early third century, it would be the earliest witness we have of ordination in the Christian tradition. However, since the notion of ecclesiastical orders is historically more congruent with church organization in the post-Nicene period, and since our concern is primarily with the language of church rituals and their theology, it is more convenient to regard it as being from the fourth century, at least in its present form. Here is what this early document tells us:

- A bishop is ordained by having hands laid on him by other bishops, even though he is chosen by all the people.

- One of the ordaining bishops prays that the new bishop will receive the power given to the apostles to shepherd the church, to forgive sins, to bind and to loose, and to be pleasing to God, whose high priesthood he is entering.[280]

279. In the east, the head of the church of Alexandria in Egypt, later the Coptic Church, has also traditionally been referred to as a pope.

280. See *The Apostolic Tradition*, 2. Since the original Greek text has been lost and the document is preserved in Coptic and Latin translations, no attempt is made here to reconstruct the Greek wording

- A presbyter is ordained by having hands laid on him by other presbyters and a bishop, who prays that he receive the spirit of grace and wisdom in the tradition of the elders chosen by Moses to help and guide the people.[281]

- A deacon is ordained by a single bishop, whose minister he will be, and who will serve in whatever capacity the bishop chooses.

- A deacon is not ordained to the priesthood shared by bishops, nor does he receive the spirit shared by presbyters, for he is only a manager or administrator.[282]

- Someone who has suffered for the faith is already a presbyter (in the sense of being an elder?) in virtue of his public witness, but to be given the office of bishop he must receive a laying on of hands.[283]

- Widows, lectors, virgins, sub-deacons and healers are not ordained even though they perform the duties of their respective offices.[284]

The ancient church order known as *The Teaching of the Twelve Apostles* (because it purported to have been written by them) but commonly referred to by its Latin title, *Didascalia Apostolorum*, talks about the qualifications for bishops (similar to those found in the pastoral epistles) and about the appointment of widows, deacons and deaconesses, but it makes no direct reference to ordination as such. The lengthier *Apostolic Constitutions* likewise claimed apostolic authorship and dates from the last quarter of the fourth century, but it is largely a reworking and expansion of *The Apostolic Tradition* and the *Didascalia Apostolorum*, and so it does little to further our knowledge of ordination and holy orders. From the absence of liturgical texts, especially of Latin texts that would represent the tradition of western Christianity, it can be inferred that during this period the orders themselves were more important than the rites that initiated people into them. Even the prayers in *The Apostolic Tradition* are presented as models for the types of prayers that should be said in ordination ceremonies, not as texts that are to be recited verbatim.[285] According to Edward Schillebeeckx, during this period the ritual blessing or laying on of hands was not essential for ordination; rather, the decisive factor was being called by the community and being appointed to the office.[286]

The Council of Nicaea in 325 spoke of ordination, but all of its canons can be understood as referring to entering the episcopal order. Canon 4 says that bishops should be appointed by all the bishops in a province, or at least by three of them, but

---

of these prayers.

281. See ibid., 7.
282. See ibid., 8.
283. See ibid., 9.
284. See ibid., 10–14.
285. See ibid., 9.
286. See Schillebeeckx, *Ministry*, 46–48.

this seems to have been a provision to ensure that new appointees would have the approval of other bishops as well as the approval of their people.[287] Moreover, canon 6 of the Council of Chalcedon in 451 declared, "No one may be raised to the order of presbyter or deacon at large (ἀπολελυμένως) without being specifically appointed to a church in a city or village, or to a shrine or monastery. If any have been ordained without such a charge, this holy Council decrees, reprimanding the one who made the appointment, that their ordination is of no effect, and that they are not to officiate anywhere." Schillebeeckx observes that this prohibition against what was later called absolute ordination—ordination that was not tied to ministry in a specific Christian community—lasted until the twelfth century, when the notion of priestly power led to the understanding that such power was independent of where it might be exercised. This meant that someone who was unable to function as a presbyter or deacon automatically reverted to being a member of the laity without having to be laicized when they were relieved of their office. There was as yet no concept of priestly powers inherent in the soul of the ordained.[288]

All the same, the power of bishops and priests steadily increased in the Christianized Roman Empire. As the number of Christians increased, the prestige of their leaders increased. As more people turned to them for religious instruction, their religious authority increased. They already had the power to bind and to loose within the Christian community, but the emperor Constantine increased their judicial power by making them local magistrates with the power to resolve civil disputes.[289] Usually episcopal power was spoken of in terms of authority (ἐξουσία) rather than power, even though that Greek word would often later be translated as *potestas* rather than as *auctoritas*. Thus bishops had the power to forgive sins and the power to consecrate, but they recognized that this meant only that they had the authority to do certain rituals, whereas the effects of those rituals were produced by the power of God. For this reason, perhaps, there are no patristic writings about priestly powers, and even John Chrysostom's treatise on priesthood (περί ἱερωσῦνης), which mixes reflections on Christian ministry with references to priesthood in the Old Testament and the priesthood of Christ, speaks only briefly of priestly power as it would later be understood, and this mainly with regard to the power to forgive sins.[290]

Because the spiritual power of the clergy was universally accepted in the Christian Roman Empire, it was not contested by heretics or schismatics, and hence it did not draw the attention of patristic authors. Even heretics like Novatian, who taught that

---

287. See Bernard Cooke, *Ministry to Word and Sacrament* (Philadelphia: Fortress Press, 1976), 430.

288. See Schillebeeckx, ibid., 38–41. As we shall see below, Augustine was of a different opinion, but there is no evidence that his opinion was widespread during the patristic period.

289. See Cooke, *Ministry*, 428–431.

290. See John Chrysostom, *The Priesthood*, 3.6: "God gave to priests a power (ἐξουσίαν) greater than that given to our natural parents."

apostates could not be forgiven, and schismatics like Donatus, who taught that they had to be rebaptized, never questioned the fundamental assumption that God had given the church and its ministers the authority or power to forgive sins in baptism and penance, the authority or power to bestow ministerial orders, and the authority or power to offer the eucharistic sacrifice. In their minds, the question was always the proper exercise of such powers, not their existence.

We have already seen that Augustine sometimes referred to ordination as the sacrament of giving baptism, and so he claimed that neither baptism nor the right to give it (*jus dandi baptismi*) could be lost:

> Each is a sacrament and each is given to a person by a type of consecration, one by being baptized and one by being ordained, which is why neither is allowed to be repeated in the Catholic Church.[291]

> If an ordained man is removed from his office because of some wrongdoing, the sacrament of the Lord that was bestowed on him will not be lost, but it will remain to his discredit (*quamvis ad iudicium permanente*).[292]

Centuries later, when medieval universities were being founded and quotations from church fathers were being collected in books of theological opinions (*libri sententiarum*), sentences such as these could be invested with patristic authority. As we saw above, Augustine was arguing from the practice of not repeating church rituals to a reason that would make sense of the practice. The schoolmen would see in Augustine's reasoning not only a justification for not reordaining but a proof that ordination is a sacrament.

(5) Marriage

The understanding of marriage became increasingly Christianized during the fourth century and fifth centuries, but the celebration of marriage remained predominantly secular. People might ask a local presbyter (or the bishop, if the family was socially prominent) to bless a marriage, but such a blessing was regarded as an honor and not a necessity, and clerical blessings were not given when the moral character of one or both spouses was questionable.[293] In Rome, and perhaps in other places, the clergy became obliged to have their own marriages blessed, but this obligation did not extend to lay people.[294] In addition, prayers for the celebration of marriage began to appear in

---

291. Augustine, *Against the Letter of Parmenian*, 2.13.28. Parmenian was a Donatist bishop.

292. Augustine, *The Good of Marriage*, 24.32.

293. See Schillebeeckx, *Marriage*, 260–262.

294. See ibid., 255.

Roman liturgical books, but such nuptial masses took place apart from the wedding, which was still a family affair.[295]

Patristic letters and sermons on marriage were often concerned with affirming the goodness of marriage against the puritanical teachings of Christian sects such as the Montanists and against the dualistic views of other religions such as the Manicheans.[296] To support their claim, bishops pointed to the facts that marriage was instituted by God at the creation and that Jesus had shown approval of marriage by attending the wedding feast at Cana. They argued strenuously in favor of marital fidelity, citing the gospel texts in which Jesus condemns divorce.[297] For the most part, divorce was regarded as a sin, and an unjust divorce might require public repentance, but marriage was not regarded as indissoluble. Divorce was legal in the Roman Empire, even after Christianity was proclaimed the official religion of the state in 380.[298]

When the linguist and theologian Jerome produced the first Latin translation of the Old and New Testaments from their original Hebrew and Greek, he followed the tradition of translating μυστήριον as *sacramentum* which, like its Greek counterpart, could mean either a hidden reality or its symbol (usually a symbolic ritual). Translating Ephesians 5:32 he wrote, *Sacramentum hoc magnum est; ego autem dico in Christo et in ecclesia,* for the Greek, τὸ μυστήριον τοῦτο μέγα ἐστίν, ἐγὼ δὲ λέγω εἰς Χριστὸν καὶ εἰς τὴν ἐκκλησίαν —virtually a word for word rendition. It is clear that, in Jerome's mind, *sacramentum* did not mean a symbol but a mystery because in his commentary on that verse he explains that the relationship between Christ and the church is a *sacramentum,* but he does not refer to the husband-wife relationship as a *sacramentum.*[299] Jerome's contemporary, Augustine, went further and saw a *sacramentum* in both relationships.

According to Theodore Mackin, whose three-volume study of marriage, divorce and the sacrament of matrimony is the definitive work in English on the subject, Augustine's use of the word *sacramentum* was not consistent.[300] In this respect, however, Augustine was no different from other fourth-century Christians who wrote about marriage and Ephesians 5. Marriage was called a *mysterium* and a *sacramentum,* but never in the same way that baptism and eucharist were regarded as mysteries and sacraments.[301]

Like other bishops of his era, Augustine rose to the defense of marriage against its detractors in a number of writings, but most explicitly in *The Good of Marriage*

---

295. See Mackin, *Marital Sacrament*, 162.

296. See ibid., 250. Also Martos, *Doors to the Sacred*, 414–415.

297. See Mackin, ibid., 164–170.

298. See Theodore Mackin, *Divorce and Remarriage* (Mahwah, NJ: Paulist Press, 1984), ch. 4–7.

299. See Mackin, *Marital Sacrament*, 182–83.

300. Mackin found that Augustine used the following terms "diffusely and often interchangeably: *figura, allegoria, prophetia, velamen* (veil, screen), *symbolum, mysterium, sacramentum*." Ibid., 197.

301. See ibid., 191.

(*De bono conjugali*), written around 401. Toward the end of that work, he summarizes what he has argued are the benefits or goods of marriage, in contrast with fornication and concubinage. The first of these is *fides* or fidelity, which is lacking in more casual relationships. The second is *proles* or legitimate offspring, for children are either avoided or illegitimate in extra-marital affairs. These two are found in all marriages, says Augustine, but Christian marriages have a benefit that is not available to pagans, namely, a *sacramentum*.[302]

As already indicated, however, Augustine is not very clear about what he means by this term, having referred to it earlier as a certain sacrament or a kind of sacrament (*quoddam sacramentum*), which remains even after divorce.[303] Later, Augustine argues that marriage in the church creates a sort of nuptial sacrament that cannot be dissolved unless one of the spouses dies.[304] But shortly thereafter he claims that the *sacramentum* is found only in monogamous first marriages and not at all in a second marriage, even if it takes place after a spouse's death. The logic behind this claim is that the *sacramentum* is an image of the singular relationship between the one Christ and the one church, and it can be such only between a man or woman and his or her first spouse.[305] Finally, Augustine ascribes a certain holiness to the *sacramentum*, which makes it indissoluble. According to Mackin,

> An effect of this holiness is that not only may one spouse not desert the other, but no desertion by either for whatever motive has the power to dissolve the marriage. Because of the *sacramentum*, or of its holiness, Christian spouses are married to one another until at least one of them dies.[306]

Like Mackin, we have been using the Latin word *sacramentum* instead of an English translation because, as was noted earlier, Augustine's use of the word is ambiguous, so one has to infer its meaning in each case from the context in which it is used. This is a good place to point out, however, that in the few cases cited here (where *sacramentum* clearly does not mean prefigurement, analogy or symbol) the word can easily refer to a mystery, a hidden reality that is somehow received by married people if they are Christians but not if they are pagans. Augustine is therefore not thinking of this hidden reality as a marital sacrament in the same way that the scholastics did

---

302. See Augustine, *The Good of Marriage*, 24.32. For other arguments in favor of marriage, see *The Literal Meaning of Genesis*, 9.7.12 and *Original Sin*, 2.9.

303. See Augustine, *The Good of Marriage*, 7.7; also Mackin, ibid., 216.

304. See Augustine, ibid., 15.17: *Semel autem initum connubium in civitate Dei nostri, ubi etiam ex prima duorum hominum copula quoddam sacramentum nuptiae gerunt, nullo modo potest nisi alicuius eorum morte dissolvi.*

305. See Augustine, ibid., 17.20; also Mackin, ibid., 217. Curiously, Augustine does not cite Ephesians 5:32 in any of his discussions about the sacrament that he believes is found in a Christian marriage, so it cannot be argued that his reasoning was based on a misreading of that passage.

306. Mackin, ibid., 218. See Augustine, ibid., 24.32.

centuries later. But this did not prevent them, when they read these Augustinian texts, from thinking that he meant what they meant by the word.

Almost twenty years after writing *The Good of Marriage*, Augustine again took up the question of marital relationships. Like many patristic writings, they are occasional pieces, written for a specific occasion—in this case, responding to questions that had been put to him as the bishop of Hippo and, by now, a locally well known theologian. The first of these pieces, *Adulterous Marriages* (*De conjugiis adulterinis*), gave a lengthy answer to the question of divorce, which was still an unresolved moral issue in the late Roman Empire. Despite the title, Augustine's concern is not with adulterous affairs but with remarriage—which Jesus in the synoptic gospels calls sinful. He argues primarily from New Testament texts that deal with divorce and remarriage, but he buttresses these proof texts with the idea he introduced decades before, namely, that in a Christian marriage there is a something which, like the baptismal character, can never be lost.[307]

The occasion for Augustine's final work on marriage, *Marriage and Concupiscence* (*De nuptiis et concupiscentiae*), was a slanderous charge that he regarded marriage as evil. What he had actually written was that marriage makes good use of the evil of concupiscence—Augustine's word of choice for selfish desire, especially in sexual matters. Never one for succinct refutations, Augustine used the accusation as an opportunity to compose a lengthy essay setting forth his views on many matters pertaining to marriage.

At one point, Augustine presents a short list of things that make marriage good:

> Fertility makes marriage good; its fruit is offspring. Chastity makes marriage good; its bond is fidelity. And a certain *sacramentum* also makes it good where the marriage is of Christians.[308]

He goes on to say that the reality or substance of the sacrament (*sacramenti res*) is such that men and women who are joined in marriage remain inseparable as long as they live, and they are not allowed even to separate from their spouse unless one of them commits adultery (*excepta causa fornicationis*).[309] Nonetheless, even though he is adamant about the effect of the *sacramentum*, he never fully clarifies what it is.

> So firmly does a certain conjugal something (*quiddam conjugale*) remain between the spouses while they both live, that neither separation nor union with

307. See Augustine, *Adulterous Marriages*, 2.5. Mackin notes that in the earlier work, Augustine said that it is the marital *sacramentum* which remains as long as both partners are alive, whereas in this later work, it is the marital bond that cannot be broken unless one of them dies. Augustine nowhere identifies the *sacramentum* with the *vinculum*—another instance of his lack of concern for terminological preciseness—but this ambiguity made it possible for the scholastics to identify the two.

308. Augustine, *Marriage and Concupiscence*, 1.10.11 (Mackin's translation). See also another summary in 1.17.19.

309. Ibid. Augustine interpreted the exception for πορνεία in Mt 5:32 as permitting separation but not divorce and remarriage in cases of marital infidelity.

another can remove it . . . just as the soul of an apostate, deserting as it were its marriage with Christ, even though it loses its faith it does not lose the *sacramentum* of faith that it received in baptism. If he lost the *sacramentum*, it would without doubt be restored to him provided he returned. But in fact he keeps it, unto the increase of his punishment, not for the earning of his reward.[310]

Here Augustine emphasizes the similarity between the marital *sacramentum* and the baptismal *sacramentum* about which he had written decades earlier. Yet just as he had to resort to similes and analogies when writing about the permanent effect of being baptized, likening it to a brand or a tattoo, so here he argues that there is a permanent effect of being married. In some places he says that it is a marital bond but he never consistently identifies the *sacramentum* with that.

How could Augustine be so sure that there has to be an invisible reality that unites Christians in marriage for life? It is because he read the scriptures literally, and he took the gospel prohibitions of divorce at face value.

We saw earlier that Augustine was convinced that there had to be a reason why the church did not rebaptize apostates and heretics. If the church is led by God, he believed, then its practices have to be correct and there has to be an explanation for their correctness. Similarly, if the scriptures are inspired by God, he believed, then what they say is true and there has to be an explanation for why they are true. In the case of baptism, the traditional talk of giving and receiving baptism led him to the insight that there has to be a baptism that is received, one that is permanent like a brand or tattoo. In the case of marriage, the gospel prohibitions of divorce led him to the insight that something similar must also be at work.

Such thinking is scientific in an elementary sort of way. Medical science, even in the ancient world, assumed that symptoms have causes. Just as health can be attributed to healthy eating and living habits, so aches and pains, fevers and irregularities must be attributable to some causes such as bad food or an imbalance in the body's humors. Classical physics and astronomy likewise tried to explain why objects fall, why some heavenly bodies change their position in the sky, and so on. Moreover, this assumption was at work at the beginning of modern science during the seventeenth century Enlightenment as well. The observation that a candle goes out after being covered by a bell jar led to the discovery of oxygen. The observation that a prism can split sunlight into different colors led to the discovery of light waves. The scientific mind looks at something and says there has to be a reason for it. Augustine's mind worked the same way.

The second step in modern scientific reasoning is to pose a theory or hypothesis for the observed phenomenon. The third step is to verify the proposed explanation by adjusting variables (e.g., seeing if two candles go out twice as fast as one, or adjusting the shape of the prism) and by having the explanation tested by other individuals. But

310. Ibid. (Mackin's translation)

ancient science, unlike modern science, had not yet realized these later steps should be part of a scientific method. Instead, it relied on plausibility and authority. The idea that the sun and moon circled the earth fit the observed data, and it was supported by the authority of the Bible. The notion that heavy objects fall faster than light ones was plausible, and it was supported by the authority of Aristotle, the Greek polymath who theorized about almost everything in the visible world. In patristic theology, therefore, explanations were regarded as plausible if they fit the data of scripture and tradition, and they were believed if they came from someone in authority. The practice of mystagogical catechesis is a perfect example of this. Bishops gave differing explanations about the Trinity, the church, baptism, ordination, marriage, and so one, but if they were plausible they could be confidently accepted by the faithful who recognized the authority of their bishop. Not until different theologies came in contact with one another was there any thought that a particular explanation might be incorrect.

The centuries-long conflict between the Donatist bishops in north Africa and the Catholic bishops (of which Augustine was one) illustrates how theological debates could not be resolved on the basis of plausibility and authority alone. Despite the plausibility of his arguments, Augustine's theology of baptism was never accepted by those who did not recognize his authority. In medieval Europe, however, Augustine's authority would be unquestioned and his explanation for why baptism, ordination and marriage are not repeated would become a central concept in scholastic sacramental theology.

d. Summary and Conclusion

In the Christianized Roman Empire, baptismal initiation began by being a long catechumenate that concluded with a ritual immersion and anointing, followed by a first participation in the eucharistic liturgy. As time went on, however, this sequence got reversed and initiates received (note the word) the sacraments of baptism, confirmation and eucharist, after which they were instructed in the meaning of those mysteries. Mystagogical catechesis, however, used the theological language associated with the rituals (e.g., baptism brings new life and the remission of sins, the laying on of hands is for reception of the Holy Spirit, and the eucharistic elements are the body and blood of Christ), so the meanings became increasingly spiritualized and the thinking about them became increasingly magical. This same dynamic can be observed in the history of public repentance, which had been a lengthy process of reconversion and recommitment before 312, but which slowly became a legalistic ritual that was often postponed until the last minute so that sins could be forgiven without lives having to be changed. Anointing of the sick continued to be something practiced by the laity, although it was sometimes done with oil blessed by a bishop. Likewise, marriage continued to be a lay-led ritual, although bishops increasingly applied scriptural passages (interpreted literally) to marriage and divorce. Ministry, however, became increasingly clericalized, and the laying on of hands that had originally been understood as a blessing got interpreted as an ordination, that is, as an initiation into a ministerial order. These practices remained fairly stable or evolved relatively slowly in the eastern half of the empire, and within five centuries the eastern church split from the west and called itself Orthodox Christianity. But the church in the west, as we shall see, experienced enormous changes as a result of the barbarian invasions and the collapse of the Roman infrastructure.

4. Sacraments in the Dark Ages

Church history books often date the beginning of the Middle Ages from the papacy of Gregory the Great (590–604), but from the perspective of this study, the last year that there was an emperor in the west (476) makes more sense. The early Middle Ages are sometimes called the Dark Ages, not because the sun shone any less, but because the intellectual light that had illuminated Christian beliefs and practices during the patristic period was severely dimmed. Augustine was the last patristic theologian of any stature in the west, and he died in 430.

It could be argued that the eastern part of the empire did not have a medieval period, a period in the middle between the ancient and the modern worlds, for its culture remained largely intact even though its size was continually shrinking. Its self-confidence was severely shaken in 1204 when Constantinople was looted by crusaders who needed extra money to pay for the ships that were taking them to the Holy Land. But the so-called Byzantine Empire and its successor states maintained their cultural identity until conquered by the Ottoman Turks in 1453. By that time in the west, the Renaissance was ushering in the modern era, but in the east, Muslim culture remained scientifically and technologically an extension of ancient Mediterranean culture. Orthodox Christianity continued to produce theologians of great stature in the style of the Greek fathers of the church, but its organizational structure and liturgical style continued largely unchanged. The modern world did not intrude on the Near East (which today is called the Middle East) until the twentieth century, when the Ottoman Empire was carved up and subjected to the rule of its European conquerors in the aftermath of World War I.

If anything, Pope Gregory was the first leader of the western church to size up the new situation correctly and to start reshaping Latin Christianity into what would eventually become Roman Catholicism. Having been a monk himself, he persuaded monks to become missionaries to the barbarians of Europe, which eventually led to the continent's religious if not political unification. Monks were celibate because they lived in community with other men, and their example was influential in establishing a belief in celibacy for the clergy. Gregory also began a simplification of the liturgy from the elaborate ceremonies of the patristic era to a simpler style of worship that fit both the Roman temperament and the somewhat diminished papal purse. Simplified even further, mass books could be carried by missionaries into the heart of Europe. Perhaps indicative of what was to come, he wrote more than any other pope in the next five centuries, and although he is was an able administrator, his writings are those of a rather limited theologian.[311]

Gregory began what was to continue for the next half millennium, namely, adaptation of the church's rituals to the social realities and pastoral needs of a rural agrarian culture. In medieval Christendom, baptism became infant baptism, confirmation became a separate rite, the eucharistic liturgy became the mass, public reconciliation was replaced by private confession, anointing of the sick became extreme unction, ordination split into seven holy orders, and matrimony became an ecclesiastical ritual. As far as can be determined (for written records from this period are scanty), none of these changes resulted from extensive theological reflection. For the most part, the theology of these rituals was to be found in the words of the rites themselves, supplemented with scriptural and patristic phrases such as "baptism is necessary for salvation" and "whoever divorces and remarries commits adultery." What these words originally meant was not retrievable, so they were invested with meanings that made sense in the new cultural context.

a. Baptism

The normal age for baptism had been going down in the later patristic period, as evidenced by the questions about infant baptism that Augustine attempted to answer with his theory of an original sin that was inherited by all the descendants of Adam and Eve. Nonetheless, baptisms were still held annually, usually at Easter and in some places on the feast of Pentecost, but since infant mortality was high, provision was made for the emergency baptism of babies who were sick and in danger of dying.

The Germanic tribes that invaded Italy and the more northern areas of Europe were led by chieftains who made decisions for all in the group—whether to migrate, whether to settle down, and whether to worship a new god. Their baptism was a simple water ritual with neither catechumenate nor mystagogical catechesis, so it was undergone without much understanding of the teachings of Christ or the demands of Christian morality. But even the remnants of the old empire were impressive to hunter-gatherers, and the missionaries preached with a courage and conviction that made the Roman religion plausible.

The absence of bishops in many mission lands made the separation of clerical baptism from episcopal confirmation a common occurrence. The city of Milan and much of the Iberian peninsula adopted the eastern practice of allowing priests to administer oil blessed by the bishop, but in the rest of Europe initiation into the faith was through baptism alone.

---

311. Such is the appraisal of Norman F. Cantor in *The Civilization of the Middle Ages* (New York: Harper Collins, 1993), 157.

These developments were driven by necessity and ingenuity—the necessity of bringing the faith to all and finding creative ways to do that. If driven by any theological ideas at all, they would have been a magical appreciation of the effects of baptism: the reception of the Holy Spirit, forgiveness of sins, and salvation in the afterlife. Since being blessed by the bishop afterward promised no such rewards, it was easily neglected.[312]

b. Confirmation

The eighth century witnessed the expansion of the kingdom of the Franks under Charles Martel, Pepin the Short, and Charles the Great, or Charlemagne, who did his best to establish a northern European empire in the image of the former Roman one. Besides founding schools and importing scholars from distant monasteries, Charlemagne insisted that the Catholic rituals in his lands be modeled on those used in the city of Rome, which at the time used an imposition of hands rather than an anointing with oil in the rite of confirmation. Baptisms could easily be confirmed if the bishop lived nearby, but since roads were almost nonexistent in the continental forests, most children were never brought to the bishop.

For centuries, the church had been the largest institution in Europe, but the rise of feudal kingdoms began to threaten episcopal prerogatives. Charlemagne, for instance, wanted to collect revenue from church lands, but he agreed to follow ecclesiastical laws from the old Roman Empire in his new Holy Roman Empire. Some of the documentation needed by the French bishops to protect their privileges could be found in monastery libraries, but others could not, so the creative bishops resorted to a clever bit of falsification. Isidore of Seville, a seventh century bishop in Spain, had been widely regarded as a scholar, which is why, when clerics working for the bishops "discovered" a collection of ancient imperial and papal decretals (some of which were in fact genuine), they attributed it to a certain Isidore. Among these was the Donation of Constantine, which showed that the emperor in the fourth century had given the pope dominion over the western half of the Roman Empire. Other documents demonstrated that church lands were exempt from taxation, that bishops had certain privileges, and so on.[313]

Not content with finding precedents for secular legislation, the bishops also tried to bolster various church practices with similar discoveries. Among these were directives from third century popes insisting on the necessity of confirmation to receive the fullness of the Holy Spirit and to be strengthened for spiritual combat. These ideas about confirmation were actually from a sermon by a fifth century bishop named Faustus of Riez hoping to persuade parents to have their children confirmed, but they

---

312. See Milner, *Theology of Confirmation*, 42–49; also Martos, *Doors to the Sacred*, 183–85.

313. Needless to say, the Donation of Constantine and other documents were later found to be spurious.

turned out to be no more persuasive in the ninth century than they had been in the fifth. What the false decretals did do, however, was give scholastics in the twelfth century a rich vein of ideas from which to mine a theology of confirmation.[314]

c. Eucharist

Whereas bishops in the early patristic period did not use written texts when presiding at community worship, bishops in the fourth and fifth centuries came to rely on words that were written out for them to read. In the east, liturgies attributed to John Chrysostom and Basil the Great were used then and are still used in Orthodox churches. In the west, collections of texts were often attributed to popes, perhaps to suggest their importance, but in the absence of corroborating information, scholars are forced to speculate about who wrote the prayers and to make educated guesses about when and where they were compiled.

The oldest of the western sacramentaries was attributed to Pope Leo I (d. 461) but it dates from somewhere in the seventh century. Only part of it remains, and it is not a true ceremonial book but a collection of prayers for use on various occasions. An early eighth century sacramentary was attributed to Pope Gelasius I (d. 496), but the text itself contains liturgical prayers of both Roman and Frankish origin. A late eighth century work known as the Gregorian Sacramentary was sent to Charlemagne for use in his empire by Pope Adrian (or Hadrian) I, but the copies that remain contain Frankish interpolations and parts of the original may not have been preserved in the extant manuscripts, so it is impossible to fully reconstruct the original text.[315]

In these books, the eucharistic liturgy is referred to in Latin as *missa*, whence the English word "mass." The precise origin of this word is lost in history, but the first edition of the *Catholic Encyclopedia* suggests that it is an instance of synecdoche, a figure of speech that allows something to be named by one of its parts, for example, referring to a car as wheels or calling a sailor a hand.[316] Since the patristic era, Christian worship included two dismissals, a dismissal of catechumens after the scripture readings and sermon, and a dismissal of the faithful after communion. The Roman liturgy ended with the words, *Ite, missa est,* which can be translated literally as "Go, it is the dismissal," but to medieval ears not fully conversant in Latin, it could sound like "Go, it is the mass." In any event, in medieval and modern times, the primary form of Catholic worship was called the mass. The word "liturgy" returned to scholarly use during the liturgical movement of the late nineteenth and early twentieth centuries, and it entered popular usage only after the Second Vatican Council.

---

314. See Milner, *Theology of Confirmation*, 53–65. Also Martos, *Doors to the Sacred*, 219–23.

315. See Josef Jungmann, *The Mass of the Roman Rite: Its Origins and Development (Missarum Solemnia)* (New York: Benziger Brothers, 1950), Vol. 1, 63.

316. See "Mass, Sacrifice of the" in *The Catholic Encyclopedia* (New York: Robert Appleton, 1910), Vol. 10, 6; also Vol. 9, 790–792.

Coincident with the introduction of the word *missa* was its association with the word *sacrificium*, as in *sacrificium missae* or sacrifice of the mass. Peruse any of the sacramentaries mentioned above, and it is clear that the mass was seen as a sacrifice that was offered by a priest to God.[317]

Also shrouded in darkness is how the Latin *eucharistia*, a transliteration of the Greek εὐχαριστία, morphed in meaning. The Greek word had meant thanksgiving and it referred to what Christians did when they worshiped. Now the Latin word became a proper noun—the Eucharist, also the Blessed Eucharist or the Most Holy Eucharist—and it referred to the consecrated elements that were offered to God and distributed to the faithful during the mass.[318]

It is important to realize that these developments in language, like many of the ritual developments in the Dark Ages, just happened. They were not decreed by popes and councils. They were not discussed and decided by theologians. Their evolution can be documented, but why these and other words evolved as they did is a puzzle that will never be solved, given the linguistic data that are available in medieval manuscripts. No one argued that Christian worship should be called the mass or that the consecrated bread and wine should be called the Eucharist. Nonetheless, these altered meanings became, in part, the foundation on which the elaborate edifice of scholastic sacramental theology was built.

Our main concern is with the language of sacramental theology, but to understand the meaning of the words that were used by the scholastics, it is vital to understand what the users of the words were referring to. What they had in mind was a form of worship that was drastically different from the episcopal liturgies about which patristic authors had written. Very likely, what they thought of as the mass was not the elaborate rites of the aforementioned sacramentaries, but the mass that was celebrated by missionary monks and parish priests. Indeed, it may have been the mass that they themselves offered, probably daily, since all of the medieval Catholic theologians were priests.

Briefly, then, the typical mass in the Middle Ages was a ritual performed in Latin for a congregation that did not, for the most part, understand Latin. The altar was not free-standing but placed against one wall, perhaps a remnant of the time when small

317. For example, in the Gelasian Sacramentary, the canon or fixed part of mass refers to the bread and wine as "these gifts, these presents, these holy and unblemished sacrificial offerings," and asks God to remember those "who themselves offer up this sacrifice of praise" as well as those on whose behalf this sacrifice is offered. Translation by R. O'Connell and H. Finberg in Palmer, *Sacraments and Worship*, 63. A perusal of the Latin text reveals many places where what is being offered to God is called a sacrifice. See H. A. Wilson, ed., *Liber Sacramentorum Romanae Ecclesiae* (Oxford: Clarendon Press, 1894), reissued in a facsimile edition as *The Gelasian Sacramentary* under the auspices of the Harvard College Library in 2003. An electronic scan of this edition on the internet reveals that the word *eucharistia* is not found in any of the Gelasian prayer texts.

318. It is possible that the early Latin translators of Greek patristic texts did not understand the meaning of εὐχαριστία, which is why they transliterated it. This still happens when early Christian texts are translated from Greek to English: offering the thanksgiving becomes offering the eucharist.

chapels were crowded with recent converts and the use of space had to be maximized. What had once been a dialogue between celebrant and congregation in a language known to both was now a dialogue between priest and mass server in an unknown tongue. If no server was available, the priest could recite both parts. The ritual could even be performed in solitude, with no one at all in attendance. The constant or common parts of the mass were probably memorized from frequent repetition, while the changing or proper parts—prayers of the day or season, scripture readings, and responsorial psalms—were read from a missal. The priest performed these rites with his back to the congregation and in a voice that was not necessarily audible. Nor was there ordinarily any sermon or homily. After the bread and wine were brought to the altar, prayers of offering referred not to the consecrated elements but to what they would become—the Eucharist, the body and blood of Christ. Bending over the bread first and then the wine, the priest recited the words of Christ at the last supper: *Hoc est enim corpus meum* and *Hic est enim calix sanguinis mei*. When the priest genuflected and lifted the consecrated elements over his head so they could be seen by the worshipers behind him, a bell was rung to call attention to the sacred transformation that had just taken place. After additional prayers and remembrances, the priest consumed the eucharistic bread and wine at the altar. Communion was not regularly offered to the laity, and when it was, it was given only in the form of bread. At the end, he turned to those in attendance and said, *Ite, missa est.*[319]

This religious ritual, repeated weekly and even daily, was offered without interpretation, for in a sense everyone knew what it meant: the priest was offering Christ to God the Father, just as the Son had offered himself to the Father on the cross for the redemption of humankind. It was a re-presentation in the here and now of the sacred moment in which Christ had wrought the salvation of the world. With the meaning of the mass being taken for granted, and with no one raising questions about it, there was virtually no theological activity about it during the Dark Ages.

There was one exception to this. In the ninth century monastery of Corbie, north of Paris, Abbot Paschase Radbert wrote *The Body and Blood of the Lord* (*De corpore et sanguine Domini*)at the request of another abbot who wanted to teach his monks about this mystery of the faith. He explained that, even though the consecrated elements did not have the appearance (*figura*) of flesh and blood, in truth (*veritas*) God transforms the bread and wine into the same natural body and blood of Christ that had ascended into heaven. About ten years later, a monk in the same monastery composed another work with the same name, but giving a different explanation. According to Ratramnus, the consecrated elements are not the actual body and blood of Christ; nevertheless, the invisible reality (*invisibilis substantia*) of Christ's body and blood is present, even though they look like bread and wine.[320] These divergent views appar-

---

319. See Martos, *Doors to the Sacred*, 263–68. For more detail, see Jungmann, *Mass of the Roman Rite*, 74–126.

320. See Macy, *Banquet's Wisdom*, 28–30.

ently stirred no controversy at the time; they were simply different ways of explaining the Catholic faith.

d. Penance

By the sixth century, public repentance (with the exception of deathbed reconciliation) had almost disappeared from Catholic ritual life. In the westernmost missionary lands, however, a new penitential practice was being introduced by Irish monks who had not been taught that only bishops could reconcile sinners to God. Initially, it was a form of spiritual training for novice monks who needed help in living up to the demands of the gospel and the monastic rule, but it was later extended to lay people as a means of consolation and reparation for those burdened with the guilt of sin. It entailed confessing one's sins to a spiritual father who assigned appropriate works of repentance (e.g., fasting to counteract gluttony, making restitution for stolen goods, or practicing sexual abstinence to work against sins of the flesh) for a period of time. At the end of that time, he assured the penitent of God's forgiveness.

Individual bishops and regional councils objected to this innovation on a number of counts. Not only were people confessing their sins to monks (many of whom would not have been priests) instead of to bishops, but they were confessing minor sins as well as major ones, and they were able to do this time and again instead of only once in a lifetime. Despite the protests of the hierarchy, private confession spread throughout Europe, and by the middle of the seventh century it was being commended in some places as a helpful spiritual practice, at least if it was done by priests.[321]

It was never understood that confessors forgave sins. Rather, as in the older system of public repentance, they made a judgment based on the sincerity of the penitent and the completion of the penitential works that the sinner was forgiven by God and could therefore be readmitted to communion, that is, if the sin had been serious enough to warrant exclusion from the Eucharist. As time went on, however, confessors began to absolve penitents from any undone works of penance in the event that the penitent would die before being readmitted to the altar, the idea being that the person would not have to die with the guilt of sin still on their soul. This was a somewhat magical idea, to be sure, but it made sense in a world in which people believed that the salvation of their soul could hang on the judgment of a religious authority.

It should also be noted that, apart from the understanding that God forgives the repentant sinner, there was no theological explanation of the transition from public to private penitential rites, nor was there any well-developed theology of the practice of

---

321. Nevertheless, confession to lay monks continued into the thirteenth century, as did the confession of nuns to abbesses, despite attempts by some bishops to give priests exclusive control over the practice. See Gary Macy, *The Hidden History of Women's Ordination* (New York: Oxford University Press, 2008), 41, 51, 82–83, 86.

private confession. As with many other church rituals, the practice developed first and the theological interpretation came later.[322]

e. Extreme Unction

During the Dark Ages, anointing the sick became a clerical prerogative and evolved into an anointing of the dying. Moreover, this anointing gradually got postponed until shortly before death, hence the name, *extrema unctio*, or last anointing.

Until the eighth century, anointing the sick was a widespread if not uniform practice. It was sometimes done by people for their relatives, by monks, nuns and priests, and also by men and women with a reputation for healing. The oil used was sometimes blessed by a bishop, but not always, and blessed water could also be used. In a world without many medical alternatives, people used any means available to find healing for themselves and their loved ones.

In England, the Venerable Bede wrote a commentary on the Epistle of James and assumed that James 5:14–15 referred to the priestly practice that was known to him.[323] Also, when Charlemagne received for a copy of the Gregorian Sacramentary, his clerics told him that it did not contain a rite for anointing the sick, so he ordered a priestly ritual to be inserted when copies of the sacramentary were made for use in the Holy Roman Empire. At the time, there was no such clerical ritual in Rome, but when copies of the expanded sacramentary were sent to Italy a few centuries later, the Frankish ritual became a Roman ritual.

During those intervening centuries, moreover, the Frankish ritual had become an anointing of the dying. The ninth century reformers who tried to promote the rite of confirmation also tried to promote anointing of the sick by the clergy, but the clerical rite of anointing called for the sick to be brought into a church and to be prayed over by a number of priests. Both the cost of multiple stipends and the difficulty in transporting the bedridden led the laity to attempt other remedies before resorting to the ecclesiastical one, and as a result, most people who were anointed in church died shortly afterward. Copyists, noticing the anomaly of prayers for healing in such circumstances, gradually substituted prayers commending the soul to God instead. In this way, the final anointing became one of the church's last rites, along with confession and viaticum.[324]

---

322. See Martos, *Doors to the Sacred*, 335–41; also Poschmann, *Penance*, 122–45.

323. We have already seen that *presbyteres* were becoming regarded as *sacerdotes* because the Christian worship was increasing regarded as a sacrifice, which was a priestly duty. By the eighth century, all New Testament references to presbyters were regarded as speaking about Catholic priests.

324. See Martos, *Doors to the Sacred*, 383–86; also Poschmann, *Penance*, 242–49

f. Ordination

Although ecclesiastical ranks or holy orders could be found in the church since the fourth century, rituals investing people with the authority to perform certain tasks were not yet perceived as sacramental except in the broad sense of being sacred and symbolic.[325] The disintegration of organizational structures affected both secular and ecclesiastical governance. Europe during the Dark Ages transitioned from being organized along classic imperial lines to being organized into a somewhat fluid feudal system of ever-shifting alliances between lords and overlords who dominated whatever territories they could conquer and control. In the midst of this system, the lord bishops sometimes ruled over their own vassals, but more often than not they ruled at the behest of the nobles who appointed them.

Although chosen by secular authorities, bishops were still ordained by other bishops, and this bifurcation of power in medieval society eventually led to political tensions on a large scale as kings consolidated their power over the state and popes consolidated their power over the church. Secular rulers viewed the church as a branch of civil government (as did Constantine and other Roman emperors), whereas powerful bishops (especially the pope in Rome) saw the state as subject to the laws of God and the authority of the church. Except for monasteries and cathedrals, however, church buildings and clerical salaries were supplied and maintained with funds from the landed gentry or lay confraternities. There being no concept of pastoral care, priestly duties were limited to ritual functions such as baptizing the newborn, offering the sacrifice of the mass, and presiding over funerals. This was clearly not a full-time occupation, so most priests supported their families by farming or practicing a trade.[326]

Lesser tensions between secular and religious authorities and also between bishops and clergy arose from the fact that money in the form of coinage was scarce and therefore land constituted the only real wealth in the early Middle Ages. Married priests who farmed rural lands often wanted their sons to inherit property which a local noble or bishop viewed as rightfully theirs. Practical concerns such as this, and the Old Testament precedent that temple priests refrained from sexual activity when they served at the altar, plus the monastic ideal of total dedication to God gave growing support to the concept of clerical celibacy. Even when local councils ordered priests to practice sexual restraint, however, they had no realistic way to enforce their mandates.[327]

Holy orders at this point in time included not only the episcopacy and the presbyerate but also lower clerical ranks such as the diaconate and subdiaconate, which were now viewed as transitional and preparatory to priestly ordination. Abbots were

---

325. Although Augustine had referred to ordination as a sacrament, at this time the works of this north African bishop were not widely known in Europe.

326. See Cooke, *Ministry*, 362–66.

327. See Anne Llewellyn Barstow, *Married Priests and the Reforming Papacy: The Eleventh Century Debates* (New York: Edwin Mellen Press, 1982), ch. 1; also Martos, *Doors to the Sacred*, 494–96.

also ordained, even if they remained lay brothers, as were abbesses who ruled over monasteries of nuns. In some respects, abbots and abbesses had power and authority similar to that of bishops; in other respects, they had duties and responsibilities similar to those of priests. All of this indicates that ordination was still regarded as an elevation to a sacred order rather than as a bestowal of specifically priestly power.[328]

g. Marriage

The hierarchy did not gain control over marriages in Europe until the twelfth century, but during the Dark Ages Christendom was slowly moving in that direction. At work from the sixth to the tenth centuries were a clash between Roman law and Germanic customs, the possibility of secret or clandestine marriage, and the desire of nobles (always men) to divorce and remarry for political or carnal reasons. In the absence of a central civil authority such as had existed under the Roman imperium, bishops were often asked to decide cases of marriage, divorce, inheritance, etc. in the hope that they would less biased than civil rulers in these matters.

According to Roman law, a marriage was created by consent between the spouses, and before Christianity began to exert its influence in the empire, a divorce could result from the withdrawal of marital consent by either party. Bishops in the Christianized empire struggled to restrict the grounds for legal divorce, but they accepted without question the notion that a marriage began when a man and woman vowed fidelity to one another. Parents who wanted to have a greater say in their children's marital future might appeal to a bishop, arguing that the children did not have their consent to marry. According to Germanic custom, on the other hand, marriage was an arrangement between families, not between individuals. In northern European tribes, children were betrothed (often at an early age) by parents (usually the fathers) until they were old enough to start their own families, so the marriage officially came into existence only when the bride was handed over to the groom and they performed their first act of sexual intercourse. Betrothed youngsters who had heard of Roman customs might try to get out of their parents' arrangement by pronouncing wedding vows with someone with whom they had fallen in love, and then appealing to the bishop to recognize their marriage.[329]

Related to what has just been said is the fact that no public ceremony, not even a civil one, was needed to create a marriage under Roman law. Thus, in addition to the above-mentioned situations, problems could arise if a couple started living together, and then one of them left the home claiming that they had never actually married by

---

328. See Macy, *Hidden History*, ch. 2.

329. These cultural paradigms and marriage cases are simplifications, but they reflect the broad lines of what was going on during the early Middle Ages. For a more detailed account, see Mackin, *What is Marriage?* 145–52.

vowing fidelity to each other. The injured party might gather testimony to the contrary and appeal to the local bishop for a decision.[330]

Because the Gospel According to Matthew (5:32 and 19:9) offers an exception to Christ's command not to put away one's spouse, men readily divorced adulterous wives and then remarried. But what if the adultery was only suspected and not proven? Or what if the wife charged that her husband had lied about her in order to marry someone else? Appeal might be made to an episcopal court to decide the matter.[331]

Other sorts of cases arose as well. What if a husband were captured in battle or a wife were abducted by marauders? When, if ever, could they be presumed dead so that the other spouse could remarry? And what about the status of children or property after a divorce? Into whose possession should they be given? Over time, as cases were decided, a body of case law developed, and afterwards decisions and decrees where gathered into collections in episcopal libraries. Moreover, the higher the social status of the appellants, the higher would be the court to which they appealed, and even if they did not appeal directly to Rome, a bishop might write to the pope for advice. Thus, even though there was as yet no church wedding ceremony, the church was becoming increasingly involved with questions surrounding the nature and consequences of marriage.[332]

h. Summary and Conclusion

While Christian rituals in the east continued to evolve slowly into today's Orthodox liturgies, ritual life in the Latin west underwent a radical transformation as Catholics grappled with the collapse of Roman civilization and the imposition of Germanic culture on Europe. At the time, the changes in ritual must have seemed gradual—adaptations to new pastoral needs each time a sacramentary was copied for use by the next generation—but when telescoped into a brief narrative covering 500 years, the changes are remarkable. Although the average age for baptism had been coming down in the late Roman Empire, by the time of the Holy Roman Empire baptism was used exclusively for infants (except for when it was used for the forced conversion of conquered pagan tribes). The bishop's post-baptismal anointing became a separated ritual and was given a new name, but it fell into general disuse nonetheless. The lengthy and elaborate eucharistic liturgy, performed as a public work by bishops (and eventually by presbyters) in huge basilicas with torches and processions, gold vestments and vessels, incense and choirs, was stripped to its bare essentials so that it could be done by a single priest, even with no assistants if necessary, in an outdoor clearing or a crude chapel. The process of public repentance, supervised by bishops, governed by canons and available only once in a lifetime slowly disappeared and was replaced with

---

330. See Martos, *Doors to the Sacred*, 427–28; also Mackin, *Marital Sacrament*, 255–56.

331. For greater detail, see Mackin, *Divorce and Remarriage*, 228–48.

332. See ibid., 252–60.

a process of private confession to a priest, invented by pastoral insight and available as often as needed. The practice of anointing the sick was forbidden to the laity and entrusted to priests, after which it became a last anointing of the dying. Ordination continued to be a rite of passage for entrance into ministerial orders as well as initiation into monastic leadership. And although the wedding remained a family ritual, marriage and its consequences were becoming increasingly subject to ecclesiastical scrutiny and supervision.

As has already been noted, these developments took place largely with little theological justification and without any ecclesiastical regulation except for what could be exercised within a small geographical region. Even Charlemagne's attempt to legislate for his entire Holy Roman Empire was short lived, for after his death his patrimony was divided among his three sons. But the seeds of a consistent theological reflection on a loosely uniform liturgical practice had already been planted.

5. Sacraments in the High Middle Ages

Western culture lay dormant for roughly half a millennium until the year 1000, which saw the last major Viking raid on continental Europe.[333] For centuries, Europeans had lived near walled castles or cities in which they might take refuge from the pillaging Northmen, but as the danger lessened and temperatures became more mild, farming increased, the population grew, and cities expanded beyond their fortified boundaries. The missionary efforts begun by Gregory I in the seventh century had at last succeeded in converting the barbarians from paganism to Christianity, at least nominally. Monks who had preserved agricultural methods that had been common centuries earlier taught these methods to peasants whose forest-dwelling forebears had been hunter-gatherers. In addition, monks who had copied and recopied the literature of the past now opened libraries and schools to study those manuscripts, and bishops soon followed suit by establishing cathedral schools. In time, city schools merged together into larger institutions where the entire universe of knowledge could be accessed—the first universities. Founded in 1088, the University of Bologna specialized in civil and canon law. Other universities also became centers of specialized studies even though each of them also taught the liberal arts, so called because language and mathematics courses provided the thinking skills that liberated the mind. Padua was famous for the study of medicine, Oxford and Cambridge for the study of philosophy, and Paris for the study of theology. The eleventh century saw the start of what is sometimes called the medieval renaissance, a rediscovery of classical culture that was eventually cut short by bubonic plague in the fourteenth century.

333. Although anthropologists would say that every society has a culture (and so one can speak legitimately of Celtic, Germanic, Slavic cultures, and so on), normative culture in the sense of highly developed standards in art and literature, science and engineering, economics and politics in Europe had declined in the fifth century and did not begin to recover until the eleventh.

One of the seemingly insurmountable tasks was the collection and organization of ancient Christian writings which had usually been produced by bishops, councils and intellectuals to address topics of immediate concern. Even the Bible was not organized by topic, for each book treated a variety of topics. Early in the twelfth century, Peter Abelard attempted to address this confusion of sources in *Sic et Non*, a compilation of patristic texts pro and con about faith, reason and God. Following his example, other professors and students created collections of texts—the predecessor of today's textbooks—by grouping them around theological topics such as the Trinity, the Incarnation, morality, salvation, the world and the church. But the first compilation to be recognized as truly excellent was not a theological work but a juridical one, *The Agreement of Disagreeing Canons* (*Concordia discordantium canonum*) edited in the mid-twelfth century by John Gratian in Bologna. Combining biblical precepts with ecclesiastical decrees, it is commonly referred to as Gratian's *Decretum* or *Decree*. Shortly after that, and perhaps influenced by the design of the *Decretum*, Peter Lombard in Paris produced a theological anthology that was to enjoy similar success. His *Four Books of Opinions* (*Sententiarum libri IV*) was not the largest compilation of original texts, but its systematic organization of quotations and ideas made it ideal teaching resource.[334] For decades, students at the University of Paris completed their theological training by writing a commentary on Lombard's *Sentences*, as it is commonly known in English.[335]

Around the same time that Gratian was working in Bologna, Hugh of St. Victor (a monastery school that was eventually incorporated into the University of Paris) wrote a book titled *The Sacraments of the Christian Faith*, but Hugh's notion of sacrament was very broad: Augustine's "sign of a sacred thing."[336] By this definition, all of creation is sacramental for all created things are signs of the God who made them, and so Hugh's work covers not only church rituals but also the incarnation, the church, religious feast days, liturgical symbols and vestments. In contrast, Lombard used a more restricted definition which enabled him to limit his treatment of sacraments in Book Four of the *Sentences* to seven ecclesiastical rituals that were understood to have invisible effects.[337]

---

334. Unlike earlier collections of opinions, Lombard paraphrased many of his sources, in effect creating a condensed version of the many theological ideas available in early medieval libraries. See Philipp W. Rosemann, *The Story of a Great Medieval Book: Peter Lombard's Sentences* (Peterborough, ON: Broadview Press, 2007), 23–26. Rosemann gives the original title as *Sententiae in quattuor libris distinctae*, or "Sentences divided into four books." He seems unaware that, despite the traditional transliteration of the book's title, *sententia* in Latin means opinion or sentiment.

335. Ibid., 60–83. Another feature of Lombard's collection that made it so user friendly was his inclusion of a table of contents, an innovation found in few other books before that time. The table of contents was improved by later editors, making the individual topics even more accessible to readers.

336. See Augustine, *The City of God*, 10.5.

337. This definition also came from Augustine: "a visible form of an invisible grace," from *Questions About the Heptateuch*, 3.84.

a. Defining the Sacraments

The Sacraments of the Christian Faith was written ten or fifteen years before the *Sentences*, but it was not a compilation of patristic opinions. Hugh of St. Victor was an Augustinian monk who followed Augustine's thinking in most matters, and so this work is to some extent a systematic presentation of what his theological forebear had written in a variety of treatises, scripture commentaries, essays and letters. Toward the end of Book One, he introduces the topic of sacraments and, after citing the short definition already quoted, he says,

> A sacrament is a corporeal or material element set before the senses without, representing by similitude and signifying by institution and containing by sanctification some invisible and spiritual grace.[338]

According to this definition, there are two dimensions or aspects to a sacrament: first, a corporeal, material, sensible or outer dimension, and second, a spiritual, invisible or inner dimension. In this, Hugh's understanding of a *sacramentum* parallels that of the church fathers prior to Augustine, who went beyond this twofold definition to speak in some places about a *sacramentum* that is received, and which is neither of the two aspects in Hugh's definition (or in Augustine's short definition, given above).

> For just as in man there are two things, body and soul, and in one Scripture likewise two things, letter and sense, so also in every sacrament there is one thing which is treated visibly without and is seen, and there is another which is believed invisibly within and is received. What is visible without and material is a sacrament, what is invisible within and spiritual is the thing or virtue of the sacrament; the sacrament, however, which is treated and sanctified without is a sign of spiritual grace and this is the thing of the sacrament and is received invisibly.[339]

To illustrate what he means by this definition, he says with regard to baptism, "visible water is the sacrament, and invisible grace the thing (*res*) or virtue (*virtus*) of the sacrament."[340] Here we find terminology that will become standard in scholastic sacramental theology: speaking of the church ritual as a *sacramentum*, and speaking about its spiritual effect as *res sacramenti*, or the thing of the sacrament, which is found here and there in the works of Augustine.[341] But he nowhere talks about the

338. Hugh of St. Victor, *The Sacraments of the Christian Faith*, Bk. 1, Pt. 9, sec. 2. The translation is by Roy J. Deferrari and can be found in *Hugh of St. Victor on the Sacraments of the Christian Faith* (Cambridge, MA: Medieval Academy of America, 1951), 155.

339. Ibid.

340. Ibid. Here and elsewhere I have inserted in Deferrari's translation some Latin words in parentheses.

341. Hugh and the other early schoolmen needed a general term to designate the invisible reality symbolized by the visible sacrament. He and Lombard call it a *res*, which literally means a thing, and is usually rendered as "thing" in English translations of scholastic works. But *res* needs to be taken very

sacramentum et res, a concept that will become standard in Catholic theology some decades later.[342] The same could be said about referring to the spiritual effect as a *virtus*, meaning a virtue in the sense of a power to do good.

In Hugh's mind, therefore, a sacrament is a sign that has been sanctified (*sanctificatum*, made holy) by God, but it still has a rather broad extension. For in addition to treating the church rituals that Catholics today call sacraments, he devotes separate parts of his work to clerical vestments, the dedication of churches and the profession of vows. Moreover he regards marriage as having been a sacrament before the Fall, since God gave Adam and Eve the duty (*officium*) to increase and multiply.[343]

The first edition of Gratian's *Decretum* appeared about the same time as Hugh's *Sacraments*, but Gratian was working in Bologna and Hugh in Paris, so neither would have seen what the other had written. It is possible that Lombard a decade later was aware of what Gratian had written, although theologians were generally not interested in the details of canon law. It is more plausible that Lombard heard about Gratian's attempt at synthesis and, since sacramental rituals were governed by ecclesiastical regulations, he may have gotten some ideas from Gratian and his sources.

Gratian's canonical compilation looks back to what has been said in the past, but unlike Lombard's theological compilation it did not become a platform for future conceptual construction, for it was never used as a basis for commentaries by students of canon law. Gratian is content with repeating Augustine's broad definition of sacrament as a sacred sign or a visible form of invisible grace.[344] He does not offer a comprehensive list of sacraments, and when he provides examples of what he is talking about he lists only three—baptism, chrism, and the body and blood (i.e., of Christ)[345]—although he also treats canons referring to confirmation, penance, ordination and marriage. He says that sacraments are so called because under the cover of corporeal things (*sub tegumento corporalium rerum*) divine power effects salvation in a hidden manner (*divina virtus secretius salutem . . . operatur*).[346] Thus for Gratian, as for Hugh, sacraments have only two dimensions or aspects: an outward or material one and an inner or spiritual one. In addition, Gratian accepts the convention that

broadly as meaning a spiritual something or spiritual reality.

342. In fact, the term *sacramentum et res* first appeared in the *Summa Sententiarum*, an anonymous compilation produced around the same time that Hugh was writing.

343. See Hugh, *Sacraments*, Bk. 2, Pt. 4 (sacred garments), Pt. 5 (dedication of a church), Pt. 11 (marriage) and Pt. 12 (vows). Hugh also speaks about the sacraments of the natural law and the written law (the Decalogue) in Bk. 1, Pt. 11 and 12. And in Bk. 2, Pt. 9 he distinguishes between sacraments instituted for practice (e.g., the sprinkling of holy water, the reception of ashes, the blessing of palms), the sacraments that consist of words (e.g., prayers and hymns), and things that are sacred but not sacraments (e.g., church lands and property).

344. John Gratian, *Decretum*, Pt. 3, dist. 2, can. 32. This work has never been translated into English, so any translations provided here are my own.

345. Ibid., Pt. 2, case 1, q. 1, can. 84.

346. Gratian also accepts the Augustinian notion that the corporeal aspect of a sacrament consists of material elements and spoken words. See Pt. 2, case 1, q. 1, can. 38.

there were sacraments before the coming of Christ. He refers to Jewish temple rituals and the anointing of kings as sacraments.[347]

In the *Decretum* there is an abundance of language describing sacraments as given and received. A quick word search of the Latin text reveals that sacraments are said to be given (*dare*) six times, conferred (*conferre*) once, bestowed (*tradere*) once, ministered (*ministrare*) three times, administered (*administrare*) twice, and dispensed (*dispensatio*) once. Sacraments are also said to be received (*suscipere*) four times, accepted (*accipere*) ten times, and taken (*sumere*) twice.[348] Sometimes the sacrament that is given and received is the body and blood of Christ, but the same terminology is used with regard to the other sacraments as well. Thus sacraments such as baptism and marriage are said to be had (*habere*) ten times, and it is argued that they cannot be lost (*non amittere*) four times.[349] Even heretics can have sacraments, says Gratian, but the effects of their sacraments cannot always be guaranteed.[350]

Gratian is not clear about the nature of sacraments that are given and received. Sometimes it appears to be a material element such as water or oil, but sometimes it is definitely something immaterial, as in the cases of marriage and ordination. Thus, although Gratian acknowledges that visible sacraments are to be distinguished from their invisible effects, he also refers to the effects as sacraments.[351] Nowhere, however, does he use the term *sacramentum et res*, a precision that would later be added by theologians and eventually by canonists as well. Nor does he link the idea that some sacraments cannot be lost with the rule that those sacraments should not be repeated.[352]

The *Decretum* provides evidence that by the mid-twelfth century, *sacramentum* was no longer understood as a Latin translation of the Greek μυστέριον. In one place, Gratian speaks about the mysteries of the sacraments (*sacramentorum mysteria*), and in another he talks about sacraments (*sacramenta*) on the one hand and the possibility of a sacrilege of the great mystery (*mysterii grandi sacrilegio*) on the other.[353]

Moving forward to around 1150, when the *Sentences* first appeared, we find Lombard introducing a definition with a more restricted extension. After distinguishing between signs and sacraments, Lombard explains what he believes is properly (*proprie*) a sacrament:

---

347. See Pt. 1, dist. 21, can. 1; Pt. 2, case 1, q. 1, can. 37; Pt. 2, case 1, q. 1, can. 87; Pt. 2, case 23, q. 4, can. 1 and 9.

348. For the sake of simplicity, only the infinitive forms of the verbs are given here.

349. Again, these Latin verbs appear in various forms, for which I have given only the infinitives.

350. A good number of examples can be found in Pt. 2, case 1, q. 1, can. 31–97 passim.

351. See, for example, Pt. 2, case 1, q. 1, can. 38, 39, 48, 70, and 97.

352. In Gratian's usage, the sacraments that cannot be lost are invisible realities, whereas the sacraments that should not be repeated are visible rites. See Pt. 2, case 1, q. 7, can. 23; Pt. 2, case 24, q. 1, can. 37; Pt. 2, case 27, q. 2, can. 51; Pt. 2, case 32, q. 7, can. 28; Pt. 3, dist. 4, can. 32 and 36.

353. See ibid., Pt. 3, dist. 2, can. 7 and 12.

> For a sacrament is properly so called because it is a sign of God's grace and a
> form of invisible grace in such manner that it bears its image and is its cause.
> And so the sacraments were not instituted only for the sake of signifying but
> also to sanctify.[354]

This strict definition was apparently the result of Lombard's own reflection for it appears nowhere else, although it contains elements taken from various sources.[355] This definition was probably also the product of his desire to restrict its applicability so that it includes only the seven that will be the object of his attention in this volume. Thus Lombard insists that sacraments are both signs and causes of grace, that they were explicitly instituted (i.e., introduced by God, meaning that they were not invented by human beings), and that their proper effect is to sanctify (*sanctificare*). By so doing, he excludes from consideration many of the things that Hugh called sacraments. Also on the basis of this definition, he argues that what the fathers had called sacraments of the Old Law (circumcision, temple sacrifices, etc.) should be called signs and not sacraments.[356]

A few facts should be noted here. The first is that everything that Lombard says about sacraments and their effects is taken from authorities such as the fathers of the church. The second is that Lombard uses these sources uncritically, that is, he interprets them literally and assigns them meanings that are helpful for his project.[357] The third is that he applies the ideas taken from ancient sources to twelfth century rituals rather than to the church practices to which his sources were referring. Looking at this from a different angle, we could say that Lombard is writing about twelfth century religious rituals, but his ideas do not come from experience with and reflection on those rituals. Instead, his ideas come from his reading of texts written in a different age about sometimes very different rituals, and he applies the ideas to rituals in his own day with no awareness that the application may be inappropriate. A clear example of this is how Lombard and other schoolmen applied James 5:14–15 to the

354. Peter Lombard, *Sentences*, Bk. 4, Dist. 1, ch. 4. The translation is by Giulio Silano and can be found in Peter Lombard, *The Sentences, Book 4: On the Doctrine of Signs* (Toronto: Pontifical Institute of Medieval Studies, 2010), 4. Unless otherwise noted, all quotations in this section are Silano's translations.

355. For example, Lombard cites Augustine's letter to a bishop named Boniface: "For if sacraments did not have the likeness of the things whose sacraments they are, they would not properly be called sacraments" *Letters*, 98. See my translation above, page 53. The notion that sacraments bear some resemblance to what they signify is about as close as early theologians got to the concept of symbolism, and so sacraments were always called signs rather than symbols. Thus baptismal water cleanses, confirmation oil strengthens, bread and wine somewhat resemble flesh and blood, etc.

356. He allows, however, that circumcision had a beneficial effect for the Jews. See Lombard, *Sentences*, Bk. 4, Dist. 1, ch. 4, 7–9.

357. For example, Lombard accepts what Augustine says about sacraments bearing a likeness to what they are signs of, but he does not accept Augustine's extension of this notion to the Easter liturgy. See above, page 53.

rite of extreme unction even though the author of that first-century epistle could not have had the medieval rite in mind when he wrote.

This methodology, if we may call it that, both allowed and encouraged the schoolmen to engage in what can be called magical thinking, that is, the attribution of invisible effects to the performance of visible rituals. It could also be called legalistic or mechanical or ontological thinking, for these alternatives all could suggest the inferring of invisible results from the observation of visible actions. But magical thinking, psychologically speaking, is a matter of perceiving cause and effect without understanding anything more than the idea that one is the cause and the other is the effect. In our everyday lives, for example, we may know that flicking a wall switch causes the overhead lights to go on, or that turning the key in the ignition causes a vehicle's engine to start, but most of us do not understand how performing the causal action actually produces the resulting effect. This is why, when the expected result does not occur, we often have to resort to an expert (e.g., an electrician or mechanic) who does understand the relationship between the two and who can therefore investigate and solve our problem.[358]

Christians in the Middle Ages "saw" religious causes and spiritual effects all the time; that is, they perceived babies being baptized and they perceived original sin being washed away, they perceived bread and wine at the beginning of mass and they perceived the body and blood of Christ when they were elevated over the priest's head after the consecration, and they perceived themselves as condemned to hell before confessing a mortal sin and as only having to endure purgatory after receiving the priest's absolution. Likewise, they regarded a man and woman as unmarried before a wedding ceremony and as married to each other afterward, and they regarded a man as a bachelor before he professed monastic vows and as a monk afterward. Their religious culture informed their perception of what happened as a result of a ritual, just as our secular culture informs our perception when we see people being married before a judge or inaugurated into public office. We see the ritual and we perceive the effect, but we do not (and do not need to) understand the complex relationship between the two, that is, we do not understand the social, linguistic and mental factors that make it possible for rituals to produce their results.

---

358. According to Swiss child psychologist Jean Piaget, magical thinking is one of the first forms of inference that we become capable of as children, and it remains a handy inferential short-cut throughout our adult lives. Were it not for our ability to perceive cause and effect without being aware of all the intermediary steps between them, our practical intelligence would be severely hampered by our lack of theoretical knowledge. "This early notion of causality may be called magical-phenomenalist: 'phenomenalist' because the phenomenal contiguity of two events is sufficient to make them appear causally related, and 'magical' because it is centered on the action of the subject without consideration of spatial connection between cause and effect." Jean Piaget and Bärbel Inhelder, *The Psychology of the Child* (New York: Basic Books, 1969), 18. For a more detailed account of the genesis of the ability to perceive causal relations, see "The Development of Causality" in Jean Piaget, *The Construction of Reality in the Child* (New York: Basic Books, 1954), ch. 3.

Returning briefly to the definitions given by both Hugh and Lombard, it should also be noted that the invisible effect of all the sacraments is given the generalized name, "grace." Whereas χάρις or *gratia* had in earlier centuries been a predicate (e.g., this or that is a gift), it is now regarded as something substantive, a thing or *res* in itself, and it is something that comes in a variety of forms. This shift in language would allow later schoolmen to distinguish between actual and habitual grace, operative and cooperative grace, prevenient and consequent grace, etc.[359]

The schoolmen in the Middle Ages were the scientists of their day, just as the philosophers in ancient Greece had been the scientists in theirs. That is, they were interested in categorizing what they saw, defining what they categorized, discovering the causes of what they observed, and generalizing the effects of these causes. Ancient botany and biology were primarily a matter of classifying plants and animals into various genera and species, discovering what caused them to be born, mature and die, observing what happened when they were eaten, and so on. Ancient astronomy divided the points of light in the night sky into stars and planets, theorized about what caused the planets to move, and pictured the relationship between the earth and the heavens. Ancient politics classified governments into different types, discerned how aristocracy, democracy, oligarchy and so on came into being, and worked out what happened to people under these different forms of government. The schoolmen in the twelfth century had Latin translations of a few Greek philosophical works (mainly Aristotle's logic, which involved classification and inference), and in the thirteenth century the rest of Aristotle's corpus came into their possession, generating a flurry of scientific activity in both the natural and supernatural sciences.

Lombard's short list of *sacramenta* in his fourth volume of the *Sentences* is given at the beginning of Section (*Distinctio*) 2: baptism, confirmation, the blessing of the bread that is Eucharist (*panis benedictio, id est, Eucharistia*), penance, extreme unction, orders, and marriage (*conjugium*). Lombard lists them as though all Catholics at the time knew that these were the seven sacraments. In fact, however, earlier compilations sometimes excluded marriage because it was in existence before Christ or because it involved potentially sinful acts, or they included many additional symbols and symbolic actions (as Hugh did) that would later be classified as sacramentals or sacrament-like (*sacramentalia*). Historically, it was because Lombard listed seven sacraments and because the *Sentences* became the standard theology textbook of thirteenth-century scholasticism that his list became the Catholic standard.[360]

Lombard does not give a rationale for selecting just these seven, but we can surmise that his motivation was scientific in the way that ancient philosophy and

---

359. The absence of the indefinite article in both Greek and Latin may have contributed to this misunderstanding. Whereas Paul, for example, may have been thinking of something as being a gift from God, medieval scholars, reading the epistles in Latin, interpreted him as talking about something spiritual called *gratia*. See, e.g., Rom 12:3–6; 1 Cor 15:10; 2 Cor 6:1; Gal 2:9; Eph 2:8.

360. See Rosemann, *Lombard's Sentences*, 60–63; also Martos, *Doors to the Sacred*, 52–56.

medieval theology were scientific. All of the seven were perceived to have invisible effects: the remission of sins, the confection of the body and blood of Christ, the forging of the marriage bond, the conferral of priestly powers, etc. Hence they were legitimate objects of scientific inquiry. How do we know that these visible rites produce invisible effects? What are those effects? How can physical actions produce metaphysical effects? Similar investigative questions could be and were indeed posed by the early schoolmen. Interestingly, some medieval rituals that were believed to produce spiritual effects (for example, the consecration of churches and monarchs, and the ordination of abbots and abbesses) did not make it into Lombard's list. Perhaps their absence is due to the fact that the fathers had not written about those rituals, and thus there were no patristic sentences about them to include in the *Sentences*.

b. Baptism

As we have just seen, what was called baptism in the Middle Ages was a brief ritual for infants. Water was sprinkled or poured on the child's head, while the formula derived from Matthew 28:19 was said aloud: *Ego te baptizo in nomine Patris, et Filii, et Spiritus Sancti*. Although baptisms in the early Middle Ages were still conducted once a year, as they had been during the patristic centuries, increasing awareness of Augustine's idea of original sin intensified the fear that the souls of children who died without baptism would be damned for all eternity. In addition, increasing familiarity with the scriptures led to baptism being likened to circumcision and performed on the eighth day after birth.

If this ritual was the schoolmen's *explicandum*, the source of ideas for their *explicationes* were the Bible and the writings of the church fathers—although, realistically, most of the works of the Greek fathers were unavailable since the schoolmen could not read Greek. And as a matter of historical record, Augustine was the Latin father who is quoted most often in their research because he wrote more than any of the others from Tertullian to Ambrose. It would be a gross oversimplification to say that early medieval sacramental theology was an application of biblical proof texts and Augustinian quotations to medieval church practices, but it also would be false to say that it was not that at all.

Despite his dependence on Augustine, Hugh of St. Victor defines baptism very much the way Tertullian did, focusing on the water:

> Baptism is the water sanctified by the word of God for washing away sins.[361]

Thus, when Hugh asks "whether anyone can be saved without actually receiving the sacrament of baptism," he is thinking about the sacramental ritual composed of water and word, not about an inner *sacramentum* or *character*, as Augustine

---

361. Hugh, *Sacraments*, Bk. 2, Pt. 6, sec. 2.

did.[362] In other words, he is thinking about receiving the water in a ceremony during which appropriate words are pronounced. Indeed, most of the things that Hugh writes about baptism regard its liturgy, not its theology. In particular, he never talks about what is received through the baptismal ritual as a permanent *sacramentum*, *baptisma*, or *character*.

Gratian does not use the word *character*, but he does speak about giving and receiving baptism, as well as about giving and receiving a sacrament in the context of talking about baptism.[363] Although he speaks about the sacrament of baptism (*sacramentum baptismi*), he makes no attempt to clarify whether he is talking about the performed sacrament (i.e., the rite) or the received sacrament.[364] Gratian seems to be content with collecting texts and with finding some order and regularity within them (as the full title of his work, *The Agreement of Disagreeing Canons*, implied) rather than with explaining them.

Many of the texts that Gratian cites are quotations from Augustine, although he does not always note that Augustine is the source. What appears to be most important for him is coming up with a consistent set of rules, not with documenting where the rules come from, nor with giving theological explanations for the rules (except the explanations provided by his sources). Thus baptism is not to be repeated, not even those done by heretics and schismatics, because it is Christ and not the minister who gives the baptism, and because baptism cannot be lost.[365] What can be lost by those who sin, however, and what is never had by those who are baptized outside the church, are holiness (*sanctificatio*), the true faith (*fides*) and unity (*unitas*) with the church.[366] Baptism effects the forgiveness and remission of all sins, including original sin, but it does not prevent the commission of future sins for which penance must be done.[367]

Lombard defines baptism as "an intinction (*intinctio*), that is, an exterior washing of the body made under a prescribed form of words. For if the washing is done without the word, there is no sacrament there; but with the addition of the word to the element (*elementum*), the sacrament is brought about; it is certainly not the element

---

362. Ibid., sec. 1. See also sec. 7, where he asks that question again.

363. For giving and receiving baptism, see Pt. 2, case 1, q. 1, can. 48, 51 and 89. For giving and receiving the sacrament, see Pt. 2, case 1, q. 1, can. 53; Pt. 2, case 32, q. 7, can. 28; Pt. 3, dist. 4, can. 151.

364. See Pt. 1, dist. 26, can. 3; Pt. 2, case 1, q. 1, can. 53; Pt. 3, dist. 4, can. 32.

365. For not repeating baptism, see Pt. 2, case 1, q. 1, can. 46 and 57; Pt. 2, case 32, q. 7, can. 28. For accepting baptisms performed by heretics and schismatics, see Pt. 2, case 1, q. 1, can. 35 and 51; Pt. 3, dist. 4, can. 43. For the sacrament coming from Christ rather than from the minister, see Pt. 2, case 1, q. 1, can. 46, 75 and 89. For baptism not being able to be lost see Pt. 2, case 32, q. 7, can. 2 and 28; Pt. 3, dist. 4, can. 32 and 36. Gratian also uses the *unum baptismam* of Eph 4:5 as a proof text for baptizing only once.

366. For sanctification see Pt. 2, case 1, q. 1, can. 89; Pt. 3, dist. 4, can. 36. For faith see Pt. 2, case 1, q. 1, can. 97; Pt. 2, case 32, q. 7, can. 28. For unity see ; Pt. 3, dist. 4, can. 32.

367. See Pt. 1, dist. 23, can. 2; Pt. 2, case 1, q. 1, can. 47; Pt. 3, dist. 4, can. 36. For Gratian, there is apparently no difference between sins being forgiven (*peccata dimittantur*) and the remission of sins (*remissionem peccatorum*): by this time, both phrases have come to have the same meaning.

itself that constitutes the sacrament, but the washing performed in the element."[368] The element involved here is, of course, water. When he calls it an element, Lombard is looking for a generalized term for the physical dimension of the sacrament, which later schoolmen, following Aristotle, would call *materia* or matter. Here he is attempting to specify what would later be called the *sacramentum tantum* or the sacramental rite. His thinking is rather legalistic or ritualistic, for he discusses at length whether the intinction or moistening must be done while pronouncing a Trinitarian formula. This is a far cry from thinking of baptism as an immersion in a Christ-like way of life. Rather, it is a ritual that produces spiritual effects if it is performed properly. In this case, it is a ritual that "wipes away and cleanses the stains of the soul and the uncleanness of vices."[369] But baptism also adorns the soul with virtues, as can be learned from the scriptures.[370] Together, these effects may be regarded as the grace of baptism.

In the next section, Lombard adopts the language of receiving the sacraments, and he refers to the grace of the sacrament as its proper "thing" (*res*).

> Here it is to be said that some receive (*suscipere*) the sacrament and thing, others the sacrament and not the thing, others the thing and not the sacrament.[371]

Clearly Lombard is following Augustine's language here, for Augustine wrote about receiving baptism and receiving the sacrament. But the nature of the received sacrament is not clear here. Although it must be certainly different from the sacramental ritual (One does not talk about receiving a ritual.), Lombard does not attempt to clarify what he is talking about. Further on in the *Sentences* he himself introduces the term *sacramentum et res* in his discussion of the Eucharist, but he does not apply that term to baptism, and it will be up to later schoolmen to interpret the *sacramentum et res* as a supernatural ability to receive supernatural grace. Here Lombard is in effect summarizing the Augustinian contribution to sacramental theology and inviting others to address the issues that Augustine left unresolved.[372]

368. Lombard, *Sentences*, Dist. 3, ch. 1. Here and in other citations of Silano's translation, I have inserted relevant Latin terms in parentheses.

369. Ibid., ch. 6.

370. Ibid., ch. 9. Later editors referenced Rom 6: 2–11, Eph. 4: 22–24, and Col 3: 9–10. These were originally attempts to describe the changes that took place in adults who converted to the way of life preached by Jesus, but they were taken by the fathers and the schoolmen as automatic effects of going through the baptismal ritual.

371. Ibid., Dist. 4, ch. 1. Lombard goes on to say that infants receive both the sacrament and its grace (which is the "thing" or reality in question), those who ask for baptism under false pretenses receive the sacrament but not its grace, and catechumens who are martyred for the faith receive the grace even though they were not able to receive the sacrament.

372. Quite possibly, Lombard's source was not the works of Augustine but the *Summa Sententiarum*, long attributed to Hugh of St. Victor but now regarded as having been produced by other monks at the school of St. Victor. With regard to baptism, this *Summa* distinguishes between the *sacramentum* and the *res sacramenti* in Tract 5 (*De sacramento baptismi*), ch. 5 and 8. It also distinguishes between the two when treating extreme unction, but there the received sacrament is clearly the anointing. See Tract 6, ch. 15: *Sacramentum ipsa inunctio, res sacramenti remissio quae ex interiori unctione confertur.*

In Section 5, Lombard takes up the question behind the Donatist controversy, namely, whether the effectiveness of a sacramental ritual depends on the status of the person who performs the ritual. The schoolmen will eventually introduce the phrase *ex opere operato*, meaning that a ritual's effectiveness depends on its proper performance. Here our interest is in noting that the question is phrased in terms of giving and receiving the sacrament.

> That said, it should be known that the sacrament of baptism is given (*dari*) by good and bad ministers, and it is received (*sumitur*) by good and bad persons. Now, a baptism is not better if it is given (*datur*) by someone who is good, nor is it less good if given (*datur*) by someone who is not so good, nor is it bad if given (*datur*) by someone who is bad. Also, a greater gift (*munus*) is not given (*datur*) in a baptism given (*dato*) by someone who is good, and there is not a lesser gift in a baptism given (*dato*) by someone who is bad. Rather, it is an equal one, because it is not the gift of a human being, but a gift of God.[373]

Next, Lombard discusses the God-given gift just mentioned, which was also known as the power of the sacrament. Again, Lombard quotes extensively from Augustine to support the view that the sacrament's power is not a human power but a divine power. The Latin word used throughout is *potestas*, but it would take the introduction of the Aristotelian concept of natural powers before Aquinas and other schoolmen would come up with the idea that this is a supernatural power. At this point, all Lombard can do is quote the tradition in support of the position that the power of baptism is a gift from God.[374]

The rest of the *Sentences*' treatment of baptism is concerned with ritual matters (e.g., the words to be used) rather than theological ones, so they need not concern us here.

c. Confirmation

In the twelfth century, the rite of confirmation was as simple as the one for baptism: it was an anointing with chrism, often as a small sign of the cross that a bishop made with his right thumb on the forehead of the candidate. The bishop might also rest his hand on the top of the candidate's head when he did this, or he might extend one or both hands over the candidate in prayer, in order to signify the laying on of hands. As already indicated, however, it was not a ritual that was performed very often, partly because of the difficulties of travel and partly because of questions about its necessity.

---

373. Ibid., Dist. 5, ch. 1 (my translation). In support of this position, Lombard supplies multiple quotations from Augustine that frame the question in terms of giving and receiving. Lombard also uses the language of giving and receiving when he discusses whether heretics should be rebaptized in Dist. 6, ch. 2.

374. Ibid., ch. 2–3.

Hugh of St. Victor's treatment of confirmation is very brief. He calls it "the imposition of the hand" and says it is a sacrament "by which the Christian is signed on the forehead with the unction of chrism." He talks mostly about the ceremony, the candidates, and chrism, which is the oil used by the bishop. He says that the sacrament should not be repeated, but he gives no reason for this. When he talks about receiving the sacrament, he appears to be speaking about the chrism or the hand-laying. [375]

Being a canon lawyer, Gratian is concerned with how the confirmation ceremony is performed.[376] It should be done by a bishop with a laying on of hands or with an anointing with oil on the forehead.[377] It is something that is done for the baptized, and for those who repent of heresy and want to join the true church.[378] In only one place does he say that the sacrament is conferred;[379] more often he says that it gives the Holy Spirit.[380] But his theological support for this claim comes from quotations wrongly attributed to the early popes Urban and Melchiades (or Miltiades), and found in a ninth century collection of decretals falsely attributed to Isidore of Seville.[381] In one place, he says that confirmation should not be repeated (*iterari minime debere*), but he give no theological explanation for this rule.[382]

Since confirmation was not a separate ritual during the patristic period, Peter Lombard had few patristic sources to quote, apart from those found in the false decretals. He cites Augustine with regard to the nonrepeatability of baptism and assumes that the reasoning also applies to confirmation, since it too is "conferred" only once. In this way, Lombard takes Augustine's rationale for the Roman practice of not rebaptizing and makes it a general principle that stands on its own, with applicability to other sacraments.[383]

There were not many theological issues concerning this sacrament, so Lombard could not adduce many texts from the early Middle Ages. He quotes Gregory the Great, who was of the opinion that priests could confirm in case of necessity. And he cites Raban Maur, who said that the Holy Spirit is given in this sacrament for strengthening.[384]

Lombard's theology of confirmation comes almost entirely from the false decretals. A sentence attributed to Pope Urban says that it enables the faithful to become

---

375. See Hugh, *Sacraments*, Bk. 2, Pt. 7.

376. Unlike theologians, canonists think about details such as godparents and fasting before the ceremony. See Gratian, *Decretum*, Pt. 3, dist. 4, can. 100 and 102; also dist. 5, can. 7.

377. See ibid., Pt. 2, case 30, q. 1, can. 1; Pt. 3, dist. 4, can. 102; Pt. 3, dist. 5, can. 4.

378. See Pt. 1, case 1, q. 1, can. 51; Pt. 3, dist. 5, can. 5.

379. See Pt. 3, dist. 5, can. 5.

380. See Pt. 3, dist. 5, can. 1, 2 and 7.

381. See above, page 162.

382. See Pt. 3, dist. 5, can. 8.

383. See Lombard, *Sentences*, Dist. 7, ch. 5. The reference is to Augustine's *Against the Letter of Parmenian*, 2.13.28.

384. See ibid., ch. 2–3.

full Christians (*pleni Christiani*), and one attributed to Pope Melchiades says that confirmation is to be held in greater veneration (*majore veneratione*) than baptism. Lombard hypothesizes that this is the case because it offers increased virtue (*augmentum virtutum*) such as the seven gifts of the Holy Spirit.[385]

Notice that Lombard never doubts any of his sources. When he reads that confirmation offers spiritual strengthening and that it makes people more fully Christians, he never wonders if these claims might not be true. Instead, he assumes their veracity based on the authority of those who made them. The question is never whether they are true but only how they are true, or how they can be interpreted in such a way that the authority of the writers is maintained. Here we see another example of how medieval theology was uncritical of its sources.

Only one of Lombard's citations speaks of confirmation being conferred, but he is quite comfortable with that language, for he says in another place that he is of the opinion that the sacrament "ought be conferred (*tradi*) and received (*accipi*) by people who are fasting, just like baptism, unless necessity compel otherwise."[386]

d. Eucharist

As we have seen, the word *Eucharistia* in the Middle Ages came to refer to the body and blood of Christ, the consecrated elements after they were transformed during the mass. It was therefore not a ritual sacrament, like the others, but a substantive one, for it was the substantial presence of a divine person under the appearances of bread and wine. It was in a very basic sense an object of faith, for it was perceived by people of faith when they gazed upon the host or the chalice.[387]

For a thousand years, Christians had accepted the notion that bread and wine became the body and blood of Christ when they ritually celebrated his death and resurrection. During the patristic period there were no theological controversies about it, so we do not really know how people understood it. We can say that they probably took the teaching literally, for this is the way most people understood biblical texts, but we actually do not know what it meant to take this doctrine literally since no one wrote of it, except to say that it was true, that it was miraculous, and that it should be accepted on faith. Nonetheless, we can glean some insight from the late patristic trend of abstaining from communion, since this was commented on by various bishops. It

---

385. See ibid., ch. 3–4; also Isaiah 11:2–3.

386. Ibid., ch. 4.

387. Although the bread used in patristic liturgies had been leavened bread, the bread used in the medieval mass was an unleavened wafer that came to be called a host (from the Latin *hostia*, meaning a sacrificial victim) because the mass was interpreted as a sacrifice in which Christ was offered to God the Father.

seems that the more they insisted that Christ was truly God, the more people hesitated to come in personal contact with the Almighty (Χρίστος Παντοκράτωρ).[388]

It was not until the ninth century that anyone of note asked how this doctrine should be understood. Radbert and Ratramnus, two monks living in the same French monastery at Corbie, gave their own interpretations of how what appeared to be bread and wine were really the body and blood of Christ. Their interpretations did not agree, but this aroused neither suspicion nor controversy at the time.

Two centuries later, the situation was quite different. The works of Aristotle on logic had been translated into Arabic and carried into Moorish Spain, from where they were translated into Latin and carried into Catholic Europe. These translations of translations aroused great interest among the early schoolmen who, until then, knew about the Greek philosopher only by reputation. Beregar of Tours, a canon of the cathedral and head of its school, applied Aristotelian logic to the Eucharist and concluded that both Radbert and Ratramnus were wrong. The natural body and blood of Christ could not be both in heaven and on earth, he reasoned, nor could the qualities (*accidentalia*) of bread and wine inhere in a hidden reality (*substantia*) that did not have those qualities. He therefore concluded that the only logical explanation for the experience of Christ in the Eucharist is that the intelligible reality (*forma*) of Christ is added to the reality of bread and wine when the words of consecration are spoken, thus enabling the believer to perceive Christ in the eucharistic elements. To his contemporaries, however, this was heresy because it denied the traditional belief that the bread and wine actually became the body and blood of Christ. According to Beregar's explanation, the bread and wine remained, and Christ became only formally, even if really, present in them.[389]

Around 1050, Berengar's views began to come to the attention of various bishops, with some supporting him and others condemning him. Although excommunicated by the pope, he continued to teach and write, and in 1059 he went to Rome to defend his position before a synod of bishops. Instead of being granted a hearing, however, he was forced to sign a profession of faith stating that "the bread and wine which are placed on the altar after the consecration are not only the sacrament but also the true body and blood of our Lord Jesus Christ, and that they are palpably handled and broken by the hands of the priest and torn by the teeth of the faithful, not simply as a sacrament but as a true fact."[390] Returning to France, Berengar stubbornly continued to defend his interpretation of the Eucharist, but to no avail. Most church-

388. See Gregory Dix, *The Shape of the Liturgy* (London: Dacre Press, 1945) 436–443. Christos Pantocrator or Christ the Almighty, usually depicted in the dome or above the altar in Orthodox churches, is a powerful image of the divine in human form.

389. See Macy, *Banquet's Wisdom*, 75–81. Also Maria J. Gondek, "Berengar de Tours (Beringerius Turonensis)" in *Powszechna Encyklopedia Filozofii* (Lublin, Poland: Polish Society of Thomas Aquinas, 2000), English translation available at http://peenef2.republika.pl/angielski/hasla/b/berengartours.html.

390. See Denzinger, *Enchiridion symbolorum*, 690.

men at the time were more comfortable with a simple explanation such as Radbert's, which was congruent with the tradition of calling the consecrated elements the body and blood of Christ.

Hugh of St. Victor's section on the Eucharist in *The Sacraments of the Christian Faith* is titled "The Sacrament of the Body and Blood of Christ," and it focuses entirely on the eucharistic elements.[391] In discussing the sacrament of the altar, however, he distinguishes not two but three things (*res*). "For the visible species which is perceived visibly is one thing, the truth of the body and blood which under visible appearance is believed invisibly is another thing, and the spiritual grace which with body and blood is received invisibly and spiritually another."[392] Hugh does not quote sources when making this distinction, but the first two "things" were already taken for granted, and indeed they could be verified experientially, for the appearance (*species*) could be seen with the eyes, and the truth which is believed could be seen with the mind. But the third is also likely to have been found in Hugh's experience, for he writes,

> When you hold His sacrament in your hands, He is with you corporeally. When you eat it and when you taste it, He is with you corporeally. Finally in sight, in touch, in taste, He is with you corporeally. As long as the sense is affected corporeally, his corporeal presence is not taken away. But after the corporeal feeling in receiving fails, then the corporeal presence is not to be sought but the spiritual is to be retained; the dispensation is completed, the perfect sacrament remains as a virtue; Christ passes from mouth to heart. It is better that it pass into your mind than into your stomach. That food is of the soul not of the body.[393]

To people who grew up in the Catholic Church before the Second Vatican Council, and to devout Catholics since then who have retained a traditional eucharistic spirituality, Hugh's description is quite recognizable. Initially after receiving communion, we have bodily sensations of eating and tasting bread. But after we swallow the sacrament and no longer feel the bread in our mouth, we intentionally seek and find a spiritual presence—the presence of Christ in our mind and heart. The sacrament is received and remains as an experienced strengthening—what Hugh calls a virtue (*virtus*)—of our relationship to Christ.

Although Hugh and Catholics in general have identified the consecrated elements and the receiving of communion as that which makes it possible to have an experience of the presence of Christ, the Catholic tradition also acknowledges that it is possible to experience the presence of God quite apart from the sacraments, and it also talks about the ability to "make a spiritual communion," that is, to invite Christ

---

391. The very last section of Hugh's treatment talks only about why "the commemoration of the passion of Christ" is called the mass, and about when it was instituted. See Hugh, *Sacraments*, Bk. 2, Pt. 8, sec. 14.

392. Ibid., sec. 7.

393. Ibid., sec. 13.

into one's heart and to experience the divine presence when the Eucharist is not available.[394] This experience of God's presence is shared by Orthodox Christians and by devout Protestants, especially evangelicals, for whom having a personal relationship with Christ is an important part of their spirituality. Indeed, the experience of divine presence is arguably shared by devoutly religious people of many faiths—Jewish, Muslim, Hindu, etc.[395]

Hugh does not use the word "transubstantiation," but he reasons that since the bread and wine are said to be changed into the body and blood of Christ, it follows that nothing of the bread and wine remains after the consecration except their appearance.[396] Then, when he asks how the body of Christ can seem to be divided (into many hosts, or on many different altars) and yet still be wholly present in each, he answers, "Do not wonder. This is the work of God."[397] Hugh does not give a philosophical explanation for this apparent miracle, but in both cases his answer makes sense in terms of eucharistic spirituality. When gazing upon the consecrated host, as during Exposition of the Blessed Sacrament, a devout Catholic does not perceive unleavened bread but rather perceives Christ present where (to someone without faith) a white wafer appears to be. In other words, one's perception is not of bread at all, but only of Christ. Nor does this perception of Christ's presence vary when one sees communion being distributed first to one person, and then to another, and then to another. One does not think of holy communion as "bits of Jesus," but one thinks "This is Jesus" every time one looks at a consecrated host, if one sees with the eyes of faith. Today it is possible to develop this somewhat phenomenological analysis of eucharistic devotion, but Hugh could only describe what he saw in objective terms such as "He is here" and "He is there."[398]

As a canonist, Gratian is less concerned with explaining the transformation of bread and wine than he is summarizing the beliefs and practices surrounding them. Among other things, he says that priests are the ones who confect the sacrament, that it should not be done in a wooden vessel, and that only bread and wine can be used for the offering.[399] Like Hugh of St. Victor, Gratian calls the sacrament the body and blood

394. See Gary Macy, "Theology of the Eucharist in the High Middle Ages," in Ian Christopher Levy, Gary Macy and Kristen Van Ausdall, *A Companion to Eucharist in the Middle Ages* (Boston: Brill, 2012), pp. 365, 379–80, 392–93.

395. On religious experience, see Martos, *Doors to the Sacred*, xvii–xviii, 7–13. Arguably, Theravada Buddhists neither seek nor find an experience of divine presence, but devout practitioners in various Mahayana sects could have such an experience when they pray in front of an image of the Buddha.

396. See Hugh, *Sacraments*, sec. 9. The term *transubstantio* was probably coined around the same time that Hugh was writing his book on sacraments, that is, around 1140, so it was not yet in common usage. See Joseph Goering, "The Invention of Transubstantiation," *Traditio* 46 (1991), 147–70.

397. Sec. 11.

398. Phenomenology was first introduced as a philosophical method by Edmund Husserl (1859–1938) in the early twentieth century.

399. See Gratian, *Decretum*, Pt. 1, dist. 25, can. 1; Pt. 3, dist. 1, can. 44; Pt. 3, dist. 2, can. 1.

of Christ, although he is aware that there is another word for it, *Eucharistia*, which is derived from the Greek.[400] The closest he gets to offering a theology of eucharistic change is to say in one place that the Holy Spirit mysteriously enlivens the bread and wine (*Spiritus sanctus mystice ille vivificat*).[401]

The verb used most frequently in association with the sacrament is to confect (*conficere*), the understanding being that a priest makes the sacrament or causes it to come into being by pronouncing the words, "This is my body" and "This is my blood." The words effect the consecration (*consecratio*) of the bread and wine, which can then be dispensed (*dispensare*) or ministered (*ministrare*) to others. They in turn accept (*accipere*) the sacrament, eating (*manducare*) the visible bread while receiving the body of Christ spiritually, and drinking (*potare*) the visible wine while receiving the blood of Christ spiritually. Before the distribution of communion, however, the sacrament is offered (*offere*) as a sacrificial gift (*oblatio*) to God.[402]

Gratian distinguishes the sacrament from the reality it signifies, but the distinction is not clear. In one place he says that Christ is in the sacrament,[403] in another place he says that the bread itself is the flesh of Christ,[404] and in a third he says that the consecrated bread is a sacrament of that flesh.[405] Yet again, the bread is called the body of Christ but it is actually a sacrament of the body of Christ.[406] Gratian does not attempt to resolve these ambiguities.

Only occasionally does one catch a glimpse of Gratian reflecting on his own experience in order to sort things out. He says in one place that the consecrated elements are called sacraments because one thing is seen in them while something else is understood,[407] which suggests that he is comparing what his eyes see with what his mind thinks. Similarly, when he says that Christ is spiritually eaten and drunk,[408] he seems to be articulating the experience of feeling a divine presence within oneself after eating and drinking the visible bread and wine. Gratian's brief reference to the remission of sins through the receiving of communion may reflect his own experience, or it

---

400. See Pt. 1, dist. 25, can. 1; Pt. 2, case 1, q. 1, can. 84; Pt. 3, dist. 2, can. 5; Pt. 3, dist. 2, can. 35; Pt. 3, dist. 2, can. 48; Pt. 3, dist. 2, can. 72.

401. See Pt. 2, case 1, q. 1, can. 84.

402. For sentences in which these verbs are used, see Pt. 1, dist. 25, can. 1; Pt. 1, dist. 32, can. 6; Pt. 2, case 1, q. 1, can. 84; Pt. 3, dist. 1, can. 44; Pt. 3, dist. 2, can. 1; Pt. 3, dist. 2, can. 5; Pt. 3, dist. 2, can. 35; Pt. 3, dist. 2, can. 36; Pt. 3, dist. 2, can. 46; Pt. 3, dist. 2, can. 48; Pt. 3, dist. 2, can. 52; Pt. 3, dist. 2, can. 58; Pt. 3, dist. 2, can. 69; Pt. 3, dist. 2, can. 72; Pt. 3, dist. 2, can. 75.

403. See Pt. 3, dist. 2, can. 40: *In illo sacramento Christus est.*

404. See Pt. 3, dist. 2, can. 48: *celestis panis, qui vere caro Christi est.*

405. See Pt. 3, dist. 2, can. 69: *Vere ergo illius carnis sacramentum est.*

406. See Pt. 3, dist. 2, can. 48: *Sicut ergo celestis panis, qui vere caro Christi est, suo modo vocatur corpus Christi, cum revera sit sacramentum corporis Christi.*

407. See Pt. 3, dist. 2, can. 58: *Ista ideo dicuntur sacramenta, quia in eis aliud videtur, et aliud intelligitur.*

408. See ibid.: *Quod Christus visibiliter in sacramento spiritualiter in veritate manducatur et bibitu.r*

may be an echo of something he has read elsewhere.[409] But he is most likely drawing on his own experience when on the one hand he acknowledges that one eats only a piece of the sacrament but the whole Christ is present in the heart.[410]

Like Hugh and Gratian, Peter Lombard refers to the Eucharist as the sacrament of the altar and the sacrament of the body and blood. Also like Hugh and Gratian, he may have been describing his own experience when he said that "the Eucharist restores us spiritually." But his limited knowledge of Greek led him to conclude that the sacrament is called Eucharist because it is derived from words meaning "good grace, because in this sacrament there is not only an increase of virtue and grace, but he who is the font and origin of all grace is wholly received."[411]

Peter borrows from the canonists the notion that the words of the consecratory ritual are to be called the form of the sacrament, and he understands that the words "This is my body" and "This is my blood" are automatically effective: "When these words are pronounced, the change of the bread and wine into the substance of the body and blood of Christ occurs." Moreover, this is the important part of the mass, for "the rest is said to the praise of God."[412] What counts is that the sacrament is confected, and what makes that happen are the words of consecration. He makes no attempt, however, to explain in philosophical terms how the change takes place. Instead, he is content to quote Augustine and call it a mystery.[413]

Nonetheless, the *Sentences* does show evidence of the philosophizing that earlier schoolmen had begun to do when reflecting on the Eucharist. Gratian and other writers had distinguished between the sacrament and its "thing," the *res sacramenti*, the reality effected by the sacramental ritual. Hugh of St. Victor had gone beyond that to distinguish two things: the body and blood of Christ and the grace that is received and remains as a virtue. Lombard accepts that there are two invisible realities (things) associated with the Eucharist, and then summarizes the matter by making a threefold distinction that is parallel to Hugh's but worded differently.

> And so three factors can be distinguished here. One is a sacrament alone; another is both a sacrament and something real; and a third is something real but not a sacrament. The sacrament that is not a reality as such is the visible appearance of bread and wine; that which is both sacrament and something

409. See Pt. 3, dist. 2, can. 40: *Qui manducaverit hoc corpus, fiet ei remissio peccatorum.*

410. See Pt. 3, dist. 2, can. 75: *per partes manducatur in sacramento . . . ; manet integer totus in corde tuo.*

411. Lombard, *Sentences*, Bk. 4, dist. 8, ch. 1. As we have seen, although the transliteration *eucharistia* derives from Greek roots meaning good and grace (or gift), the original word in Greek actually meant thanksgiving. Gratian also provides this fictive etymology in the *Decretum*, Pt. 2, case 1, q. 1, can. 84.

412. Ibid., ch. 4. This instantaneous change in perceived reality is phenomenologically analogous to the change in one's perception of someone being sworn in as a public official. Before taking the oath of office, the person is an ordinary citizen; immediately after, he or she is someone with power.

413. Ibid., ch. 7, par. 3.

real is Christ's own flesh and blood; that which is real and not a sacrament is his mystical flesh.[414]

As observed above in note 372, the source of this terminology was quite likely the School of St. Victor near Paris, where unknown monks compiled the *Summa Sententiarum* (*Compendium of Opinions*) some time between Hugh's *Sacraments* and Lombard's *Sentences*. Because of the anonymity of the authors, we do not know who first came up with the idea of the *sacramentum et res* as a third something in addition to the *sacramentum tantum* and the *res sacramenti*, but their contribution was clearly articulated in the chapter on the Eucharist titled, *Quod tria sint in sacramento altaris.*

> Here there are three that need to be considered: one is that which is only a sacrament, another is that which is both a sacrament and the reality of the sacrament, and a third which is only a reality. The visible appearances of bread and wine are a sacrament but not a reality, for these are visibly broken, placed on the altar, and raised during the celebration. Indeed, a sacrament is a sign of a sacred reality. But a sign makes something that is beyond the appearances come into the mind.[415]

The author repeats Augustine's definition of a sacrament as a sign of a sacred reality, but then he goes beyond Augustine to say something that can be verified in experience, namely, that a sign brings to mind something more than the physical aspects of the sign itself. What the bread and wine bring to mind are the body and blood of Christ, or perhaps more carefully put, the outward appearances of bread and wine bring into consciousness the body and blood of Christ. The *sacramentum et res* is the very body and blood of Christ (*ipsum corpus Christi et sanguis*) but it is not Christ's physical body. Rather it is Christ's spiritual flesh (*spiritualis caro Christi*) alluded to in John's gospel (Jn 6:48–58).[416] Nonetheless, the author asserts that Christ's spiritual flesh is real (i.e., it is a *res*), so it is both real and in the mind, a reality that is found in consciousness, or a reality of which one is consciously aware. Like Hugh's description

414. Ibid., par. 2 (my translation): *Sunt ergo hic tria distinguenda: unum, quod tantum est sacramentum; alterum, quod est sacramentum et res; et tertium, quod est res and non sacramentum. Sacramentum et non res est /species visibilis panis et vini; sacramentum et res, caro Christi propria et sanguis; res et non sacramentum, mystica ejus caro.*

415. *Summa Sententiarum*, Tract 6 (*De sacramentis confirmationis, eucharistiae et extremae unctionis*), ch. 3: *Tria hic considerare oportet: unum quod est sacramentum tantum, alterum quod est sacramentum et res sacramenti, tertium quod est res tantum. Sacramentum et non res, sunt species visibiles, id est panis et vini; et ea quae ibi visibiliter celebrantur, ut fractio, depositio, elevatio. Sacramentum enim est sacrae rei signum. Signum autem est quod praeter speciem quam ingerit facit aliquid in mentem venire.* Here, as above, I have translated *res* as something real or as reality, and not as thing, which is the preference of most translators. The reference is to something that is real but not material, that is, to a spiritual or invisible reality. Note also that the name of the *tertium quid* is not yet what it would become, for here it is called *sacramentum et res sacramenti* rather than *sacramentum et res*.

416. See ibid.

of receiving Christ in communion, this seems to be an attempt to articulate the experience of being aware of Christ's real presence in the sacrament.

This chapter of the *Summa Sententiarum* concludes,

> And so in this sacrament there is a threefold consideration, as we said above. There are the visible appearances that are signs rather than realities; there is the true body of Christ under the appearance of bread and wine; and thirdly there are what can be called the spiritual flesh of Christ and the power of the sacrament, or the efficacy of the sacrament.[417]

By the early thirteenth century, this threefold consideration became standard in Catholic sacramental theology. Lombard's *Sentences* was but one of many textbooks when he wrote it, but fifty years later it had become the textbook of choice among the theology faculty at the University of Paris.[418] Today, writing a thesis is the ordinary requirement for completing a master's degree; then, teaching a course on the *Sentences* was required to become a *magister*. As a result, the threefold distinction between *sacramentum tantum*, *sacramentum et res* and *res tantum* became the standard way to think about the Eucharist and, eventually, the other sacraments as well.[419]

One aspect of this twelfth-century analysis did not become standard, however. The author of the *Summa Sententiarum* refers to the spiritual flesh of Christ and Lombard refers to the mystical flesh of Christ. Could they have been talking about a religious experience, that is, about an experienced immaterial reality? Lombard notes that "the flesh of Christ, more than other graces, spiritually restores and nourishes a person inwardly."[420] How did he know this? Unlike Hugh, these two authors do not describe the experience of receiving communion, but it is quite possible that this reference to a spiritual reality that results from receiving communion reflects their own religious experience. One author makes a reference to the bread of life discourse, and the other was aware that Augustine and others had identified the flesh of Christ with the spiritual nourishment that can be experienced through the receiving of communion.[421] Indeed, one could surmise that the threefold distinction, although made on the basis of authoritative texts, gained plausibility from being able to verified in experience. With one's eyes, one could see the outward appearances of bread and wine; because of one's faith, one could perceive the presence of Christ in the consecrated elements; and if one received communion devoutly, one could feel inwardly nourished and restored.

---

417. Ibid.: *Itaque tria in hoc sacramento consideranda sunt: species visibiles, quae sacramentum sunt et non res, et verum corpus Christi quod sub specie est panis et vini, tertium ipsa efficacia sacramenti, quae spiritualis caro Christi et virtus sacramenti appellantur, ut diximus.*

418. See Rosemann, *Peter Lombard's Sentences*, 60–61.

419. Interestingly, Lombard himself did not generalize on the threefold distinction and apply it to the other sacraments, which would be done by later schoolmen. In his treatment of baptism, for example, he does not identify the received sacrament as a *sacramentum et res*.

420. Lombard, *Sentences*, Bk. 4, Dist. 8, ch. 7, par. 3 (my translation).

421. See ibid., Dist. 9, ch. 1.

Needless to say, the *Sentences* talks regularly about receiving the sacrament and receiving the body and blood of Christ, and in one place he even quotes Augustine, who said, "A good person receives the sacrament and the thing of the sacrament, but a wicked one the sacrament and not the thing." Although not specifically identified here, the sacrament that is received cannot be the bread and the wine, for they are no longer present, but the *sacramentum et res*.[422] In other words, in an unworthy reception of communion, one receives the body and blood of Christ, but not the grace of the sacrament.

The combination of an inherited verbal tradition (i.e., calling the bread and wine the body and blood of Christ) and personal religious experience (i.e., perceiving the presence of Christ when looking at or ingesting the elements) also provides a basis for understanding what Lombard says about what Catholics call the real presence of Christ in the Eucharist. Lombard mocks those who deny the real presence as insane because they deny the power of God, which is unlimited.[423] But this appeal to objective logic may be his way of articulating a phenomenological fact, namely, the conscious perception of a divine presence when looking at the consecrated elements. Thus Lombard can say of Christ that "invisibly he is on the altar, because he does not appear in human form, but is veiled by the form of bread and wine."[424] Likewise, the flesh of Christ (i.e., the spiritual food that one receives when one partakes of communion) is also invisible: "it is truly on the altar, but because it does not appear in its own species, it is called invisible."[425] Significantly, Lombard also calls it intelligible (*intelligibile*), which is to say, understandable or meaningful.[426] All of these claims match what could be said if one tried to describe the experience of eucharistic adoration.

In the next section, Lombard uses language that will become standard in scholastic theology, and which harkens back to Berengar's claim that the presence of Christ was a formal presence. In Latin, the word *forma* can mean intelligibility, and in Greek philosophy it was understood to be that aspect of a thing which makes it understandable.[427] What made Berengar's explanation of Christ's real (or true) presence unacceptable is that it ran contrary to the tradition of saying that the bread and wine *become* the body and blood of Christ. This way of expressing the faith was generally taken to

422. See ibid., esp. the quotation in ch. 3.

423. See ibid., Dist. 10, ch. 1, par. 1.

424. Ibid., par. 5. Lombard believed that Christ's visible body is in heaven, having ascended there after the resurrection.

425. Ibid. Note that he does not call Christ's presence on the altar the real presence of Christ but the true presence of Christ. The terminology will change in later scholasticism, but the referent is the same.

426. Ibid., par. 7.

427. When the works of Plato and Aristotle were translated into Latin, εἶδος was usually translated as *forma*, but what the Greeks were referring to was an object's intelligibility, or the idea of the thing, which was interpreted as inhering in the thing itself. Material objects were thus said to be composed of matter and form, that is, they were both sensible and intelligible.

mean that what is really and truly bread and wine become really and truly the body and blood of Christ. In scholastic terminology, influenced as it was by Aristotelian metaphysics, the substance of bread and wine become the substance of Christ's body and blood. Berengar's explanation said something different; it said, in effect, that the reality of Christ is added to the reality of the elements.

Bernard Lonergan has argued that the Latin *substantia* is best understood as referring to what in English is called a thing, a "unity identity whole."[428] Transliterating *substantia* into "substance" is misleading because that word in English is commonly understood to be some sort of stuff, which is indeterminate, whereas a *substantia* is always determinate. The Greek word ουσία was usually translated as *substantia* in Latin, and it is sometimes translated as substance in English, but it is better translated as being, or even as a being. So *substantia* in scholastic writings should be understood as a being, as something that is. In Lonergan's terminology, it is a unified whole with a definite identity. When the schoolmen speak of the substance of bread and wine becoming the substance of Christ's body and blood, therefore, what they are saying in effect is that one being becomes another being or, more colloquially, that something becomes something else.

For centuries, the Christian tradition had affirmed that the bread and wine become the body and blood of Christ. When the schoolmen put this idea into the Greek philosophical categories that they were using, they said that the *substantia* of bread and wine became the *substantia* of Christ's body and blood, but they were only expressing the same belief in different terms. To put it in ordinary language, they were saying that what had been really and truly bread and wine became something really and truly different, namely, the body and blood of Christ. If it is correct to assume that the words of their tradition shaped their perception of reality, then they were talking about something that they experienced as real, not merely something that they believed was true.

In the past, some had argued, "The mystery of faith may be healthily believed; it cannot be healthily investigated."[429] But the schoolmen were not daunted by this warning, and in the twelfth century at least two explanations competed for acceptance. One later became known as transubstantiation, meaning that the substance of the bread and wine are changed into the substance of Christ's body and blood while the accidents remain the same. More colloquially, that actual bread and wine are changed into the body and blood of Christ even though their appearance is not changed. The other became known as consubstantiation, meaning that the substance of Christ's body and blood is added to the substance of bread and wine, whose accidents remain. More colloquially, Christ becomes really and truly present in the bread and wine, which continue to be what they were before, and so they still look like bread and wine. Lombard expressed his preference for the former view, not on philosophical grounds,

428. See Lonergan, *Insight*, 245–250; also 367 and 436.

429. Cited in Lombard, *Sentences*, Dist. 11, ch. 2, par. 2.

but because it better corresponded to the doctrine that the bread and wine become the body and blood of Christ.[430]

As mentioned earlier, the *Sentences* does not treat the mass as such, and it does not even have much to say about the mass as a sacrifice, a notion that would become greatly amplified during the Catholic counter-reformation following the Council of Trent. In one chapter of one section, Lombard affirms the tradition, citing Ambrose and Augustine, that "what the priest does is properly called a sacrifice or immolation."[431] He then asks the question, "whether Christ is immolated every day, or if he was immolated only once," giving the answer that later became standard among the schoolmen:

> To this, it may be briefly said that what is offered and consecrated by the priest is called sacrifice and oblation, because it is a remembrance and representation of the true sacrifice and holy immolation made on the altar of the cross. And indeed Christ died only once, namely on the cross, and there he was immolated in himself; but he is daily immolated in the sacrament, because in the sacrament is made a remembrance of what was done once.[432]

Two things may be noted. The first is that the understanding of sacrifice implicit in this passage is quite different from the understanding of sacrifice in the ancient world. When the thanksgiving meal (εὐχαριστία) was first called a sacrifice (θυσία) in the early patristic period, it referred to a meal celebrated in the presence of a god, and it is indirect evidence that early Christians experienced the presence of Christ, if not specifically in the bread and wine, then in the sharing of them. A θυσία was also an act of devotion or self-offering, for the spiritual dynamic of offering food to the god (or, in the Christians' case, to God the Father) symbolized their dedication and devotion to the values and ideals that the god represented. It was this dimension of θυσία that provided the linguistic basis for New Testament authors to interpret Jesus' death on the cross as a sacrifice, for by allowing himself to be executed rather than denying his mission, he was showing his devotion to the will of the Father and putting himself in God's hands.[433] In the Middle Ages, however, what happened on the cross was interpreted as a bloody death (immolation) and offering (oblation) to God made by Christ

---

430. See ibid., par. 5–10. Technically, consubstantiation differed from Berengar's explanation since it said that Christ is substantially present in the bread and wine, whereas Berengar had said that he is only formally present. In Aristotelian metaphysics, substance is composed of matter and form, so Berengar's theory was, in effect, that only the form or idea of Christ is in the consecrated elements. See also, Gary Macy, *The Theologies of the Eucharist in the Early Scholastic Period* (New York: Oxford University Press, 1984), 39–40.

431. Ibid., Dist. 12, ch. 5.

432. Ibid.

433. The Epistle to the Hebrews comes closest to interpreting the death of Jesus as a propitiatory offering made on behalf of others, but even this should not be interpreted as something that frees Christians from guilt without their having to participate in his offering by devoting their lives to others, as he did. See Heb 13:15–16.

to atone for the sins of others, quite apart from the participation of these acts in a life of devotion to God and self-giving to others.

The second thing to note is that Christians in the Middle Ages were expected to participate in the sacrifice of the Mass (called an unbloody sacrifice by later writers) in remembrance of what Christ had done for them. This remembrance was not supposed to be a mere mental recalling of an event long ago, however. Eucharistic spirituality in medieval and Tridentine Catholicism called for an imaginative and emotional participation in the sacrifice that took place once and for all on Calvary. It was supposed to be a re-living of that event that was re-presented at every mass. And it was supposed to result in deep gratitude for what Christ had done for the world's redemption, as well as a firm resolution to lead a life of personal holiness.[434] In this respect, then, there was a similarity between participating in a eucharistic θυσία in the third century and participating in a sacrifice of the mass in the thirteenth century: both invited attendees to enter into a spiritual dynamic of self-giving, but the earlier ritual celebrated communal self-giving to other people and the later ritual encouraged individual self-giving to God.

e. Penance

Medieval Christianity recognized that most people could not participate in the spiritual dynamic of the mass because they could not hear, much less understand, what the priest was doing at the altar. Creative preachers sometimes offered allegorical interpretations of the mass, likening parts of the mass to events in the life of Christ, but these were few and far between.[435] Most people were told that Christ had died for their sins, that his sacrifice was made present at every mass, and that they should worship him in the eucharistic elements. Christ's sacrificial death had made grace available to them, but if they sinned gravely, they had to confess their sins and make reparation for them in order to receive it.

Private confession in the twelfth century was a religious practice rather than an ecclesiastical ritual. That is to say, there was not a single prescribed way of doing it, nor was there a specific verbal formula that had to be pronounced, such as the Trinitarian formula for baptism or the words of consecration for the Eucharist. In local parishes, only priests ordinarily heard confessions, but monks and nuns still confessed to abbots and abbesses, and lay people sometimes found confessors in monks who were not ordained.

---

434. See Thomas à Kempis, *The Imitation of Christ*, Bk. 3, ch. 15; Bk. 4, ch. 3–4; Josef A. Jungmann, *The Mass: An Historical, Theological and Pastoral Survey* (Collegeville, MN: Liturgical Press, 1975), 56–57; Adolphe Tanquerey, *The Spiritual Life: A Treatise on Ascetical and Mystical Theology* (Westminster, MD: Newman, 1948), 143–150 on communion as a means of sanctification.

435. See Jungmann, *Mass of the Roman Rite*, Vol 1, 89–90; also Martos, *Doors to the Sacred*, 269.

As we have seen, the practice had undergone considerable evolution during the Dark Ages, and by the high Middle Ages confession to a priest had become relatively standardized, judging from the ecclesiastical records that are still available. There had been four steps in public repentance during the patristic period: confession in private to the bishop, the public performance of works of repentance, ritual reconciliation with the church, and readmission to communion. People who were gravely ill were routinely absolved from any undone penances so that they could be reconciled and receive communion before their departure from this life. This sequence was initially followed when reconciliation became a priestly practice, but over the course of centuries it got changed around: the penitent confessed in private, the priest then gave assurance of God's forgiveness and assigned works of penance, and he also absolved the penitent from any undone penances in the case of a sudden and unexpected death. By the eleventh century, this absolution from penances had become an absolution from sins,[436] and it was understood to be a juridical act that could be performed only by priests. This is the state of the practice when it was approved and recommended by the Fourth Lateran Council in 1215.[437]

Hugh of St. Victor opens his treatment of confession with a lengthy argument against those who say that there is no commandment to confess sins even though Christ gave his disciples the power (*potestas*) to forgive them. Although he distinguishes between "those who have sins" and "those who have the power to forgive sins," he repeatedly quotes James 5:16, which says "confess your sins to one another," and he nowhere says that only priests have this power.[438] When he speaks of penance (*paenitentia*) he does not mention a church ritual but says, "Exterior penance is in the affliction of the flesh. Interior penance is in the contrition of the heart."[439] In this context, *paenitentia* is probably better translated as penitence. Indeed, most of Hugh's treatment deals with the dynamic of repentance and forgiveness, and the role that confessing to another might play in this process, rather than with confession as a rite in need of a theological explanation.

In only one place in the *Decretum* does Gratian make reference to penance (*penitentia*) as a sacrament that is comparable to baptism, and that is given for washing away sins,[440] and in only two places does he talk about doing penance (*penitentiam agere*) or performing works of repentance.[441] If in 1140 penance were a church ritual

---

436. Although called an absolution from sins, it was understood to be an absolution from guilt, which is another way of talking about a forgiveness of sins.

437. See Poschmann, *Penance*, ch. 2; also Martos, *Doors to the Sacred*, 340–341.

438. Hugh, *Sacraments*, Bk. 2, Pt. 14, ch. 1.

439. Ibid., ch. 2. Afflictions of the flesh might include abstaining from meat or wine, fasting completely from food or drink, kneeling for long periods of time, etc.

440. See Pt. 2, case 1, q. 1, can. 42: *ad culpas abluendas dantur, ut baptismus et penitentia.*

441. See Pt. 2, case 1, q. 7, can. 5; Pt. 2, case 2, q. 1, can. 18.

regulated by ecclesiastical canons, Gratian would have written much more about it, so we must conclude that at this point the practice was more informal than formal.

Almost everything that Gratian has to say about the forgiveness or remission of sins (*remissio peccatorum*) is related to baptism, which is said to give or confer (*dare, conferre*) the remission of sins on the baptized.[442] He appears to think rather legalisitically about this, for he says that it is done through the power of the keys rather than through any movement of the heart.[443] He says elsewhere that receiving the body of Christ also makes for the remission of sins, but in one place he says that receiving the body gives remission of sins if it is done with a wholehearted confession of sins accompanied by works of repentance.[444] Normally, baptism brings a full remission of sins, but it does not have this effect for those who are baptized outside the church.[445]

Overall, Gratian's treatment is legalistic and mechanistic rather than pastoral and introspective. Interestingly, he always speaks about the remission of sins and never about the forgiveness (*dismissio* or *venia*) of sins. He never tries to explain what he means by the remission of sins, but it appears that he must have in mind the forgiveness of guilt, unless he thinks of sins themselves as somehow inhering in the soul prior to baptism.

In contrast with Gratian's legalistic approach, Lombard's is pastoral and spiritual, treating sin and its forgiveness in eight sections, and devoting more space to penance than to baptism or the Eucharist. The broadness of this treatment is due in part to the ambiguity of the Latin word *paenitentia* (also spelled *penitentia*, *poenitentia* or *pœnitentia*), which can be translated as penitence, repentance or penance, depending on the context. When one hears the phrase, "sacrament of penance" today, one thinks of a Catholic church ritual named penance (or, since Vatican II, reconciliation), but when medieval writers talked about *sacramentum paenitentiae*, they were more often thinking about some outward sign of repentance. Thus Lombard writes,

> For there is an inner penance, and an outward one. The exterior one is the sacrament; the interior one is the virtue of the mind; and each of these is a cause of justification and salvation.[446]

During the previous thousand years, concern for the consequences of sin had gradually shifted from this life to the next, that is, from the effects of selfish and immoral behavior on individuals and communities to the effects on a person's soul in the afterlife. Moreover, thinking about sin and its consequences had become more legalistic, not only when public repentance was required for public sins in the Christian

442. See Pt. 2, case 2, q. 1, can. 47 and 48; Pt. 2, case 24, q. 1, can. 31.

443. See Pt. 2, case 32, q. 1, can. 8: *per claves regni celorum.*

444. See Pt. 3, dist. 2, can. 40; Pt. 2, 33, 3 (*De penitentia*), dist. 1, can. 52: *Ergo evidentissime Domini predicatione mandatum est etiam gravissimi criminis reis, si ex toto corde et manifesta confessione peccati penitentiam gerant, sacramenti celestis perfundendam gratiam.*

445. See See Pt. 3, dist. 4, can. 4 and 146.

446. Lombard, *Sentences*, Dist. 14, ch. 1.

Roman Empire but also when specific penances were meted out for specific sins during the Dark Ages.[447] The word *paenitentia* is closely related to *poena*, which means punishment or penalty. Lombard links it to a different word, but the meaning is the same: "It is called penance from 'punishing,' and by it each one punishes the illicit things which he has done."[448]

In the *Sentences*, penance is primarily interior penitence, which is discussed next:

> Penance is a virtue by which we bewail and hate, with purpose of amendment, the evils we have committed, and we will not to commit again the things we have bewailed. And so true penance is to sorrow in one's soul and to hate vices.[449]

When books such as the *Sentences* were being compiled, the schoolmen gained access to texts from the patristic era, and the texts that spoke of penance of course often referred to the canonical process of public repentance. Unaware of the difference, medieval scholars often applied the quotations to the process of private confession, and in doing so they sometimes attributed things to the medieval practice that had been true centuries before. Lombard was aware of what he called solemn or ceremonial penance (*paenitentia solemnis*), but he believes it was a special custom of the church (*specialem morem ecclesiae*) long ago, whereas in fact it was the canonical norm for centuries.[450]

Lombard's discussion about works of repentance such as fasting and almsgiving eventually leads him to ask whether sin can be remitted without confession if one is sufficiently contrite in one's heart. He cites a number of authorities that say sin is remitted by contrition alone and then a number that say that confession is necessary, concluding that "it is necessary for a penitent to confess, if he has the time; and yet, before there is confession by the mouth, if there is the intention in the heart, remission is granted to him."[451] He is trying to have it both ways because he does not want to contradict any of the authoritative theologians who preceded him.

Next he asks whether it is necessary to confess one's sins to a priest, or whether confession can be made to a lay person or even just to God. Lining up authorities in support of each of these alternatives, Lombard again refuses to give a definitive answer, suggesting circumstances under which each one might be correct.[452] If nothing else, this thorough examination of the questions demonstrates that their answers had not

---

447. On legalism the patristic period, see Martos, *Doors to the Sacred*, 328–334; and in the early Middle Ages, 337–339. See also Hugh Connolly, *The Irish Penitentials and Their Significance for the Sacrament of Penance Today* (Dublin: Four Courts Press, 1995).

448. Lombard., *Sentences*, ch. 2. The word used for punishing is *puniendo*, and the image is one of beating down the sins in a person's soul.

449. Ibid., ch. 3.

450. Ibid., ch. 4.

451. Ibid., Dist. 17, ch. 1

452. Ibid., Dist. 17, ch. 2–5.

yet been decided. And one reason for the lack of clear *explicationes* was the absence of a definite *explicandum*, that is to say, there was not yet a uniform sacramental ritual in European Christianity.

This lack of clarity may be one reason why Lombard does not discuss the distinction between the sacred sign (*sacramentum*) and the spiritual reality (*res*) of penance until the very end. According to the *Sentences*, "Some say that the sacrament here is that which is done outwardly alone, namely outward penance [i.e., works of repentance], which is the sign of the inner penance, namely of contrition of heart and humiliation."[453] Yet if this is the case, he notes, the spiritual reality seems to be the cause of the sign and not the other way around, for inner repentance is expressed in a demonstration of repentance.

> But some say that inward and outward penance are the sacrament: not two sacraments but one. . . . As in the sacrament of the body, so also in this sacrament they say that the sacrament alone (*sacramentum tantum*) is one thing, namely outward penance; another is sacrament and thing (*sacramentum et res*), namely inward penance; another is thing and not sacrament (*res tantum*), namely the remission of sins.[454]

Lombard expresses his approval of the simpler twofold distinction, and he says nothing about the threefold distinction, which appears to have been introduced by others in order to fit the practice of confession into the categories that were beginning to provide a convenient schema for understanding the Eucharist and other sacraments. In sum, he leaves it to later schoolmen to work out a satisfactory theology of penance, but he has given them ample material to work with.

Something that ought to be noted with regard to repentance rituals in the history of Christianity is the vagueness of words related to the words and the persons involved. In the Koine Greek of the New Testament, the word most frequently used is αφιέναι, which literally means to send forth or let go, but which by extension means to dismiss a debt or forgive a wrong. In the Vulgate, two words are used: *dimittere*, which means literally to send away or dismiss, and *remittere*, which means literally to send back or remit. All of the words can be rendered in English as forgive, which captures neither the original sense of the Greek word nor the nuance between the two Latin words.[455] Early Christian concern with sin had to do with ceasing sinful behavior by getting rid of sinful habits, and indeed the process of public repentance aimed at precisely that end. So also did the practice of private confession when it first appeared. Even the penitentials, those books that confessors used to match sins with penances, were originally intended to expunge bad habits (e.g., avarice) by prescribing virtuous

453. Ibid., Dist. 22, ch. 2.

454. Ibid.

455. In English translations of Latin works, *dimittere* is often translated as forgive (as in the Lord's Prayer) and *remittere* is often translated as remit (as when speaking about the remission of sins), but the practice is far from uniform.

ones (e.g., almsgiving). Over the course of time, however, both practices succumbed to magical thinking, with public repentance being postponed until one was close to death so that one could obtain forgiveness without having to do anything but confess one sins, and with private confession offering forgiveness in much the same way.

The *Book of Sentences* was written at a time when Christian thinkers were still wrestling with the relation between conscious remorse, demonstrations of repentance, and forgiveness by God. In time, however, logic would lead the schoolmen to embrace the view that what was most important is God's forgiveness, and that priests had the power to declare that forgiveness if penitents expressed sorrow for their sins and promised not to sin again. Thus, what had originally been an attempt to help people through a process of moral conversion became a ritual for obtaining forgiveness as often as needed. It became more legalistic, for it required only the proper performance of the ritual, and it became more magical, for its invisible efficacy was guaranteed by the church.[456] In other words, the canonical approach based on church law eventually displaced more nuanced theological approaches based on experience.

f. Extreme Unction

In the twelfth century, the anointing of the sick was well on its way to becoming the anointing of the dying. Whether the anointed recovered from their illness or not, however, the purpose of the ritual was increasingly regarded as preparation for eternal life, not physical recovery. In the copying and recopying of sacramentaries, the order of the last rites got changed from anointing-confession-viaticum to confession-viaticum-anointing, which led the schoolmen to speculate about what there was left for the anointing to do after someone made their last confession and received their last communion.

Perhaps the continuing evolution of this ritual and its relative unimportance in the lives of most Christians explain why it is nowhere mentioned in Gratian's *Decretum*. There are about fifty references to anointing (*unctio*) in his work, but none to an anointing done for the sick or to a final anointing (*extrema unctio*) performed by priests. All are references to the anointings and oils that are used in baptism, ordination, the consecration of churches, and so on.

In *The Sacraments of the Christian Faith*, Hugh of St. Victor refers to this ritual by its traditional name, anointing of the sick. He believed that the practice was instituted by the apostles because of what is found in James 5:14–16, which he says shows that "this sacrament was established for a twofold reason, namely, for the remission of sins

---

456. Thus Lombard notes, "But it is asked whether a priest can absolve from sin, that is, from guilt, so as to wipe away the stain of guilt; or whether he is able to dissolve the debt of eternal death." *Sentences*, Dist. 18, ch. 4. For the purpose of this study, his answer to the question is less significant than the way the question is posed, for it assumes that the ritual has a hidden spiritual effect. (His answer is that the priest performs the ritual but God remits sins and their punishment.)

and for the alleviation of sickness."[457] He argues for the repeatability of the sacrament not because of church practice (since it was usually not repeated) but because of the pastoral possibility that a person who was anointed might recover, only to fall sick later from a different illness. He appears to assume that the anointing will be done by priests, not only because of the proof text taken from the Epistle of James, but also because the anointing is to be done using "the oil of the sick," which is blessed by the bishop. He devotes only three short chapters to this sacrament.

The treatment in the *Sentences* is equally abbreviated, but the practice is here called *extrema unctio*, and Lombard explains that it is "done at the end of life with oil consecrated by the bishop."[458] As with confession, there does not seem to have been a uniform rite, which was not unusual at a time when sacramentaries were copied by hand and each new copy was amended as seemed appropriate. Perhaps for this reason, Lombard deems it necessary at the beginning of his treatment to distinguish it from the anointings that take place in baptism and confirmation, as well as from the anointings given to kings and bishops.

In this ritual, oil is literally given by one person to another, and so Lombard speaks naturally of receiving the anointing and receiving the sacrament. But availing himself of the distinction between *sacramentum* and *res sacramenti*, he writes,

> The sacrament is the outer anointing itself; the thing of the sacrament is the inner anointing, which is brought about by the remission of sins and the increase of the virtues.[459]

Lombard allows, nonetheless, that the sacrament might bring relief in body as well as in soul, "so long as it is expedient that he should be relieved in both."[460] When it comes to the question of whether the sacrament can be repeated, he agrees that it can be, but not on theological or pastoral grounds. Rather, it can be repeated because it is the custom of the church to do so.[461]

g. Ordination

Even though *The Apostolic Tradition* had prohibited women who served in the ministries of widows and virgins from being ordained, women in the east continued to be ordained deacons, and in the west women were ordained to a variety of ministries. As already noted, ordination in the patristic and early medieval periods was a matter of

---

457. Hugh of St. Victor, *Sacraments*, Bk. 2, pt. 15, ch. 2.

458. Lombard, *Sentences*, Dist. 23, ch. 1.

459. Ibid., ch. 3. Later schoolmen speculated that the effect of extreme unction was the forgiveness of venial sins, especially those which had never been confessed, since only mortal sins had to be revealed in the sacrament of penance.

460. Ibid.

461. Ibid, ch. 4.

being publicly enrolled in an *ordo* or class of people who were of service in the church. Also during this lengthy period, the terms *ordinare, consecrare* and *benedicere* were used interchangeably in sacramentaries and other documents referring to the orders. Given this looseness of terminology, there is ample evidence that women in the west were ordained to be widows, virgins, deaconesses, cloistered nuns, and abbesses.[462]

As European society emerged from the Dark Ages and started to engage in intellectual pursuits, church leaders and scholars began to seek a coherent picture both of the world around them and also of the faith they shared. To this end, as we have already seen, texts were gathered, commented on, and interpreted in ways that minimized the differences between them. In addition, those interested in reform began to promote greater uniformity in liturgical practice and greater control of people's behavior. The collection of false decretals produced by the ninth century reformers in Charlemagne's Holy Roman Empire is a practical example of this, and Gratian's *Agreement of Disagreeing Canons* (the *Decretum*) as well as Lombard's *Four Books of Opinions* (the *Sentences*) are academic examples of this. Pope's Gregory VII in the eleventh century and Alexander III in the twelfth century were also energetic reformers.

Hugh of St. Victor's treatment of sacraments related to the clergy shows how the schoolmen's thinking about ordination was shifting from an enrollment in an *ordo* to a bestowal of special gifts. The section on clerical orders is titled "Spiritual Power," and it treats only those *ordines* related to the priesthood, namely porter, lector, exorcist, acolyte, subdeacon, deacon, presbyter, bishop, archbishop, patriarch or primate, and pope.[463] It then discusses the powers related to each of these orders, with presbyters "receiving in this sacrament the grace of consecrating" and "the power of offering hosts pleasing to God."[464] Although Hugh often speaks of *presbyteres* and *sacerdotes* interchangeably, it is clear that in his mind the upper clergy are priests even though they rank higher than presbyters. Toward the end of his treatment, he asks whether deacons and those in higher orders should be ordained "without a definite title," that is without being assigned to a particular community, but he does not answer the question.[465] Previously, people were ordained to a certain role within a given community, but with ordination now being conceived as a bestowal of special powers, the older restriction was becoming an issue.

Gratian does not even raise the question of ordination with or without a title. In the *Decretum* it is clear that holy orders (*sacri ordines*) are clerical ranks or steps through which the ordained pass from lower to higher grades of ministry, each of

462. There is also evidence that women entered the orders of presbyter and bishop, but it is less plentiful. See Macy, *Hidden History*, ch. 3

463. According to Hugh, lay monks are said to be in a religious order, but this is a concession granted to them "as a matter of indulgence," out of respect for their state in life. See Hugh, *Sacraments*, Bk. 2, Pt. 3, ch. 3.

464. Ibid., ch. 11. Note that for Hugh, *sacramentum* refers to the ceremony ("in this sacrament"); he does not speak of a received sacrament but only of powers and gifts that are received.

465. See ibid., ch. 21.

which is characterized by a certain power (*potestas*), with no reference to where that power is to be exercised. Since ordination encompassed a number of different ceremonies, Gratian speaks of the sacraments (*sacramenta*) of ordination.[466]

The orders listed in the *Decretum* correspond exactly to those found in the Catholic Church from the high Middle Ages to the middle of the twentieth century: porter, lector, exorcist, acolyte, subdeacon, deacon, and priest (*gradum sacerdotii vel levitici ordinis*).[467] Whereas in earlier centuries, people in various orders performed separate ministries, by the twelfth century the sequence of seven orders comprised something of a training program for clerics, with each order being a step (*gradus*) to the next. Clerics advance (*accedere*) and are promoted (*promovere*) through the ranks, through which they are also said to ascend (*ascendere*).[468] When they are admitted (*admittere*) to an order, they receive (*recipere*, *accipere*) the order, which they are also said to have (*habere*).[469] Augustine had called priesthood the sacrament of giving baptism, and following his example, Gratian speaks not only of orders being received but also of a sacrament being received by those who are ordained.[470] Also on Augustine's authority, Gratian says that this sacrament cannot be lost and that therefore no ordination should be repeated.[471] Gratian also speaks of ordination as a sort of consecration (*quadam consecratione*) by which men are made priests (*sacerdotes fieri*), deacons, and so on.[472] Finally, ordination is said to be celebrated (*celebrare*).[473]

Peter Lombard's treatment of clerical orders is similar to that of Hugh, focusing on the duties of each.[474] He acknowledges that only the orders of deacon, presbyter and bishop are found in the New Testament, but he conflates presbyters with bishops, thereby maintaining the number of orders at seven. He does not say that Christ ordained the apostles, but he does believe that the apostles ordained bishops, presbyters and deacons in the early church.[475]

---

466. See Gratian, *Decretum*, Pt. 2, case 1, q. 1, can. 97.

467. See ibid., Pt. 1, dist. 23, can. 11– 19; also dist. 25, can. 1.

468. See Pt. 1, dist. 34, can. 10; dist. 48, can. 2; Pt. 2, case 1, q. 1, can. 120.

469. See Pt. 1, dist. 50, can. 34; dist. 81, can. 4: Pt. 2, case 1, q. 1, can. 97 and 119; Pt. 2, case 1, q. 7, can. 2; Pt. 2, case 9, q. 1, can. 4; Pt. 3, dist. 4, can. 32.

470. See Pt. 2, case 1, q. 1, can. 43 and 97; Pt. 3, dist. 4, can. 32. At this point, it is still an open question whether ordination comprises one or seven sacraments, i.e., one for each grade. Gratian does not raise this issue, but it was debated in the thirteenth century until it was agreed that it is one sacrament but its powers are incrementally received with each advance in holy orders.

471. See Pt. 2, case 24, q. 1, can. 37; Pt. 3, dist. 4, can. 32.

472. See Pt. 1, dist. 23, can. 11; dist. 27, can. 1; Pt. 2, case 1, q. 1, can. 97.

473. See Pt. 1, dist. 67, can. 1; dist. 75, can. 5.

474. In Lombard's mind, all of the orders derive from the earthly ministry of Jesus. For example, Jesus exercised the office of porter when he drove the money changers from the temple, and that of lector when he read from the book of Isaiah in the synagogue. See Lombard, *Sentences*, Dist. 24, ch. 5–6.

475. See ibid., ch. 12.

Only toward the end of this section does Lombard say what he means by an order:

> But if it were asked what it is that here is called an order, it may truly be said that it is some mark (*signaculum*), that is, something sacred (*sacrum quoddam*), by which spiritual power (*potestas*) and office (*officium*) are granted to the one ordained. And so the spiritual character (*character*), when a promotion of power is made, is called an order or degree (*gradus*).[476]

The first seven degrees bestow powers on the ordained, whereas the ordination of bishops, archbishops, patriarchs and metropolitans convey offices or dignities. Thus the first seven orders "are called sacraments, because a sacred thing is conferred in the receiving of them, that is, grace, which the things carried out at ordination signify."[477]

In these two quotations we see a clear distinction between the sacramental rite (*sacramentum tantum*), of which here there are seven, and that which is bestowed and received, here described as a grace or gift that is a power or office, but not generalized as the thing of the sacrament (*res tantum*). Lombard says that a special character is given with each increase in power, but he does not say what the character is nor does he identify it as something that is both *sacramentum* and *res*. That development will come only later, as schoolmen commenting on the *Sentences* notice the parallels between ordination and baptism, and as they apply the threefold distinction needed to explain the Eucharist to all the other sacraments.

Once again, as with the work of Hugh and Gratian, we see scholastic theology moving in the direction of the theory that would be worked out by Aquinas and others a half century later, but it is not yet there. Nonetheless, the notion that the ordination rite confers both a character and a power is securely established by 1150, as is the understanding that the power given to the presbyter is a priestly (*sacerdotalis*) power to confect the sacrament of the Lord's body and blood and to offer God "placating sacrifices."[478]

h. Marriage

For centuries after the collapse of the Roman Empire, there had been no central civil authority in Europe except for Charlemagne's Holy Roman Empire, and then only briefly. Nonetheless, people continued to marry and to argue about the validity of marriages, the fairness of divorces, the inheritance rights of children, and so on. Disputed cases were usually decided in the court of the local lord, but if either

---

476. Ibid., ch. 13.

477. Ibid. Lombard is referring to the giving of symbolic keys in the ordination of a porter, the giving of a candle in the ordination of an acolyte, the giving of a book of the gospels in the ordination of a deacon, and so on.

478. Ibid., ch. 11.

party disputed the lord's judgment, appeal might be made to a higher authority, and very often that higher authority was the bishop of the region. Thus, in the tenth and eleventh centuries, bishops became increasingly involved with marriage cases, their decisions entered the body of ecclesiastical case law, and the regulations approved by bishops and synods to bring some order into marital matters entered into church regulations or canon law.

In order to address the problem of clandestine marriages, church laws increasingly required that all marriages be witnessed by the local priest and recorded in the parish registry, where baptisms were also recorded. This led to weddings being conducted in churches rather than in homes, and to priests being asked to bless the newly married couple. Eventually, priests displaced the parents who had previously conducted the wedding ceremony, and by the twelfth century, the exchange of wedding vows had become a church ritual, usually followed by a mass that celebrated the nuptials.[479]

Christian intellectuals had long written about marriage, not because it was a church ceremony but because in one way or another it touched the life of every Christian. The growing body of case law and ecclesiastical regulation concerning marriage, however, led Gratian to include marriage in his *Decretum*, and the newly developed priestly ritual led Lombard to include marriage in his *Sentences*. Both had an interest in defining marriage, one from a legal perspective and the other from a theological perspective, and both had an interest in determining exactly when a marriage came into being.

During the Dark Ages, ancient Roman law and traditional Germanic customs had existed side by side. Southern Europe leaned toward the Roman tradition that marriage is created by consent, and northern Europe leaned toward the Germanic tradition of marriage being sealed by intercourse, but no large portion of Christendom was totally governed by one tradition or the other. After the year 1000, as the schoolmen turned their scientific minds to discerning the order in the universe, they instinctively assumed that since there is only one God, only one human race, and only one true religion, that there ought to be one true understanding of marriage.

In the twelfth century, the legal, liturgical and theological strands of development came together. Gratian and other canonists favored the Germanic assumption that a valid marriage had to be ratified by an act of sexual intercourse. Lombard and other theologians favored the Roman belief that a true marriage comes into existence when the partners stand before each other and pronounce their wedding vows. But the theologians also had another issue to deal with, namely, the sacramentality of marriage.

Interpreting Ephesians 5:32, *Sacramentum hoc magnum est*, as referring to a sacrament rather than to a mystery, and rediscovering Augustine's insistence that marriage contains a *sacramentum*, the schoolmen concluded that marriage is a Christian sacrament. In the early twelfth century, when any sacred thing could be called a

---

479. See Schillebeeckx, *Marriage*, 256–79; also Martos, *Doors to the Sacred*, 426–29.

sacrament, the main objection to marriage being regarded as a sacrament was that it involved sexual activity, which was viewed as less than holy. But in the late twelfth century, when only seven specific church rituals were called sacraments, the discussion turned to the nature of the sacrament that Augustine claimed was indissoluble.

The three strands were woven together by Alexander III, a canonist who was pope from 1159 to 1181. Alexander proposed that a true marriage comes into existence when the spouses consent to be husband and wife, and that the marital relationship itself is a sacrament, but that it becomes indissoluble only with the couple's first act of sexual intercourse. This was a good practical solution to issues that had been bothering churchmen for decades, and the pope left it to others to determine the nature of the marital sacrament and to figure out how a carnal activity could turn a dissoluble relationship into an indissoluble one.

Writing at a time when theological terminology was still fluid, Hugh of St. Victor could say that the sacrament of marriage was established by God before the fall of Adam and Eve, not as a remedy for sin (i.e., to provide for the weakness of the flesh) but as a duty (*officium*) to increase and multiply.[480] Marriage could be considered sacramental even before Christ because it is richly symbolic, anticipating the union between Christ and the church. Hugh follows the Roman tradition in defining marriage in terms of consent, both the *consensus conjugalis* to make a life together and the *consensus carnis* to have sexual intercourse. The bond between the spouses is a *vinculum caritatis* rather than a legal bond.[481]

Most of Hugh's treatment of marriage deals with non-sacramental issues (e.g., clandestine marriages, polygamy in the Old Testament, and forbidden degrees of kinship), and his discussion of the benefits of marriage (fidelity, progeny and sacrament) closely follows the teaching of Augustine.[482] Likewise, he accepts at face value Augustine's teaching on the indissolubility of the sacrament, discussing only whether a union that is dissolved by annulment or dispensation can rightly be said to have been a marriage.[483] Nonetheless, he is not very definite about the nature of the sacrament.[484]

Gratian agrees with Hugh of St. Victor that marriage (*conjugium*) was instituted by God in the Garden of Eden, but he does not say that it was a sacrament at that time. In his mind, marriage in Paradise was so pure that conception would have taken place without ardor and childbirth would have happened without pain.[485] It was only after the Fall that men felt lust and women experienced painful labor.

Gratian defines marriage (*coniugium sive matrimonium*) as a coming together of a man and a woman in a common life. For this reason, the consent of both are

---

480. See Hugh of St. Victor, *Sacraments*, Bk. 2, Pt. 11, ch. 1.

481. See ibid., ch. 2–4; Also Schillebeeckx, *Marriage,* 320–24.

482. See ibid., ch. 7 and 8.

483. See ibid., ch. 11.

484. See Schillebeeckx, *Marriage,* 323.

485. See Gratian, *Decretum,* Pt. 2, case 32, q. 2, can. 1 and 2.

needed, and marriage cannot be contracted before the age of discretion.[486] Gratian cites a number of sources to the effect that consent makes the marriage,[487] but he is of the opinion that a marriage to which the spouses have given consent is not ratified or completed until they have sexual intercourse.[488]

Citing the authority of Augustine, he declares that for Christians there are three benefits of marriage—fidelity, offspring, and sacrament—and he hints that the mingling of the sexes (*conmixtionem sexuum*) is a sign of the nuptials (*nuptiae*) between Christ and the church.[489] Gratian does not forthrightly declare that marriage is a sacrament, however; he prefers to say that there is a sacrament in marriage.[490]

Gratian appears to identify the sacrament that is found in marriage with the marriage bond (*vinculum coniugii* or *vinculum coniugale*), a legal concept and social reality that was given metaphysical status in medieval philosophy and theology.[491] Although he nowhere equates the sacrament and the bond, he ascribes the attribute of indissolubility to it, saying that, like the sacrament of baptism, the bond of marriage cannot be taken away nor lost.[492] Because of the bond or sacrament in marriage, a legitimate and ratified marriage (*coniugia legitima et rata*) cannot be dissolved for any reason.[493] Among the proposed reasons that Gratian rejects are infidelity or violation of the marriage vow, the sickness or absence of a spouse, and the fact that a marriage was entered into secretly and without parental consent.[494] Evidently some had argued that when pagans are baptized, their marriage to a pagan spouse is dissolved, but Gratian rejects this argument.[495] The only way to lose the sacrament of marriage, he says, is the death of one's spouse.[496]

The *Decretum* treats many other aspects of marriage such as wedding customs, grounds for annulment, legitimacy of offspring, and inheritance rights, but these do not pertain to sacramentality and need not concern us here.

486. See ibid., Pt. 2, case 29, q. 1, can. 1.

487. See Pt. 2, case 27, q. 2, can. 1 and 45.

488. See Pt. 2, case 27, q. 2, can. 26: *Unde inter sponsum et sponsam coniugium est, sed initiatum; inter copulatos est coniugium ratum.* See also can. 37.

489. See Pt. 2, case 27, q. 2, can. 10, 17 and 39. Also case 32, q. 2, can. 2.

490. See Pt. 2, case 27, q. 2, can. 39: *habeat in se Christi et ecclesiae sacramentum.* Also Pt. 2, case 32, q. 2, can. 2: *Magnum ibi sacramentum.*

491. See Pt.1, dist. 23, can. 3; Pt. 2, case 32, q. 7, can. 1 and 28.

492. See Pt. 2, case 32, q. 7, can. 28: *Manet inter viventes quoddam vinculum coniugale, quod nec separatio, nec cum altero copulatio possit auferre; sicut apostata anima, velut de coniugio Christi recedens, etiam fide perdita sacramentum fidei non amittit, quod lavacro regenerationis accepit.*

493. See Pt. 2, case 28, q. 1, can. 17. Also case 27, q. 2, can. 51. Also Pt. 2, case 32, q. 7, can. 2: *Nulla ratione dissolvitur coniugium, quod semel initum probatur.*

494. See Pt.1, dist. 27, can. 1; Pt. 2, case 28, q. 1, can. 1; case 30, q. 5, can. 8; case 32, q. 7, can. 2 and 28.

495. See Pt. 2, case 28, q. 2, can. 1: *Crimina enim in baptismo solvuntur, non coniugia.* Also can. 2.

496. See Pt. 2, case 32, q. 7, can. 2.

Peter Lombard practically quotes Hugh of St. Victor when he says that the sacrament of marriage was instituted by God before the original sin, but he goes on to say that there was a twofold institution of marriage, the first being God's command to increase and multiply and the second being God's concession to the weakness of the flesh.[497] That Christ approved of marriage is clear from his attendance at the wedding feast at Cana and from his condemnation of divorce and remarriage.[498]

Earlier schoolmen had speculated whether the sacrament of marriage might be an element in the nuptial ceremony such as the blessing of the couple by the priest,[499] but the theological tradition clearly favored the notion that the marital relationship itself is somehow sacramental. Thus Lombard declares that if a sacrament is a sign of a sacred thing, there must be a sacred reality of which marriage itself is a sign, and indeed that reality is proclaimed in the Epistle to the Ephesians to be "the joining of Christ and his Church."[500] Thus the evolution of language that began in the fourth century comes to completion in the twelfth century. When Jerome translated μυστήριον as *sacramentum*, what he meant was a mystery, the mystery being the relationship between Christ and the church. When Augustine reflected on this passage, he saw a *sacramentum* or mystery in both the husband-wife relationship and the Christ-church relationship. But now in the *Sentences*, the *sacramentum* is only the husband-wife relationship which is a sacred sign of a sacred reality, namely, the Christ-church relationship. The latter is not a *sacramentum* but something that is signified, namely, the joining of the church as bride with her bridegroom, who is Christ.

> And so the bride is joined to the bridegroom spiritually and corporeally, that is, by charity and by the conformity of nature.—There is a symbol of this two-fold joining in marriage: for the consent of the partners signifies the spiritual joining of Christ and the Church, which happens through charity; but the intermingling of the sexes signifies that union which happens through the conformity of nature.[501]

Lombard insists that what brings the marriage into being (in other words, what causes the marital sacrament) is the expressed consent of the couple, and that everything else in the wedding ritual (e.g., the priest's blessing) is merely decorous. Like Hugh and Gratian, he discusses many other issues of importance to marriage in the Middle Ages (e.g., who may and may not marry, the rights and duties of husband and wife), returning to the matter of sacramentality only briefly when appealing to the authority of Augustine that there are three benefits or goods of marriage, namely

497. Lombard, *Sentences*, Dist. 26, ch. 1–4.

498. Ibid., ch. 5.

499. See Schillebeeckx, *Marriage*, 312–15.

500. Lombard., *Sentences*, Dist. 26, ch. 6.

501. Ibid., Dist. 27, ch. 3; Dist. 28, ch. 2. Also Dist. 31, ch. 2, par. 3: "And note that the third good of marriage is called 'sacrament' not because the marriage itself is a sacrament, but because it is a sign of its sacred thing, that is, the spiritual and inseparable conjoining of Christ and the Church."

fidelity, offspring, and sacrament. But for Lombard, like Gratian, naming one of the benefits of marriage as sacrament basically implies that the union cannot be severed:

> But sacrament so inseparably inheres in the marriage of lawful persons that there does not seem to be a marriage without it, because a conjugal bond always remains between living partners, so that, even when there is a divorce because of fornication, the firmness of the conjugal bond is not dissolved.[502]

In other words, marriage is a sacred sign of the union between Christ and the church. But the union between Christ and the church is indissoluble. Therefore the sign that points to it must also be indissoluble.

Apart from the fact that this argument is formally fallacious, that is, it has a faulty logical form, it might be noted that the scholastic position on the indissolubility of marriage was also logically inconsistent. For logically, if a sacramental marriage, like the union of Christ and the church, is indissoluble, and if death is not the end of life but a transition to a different mode of life, then a sacramental marriage should continue to exist even after the death of one of the spouses. But neither Augustine nor the schoolmen ever considered this argument, probably because it would have been glaringly countercultural to propose that widows and widowers could not remarry.

Here then we have another instance of lived experience shaping theology. Augustine had explained the practice of not rebaptizing by postulating the existence of a baptismal *sacramentum*, and he argued against remarriage by postulating the existence of a marital *sacramentum*. In the case of marriage, however, his argument did not fit the times, and Christians continued to divorce and remarry in the Roman Empire. Later, in medieval Christendom, divorce was virtually impossible because marriages were generally arranged by parents for their children and separation from one's spouse was socially stigmatized. Then, in the twelfth century, the institutional church found itself in complete legal control of marriage, so it ratified the status quo by making divorce legally impossible and resurrecting Augustine's theory of indissolubility to explain it.[503] But just as Augustine had not considered the logical implication of his own theory, namely that it would forbid remarriage in all cases, so the medieval churchmen never realized that if Augustine's theory were true, then remarried widows and widowers had to be living in sin. They never realized this because they never even thought it, for thinking it would have run counter to their experience of a society in which surviving spouses were free to remarry.

---

502. Ibid., par. 4. In the ancient church, as in Orthodox churches today, divorce severs the bond of marriage, but on the strength of Augustine's authority, the medieval schoolmen accepted that a legal divorce does not dissolve the sacramental bond. Lombard refers to lawful persons here because a little later he will say that no sacrament exists in the union of those who have no legal right to marry.

503. Appeal was also made to the gospel condemnations of divorce, but in the early church these condemnations were taken to mean that divorce (especially unjust divorce) is a sin, whereas in the medieval church they were taken to mean that divorce is impossible.

i. Concluding Summary

The high Middle Ages, especially the twelfth century with which we have been dealing, and the thirteenth century which produced the synthesis already presented in the first chapter, marked the summit of liturgical and theological development for the Catholic sacraments. Before the twelfth century, there was no talk of seven sacraments because all religious rituals and symbols could be called *sacramenta*. By the end of the thirteenth century, Catholic discussion of *sacramenta* was limited to the familiar seven, and with the help of philosophical concepts borrowed from Aristotle (matter and form, substance and accidents, potency and act, essence and existence, etc.) these seven had an intellectually sophisticated explanation of what they were and how they produced their effects. In time, both the liturgical form of the sacraments and their theological explanation would become matters of Catholic doctrine when the church's bishops convened to combat the Protestant Reformation at the Council of Trent.

Some important observations need to be made, however, about the medieval synthesis, the Tridentine doctrines, and the Catholic sacraments during the centuries preceding the Second Vatican Council.

- The number of rituals called sacraments in the Latin church was not fixed at seven until later in the twelfth century at the earliest. Prior to 1140 any number of religious rituals could be called *sacramenta*, as evidenced in *The Sacraments of the Christian Faith* by Hugh of St. Victor.

- The schoolmen were familiar with the language of giving and receiving with regard to the sacraments, and they did not question it. Sometimes what was said to be given and received was some material element such as water or oil, but it was understood that something immaterial was also received through these rituals, and the general name for it was *gratia* or grace.

- This immaterial effect began to be spoken of as the *res* of the sacrament, following a usage introduced by Augustine and consistent with his broad definition of a sacrament as a sign of a sacred thing. Although translators usually render *res* as "thing," the *res* that Augustine and the schoolmen had in mind is better thought of as a reality, that is, as an immaterial or spiritual reality.

- The devout schoolmen not only believed that material rituals had immaterial effects, but they also perceived those effects. That is, they perceived the effects "with the eyes of faith," which enabled them to see Christ in the consecrated elements, to experience forgiveness after receiving absolution, and so on.

- In his discussion of baptism, Lombard speaks about receiving the *sacramentum* and the *res*, but he does not explain what the *sacramentum* is. Although he later applies the term *sacramentum et res* to the consecrated Eucharist, in the *Sentences* it is not a term that has a general applicability to all the sacraments.

- When Lombard speaks about receiving the sacrament of confirmation, again he is not clear, but he may be referring to being anointed with chrism.

- Since Christians are confirmed only once, Lombard begins to generalize on Augustine's explanation of why they are baptized only once, that is, they receive a spiritual character.

- Although it cannot be proven, there is sufficient textual evidence to suggest that when the schoolmen spoke about Christ's presence in the Eucharist, and when they proposed philosophical explanations for that presence, they were thinking not only about texts (e.g., "This is my body.") and beliefs (e.g., the consecrated bread is the body of Christ) but also about their own personal experiences of divine presence associated with the Eucharist.

- When scholastic theology speaks about the substance of bread and wine being transformed into the body and blood of Christ, or when it says that the substance of Christ's body and blood are in the Eucharist under the appearance (or species) of bread and wine, the word *substantia* is best thought of as a "unity identity whole," or as an individual reality.

- Although the schoolmen inherited the teaching that the mass (what had been earlier called the eucharistic liturgy) is a sacrifice, they misinterpreted the meaning of *sacrificium*, taking it to be the immolation of a sacrificial victim rather than a meal shared in the presence of God, which had been the early patristic understanding. This misunderstanding formed the core of much medieval eucharistic theology, and indeed of much subsequent Catholic and Protestant thinking about salvation.

- The twelfth century understanding of ritual repentance (*sacramentum paenitentiae*) was largely experiential, reflecting on the relationship between interior conversion and external signs of it. In time, however, the theology of penance would become more ritualistic and link the remission of sins to the words of absolution pronounced by the priest.

- Extreme unction appears to be unknown to Hugh and Gratian in 1140, but it is named by Lombard as one of the seven sacraments in 1150. On the authority of others, he says that the sacrament is for the remission of sins and an increase in virtue, but he makes no attempt to explain how this happens.

- Hugh, Gratian and Lombard all regard ordination as a bestowal of spiritual powers, especially the power to consecrate the Eucharist and offer the sacrifice of the mass. The arrival of this theory of ordination brings to a close the era of ordination to a specific local ministry and opens the era of absolute ordination, with the idea that priestly powers can be exercised anywhere.

- The twelfth century theology of marriage likewise reflects an ecclesiastical situation in which there is a new wedding ceremony and canons regulating marriage. Ephesians 5:32 is misinterpreted as referring to the sacrament of marriage and, on the authority of Augustine, the sacrament is regarded as indissoluble.

6. Complex History and Theological Method

According to scholars who translate Latin texts, a vast quantity of medieval manuscripts referring to Christian beliefs and practices have yet to be translated into modern languages. Understandably, when Catholic theology was conducted primarily in Latin (that is, until the mid-twentieth century), the texts that made it into print were mainly those that supported Catholic doctrines. These included the early scholastic works cited in this chapter, the patristic texts cited in various *summae* and collections of *sententiae*, and post-Tridentine writings by orthodox theologians that conformed to the conclusions of the scholastics and the increasingly uniform practices of the Roman Catholic Church. Occasionally, Protestant scholars discovered ancient and medieval documents that called Catholic sacramental practices into question, but these were usually able to be explained away by Catholic historians and theologians. Overlooked and left out of Catholic books and periodicals, quite understandably, were texts that might have called into question Catholic beliefs and practices during a period when adherence to a lengthy uniform tradition was regarded as proof that Protestant innovations were wrong.

Prior to the thirteenth century, however, church practices and Christian beliefs were far from uniform and far from what they would later become. Some of that variety has been brought to light in this chapter, which has argued that early texts about the remission of sin through baptism referred to the elimination of sinful practices through immersion in Jesus' way of life, that early texts calling Christian gatherings sacrifices were explaining that they were festive meals shared in the presence of God, and that early texts mentioning healing through anointing were not referring to an exclusively clerical practice. In other words, what early Christians meant when they wrote about their religious rituals was probably something quite different from what those texts were later taken to mean. Even in the area of doctrine, Christians held a variety of beliefs about God, Jesus, and the Holy Spirit that were molded into an orthodox uniformity by seven ecumenical councils convened by Roman emperors who were keenly interested in imperial unity. The controversy over rebaptism and reordination did not go away until north African Christianity was lost to Islamic expansion in the eighth and ninth centuries, leaving the Roman practice and the Augustinian theory dominant in Europe.

What is less well known is that for centuries women had been ordained as deacons and abbesses, and perhaps even as presbyters and bishops, although the data supporting the latter are more sparse and less clear. By delving into previously uninvestigated and untranslated documents from the early Middle Ages, however, Gary

Macy and others have been able to demonstrate that women were ordained until the twelfth century, when a new theory of priestly powers was used to exclude women from ordination.[504] This may be only the tip of the iceberg, for if other early medieval texts are unearthed and translated, they are likely to confirm that during the first thousand years of Christianity, Catholic ritual practices were much more diverse than they have been for the past five hundred years. This would have wide ranging implications both for ecumenism and for liturgical inculturation.

Thanks to Theodore Mackin, we already know that Christians were able to divorce and remarry before the twelfth century,[505] and thanks to Bernard Cooke, we know that Christian ministers were neither regarded as nor called priests before the third century.[506] It has been clear for some time, therefore, that sacramental or liturgical theology has always been a reflection on and a reflection of the church's ritual practices, as well as of the surrounding social practices, in any given era. Thus, when divorce was legally permissible, divorce was regarded as theologically possible even if sometimes sinful (in the case of an unjust dismissal of a spouse), but when divorce became legally impossible, marriage came to be regarded as indissoluble. As has already been noted, the ability of people to remarry after the death of their spouse has never been questioned even though the theory of indissolubility should have logically prohibited it. Analogously, it can be argued that the theology of marriage proclaims it to be monogamous because it was developed at a time and in a culture when monogamy was the social norm. In other words, the classic Christian theology of marriage is actually a theology of monogamy. Had Judaism at the time of Christ allowed polygamy, the early Christian understanding of marriage would likely have been something like a theology of polygamy. Then, had medieval society, contrary to an earlier cultural practice, later adopted monogamy as a social norm, its academics could have developed a scholastic theology of monogamy despite the earlier social practice of polygamy. For this is precisely what happened in actual history, when the schoolmen were unaware that for eleven centuries Catholics had been able to divorce, and that Orthodox Christians in the distant Byzantine empire were still allowed to divorce and remarry. Granted that divorces in early Christianity and in the eastern churches were few and far between, they were still possible, and the theology of marriage in those societies reflected their respective cultural realities. But the scholastic theology of marriage buttressed the cultural reality of marriage as it was lived in medieval Europe, and since divorce was legally impossible, it was reasonable to say that marriage is indissoluble.

So too with the other sacraments. Priests in the Middle Ages were religious functionaries who had special duties with regard to baptisms, masses, confessions, weddings, and funerals, but ministry for most clergy was not a full-time occupation. Many supported themselves by farming and had a family to help with the work, even

---

504. See Macy, *Hidden History*, ch. 4.

505. See Mackin, *Divorce and Remarriage*, ch. 10.

506. See Cooke, *Ministry*, 351, 528–534, 537–538.

after the twelfth century when the church declared clerical marriages to be invalid. Since there were no seminaries, priests learned their trade the way other tradesmen did, that is, through an apprenticeship system through which trainees rose through the holy orders from porter to lector to acolyte to exorcist to subdeacon to deacon to priest. Priests had sacred powers conferred on them through ordination, most notably the power to forgive sins, the power to confect the Eucharist, and the power to administer extreme unction. Bishops, archbishops, cardinals and so on had the same sacramental powers that priests had, but they had greater temporal powers to rule over the church, and they had jurisdiction to confirm and ordain. Given this state of affairs, it was logical to conceive of holy orders as a sacrament that was incrementally received through a series of ordination rituals, that bestowed an indelible character that could be received only once, and that was the source of the sacerdotal powers that made priests truly different from lay people.

Baptism was a ritual that was performed almost exclusively on children. Being one of the two oldest Christian rituals, it came with theological concepts inherited from earlier eras, notably the ideas that baptism is necessary for salvation, that baptism washes away sin, and that baptism bestows new life. These ideas explained why only Christians could receive the other sacraments and why only Christians could be buried in consecrated ground. Baptism gave Christian souls special powers in the same way that ordination gave priests the powers that they exercised when they performed their sacerdotal functions. By conferring the virtues of faith, hope and charity, it enabled Christians to believe what pagans did not, to hope for an eternal reward in heaven, and to achieve true sanctity if they cooperated with the grace that God gave them. In contrast, the unbaptized (such as Jews and Muslims) were destined for eternal damnation and could be treated as such. Since baptism conferred an indelible character on the soul, it could be received only once, and those who received it were permanently members of the one true Church.

Unlike baptism, confirmation had little theological content. Since it was not necessary for salvation, parents often neglected to have their children confirmed, and it is likely that the majority of Christians in the Middle Ages never received this sacrament. Once they did receive it, however, custom dictated that they could not receive it again, and so confirmation too was understood to bestow an invisible character on the soul. The fact that the clergy were required to be confirmed before receiving holy orders may have contributed to the notion that confirmation gave additional strength to the baptized and made them soldiers of Christ.

The scriptures say that only the pure of heart shall see God, so those who lost their baptismal purity needed a way to have sins forgiven and, if possible, to make satisfaction for their sins in this life before entering the next one. The sacrament of penance assured penitents of God's forgiveness and enabled them to perform works of repentance and thus shorten their stay in purgatory. In time, indulgences were introduced as a means of reducing the length of punishment in the afterlife by substituting works of charity for more severe penances. Nonetheless, people tended to put off receiving this sacrament for years on end, so the hierarchy made yearly confession a matter of church law in order to ensure that as many people as possible died in a state of grace.

Extreme unction was another sacrament that was avoided by many, in part because, in an age without modern medicine, death often came swiftly and without notice. In addition, the sacrament had to be administered in a church by a small assembly of priests, so both the distance to be traveled and the stipends to be paid were obstacles to its being regularly sought by the peasants who made up about ninety percent of the population. Moreover, it was difficult to specify the theological effects of the sacrament, so the last rites for most people, if they could see the end coming, were a last confession and a final reception of communion.

Since the later patristic period, when the fathers of the church greatly emphasized the divinity of Christ in order to combat the Arian heresy, a sense of unworthiness led lay people to avoid receiving holy communion with any regularity. In reaction, the hierarchy responded in the same way that they had to the avoidance of confession—by mandating (at the Fourth Lateran Council) the reception of communion at least once a year at Easter time. Noting the link between penance's purification of the soul and the necessity of receiving the Eucharist in a state of grace (lest a sacrilege be committed), most people took care of both obligations at the same time, performing what was popularly called the Easter duty.

The Eucharist in the Middle Ages was thus not a sacrament to be received, but a sacrament to be adored. People were taught that Christ was present in the Eucharist, and the Blessed Sacrament was reserved in a tabernacle on or above the main altar of every church. A lit candle signified the divine presence, so Catholics were told to show reverence by genuflecting in front of it, and the devout were encouraged to adore Christ in the Eucharist by kneeling and praying in spiritual communion.

The mass itself, a ritual shadow of the great liturgies of earlier centuries, was opaque to most people, for they did not understand Latin and, even if they did, they could not have heard the priest standing at the altar with his back to them. But they were enabled to penetrate the mystery of the Eucharist when a bell signaled that the priest was about to lift it high, right after it was consecrated, so that they could adore it. Inevitably, superstition got mingled with this pious practice, leading to the belief that saying the right prayer during the elevation of the host would bring good fortune.

The purpose of the mass was to consecrate the Eucharist and to offer it in sacrifice to God the Father. This unbloody sacrifice was not a repetition of Christ's sacrifice on Calvary but a participation in it, making that unique event present in the here and now, and perceivable to those who had faith. Weekly attendance at mass was a moral requirement, and absence without a compelling reason was seriously sinful, leading to regularly high church attendance. But the legal requirement covered only that portion of the mass from shortly before the consecration until shortly after the priest's communion, so it was possible to fulfill one's Sunday obligation in a relatively short amount of time.

In summary, the sacramental theology of the Middle Ages went hand in glove with medieval sacramental practices, especially with the way the Catholic sacraments were practiced in Paris, where the great schools of theology were found. In the same way, scholastic sacramental theology during the Tridentine era mirrored modern sacramental practices, and vice-versa. In general, we can say that sacramental theology (even before there was an academic discipline called by that name) was a reflection on and a reflection of the ritual, ecclesiastical and social practices of the eras in which they developed, and that this was true for the better part of twenty centuries. In the twentieth century, however, this began to change.

Even prior to the Second Vatican Council, some theologians had begun looking for alternatives to scholastic theology in order to explain the sacraments to an increasingly educated Catholic audience. Earlier in the twentieth century, neo-scholasticism and neo-Thomism had attempted to address issues raised by modern philosophy and science, but they offered no new insights with regard to theological matters. After World War II, Edward Schillebeeckx in Holland and Karl Rahner in Germany introduced ideas from the philosophies of existentialism and phenomenology in developing new explanations of the sacraments, arguing that they were doing nothing different from what Thomas Aquinas and the other schoolmen had done when they drew ideas from the philosophy of Aristotle to explain the sacraments in the thirteenth century. Schillebeeckx and Rahner were so well versed in scholasticism that they were able to show that their new approaches did not contradict Catholic doctrine but were simply new ways of explaining Catholic doctrine. Schillebeeckx, for example, used the language of interpersonal encounter to interpret the real presence of Christ in the Eucharist, and Rahner used a phenomenological analysis of symbolism to explain how God acts through symbolic rituals such as the sacraments.

In many ways, the Second Vatican Council vindicated the efforts of these two theologians and others like them who had been seeking to promote new thinking not only in sacramental theology but in all areas of Catholic teaching. Popular appreciation for new ideas encouraged the development of additional explanations of the sacraments in subsequent decades, including a postmodern approach elaborated by French theologian Louis-Marie Chauvet. All of these efforts preserved Catholic sacramental doctrine while offering different explanations by using concepts derived from different philosophical systems.

During the decades following the council, however, Catholic sacramental practice changed, some of it intentionally and some of it unintentionally. The intentional changes were found in the new rites that were drawn up by Vatican liturgical commissions, translated into vernacular languages, and promulgated throughout the world. Infant baptism moved from being a private ceremony performed shortly after a baby's birth to being a communal ceremony in conjunction with a Sunday liturgy and performed weeks or even months after the birth. Adult baptism was promoted with the new Rite of Christian Initiation of Adults, which included months of catechesis prior to formal reception into the church. Changes in the mass included the location of the altar, greater lay involvement in the liturgy, the introduction of popular music, and the inclusion of cultural elements such as dress and dancing, especially in non-European countries. The confession box was replaced with a reconciliation room, and three different forms of the rite were introduced, some of which included public liturgical elements. Extreme unction was renamed anointing of the sick, and its use was expanded to include all those who are seriously or chronically ill, not just the dying. The rite of marriage was revised to allow greater investment by the bride and groom in the design of their own wedding. The holy orders were reduced to three—deacon, priest, and bishop—and ordination rites put more emphasis on commitment to ministry than on the reception of priestly powers. Moreover, the diaconate was expanded to include married men who did not intend to become priests. The rite of confirmation was reshaped, but uncertainty about the proper age for confirmation let to celebrations ranging from before first communion to the last year of high school.

Partly as a result of the new rites themselves, partly as a result of changes in other areas of Catholic theology, and partly as a result of cultural changes that swept through Europe and America during the sixties and seventies, an array of unintended changes also ensued. Ecumenical dialogue increased Catholics' appreciation for Protestants, and interfaith dialogue increased their respect for people of other religions, diminishing the belief that only Catholics could go to heaven and that baptism was necessary for salvation. The notion of original sin became less prominent in Catholic thinking, leading to the delaying of infant baptism, as noted above. Moral theologians suggested that it was not very easy to commit a mortal sin, and liturgical theologians promoted the idea that communion as well as confession could be a remedy for venial sin; as a result, confession lines dwindled and communion lines swelled. The new mass promoted active participation by the laity by encouraging singing even during the reception of communion, preventing many from having a deep experience of Christ in the Eucharist and promoting instead an experience of Christ in the worshiping assembly. Priests, whose lives and duties had been stable since the Council of Trent, began to leave the priesthood in large numbers for a variety of reasons, the most prominent of which was the desire to marry. The percentage of Catholics who divorced and remarried shot up and leveled off at the same rate as that of non-Catholics in most countries. Respect for the Vatican as a moral authority was diminished when Pope Paul VI reaffirmed the traditional prohibition of artificial birth control almost a decade after most lay people and many priests had concluded that using a contraceptive pill was morally acceptable. The automatic acceptance of priests as sacred persons was shaken in the wake of multiple pedophilia scandals in the eighties and nineties, and respect for bishops as pastoral leaders was reduced when they were perceived as being more concerned about the church's reputation than about the children who had been molested. Many Catholics stopped going to mass and many left the church, making ex-Catholics the largest religious group in the United States after the Catholic Church itself. Some of those who left were rebaptized in evangelical Protestant churches, and others became Muslims or Jews, atheists or agnostics, thereby unsettling the notions that baptism can occur only once and that it makes a person a Christian forever. Older Catholics gradually accepted the idea that they could receive the anointing of the sick whenever they were seriously ill, but the reduced numbers of priests made the sacrament increasingly unavailable. Younger Catholics might find themselves being confirmed anywhere from age eight to age eighteen, but many parents lost interest in their children's religious education after they had "received all their sacraments," and most teenagers lost interest in attending church after they were confirmed.

Other changes in attitude and behavior could also be cited, but these are enough to make the point that both the sacramental rituals themselves and the experiences related to the sacraments changed drastically during the five decades after Vatican II. The result has been a growing gap between Catholic sacramental theology and Catholic sacramental experience. As noted above, the new sacramental theologies were for the most part alternative explanations of Catholic sacramental doctrine which left the doctrines themselves unquestioned. At the beginning, when Schillebeeckx and Rahner were doing their work, this was a great advantage because it blunted the attacks of conservative critics, but in the long run it has reduced the credibility of all sacramental theology, both scholastic and contemporary.

Until very recently, sacramental theology has been both a reflection on and a reflection of Catholic sacramental practices. To use the terminology of the schoolmen, the *explicandum*—that which was to be explained—were the rites themselves and their results in Catholic society, and the *explicatio*—the explanation—was the theology that showed how the sacraments worked, that is, how they produced the results that they were perceived to produce. Recent sacramental theologians, however, have not done that. Instead, they have made Catholic sacramental doctrine, at least in its basics, the *explicandum*, and they have offered various *explicationes* (existential, phenomenological, postmodern, etc.) showing how the traditional doctrines can be understood in non-scholastic terms. Thus the effects explained by the new theologies are the same effects that were explained in scholastic theology and enshrined in Catholic sacramental doctrine—for example, the permanence and unrepeatability of baptism, the belief that only the baptized can be saved, the effectiveness of confirmation, the importance of going to confession for forgiveness and of being anointed for healing, the supernatural powers of the priest, the indissolubility of marriage, and the presence of Christ in the eucharistic elements. The problem is that these effects no longer occur, as far as many Catholics can see. So it does not matter whether one offers a scholastic explanation, an existentialist explanation, a phenomenological explanation, or a postmodern explanation. There is nothing wrong with the explanations, but for many people there is no longer anything to explain. Catholic sacramental doctrine has become, for the most part, unintelligible in any intellectual context, medieval or contemporary. It simply no longer corresponds to what large numbers of Catholics experience in connection with the sacraments. Therefore any theologies that attempt to explain the doctrines are likewise out of touch with the lived experience of many Catholics today.

If this is the case, then what can be done? Has sacramental theology outlived its usefulness? Or must sacramental theology be reduced to anarchy, with each worshiping community, or perhaps even every individual Catholic, reflecting on their own ritual experience and developing their own sacramental theology?

Having deconstructed not only scholastic sacramental theology but also, as it turns out, Catholic sacramental doctrine, it is time to envision the task of reconstruction.

IV

Reconstruction

*Sacraments in the Future**

For doing sacramental theology in the twenty-first century, the most important book to read is *Christianity Rediscovered* by Vincent Donovan.[1]

Donovan was a Holy Ghost father who was sent as a missionary to Tanzania in the 1950s, where he learned that the Masai still practiced their tribal religion even though his religious order had been there for a hundred years, and even though many Masai children had graduated from the local Catholic school. What was wrong, he asked, with this approach to missionary work? St. Paul had spent perhaps a few months in Thessalonica, in Corinth, in Galatia and other places before pushing on to the next city, and yet his method of evangelizing had planted the seed of Christianity in much of Asia Minor. What would happen if someone followed Paul's example in the twentieth century?

The Masai at the time were a herding people who lived in clans, and their wealth was measured in cattle. Donovan drove to their villages in the morning to share stories after the cattle had been put out to pasture. He talked about twelve clans of the tribe of Abraham that had herded sheep and goats, how they had escaped from slavery under a cruel king, and how they eventually settled in a land that God had shown to them. A young man named Jesus from the clan of Judah was called by God to show his people the true way to live. Both by his example and by the stories he told, he showed God's way to whomever would listen.

When Donovan shared stories with the Masai, occasionally he would ask, "Do you accept this teaching?" Sometimes they did, sometimes they didn't, and sometimes they said, "We'll think about it." They would talk about it among themselves, and during his next visit, he would hear their answer.

---

* For an abstract of this chapter, please read the summary of the argument that begins on page 298.

1. Vincent J. Donovan, *Christianity Rediscovered* (Chicago: Fides Claretian, 1978).

One time, after receiving a teaching about the Christian eucharist, the men said, "If we accept this story, we will have to let the women eat with us." The Masai custom was for women to serve the men, then to eat with the children after the men had had their fill. Donovan agreed that the interpretation was correct. He was told, "We'll think about it."

After many months, if a village had come to accept Jesus' teaching, Donovan would ask if they wanted to be baptized as the early Christians had been, in order to symbolize their commitment to God and to this new life. If the village elders agreed, even the children and those not able to fully understand the message were baptized. The elders said, "We will teach them. They will learn from our example." After the baptism, Donovan would spend more time with the next village, returning only occasionally to see how the new Christians were doing.

Before he left, however, Donovan talked about ceremonies and rituals. They had a ritual for reconciliation, but in order to accept the teaching of Jesus, they had to agree that every sin could be forgiven. Until then, some offenses were unpardonable. But they accepted the message of Jesus as good news—that it is right to forgive any wrong that is done to them.

Donovan accepted the Masai ritual of asking for and giving forgiveness. He did not insist that they practice the rite of penance. Nor did he insist on the ordination of priests. Like Paul, he just left the elders in charge and asked them to remain true to the message of Jesus.

According to their own custom, each week they celebrated their unity in Christ and their thankfulness for the way of life he had show to them. In each village, the huts were in a circle, and on Sunday morning a clump of grass would be passed from one family to the next. Since grass was life for their cattle, the passing of grass symbolized a willingness to share life with the recipient.

When the grass completed the circle from family to family, they would celebrate the life and unity for which they were thankful. If the grass did not make it around the circle, there was no celebration that week. Instead, the families worked on reconciliation.

Although I did not fully realize this book's significance the first time I read it, the lessons it teaches have remained with me. The first is that reality is more important than symbolism. The second is that symbols have meaning only in a cultural context. What these lessons imply for Catholic sacraments and their theology is the topic of this chapter.

1. Symbols and Meaning

We sometimes say things in ways that are perfectly acceptable in ordinary conversation but that present problems when we try to think about them scientifically. We talk about the sun rising and setting, and for thousands of years this was all right. Even when ancient astronomers first calculated the motions of the sun and moon relative to the earth, thinking that heavenly bodies revolved around a stable earth, it was still all right. But when medieval astronomers began to make more accurate calculations about heavenly bodies, and when the newly invented telescope made even more precise calculations possible, the traditional picture had to be discarded in favor of a model that put the sun at the center and made the earth one of the planets.

Similarly, this book opened with the observation that Catholics talk about administering and receiving sacraments. Around the turn of the fifth century, Augustine understood the reception of baptism to mean that something permanent is received in the soul whenever a child or adult is baptized with water in the name of the Trinity. Then in the twelfth and thirteenth centuries, schoolmen generalized this idea so that it easily covered confirmation, ordination and marriage, and with some difficulty it could also apply to penance and extreme unction. In the twentieth century, Catholic theologians began to question the notion of a sacrament that is received (the *sacramentum et res*) and to offer alternative theories or explanations of how the sacraments produce spiritual effects. This book, being written early in the twenty-first century, has shown how the concept of a received sacrament presents both theological and pastoral problems today, and it has argued that it is best to abandon this concept because, among other reasons, the permanence that it was meant to explain no longer exists.

Pushing this type of analysis further, let us ask about symbols and meaning. We can ask, "What does that symbol mean?" When we do that, we are assuming that the symbol has some objective meaning. We can pose the same type of question about the meaning of words, which are linguistic symbols. We can even look in the dictionary for what we assume is a word's objective meaning. At the same time, however, we are aware that words can have different meanings, that they can have nuances of meaning, and that their meaning can change over time. The assumption that words and other symbols have simple, objective meanings is problematic.

Consider the possibility that symbols have no meaning in themselves, and that the meanings commonly ascribed to symbols are actually in people's minds. A teacher once told his astonished students, "There is no knowledge in the library. All that's in the library are books, and all that's in books are paper and ink." In the same way, all that is in a drawn symbol are lines and colors, and words are literally just sounds in the air or squiggles on a page. In other words, there is no meaning *in* symbols, and there is no meaning *in* words. Talking about them having meaning is just a manner of speaking, like talking about the sun rising and setting, based on how things appear to be. Actually, meaning is something that happens in people's minds; it is an activity of human consciousness. Accordingly, the teacher was contending that there is knowledge in the library only when there are people in the library and they are using their minds. I am likewise contending that meaning is something that is found in an active human consciousness. You are not aware of any meaning when you are dead asleep.

If words literally had meaning, that is, if there were meaning in words themselves, then no one would ever wonder what someone else was saying; the meaning would be evident. Likewise, no one would ever have to learn a foreign language; one could understand what was being said by perceiving the meaning in the words. But the meaning is not actually in the words. The meaning is in the mind of the speaker who is trying to communicate something, and if the communication is successful, the listener will know what the speaker means. We do not literally hear meaning; we hear sounds that we interpret as meaningful if we know the language and can understand what the speaker is talking about. Although "I hear what you're saying" is a common expression, it is not literally true. We hear a certain pattern of sounds, and if the conditions are right, we understand the meaning represented by that pattern.

The same can be said of symbols. If symbols literally had meaning, and if there were meaning actually in symbols, no one would ever wonder about their meaning, for one could look at the symbols and see the meaning in them. But this does not happen. We have all had the experience of looking at a symbol and not understanding what it meant. Staring intently at a symbol does not reveal its meaning. Someone who understands the symbol has to communicate the meaning to us; otherwise we have to look for clues in order to figure out what the symbol might mean.

This holds true *a fortiori* for symbolic rituals, which are ceremonies that usually contain a number of symbolic actions, symbolic objects, and words (which are symbols, as we have already noted). A symbolic ritual has no meaning in itself, that is, the ritual as a dynamic collection of symbols is not inherently meaningful. If it were, we could never have the experience of attending a ceremony and wondering what it means. Usually, those participating in the ritual understand what it means, and people who are familiar with the ritual can communicate that meaning to us. Otherwise we have to look for clues as to its meaning. If the focus of attention is on a man and a woman, it may be a wedding ceremony. If someone in the ceremony is being given symbolic objects or invested with symbolic garments, it may be an induction ritual. We have to do some mental work to understand a ceremony—minimally, at least, asking a question—in order to arrive at its meaning.[2]

What Donovan did with the Masai was communicate biblical ideas or meanings to his listeners through scripture stories, and through stories about Jesus and what he had taught. This is precisely what Paul must have done since his Gentile listeners were not familiar with the Hebrew scriptures and the New Testament had not been written yet. Some of these were meanings with which they were already familiar, such as the meaning of community and the meaning of forgiveness. Sometimes an idea needed to be stretched or added to, as when he said that Jesus taught that all sins can

---

2. Although this analysis is nowhere presented by Bernard Lonergan, it is consonant with his cognitional analysis and it is dependent on what he calls self-appropriation or the appropriation of one's own rational self-consciousness. See *Insight*, Introduction and ch. 1–11; "Dimensions of Meaning" in *Collection: Papers by Bernard Lonergan* (New York: Herder and Herder, 1967), 252–67; and "Meaning" in *Method in Theology* (New York: Herder and Herder, 1972), ch. 3.

be forgiven. But once the Masai understood the meaning, Donovan left it up to them to ritualize the meaning in a way that was culturally appropriate for them. Donovan understood that the meaning is more important than the symbolism. In our culture, one can express love with daisies as well as with roses, but in the absence of genuine love, even orchids are an empty symbol.

2. Meaning and Context

It is often assumed that words, concepts, thoughts and meanings coincide, but this is demonstrably not the case. It is true that most of us think by using words to frame our thoughts, but we may be able to remember a time when we had an idea but words failed us. Or perhaps we can remember writing out an idea and then rewriting the sentence because the first sentence did not accurately express what we meant to say. Then again, there are times when we have seen a smile or a scowl on someone's face, and we knew what it meant even though we did not formulate that meaning in words. Examples such as these indicate that it is possible to be aware of meaning without thinking words and without making use of concepts represented by words.

By the same token, a meaning can often be expressed in different words. The easiest example of this is how an idea can be expressed in different languages. Although linguists assure us that it is difficult to translate complex thoughts in a poem or a novel from one language into another, it is equally true that the same relatively simple idea can be expressed as *La voiture est noire*, *Das Auto ist schwartz*, and *The car is black* with little or no difference in meaning from one language to another. And if language can be thought of as a context within which an idea is expressed, then this example can also be seen as a simple meaning that is expressed in three different linguistic contexts. Unless one understands the language or the context in which an idea is expressed, one does not understand what is said in that language. This is true not only of different human languages such as French, German and English, but it is also true of other constructs such as scientific and technical languages that are full of unfamiliar words.

Further, if language is a context within which words are understood, culture is a context within which symbols are understood. In Europe people nod when they want to say yes, and they shake their head when they want to say no, but in parts of India both bobbing the head and wobbling it from side to side can indicate comprehension without either agreement or disagreement. In America we make a circle with the thumb and forefinger to signal OK, but in Brazil that gesture is the equivalent of raising one's middle finger straight up. Anyone who travels in other lands can discover how easy it is to make this kind of mistake.

One of the most surprising Masai rituals described by Donovan involves the spittle of forgiveness. In any western culture, spitting on someone is an insult, but in the dry savannah that the Masai inhabit, it is a blessing. It means something like "I share my water with you." The gesture is performed to indicate that the one doing the spitting forgives the one being spat upon. In Masai culture, it can be shameful and heart-rending to go without the spittle of forgiveness. Needless to say, the way they sacramentalized reconciliation was far different from any of the three Roman rites of penance.

If the meaning of words depends on the context, linguistic and otherwise, and if the meaning of symbols depends on the culture or social context, there is also another factor at work, which is intention. What do people consciously intend by the words they use? What do people consciously intend by the symbols they use? We have all had the experience of having our words taken in a way we did not intend. The examples cited above show how it is possible to intend to communicate one idea and to convey quite a different meaning instead.

Who intends what a ritual should mean in theory, and who decides what it actually means in practice? Is it possible that rituals can have different meanings for different participants? If so, who or what determines the actual meaning of the ritual? And is there any way to determine that meaning?

If meaning is found in human minds, it is also expressed in words and other symbols that may be objects, images, gestures, sounds, smells, and so on. The theoretical meaning of a ritual, which is to say the meaning that the ritual is intended to have by its designers, can be determined from an examination of the ritual by those who have the expertise to do so. In the case of a Christian ritual, those who best understand the language of ritual are liturgists and liturgical theologians. Moreover, those who best understand the intended purpose of the ritual would be religious authorities, ecclesiologists, and doctrinal theologians. The minds that design liturgical rituals, however, finish their work when they produce a script of what is to be said and done during the ceremony. This liturgical script is often referred to as a rite, for example, the rite of baptism or the rite of Christian burial.

Those who produce the rite, however, are usually not its performers (its ministers or celebrants or officiants) and their attendants. Since ministers are generally conversant with the intent of the liturgical designers and with the theology expressed in the rite, what the performed liturgy means to them is probably fairly coincident with the intended meaning of the rite. With regard to the liturgical attendants, however, this is not always the case. Deacons, lectors, candle bearers, choir members and so on—especially if they are adolescents or children—are not likely to have a full grasp of the rite's purpose. The more distracted they seem to be during their service at the altar, the less they seem to know what is supposed to be going on. Here we begin to see how the actual meaning of the ritual can begin to split away from its intended meaning.

At the other extreme are the individuals in the congregation or assembly and the ideas that are going on in their minds during the religious service, say, a eucharistic liturgy in a large Catholic parish. For most of the children, the exercise probably means something like "This is where we go every Sunday," or "This is a grown-up thing and I'm supposed to be quiet." For many of the teenagers, the service can mean that they have to put up with something that they do not understand, or it can be an opportunity to meet their friends and observe members of the opposite sex. Adults in attendance can be knowledgeable about their faith or not, they can have various degrees of understanding about the liturgy, they can have a greater or lesser sense of mystery or divine presence, they can be actively engaged in the service or they can be passively listening, and they can be paying attention at some points while daydreaming at others. Were we to try to figure out what the mass means to each individual at every point in the ceremony, we would be faced with so much diversity that it would be difficult if not impossible to determine the meaning of any liturgy.

Perhaps, however, we can find some meaning that is likely to be common to most if not all of those in attendance, something that is not as explicitly detailed as the meaning embodied in the rite, yet something not as amorphous and elusive as the ideas that are coming and going in the minds of everyone in attendance. If one imagines a group activity of any sort, such as attending a sporting event, going on a family vacation, inviting some friends for dinner, or watching a holiday parade, it is easy to suppose that there are some ideas or intentions that are common to everyone there because they all wound up in the same place doing the same thing at the same time. Something meaningful has brought them together for this event, or perhaps it is a cluster of overlapping thoughts and feelings.

Before proceeding with this analysis, notice that I am not talking about liturgy in general or about the mass as such. Liturgy in general is an abstraction. No one ever participates in an abstraction, but only in actual events. Likewise, the mass as such does not exist. The only masses that do exist are ones that are going on at some place and some time. Were we to inquire about the meaning of the mass or the meaning of the eucharistic liturgy, we would be asking about the meaning of the unperformed rite, the meaning or more correctly the set of meanings that the designers had in mind when they prescribed what was to be said and done whenever the rite is performed. Such meanings are easily accessible by reading the ritual texts themselves, by reading instructional materials about the rites, by reading scholarly commentaries, and so on. What we are after is much more elusive.

More elusive but also more pertinent, for we are looking for the actual meanings of actual liturgical celebrations. Not that we can decide at a distance what any mass means for the people who are attending it, but we can propose a plausible method for finding this out in any particular case by giving examples of how it can be done.

Let's begin with something simple—a child's birthday party to which friends and relatives are invited. What are some meanings that people are likely to bring into this event? First, "This is my birthday! I'm a year older! I wonder what presents I'll get?" Second, "This is his or her birthday. I hope I brought a good present." Third, there are meaningful emotional ties all around, among the children, among the adults, and between the children and the adults. One does not usually invite strangers to a birthday party. Fourth, there are shared memories, or memories of the others that each one has.

Fifth, there are anticipations about the future ranging from "what I want to be when I grow up" to "I hope he learns to settle down in school" to "I wonder if her parents will stay married?" Realistically, though, it is the positives rather than the negatives that are being celebrated, the happy times that are remembered, and a good future that is uppermost in mind.

Even simpler might be a family supper, for those families that make it a point to eat together on a regular basis. For parents who insist on this routine, the idea of family might be uppermost, something that regularly renews the bonds of affection that ought to be present among children and adults, and a way of keeping in touch with what is going on in one another's lives. A meal together is a celebration of relationships, no matter how vaguely, and regardless of particular tensions between family members. One could say simply that the meaning of family is what makes a meal a family meal.

Somewhat more complex might be an Independence Day celebration, say, a Fourth of July band concert and fireworks display. Most people there are probably strangers, but they have some things in common: they are citizens or at least residents of the United States of America, they are politically free and socially secure, they have a job or some sort or income (at least enough to be able to come out for a public performance), and they probably identify to some extent with the myths and legends of American greatness, goodness and superiority. Were one to take a poll asking what the celebration is all about, one would most likely receive a variety of responses revolving around ideals and ideas such as these, plus (no doubt), "We're just here to have a good time and enjoy the show."

In the same way, then, one might imagine taking a poll among people attending any church service or, more specifically, a Sunday liturgy in a Catholic parish. Going further, one might try to be a bit more comprehensive and organize focus groups, the way marketing companies do, asking "Why are you here?" and "What do you get out of it?" At the very least, one might think about one's own worship community and, if one feels like a typical member of the community, ask what it is that brings people together week after week, what they think it means, and what benefit they derive from it. Although there would be no doubt a range of answers, at some point no new answers would suggest themselves, and one would have a hazy and somewhat unscientific understanding of what that Sunday mass means for the people who attend it.

Notice that in these four examples, were we actually to ask people involved in any of these ritual activities about what it meant to them, they would probably take a moment to reflect on their experience before answering the question. If a group were involved in answering the question, very likely there would be one person with a ready answer, then others would chime in, and then the answers of some would suggest additional answers from people who had already spoken.

Why would it take a while for people to articulate the meaning of an activity that, to all appearances, they found meaningful? As was said earlier, not all meaning gets articulated in ideas and expressed in words. The meaning of facial expressions, the meaning suggested by hand gestures or a tone of voice, the multiple meanings that are sensed at a public event such as a rock concert or a neighbor's funeral—most of these meanings are not conceptualized or thought out. Rather they are felt or intuited, and so it takes an added effort to articulate them, although some people are better than others at getting in touch with their feelings and expressing them in words.

Probably the most important context for the majority of people attending a ritual event, therefore, is the fabric of felt meanings that are shared by those in attendance. Moreover, if the ritual is one that is repeated on a regular basis, those who regularly attend can be expected to experience a richer weave of felt meanings than those who are attending for the first time. Sports fans, for example, are in a position to sense more of what is going on in the stadium (from the supporters of their team and from the opposing fans, from the crowd's reaction to good and bad plays, from the body language of individual players, etc.) than someone who is new to the venue or new to the sport. Most of us have had the experience of being somewhat bewildered and perhaps confused on the first day of class, the first day on the job, and so on. Such bewilderment is indicative of the absence of felt meanings which, as they begin to accrue, enable us to feel more at home. It is within that context of insights which are sensed but not articulated that we understand the particulars that happen at the event. Continuing the sports example, these particulars would be plays that are made, reactions from the crowd, and so on.

Returning now to religious rituals, the actual context for any Sunday mass is the parish community, or rather the life of the community that supplies the lived experience which people bring to their liturgical celebrations. In the worst case scenario, no one at mass knows anyone else there; they just meet at church once a week and then go their separate ways. But even in this case, unless the venue is something like an airport chapel with totally different attendees every week, people are still seeing one another and perhaps exchanging pleasantries once a week, and even this can begin to provide some sense of community over the course of time. In a large and active parish, however, it is more likely that the community is comprised of sub-communities, people who know one another and interact with one another outside of church even though they don't know most of the people in the parish. These might be ushers and altar servers, choir members and the organist, the Ladies' Guild and Holy Name Society, Boy Scouts and Girl Scouts and their leaders, religious educators and their students, catechists and catechumens, prayer groups and Bible study groups, social justice and right-to-life groups, support groups for the needy, and so on. If the parish has an elementary school, some of the children will have interacted with one another during the week. There will also be sports teams with volunteer organizers and coaches, large and small fund-raising committees, and various networks of parents dedicated to improving the quality of the school and their children's educational experience.

Examples could be multiplied, but these are enough to make the point that the lived experiences of the parishioners—minimally their weekly mass attendance and maximally hours spent interacting in committees, clubs, study groups, sports teams, school classes, and other activities—provide not one but many contexts of felt meaning within which any liturgy takes place. The greater the number of meaningful interactions that take place between parishioners during the week, the more meaningful their Sunday worship will seem to be, all things being equal. Sometimes, however, a new element is introduced that strains or tears the fabric of meaning that is expressed in the weekly ritual. A new music minister wants to introduce unfamiliar hymns, a new pastor is overly controlling or a poor public speaker, a new bishop prohibits girls from serving at the altar—and suddenly the focus shifts to the source of irritation. The normal celebration of parish life gets interrupted until the community arrives at a new normalcy. If it does not, dissatisfaction by some will become a constant source of stress in the parish.

For over a century, rituals have been recognized as facilitating social transition. Baptisms and weddings, inductions and ordinations, bar mitzvahs and bat mitzvahs, military promotions and such are rites of passage through which people pass from one status to another. But not all rituals are rites of passage. Some simply celebrate history, values, ideals and other spiritual realities that are important for society or for some community within it. Such intensification rituals do not make something happen; rather they celebrate and amplify our awareness of what is already happening or what is always going on behind the scenes. Intensification rituals, in other words, celebrate something about the context in which people live. Annual holidays such as Memorial Day and Labor Day, Independence Day and Thanksgiving, Christmas and Easter do not make anything new happen, but they remind and consciously reconnect people with what is always present, always real, and always true—at least for those who live in the social contexts founded on the events, beliefs and values being celebrated.

The Sunday eucharistic liturgy (and to a lesser extent, weekday liturgies) therefore celebrates the spiritual realities that undergird the life of the parish. In theological terms, it celebrates the life and ministry of Jesus, it celebrates the death and resurrection of Christ, it celebrates the kingdom of God, it celebrates God's love and forgiveness, and it celebrates the life of the Holy Spirit. But it does not celebrate these realities in the abstract, nor does it celebrate them as concepts or doctrines. Rather, it celebrates them in the here and now, and to the extent that they are concretely realized in the lives of people. The eucharistic liturgy celebrates the life and ministry of Jesus to the extent that Jesus' life of self-giving and service to others are happening in the parish. It celebrates the paschal mystery to the extent that parishioners are intentionally dying to self and experiencing vitality as a result. It celebrates the kingdom of God to the extent that God reigns in the hearts of parishioners and the gospel guides their decision making. It celebrates divine love and forgiveness to the extent that people are caring for others and forgiving one another. It celebrates the life of the Holy Spirit to the extent that a healthy and healing spirit pervades the individual and collective lives of the parishioners.

To the extent that these are present, the liturgical celebration is meaningful and authentic. To the extent that they are absent, it is meaningless and phony.[3]

3. Reality and Symbol

People in western culture tend to conceive of reality in physical terms. Anything that can be seen, heard, tasted, touched or smelled is obviously real. In contrast, things that cannot be perceived by the five senses tend to be regarded as abstractions and as somewhat less than real. Even ideals such as freedom and liberty, for which Americans are willing to fight and die, are not thought of as solidly real, which is perhaps why it is so easy for politicians to manipulate public sentiment about them. Americans today also worry about security, but they think of it in terms of metal detectors and closed-circuit cameras, guns and security guards—all things that can be seen and touched. Wealth too is conceived in terms of dollars and cents: money in the bank, houses, cars, jewelry, and so on.

This concept of reality, however, is extremely naïve. Physically, a hundred dollar bill is little different from a ten dollar bill; it weighs the same, and it has the same amount of ink on it. Only the printing is different, and what is printed is mainly symbolic. If words are symbols, numbers are also symbols, and ultimately the numbers on currency or on a bank statement symbolize wealth. But wealth is nothing physical. Material or economic wealth can be measured in terms of property, cash, stocks and bonds and the like, but wealth is an idea, and ideas are not physical.

But aren't ideas physical occurrences, things that happen inside our brain? Not really. We need our brain in order to think, but thoughts are not reducible to brain functions. Even in the physical world, a whole is more than the sum of its parts. Computers and automobiles are made up of many parts, but they are more complex than and different from any of their parts. One cannot look at a motherboard and call it a computer or look at a steering wheel and call it a car. A dog is more than a collection of cells, more than the molecules that make up those cells, and more than the atoms that make up the molecules. Whether we are talking about machines, plants or animals, individual things may be composed of parts, but they are not just the parts, they are more than the parts. Otherwise, we would not be able to talk about them; we would only be able to talk about their parts. Individual things are real, even individual things that are made up of parts that are also real. In Lonergan's terminology, they are unity identity wholes. In scholastic terminology, they are subsisting beings or substances.

---

3. One reason, therefore, why youngsters find mass boring is that they are not connected with parish service activities during the week. Teenagers in youth groups that challenge them to engage in ministry and grow spiritually usually do not have this problem.

In an analogous way, the mind is one thing and the brain is something else. X-rays, MRIs and CAT scans can produce images of our brain, but there is nothing that can see our mind. The brain is something that is physical, but the mind is not physical. The human mind and all that occurs in it—consciousness, thoughts, feelings, intuitions, etc.—are in a very basic sense non-material or spiritual realities. Compared to things in the physical world, things such as ideas and ideals, values and principles seem rather vague and airy. They cannot be seen, heard, touched, tasted or smelled. But they are nonetheless real.

As a matter of fact, spiritual realities pervade and surround the world in which we consciously live, that is, they make up most of what we think about and they enable us to observe the things we ordinarily think of as real, such as physical objects. Right now, you are reading this book. If you stop reading for a moment and just look at the book, you can truthfully say that the book is in your mind—which is just another way of saying that you are aware of the book or the book is in your field of consciousness. In the same way, you can think about your brain and say that your brain—or at least the thought of your brain—is in your mind. Moreover, this claim is intuitively self-evident, just as the claim that the book is in your mind is intuitively self-evident if indeed you are now looking at a book. But there is no way to make the claim that the mind is in the brain. There is no way to verify that statement. All that is literally in the brain are neurons, dendrites, blood, and other things that are physically observable. But the mind is not physically observable, nor are ideas and many of the other things that we commonly say are in our mind or on our mind.

In a very real sense, the spiritual world makes the material world possible. Unless human beings were aware of physical objects, there would be no physical objects to think about or talk about. You could say that your spiritual world is the same as your consciousness or your field of awareness. It includes not only the things you perceive with your five senses, but also your thoughts and feelings, your knowledge and beliefs, your values and ideals, and everything else that you might be aware of whenever you are awake and conscious.

The material things that we are aware of in our spiritual world are real to us.[4] But so also are the immaterial things that we are aware of, such as our thoughts, feelings and the other items just mentioned. They are real thoughts and real feelings. The things you know are real knowledge, and the things you believe are real beliefs. (Whether they are true or not is a different matter.) Likewise, your values and ideals are real if you actually live according to them, for they motivate your decisions and actions.

---

4. Whether or not the things that are real to us are also real to others is a problem that philosophers have wrestled with for centuries, and we will not try to resolve it here, although I believe Bernard Lonergan has adequately addressed it in chapter 13 of *Insight*, "The Notion of Objectivity." Ultimately, the issue is not whether there is an objective world "out there" but how it is that we arrive at knowledge that is generally understood to be objectively correct. To follow the analysis being presented here, you only have to agree that you know things that are real, even if you do not have an explanation for how this happens.

We have been taking some time to talk about spiritual realities and to establish that they are indeed real even though they are not tangible and sensible. Love and hatred, friendship and alienation, wealth and poverty, guilt and forgiveness, and most the other things that make life happy or miserable are spiritual realities. Certainly it is true that we need a basic amount of food, clothing and shelter, which are physical realities, in order to have a satisfying life, but once those physical needs are satisfied, virtually all of our other needs are non-material.[5] Acceptance, belonging, community, affirmation, forgiveness and so on are all spiritual realities. Spiritual realities such as family and friendships are so important to us that, if we have them, we can be happy even though we do not have many material goods. Conversely, if we are alone and unloved, hopeless or purposeless, we can be miserable even if we live in a mansion and have much more stuff than we need. Positive spiritual realities, not material realities, make life worth living.

As already indicated, spiritual realities can be perceived, though not by the five senses. When you read the sentences in this book, you perceive what is being talked about, but all you literally see with your eyes are black shapes on a white background. The rest is interpretation, that is, if you have learned to read and have some acquaintance with what is being talked about, you use your acquired reading skills to perceive what is being said. This is likewise true in any ordinary conversation. What your ears pick up are vibrations in the air, but you perceive the information being communicated, and information (at least in this instance) is a spiritual reality, a meaning of some sort.

Spiritual realities can be perceived through words, gestures, body language, and so on, all of which function as symbols of what they stand for. Notice, however, that in order to perform this symbolic function, the person doing the perceiving has to be somewhat familiar with what is symbolized. Symbols can connect us (remind us, reacquaint us, etc.) with spiritual realities, but since such realities are to be found in the realm of thoughts and feelings, they already have to be in the mental world of our own consciousness if symbols are going to do this for us. At a basic level, if my auto mechanic is telling me that I need new MacPherson struts and I am not familiar with a car's suspension system, I have no idea what the mechanic is talking about. At a somewhat more complex level, if I am told that God loves us the way a father loves his children, I may have no idea what that means if my own father beat and abused me.

In themselves, then, symbols have no meaning. There is literally no meaning in any symbol, nor is there meaning in any word. Meaning occurs only in human minds. It is an activity and product of human consciousness.

Ordinarily, we talk about symbols as though they had meaning. We ask, "What is the meaning of that symbol?" and we expect an answer. Volumes are written about

---

5. See Abraham Maslow, *Toward a Psychology of Being*, 3rd Edition (Hoboken, NJ: Wiley and Sons, 1998); also a lecture published as *Hierarchy of Needs: A Theory of Human Motivation* (Amazon Kindle edition, 2011).

the meaning of symbols in painting and literature, about the meaning of religious rituals, and about the meaning of facial expressions and hand gestures. Similarly, we ask, "What does this word mean?" and we go to a dictionary to find the meaning. Actually, though, all that is literally in the dictionary is paper and ink. If I wanted to find the meaning of *verloren* but all I had was a German-to-German dictionary, I would have to understand the meaning of other German words before I could find what the word *verloren* means. Dictionaries work because they present the meaning of unfamiliar words in words that we already know the meaning of.

Just as talking about the sun rising and setting has some practical value, so talking about the meaning of words and symbols has practical value. It is a linguistic shorthand that facilitates the interpretation of unfamiliar words and symbols, whether we are doing this for others or others are doing this for us. In the short run, it helps us to associate the unfamiliar (such as word in a foreign language) with the familiar (such as a word in our own language) so that the meaning of which we are already aware occurs when we see the word or symbol that we would like to understand. In the long run, it helps us to arrive at new insights that give us new ideas and thus expand the realm of meanings in our awareness. Either way, talking about words and symbols as though they have meaning in themselves helps us to understand more.

But it is also deceptive. In the same way that speaking about sunrise and sunset led to a scientific model of the cosmos that later proved to be unworkable, speaking about words and symbols as though they are intrinsically meaningful can lead to conclusions that are similarly unworkable. This is true of words and symbols in general, but here we will talk mainly about those that appear in religious discourse and liturgical ritual.

For most of Christian history, the Bible was taken literally, and biblical literalism is based on the assumption that the words in the Bible mean what they say. Protestants who call themselves fundamentalists take the words of scripture literally, but the problem is that fundamentalists do not necessarily agree on the meaning of scripture passages. Some take Jesus' references to the abundant life in John 10:10 to mean material abundance or wealth, while others take it to mean spiritual abundance or joy. Catholic conservatives interpret Matthew 16:18, where Jesus calls Peter the rock on which he will build his church, as the time when Christ founded the papacy, but no Protestant conservatives interpret it that way. Clearly the meaning is not in the words but in the interpreters.

In parallel fashion, liturgists can go through great efforts to parse the meaning of the words in the mass, writing whole books about the correct interpretation of various prayers, the true significance of kneeling or standing, and the importance of facing in a certain direction during public worship. Likewise, theologians can write books about the meaning of baptism, the meaning of confirmation, or about the meaning of other sacraments, as though the meaning were "out there" in the words of the rite or the symbolism of the ritual. One reason why new books on the sacraments keep appearing is that the sacraments, as symbolic rituals, have no meaning in themselves and so it is always possible to debate about the "true" meaning of the sacraments. Historical theologians may argue that there is an original meaning for a sacrament and that it ought to be restored (e.g., returning to the original sequence of the initiation rites), and creative theologians may suggest new meanings for some sacraments (e.g., the social justice implications of the mass). Such efforts may be persuasive, but the only ones they persuade are individual readers; it does nothing to change the meaning of the sacraments for anyone else.

As suggested at the end of the previous section, the actual meaning of any actual sacramental ritual is going to be found in the minds of the participants. Both the ministers and the congregation, or the leaders and the assembly, are participants inasmuch as they are actively taking part, to a greater or lesser extent, in the liturgical event. As we have seen, any actual ritual is going to mean different things to different people, but to the extent that groups of participants and perhaps even all the participants have something in common, the ritual can be expected to have some common meaning. In the case of the Masai, who shared a common way of life in villages of only a few hundred, and who shared a common cultural tradition, it was fairly easy for them to develop or adapt rituals whose meaning would be clear to all the participants. This is not the case with most Catholic parishes today, especially large urban and suburban parishes, where people may come from different ethnic and economic backgrounds, where they may have different degrees of secular education and religious training, and where they almost certainly do different kinds of work on the days when they are not at church. What can unite such a diversity of participants into a meaningful common worship?

Notice that with the Masai, sometimes the meaning was understood before the ritual was invented. In order to express unity among the families in the village, the elders introduced a rite of passing a clump of grass from hut to hut until everyone had assented to this meaning. Sometimes the ritual was already a cultural practice, such as bestowing the spittle of forgiveness, and everyone understood its meaning. And sometimes a new ritual was introduced, as was the case with baptism, but the entire tribe knew ahead of time what the ritual was going to mean, for they had already accepting the teachings of Jesus and they had already started to live according to them. Baptism thus symbolized something that was already meaningful for them. It was also something that was already real for them, for they had already started to live according to the gospel and its meaning was starting to live in them. Likewise, no one gave the spittle of forgiveness unless they were actually able to forgive the person who had offended them. And the unity of the tribe had to be present before the eucharistic ritual could begin.

In 2011, English-speaking Catholics debated the pros and cons of the Third Edition of the Roman Missal, which replaced the somewhat looser translation of the Latin text with one that followed the vocabulary and word order of the original more closely. Conservatives praised the new translation for making the liturgy more solemn, thus accentuating the mysteriousness of the eucharistic sacrifice. Liberals condemned it for making the liturgy less intelligible and therefore less accessible to many of the faithful. Conservatives hoped that the new translation would make the mass more meaningful. Liberals feared that it would make the mass less meaningful. Neither result occurred, because the meaning of the mass, or rather the meanings that people find in their eucharistic celebrations, do not come from the text. Texts, as we have already seen, have no meaning in themselves.

Consider the fact that prior to 1969, Catholics around the world attended mass in Latin, but very few of them could understand the words that were being said. Many, however, found the mass to be very meaningful, and nostalgia for this meaning motivates the conservatives' desire for more literal translations and the restorationists' desire for Latin masses. But where did that meaning come from, if not from the text? One could make the case that the meaning came from the catechism, which was taught to all Catholic children at the time. Realistically, however, apart from the doctrines of the mass as a sacrifice and the real presence of Christ in the Eucharist, little else from the catechism is likely to have been remembered.

Rather, the meaning (probably felt as meaningfulness rather than thought in ideas) came from the shared experiences of Catholics who, for the most part, lived apart from non-Catholics—those "who did not belong to the one true Church." In large American cities, immigrant Catholics found themselves in ethnic neighborhoods where people spoke the same language, looked out for one another, joined ethnic social clubs, established savings associations, supported the same political party, and used the same funeral home. In rural areas, it was not uncommon for Catholics to settle in one town, Lutherans in another, Moravians in another, and so on. And even though the mass was in Latin, they often attended Irish or German or Italian or Polish parishes where they could hear sermons in their own language and socialize with people who shared similar daily experiences. A large proportion of Catholic children attended parochial schools and associated mainly with other Catholic kids in sporting and social activities. Going to church on Sunday affirmed people's Catholic identity, it assured them that their lives had a transcendent meaning and purpose, and it celebrated the joys and successes that many of them experienced from week to week and year to year. The Church gave people a code of conduct, it structured their lives from cradle to grave, and it could be a refuge from terrors and uncertainties of daily life, dangerous work, and even anti-Catholic bigotry. This common shared experience, not of all Catholics in the United States but of the people in the particular parish where they lived, is what Catholics brought to their Sunday worship, and this is what gave the Latin mass meaning for them. Analogously the same could be said for most Catholic parishes around the world prior to the Second Vatican Council.

Catholics today, however, are no longer the relatively homogeneous communities that they once were. For many social, cultural and economic reasons, the people who come to church on a given Sunday (or to a Saturday vigil mass) are a diverse group that may or may not have much in common apart from the fact that they share the same space for an hour a week. Our reflections on the Masai and on pre-Vatican II Catholics have given us some clues about where the meaning of the mass will come from in the twenty-first century. In fact, if this analysis is correct, the meaning of the mass can only be in the minds of those who are participating in it, and the common meaning that it has can only come from what the participants have in common.

4. Dimensions of meaning

People can have a lot of things in common, but commonalities tend to fall into three different areas. They can share experiences, they can have similar ideas and beliefs, and they can decide to do the same things. People who have all three in common are a tightly knit community, perhaps in a family or a fire department or a sports team. Tribal communities such as the Masai also share meaning in all three dimensions: since their numbers are small, they see each other regularly if not every day; since their communication with outsiders is limited, their society provides them with ideas and ideals, values and mores in myths and rituals in which they all participate; since their range of choices are few, girls decide to be mothers and artisans while boys decide to be herdsmen and hunters. People in tribal societies, especially isolated ones, cannot avoid having a great deal in common.

People in modern and industrial societies usually do not have so much in common. Even families tend to be split by parents going off to different jobs, by children going off to different schools, by everyone having different friends, by each being interested in different sources of information and entertainment, and so on. As a result of this fracturing of relationships, people often find that they connect with others in only one or two areas rather than in all three.

One place that people find meaning is in experience. Those who live in the same neighborhood or town have similar experiences of location, youngsters who go to the same school have similar experiences across a number of years, and people who work for the same company or the same type of business find that they can compare experiences on the job. Boys talk with boys, girls talk with girls, women talk with women, and men talk with men about what they have seen and heard just by being who they are. Parents of newborns and young children can share lots of stories, as can people who have been through natural disasters such as fires and floods. They can easily find meaning in and relate to experiences that were similar to their own. Of course, everyone can talk about the weather because everyone experiences it.

It can happen that people without similar backgrounds find that they have common interests or similar beliefs and ideas. Strangers can strike up a conversation while seated next to each other in a plane and find that they are both interested in music or science or traveling, and whether they agree or not, they can share what they've learned and what they believe to be the case. Catholics may find that they can talk about religion with other Catholics more easily than with people of other faiths (or of no faith) because their common beliefs give them a basis of understanding. Of course, the same is true for Evangelicals, Jews, Muslims, and so on. Common knowledge is the basis of shop talk because you cannot address the other person's comments without understanding what they are talking about. People join clubs who may have little in common except their interest in antiques, the stock market, cooking, music, superheroes, or astrology. Likewise they may join professional associations and go to conventions to learn about and discuss marketing strategies, personnel problems, medical technology, tax regulations, social services, and so on with people who otherwise are total strangers. Men with little else in common are often able to carry on at least a short conversation about baseball, football, basketball, or whatever other sport is currently in season.

It is even possible for people from very different backgrounds and with sometimes fairly different ideas to make similar decisions. They may decide to have children or not, to convert to a certain religion, to support a political candidate, to become vegetarian or vegan, to approve or object to a government policy, and so on. They may find themselves at a political rally or social demonstration with others who have made the same decision but who in many other respects are very different from them. They may decide to serve in a soup kitchen, volunteer in a school, work with troubled teens, or join with others in disaster relief, and although in time they may build up a raft of common experiences, at the beginning they are united primarily in their common decision.

Let us take this last example as a way to understand how the bonds of community can grow. Imagine that the chamber of commerce in one town has called for volunteers to clean up tornado damage in another town a few hours away. Initially, those who answer the call have nothing particular in common except their decision to engage in disaster relief. They may attend an organizational meeting and begin to gain some common understandings about what to wear, the equipment that will be needed, and the work that they will be expected to do for, say, a long weekend. During the drive to the demolished town, they talk a bit about themselves, what motivated them to volunteer, their marital status, where they work, and generally engage in small talk. By doing so, they are beginning to build up some common ideas about each other. When they get to the job site, they are no longer interested in one another, but all the while they are building up hours and days of common experiences. When they get together for meals, they talk about what they did, the challenges and successes they ran into, ways that the townspeople have expressed their gratitude, how they feel about what they are doing, and whatever else they can think of saying until it is time to get back to work, or to get some rest and relaxation before the next day's work.

Notice that a meal is a ritual. In our culture it is not a very complicated ritual, but it meets the requirement of occurring routinely, it is governed by rules of table manners and social etiquette, and it has a certain internal structure that begins with setting the table (or passing around food boxes) and ends with washing the dishes (or disposing the food boxes). Likewise, each meal itself—whether it is breakfast, lunch or supper—is going to offer certain types of food that are appropriate. Cereal or eggs for breakfast, sandwiches and maybe fruit for lunch, and meat and potatoes for supper would not be unusual.

As we have already seen, a ritual in and of itself has no meaning, and it might seem strange to ask the meaning of a meal in this context. The volunteers, however, would very likely find their meals meaningful, and they might even talk about this when they go home and talk about their experiences on the trip. Very likely, however, much of the meaning that they would find during the meals would be felt meaning, not conceptualized and expressed meaning. Undoubtedly, most if not all of the meaning that they felt during the meals would be connected in one way or another to what they had been doing between meals, that is, their experience of working together and helping others.

Now, the eucharistic liturgy is a ritual meal, so we can apply this analysis, more or less, to what Catholics do in church on Sundays. If we begin with the dimension of decision making, we can say that all have made the decision to go to a particular mass, but this implies little more commonality than going to the same restaurant at the same time; the diners do not interact with one another, and their reasons for going there might be quite varied. In the area of understanding, it used to be true that all Catholics agreed with Church teachings in the areas of doctrine (e.g., the Trinity), morality (e.g., no meat on Friday), and worship (e.g., the mass is a sacrifice). This is no longer the case, however. Opinion polls show that not all Catholics believe that the pope is infallible, that birth control is wrong, that abortion is always a crime, or that Christ is really present in the Eucharist.[6] Still we can guess that the people who show up for mass on Sunday share the beliefs that the Catholic Church is a good one to belong to, that it promotes the teachings of Jesus and the Christian tradition, and that religious worship is important. Beyond this, people in attendance may share common

6. On infallibility, see Hans Küng, *Infallible? An Inquiry* (Garden City, NY: Doubleday, 1971); Karl Rahner and Hans Küng, "A Working Agreement to Disagree," *America*, v. 129, n. 1 (July 7, 1973) 9–12; John Allen, "Infallibility Debate Continues," *National Catholic Reporter*, v. 47, n. 16 (May 27, 2011) 10–12. On contraception, see "The Pope and Birth Control: A Crisis in Catholic Authority," *Time*, v. 92, n. 6 (August 9, 1968) 54; Garth L. Hallett, "Infallibility and Contraception: The Debate Continues," *Theological Studies*, v. 49, n. 3 (September 1988) 517–528. On abortion, see James Hitchcock, "Catholic Liberals and Abortion," *Human Life Review*, v. 37, n. 1/2 (Winter/Spring 2011) 31–43; Andrew Greeley, "The Abortion Debate and the Catholic Subculture," *America*, v. 167, n. 1 (July 4, 1992) 13–15. On the Eucharist, see Mary Gautier, "Knowledge and Belief About the Real Presence," *National Catholic Reporter*, v. 48, n. 1 (October 24, 2011) 27; Peter Steinfels, "Future of Faith Worries Catholic Leaders," *New York Times*, v. 143, n. 49714 (June 1, 1994) A1, A12. For general surveys of diversity in beliefs and practices among U.S. Catholics, see Mark M. Gray, Paul M. Perl and Tricia C. Bruce, *Marriage in the Catholic Church: A Survey of U.S. Catholics*, Center for Applied Research in the Apostolate, Georgetown University, Washington, DC, October 2007; Mark M. Gray and Paul M. Perl, *Sacraments Today: Belief and Practice among U.S. Catholics*, Center for Applied Research in the Apostolate, Georgetown University, Washington, DC, April 2008.

beliefs about God, the scriptures, and so on, but since they do not get much chance to talk about these things, they do not know who agrees with them and who does not. Finally, if they share the same space for only an hour per week, and if they don't necessarily sit in the same place or see the same people every week, they will not have much in common with the other churchgoers in the area of common experience. All in all, therefore, it is possible for Catholics to attend mass regularly without having much in common with others who are there in the church with them. The same would be true, of course, for Protestants, Jews, and others who do not have any interaction with other members of the congregation apart from weekly worship services.

Consider now the eucharistic liturgy of a vibrant charismatic prayer group. It would not take place on Sunday because there are no longer any priests to spare on weekends. This means they had to get together as a group to determine the best time for weekly worship, some of them may have to work together to prepare the worship space, and they all would have decided to get together at a time and place which is a bit out of the ordinary. Since spirituality is important for charismatics, there is a good chance that all or some members of the group get together for prayer or Bible study in addition to the regular mass, and such meetings would involve of personal interaction in the sharing of ideas and experiences. Charismatics believe in healing through prayer, and so members of the group would regularly pray over others or be prayed over themselves with a laying on of hands. They believe in prophesy and the other charisms mentioned in 1 Corinthians 12:7–10, and they may have heard prophetic utterances during mass or prayer meetings from people who are speaking in the Spirit. Charismatics also put great emphasis on certain Christian beliefs such as God's love and providence, the power of the Holy Spirit, surrender to God's grace, and praying in tongues. Thus in the area of ideas the group would have much more in common than would people in an average parish. Their uniqueness on many levels would also give them a sense of being different from the average Catholic, perhaps even an awareness of being special or called by God, an awareness of church in the literal sense of the Greek word εκκλεσία, being called out or set apart from the crowd. Their common experiences, ideas and decisions would make them a rather cohesive group, and their religious rituals (whether the mass or other forms of group prayer) would naturally amplify their sense of unity and togetherness.

Think now about a Hispanic community, not a large parish in California or Texas, but a smaller community of mostly migrant workers and their families somewhere in the American farm belt. Some families may have set down roots in the place, but most of the men are just there for the harvest, and then they will move on. They are not a parish as such, but a priest who speaks Spanish celebrates the eucharist with them after the regularly scheduled Sunday masses. In the area of experience, they have much in common: they are strangers in a strange land; they have all left their homes in Latin America to seek a better life for themselves and their children; they experience the loss of their home town and their many relatives there; they share the aches and pains of hard physical labor; and whether they have documents or not, they fear the surprise appearance of immigration authorities anytime in the day or night. In the area of mutual understanding, they share a common language and a similar culture, they remember the religious processions and devotions they grew up with, they have a special attachment to the rosary and Our Lady of Guadalupe, they know most of the people around them because the community is small and many of the pickers come back every year, they know what it is to be poor and to live from payday to payday, they know what it is like to be hungry, to ask for food, and to be asked for food and maybe a few dollars. They have made a number of common decisions: to leave their home and their extended family, to work rather than seek public assistance, to remain Catholic despite constant invitations from the Protestants who proselytize among them, perhaps to overstay their visa and become illegal, perhaps to walk some distance to get to mass. All of this resonates in their minds as they say the responses and sing the hymns in Spanish during the liturgy. All of this adds meaning to the religious ritual, and it carries over into the meal of rice and beans that the Anglo parishioners prepare for them every week.

Finally, imagine a small Catholic church in the poorer section of a large city. It is a non-geographical parish, so people come from all over town and from outside the city limits. It is also a non-discriminating parish, welcoming the divorced and remarried, gays and lesbians, former priests and nuns, unmarried couples, and even non-Catholics. Shortly after Vatican II, the pews were taken out and replaced with chairs, and the altar is now a large table that is usually in the middle of the nave, but it can be moved for different arrangements of the assembly. Where the old altar once stood is now a platform for a music ensemble and chorus of paid and volunteer musicians. In the 1970s the parish began buying run-down properties in the neighborhood, fixing them up, and then renting them at fair prices. It also saw a need to help people on welfare and disability manage their money and rebuild their lives, so it started a counseling service in what used to be the sacristy. In the 1980s the parish joined the Sanctuary movement, sheltering political refugees from El Salvador trying to reach freedom in Canada. It also started a fair trade market for Latin American crafts, and it has since become a not-for-profit store. Through an American missionary, the church established a close relationship with a rural parish in Nicaragua. Today it provides funds for a community health clinic there, it helps women grow vegetables for their families, and it supports an organic farming cooperative. Every year or so, the parish sends a delegation to visit that parish, and it pays for a delegation to come from Nicaragua to meet the parishioners here and report on progress there. The old parochial school is now a minimum security jail that provides men to do janitorial work in the church and allows them to come for worship on Sunday. The former rectory is now a retreat center for high school and college students who are interested in spiritual growth through an inner city immersion. A number of small groups meet regularly for prayer and Bible study, and during Advent and Lent additional groups are formed for short-term reading and sharing. There is only one liturgy every Sunday, which is planned and executed entirely by parishioners, with a priest from a neighboring parish as the usual sacramental minister. Children's church is held during the adults' Liturgy of the Word, divided into different age groups and led by parents of the children themselves. Besides the worship committee and the parish council, there are about a dozen committees that meet weekly or monthly, many having to do with social justice concerns. The parish's St. Vincent de Paul Conference distributes food to and pays utility bills for needy families in the neighborhood, most of whom are not Catholic. Of the 300 or so households in the parish directory, two-thirds of them are engaged in some form of parish ministry. The rest just come on Sunday for the experience of worshiping with people who sing their hearts out. During the kiss of peace before communion, it takes more than five minutes for everyone to greet and hug most of the people that they know in church. The mass always ends with applause.

The energy that gets expressed in the single Sunday liturgy comes from the effort that gets put into parish life the rest of the week. Members who have been in the parish for decades share years of worshiping and working together, working not just on committees but also on projects such as rehabilitating nearby houses and going on disaster relief missions. They share mostly liberal ideas about the church and the hierarchy, the Second Vatican Council, human rights, and social justice, and they are very aware of having decided to remain Catholic despite their disagreement with Rome on many issues. For those who are newer to the parish, there is a collective memory of what the parish has done and what it stands for, as expressed in the mission statement posted in the vestibule. They make many similar decisions about volunteering their time and being very generous with their money.

If members of the three communities just described—the charismatic prayer group, the Hispanic community, and the inner-city church—were asked if their Sunday worship was meaningful, virtually all would say yes. If asked what it meant, however, people might be hard pressed to articulate it. This is because much of the meaning is felt rather than conceptualized: it is the felt meaning of the common experiences, the felt realization of common beliefs and ideals, and the feeling of community that comes from having common values and making similar decisions. Of the three groups, those in the charismatic community might be more inclined to express their understanding of the mass in theological terms because their sense of who they are and what they are doing is closely related to scripture passages (e.g., Paul speaking about the charisms) and traditional doctrines (e.g., Christ's presence in the Eucharist). But clearly it is not necessary to have a theological vocabulary or a dictionary of doctrinal terms in order to experience meaningful worship nor to articulate that meaning if asked.

What is needed to experience meaningful worship are shared meaningful experiences and relationships, beliefs and ideas, values and decisions, most of which occur long before the liturgy begins. If the meaning is already present in the minds of the participants, the liturgy is meaningful. If there is no lived and shared meaning in their minds, the liturgy is virtually meaningless.

Where, then, does the meaning of a mass come from? Notice that I ask about the meaning of *a* mass and not about the meaning of *the* mass. When we talk about the mass, we are talking about an abstraction, a concept, an idea. It is one of those realities that exists only in our minds. We have never experienced *the* mass; we have always had experiences of this mass or that mass, of individual eucharistic liturgies. Nor have we ever decided to go to *the* mass; our decisions have always been to attend this mass or that mass, this or that particular eucharistic liturgy.

At the beginning of this chapter, I proposed that talking about meaning as though it were something contained in words and symbols is both helpful and misleading. It is helpful up to a point, but after that, it is misleading. Similarly, the analytical chapters in this book were based on the proposal that talking about sacraments as given and received was helpful in the past, but now it has become misleading. The sacraments that were said to be received are, when analyzed, not spiritual realities but explanatory constructs. These were needed in scholasticism to explain the connection between certain religious rituals that were experienced as real (baptism, eucharist, etc.) and non-material things that were also experienced as real (church membership, Christ's presence, etc.). For eleven centuries, however, western Christians affirmed that spiritual realities are brought about by church rituals without needing to think of something that mediates between the two, something that is called a sacrament. Similarly, for twenty centuries, eastern Christians have affirmed that spiritual realities are brought about by church rituals without resorting to the scholastic concept of the *sacramentum et res*. It is time to acknowledge that talking about sacraments as though they can be given and received may have been helpful in the past, but now it is misleading.

In the same vein, I propose that talking about the meaning of the mass, although it may have been helpful in the past, is now misleading. When Catholic culture was more homogeneous, it made sense to think that church rituals should always mean the same thing to everyone. And when Catholic society was more stratified, it made sense to think that the people on top should tell the people on the bottom what the sacramental rites meant. Indeed, the revisions that were introduced after the Second Vatican Council were based on the assumption that the meaning of each sacrament could be expressed in words and actions that were different from the Catholic rites that had been introduced after the Council of Trent, four centuries earlier. Pope John XXIII had said in his opening address at the Council, "The substance of the ancient doctrine of the deposit of faith is one thing, and the way in which it is presented is another." Applied to the sacraments, it meant that the meaning of a sacrament is one thing, and the way it is symbolically expressed is another.

The movement toward liturgical inculturation in the 1970s was based on this same assumption. Americans could take the meanings of the eucharistic rite, for example, and express them in folk songs and guitar masses. Africans could take those same meanings and express them using drums and dance in ways that made sense to them. In this context, Vincent Donovan's *Christianity Rediscovered* in 1978 not only affirmed what the pope had said and what the council had done, but it moved the project to the next logical stage, allowing indigenous people to create their own rituals instead of having to adopt and adapt European ones. Asians likewise believed they should be free not only to adapt the Roman rituals to their situation but even to inculturate the meaning of the mass and sacraments in ways that would be most meaningful to Catholics in the Philippines, Korea, Vietnam and other far eastern cultures. Indeed, it was a Filipino liturgist, Anscar Chupungco, who first conceptualized and proposed various degrees of inculturation.[7]

This developmental process was interrupted and curtailed by Pope John Paul II, however, who insisted that all adaptations of the Roman liturgy, both eucharistic and sacramental, be approved by the Vatican, and who forbade genuine inculturation. From the pope's writings and from other documents issued by the magisterium in recent decades, it is clear that the conservatives in Rome identify the meaning of the sacraments with the meaning of the Latin texts that are the basis of all approved translations in the Church.[8] They are simply not aware that the actual meaning of any sacramental ritual is not found in the text but in the minds of those who participate in the ritual. Thus they can insist on preserving the meaning of the mass and the meaning of the sacraments as though they were talking about something that is real. But it is not real, except in the sense that it is the real meaning (that is, a good translation) of the text and of the written rite. The only real sacraments are those that are going on at any given time, and the only real meanings that they have are the meanings that they have in the minds of those who are participating in them.

Thus the attempt to rein in liturgical development, instead of preserving the traditional meaning of the mass and the sacraments, has in fact obscured that meaning. By insisting that the form and language of the rituals (the actual performances) remain close to the officially approved rites (the written texts), the magisterium has guaranteed that Catholic rituals are becoming increasingly disconnected from the religious lives of most Catholics around the world. That is, the people in the pews for the most part do not think of the meanings of the texts when they are attending the rituals. Had the Vatican given priority to meaning over form, it could have allowed the meaning of the sacraments to be genuinely inculturated and expressed in a variety of cultural forms. Thus, if the meaning of baptism is the forgiveness of past sins and

---

7. See Anscar J. Chupungco, *Cultural Adaptation of the Liturgy* (New York: Paulist Press, 1982); *Liturgies of the Future: The Process and Methods of Inculturation* (New York: Paulist Press, 1989); and *Liturgical Inculturation : Sacramentals, Religiosity, and Catechesis* (Collegeville, MN: Liturgical Press, 1992).

8. See *Liturgiam Authenticam: On the Use of Vernacular Languages in the Publication of the Books of the Roman Liturgy* issued by the Congregation for Divine Worship and the Discipline of the Sacraments on March 28, 2001.

entrance into the church, it could have allowed the development not only of different water rituals but other rituals that might embody the ideas of forgiveness and immersion (βαπτίζειν) into the Christian community. Likewise, if the meaning of marriage is the commitment of two people to be faithful to and care for each other, it could have allowed virtually any type of indigenous wedding ritual to be adapted for use by Catholics. Moreover, control over the ritual forms themselves could have been given to local jurisdictions such as episcopal conferences, so that if the sacramental rites developed at one point became unsatisfactory a generation later, the people in those jurisdictions, under the auspices of their bishops, could adapt them to the sensibilities of the next generation.

Had such a path been followed, the illusion that meanings are somehow contained in rituals would have been perpetuated, for the meaning perceived in any given instance would have been culturally appropriate and, in a sense, obvious to anyone in that culture. Outsiders might ask about the meaning of a ritual, and a respondent would reply by reading the cultural symbolism and translating it into the language of the inquirer, much the same as translating the meaning of a word into a different language.

As things stand, however, the standardization of Catholic rituals in such a way that they must closely approximate the Latin texts approved after Vatican II guarantees that most Catholics around the world will not perceive the traditional meanings in the rites themselves, and that the meanings will have to be explained not only to outsiders but to Catholics themselves. Moreover, the symbolic opaqueness of even the translated texts will guarantee that, when Catholics attend the religious rituals of their church, the meanings in their minds will not come from the words of the rites but from their own life experiences.

5. Toward an Authentic Future

If the road taken by the magisterium is a dead end, is there any way forward? The path taken by the Masai and the analysis presented in this chapter suggest that there is. The only genuine way forward is to look away from ritual and to look instead at what is ritualized, that is, to look at life rather than liturgy and, indeed, to look at the communal lives of people in the church.

Reference was made earlier to the Tridentine mass that all Catholics attended prior to 1969, and to the fact that many found it meaningful even though it was in Latin. This is not to deny that for many people the mass was meaningless in the sense that they didn't understand the language, although they did understand that the priest at the altar was doing something serious for the salvation of the world, and they did understand that the bread and wine were changed into the body and blood of Christ, to which they should show great reverence. Nor is it to deny that many devout Catholics filled their time by praying the rosary or engaging in religious devotions which they found more meaningful than the mass. Nor is it to deny that children and adolescents attended the mass because their parents forced them to be there, and the same was probably true of many men who were there to please their wives. But the men may have drawn meaning from the experiences, understandings and decisions they shared with other men who worked in the same factory, for example, who faced the same economic challenges, who had similar problems with their kids, who faced discrimination because they were a minority, who supported the same political party, who drank at the same local bar, and who played in the same softball league or bowling club. Likewise, most of the children would have gone to the same parochial school, had the same teachers, laughed at the same jokes, talked about the same radio and television shows, played together after school, had the same gripes about their parents, and had met each other on the same confession line on Saturday. The women and men most active in the parish would have been members of the Holy Name Society, the Altar and Rosary Society, various sodalities, the Knights of Columbus, or the school's PTA. They would have been coaches for teams in the Catholic Youth Organization, and they would have been Girl Scout and Boy Scout leaders. Most of them—women and men, girls and boys—would have lived in the same neighborhood so that they could walk to school and church, and they would bump into other parish members when walking or shopping. In the traditional Catholic parish, there was a network of relationships and an overlap of experiences, understandings and decisions that invisibly linked most of the parishioners together, and that was felt just as surely as the feeling of being family at a Thanksgiving dinner or a Fourth of July picnic.

These various dimensions of meaning were actuated when they saw the people they knew at Sunday mass. Whether or not they shared stories before or after church, they shared experiences outside of church. Whether or not they talked about the same ideas, they shared the understanding of being a minority, of being Catholic, of belonging to the one true church with the pope at its head. They knew what they should believe, and they knew how they ought to behave, because it was laid out for them in the catechism. They made similar decisions about the clothes they wore, the food they ate, and even the cars they bought. All of this came together somewhat subconsciously and resonated at the level of feeling while they attended a weekly ritual that was so important that their soul would be imperiled if they missed it. When Catholics reminisce about "the good old days," they are bringing into consciousness what they loved and hated in their parish decades ago, all of which gave meaning to their lives then.

Missing these dimensions of meaning, Catholics today sometimes find themselves leaving their parish and joining a so-called mega-church nearby. Protestant churches of this sort grow in part because people are attracted to the preaching of individuals who are able to connect scriptural teachings with their personal lives, who can offer biblical certainty during uncertain times, and who can give direction to their otherwise directionless lives. Such churches maintain the people they attract, not only by offering something worth listening to on Sunday, but by providing a network of relationships through which they interact with one another during the week. Besides prayer groups and Bible studies, they offer baby-sitting for working mothers and support groups for stay-at-home moms; and they offer a variety of involvements for children and adolescents from Sunday school to vacation Bible school to youth groups to after-school clubs to summer camps to sports teams throughout the year. They often expect that every church member is going to be engaged in some kind of ministerial work, whether it is spreading the gospel in new neighborhoods, doing baby-sitting during church services, preparing the social hour afterwards, organizing and helping with youth activities, singing in any number of choirs, working in a food pantry, or visiting shut-ins. They often offer social services both to their members and to others, which then become outreach ministries that help grow the congregation, such as individual and marriage counseling, parent support groups, help with paying rent and utility bills, and help with finding a job.

Sunday worship in such a church often centers around a well prepared but lengthy sermon preached by the person whose charisma and ability caused the church to grow in the first place. But the service also includes hymn singing and public praying, it may give people an opportunity to testify how God is acting in their lives, it may call to the altar those who feel a special need for prayer, and it may contain a communion service. The flexible and non-liturgical nature of such worship suggests that it is not any pre-designed and well-worded rite that gives the service its meaning. In fact, much of the praying in such churches is spontaneous, and its very spontaneity conveys a message of sincerity and devotion on the part of the one doing the praying. Rather, as has been suggested, the meaning of the service (that is, what it means to the people in attendance) arises out of and amplifies the meanings that the members have been aware of, even if subliminally, in their actions and interactions during the week.

Notice that virtually all of the church's organized activities are related to gospel values. During the week, church members are either ministering to others or they are being ministered to, so they are feeling glad for having their needs met or they are feeling the satisfaction of meeting the needs of others. To the extent that each adult is required to participate in some ministry, and to the extent that children and adolescents are invited to participate in ministry, to that extent they are laying their lives down for others and experiencing the paschal mystery of finding life by giving it up. All of that activity is meaningful, and that meaning is felt again in the familiar surroundings of the sanctuary and the familiar faces of other church members. Some of that meaning gets echoed in the prayers that are said and in the hymns that are sung. And some of that meaning gets reaffirmed in the sermon when it touches on turning one's life over to Christ and doing God's work in the world. The Sunday service acts as a reminder and resonator for the meaning that people find in church-related activities during the week, and this is why it is experienced as meaningful.

This is not to suggest that people cannot find new meaning in church on Sunday, either in one of the scripture readings, or in something that is said by one of the ministers, or in the words of one of the hymns, or in a ritual activity such as a baptism. But it is to affirm that most of the meaning that fills the minds of churchgoers—and also the meaning that may lie just below conscious awareness—comes not from what happens in church but from what happens before any church service begins. For it is possible to walk out of church and not remember anything in particular that was said or done but still feel that it was a meaningful time of worship.

Whereas the major Protestant denominations have three types of religious ritual (sermon-centered worship, baptism, and communion—also called the Lord's supper), the Catholic Church since the Middle Ages has had seven. These seven are tradition-ally called sacraments, although in early Christianity there was no generic name for liturgical rituals. Ordinarily, when all seven sacraments are discussed, baptism and the other sacraments of initiation are treated first, then the two sacraments of heal-ing, and finally the two sacraments of vocation. Also, the treatment of any particular sacrament begins with a description of the rite and then moves on to a discussion of what it means. If it is true, however, that the actual meaning of a ritual performance arises out of what people have experienced and understood before the performance, and if the meaning of any rite of passage or transition ritual comes from decisions that have been made before the ritual begins, it is appropriate to take a different approach.

Let us assume that Christian lives lived in community with others are based on some common experiences, understandings and decisions. In discussing these com-monalities, we will not attempt to be exhaustive, but we will look for ideas and ideals, principles and values that could guide the behavior of Christian groups that are both large and small, and that would not vary much from culture to culture. Moreover, we will limit our search for such spiritual realities by looking for ones that are related to the seven sacraments as they have been traditionally performed and understood.

a. Ordination

Even a casual reading of the New Testament reveals that among its central ideas are the love of others and service to others. The Greek word for love in the Christian scriptures is αγάπη, which is better translated as care, and which is more related to action than to feeling. Living according to what the gospels and epistles say about αγάπη, therefore, means caring about and taking care of others. Thus it implies service to others, not for any reward, but because one cares about them. The life of Jesus in the synoptic gospels is characterized by his ministering to others, especially the sick and the suffering. Jesus in the fourth gospel tells his disciples in no uncertain terms that they are to love one another in the same way that he loved them. A famous section of Paul's first letter to the Corinthians sings the praises of αγάπη.[9]

---

9. See Jn 15:12–13, 1 Cor 13: 1–8.

Although ordination in medieval and Tridentine Catholicism ritualized the bestowal of priestly power, both the revised rite and its theology instead emphasize ministerial responsibility. Priests are given the office of priesthood and exhorted to live the gospel in an exemplary fashion, so that their justice and mercy can inspire others, and even their ability to consecrate the Eucharist is for the service of the people.[10] Ordination therefore celebrates a decision to be of service to the church and, through the church, to the world. Currently the orders of presbyter and bishop are limited to celibate males, but this is largely a historical development since in early Christianity men in both orders were married.[11] Moreover, there is ample evidence that, prior to the interpretation of ordination as a bestowal of priestly power in the twelfth century, women were ordained to positions of responsibility in monasteries, and in the ancient church deaconesses as well as deacons were ordained.[12] The scholastic theory of ordination as a ritual with permanent effects arose at a time when there was little social mobility and life expectancy was short, but in recent decades it has been belied by many leaving the priesthood. According to the theory, such men are still priests, but they are not allowed to exercise their priestly powers. Earlier in the church's history, however, it was understood that people were ordained to serve a certain community in a certain capacity, so they did not take their ordination with them when they traveled, so to speak, and when they left the position for which they were ordained, they simply became a member of the faithful; they did not have to be laicized. In this respect, ordination was much like being given a position in public service today: the responsibility is given for a certain time and in a certain place (e.g., teacher, school superintendent, county prosecutor, district court judge), and when people leave that position, they revert back to being ordinary citizens. It could be that way again. In this respect, ordination was once much like ordination in many Protestant churches today, where one is ordained to minister in a certain capacity for a certain congregation. When one leaves that position, one is no longer an ordained person, and if one is called to minister in a different congregation, one may be ordained again.

Ordination as a ceremony that celebrates the beginning of a professional life of ministry could therefore be much more flexible than it is today. It could be open to men and women, married and unmarried, heterosexual and homosexual who are judged by those who appoint them and by those whom they serve as having the qualities

10. See the Rite of Ordination in *The Rites of the Catholic Church*, Vol. 2 (Collegeville, MN: Liturgical Press, 1990), ch. 3.

11. See Jean-Paul Audet, *Structures of Christian Priesthood: A Study of Home, Marriage, and Celibacy in the Pastoral Service of the Church* (New York: Macmillan, 1968); also Joseph Martos, *Doors to the Sacred*, 468–494.

12. See John Wijngaards, *Women Deacons in the Early Church: Historical Texts and Contemporary Debates* (New York: Crossroad, 2006); also Gary Macy, William T. Ditewig and Phyllis Zagano, *Women Deacons: Past, Present, Future* (Mahwah, NJ: Paulist Press, 2011), 9–36. A collection of relevant texts can be found in Kevin Madigan and Carolyn Osiek, eds., *Ordained Women in the Early Church: A Documentary History* (Baltimore: Johns Hopkins University Press, 2005.)

needed to perform the duties to which they are called. Currently there are three orders in the Catholic Church, but conceivably ordination could also be extended to religious educators, youth ministers, church musicians, parish administrators, pastoral counselors, social workers, and others who receive professional training before their ministry, who must maintain a high level of professional and ethical conduct during their service to the church, and who depend for their livelihood on the income they receive for that service. For what is celebrated in an ordination ceremony is not gender or marital status or sexual orientation or permanence, but caring for others and service to others as a full-time occupation.

The vision of a variety of ordinations opens up the possibility of a variety of cultural variations as well. At present, there is a Latin text that is normative for all translations of the ordination rite, and at most, the ceremony can be adapted to local cultures through the addition of indigenous dress, music and perhaps dance—which are all peripheral to the inflexible rite itself. As long as the meaning of the rite is believed to be in its words (technically, the form of the rite), a strong argument can be made in favor of ritual inflexibility. But if the meaning is acknowledged to be in the participants, then theoretically any sort of ceremony is possible as long as it means that the ordinand is entering into a ministerial role that demands a high level of commitment and skill for a sustained period of time. Politically, however, a way would have to be found to maintain a unity of purpose and meaning amidst a burgeoning diversity of ceremonies. Regardless of the rite's cultural shape, however, the ordaining minister and the community to be served would be empowering the ordinand with the authority needed to perform the professional service. Theologically, since all power comes ultimately from God, the prayers of the rite could be very similar in form to what they already are, asking God to guide and enable the newly ordained to fulfill his or her ministerial responsibilities.

b. Confirmation

Confirmation has been called a sacrament in search of a theology. In the present context, this can be understood as a ceremony in search of a purpose.

Since the Second Vatican Council, two theologies have competed for acceptance. Both are founded on the notion that confirmation is a sacrament of initiation. One theology suggests that confirmation is a celebration of Christian adulthood, an opportunity for adolescents to publicly profess the faith that their parents accepted for them when they were baptized as infants. The other theology proposes that since confirmation is the completion of baptism, and since only the fully initiated should receive communion, children should be confirmed before their first reception of the Eucharist.

One problem regarding the two interpretations is that the rite of confirmation is so vague that it does not support or exclude either of them. The canonical form of the rite is, "Be sealed with the gift of the Holy Spirit," and the attendant prayers are hardly more specific. Since there is no particular meaning inherent in the words and gestures, the proponents of both theologies are able to propose ideas in the hope that they will be accepted by the people involved, namely the local bishop, the parish priest, the parents and the children to be confirmed. When the confirmands are adolescents, a good deal of time is spent convincing them that the sacrament will make them fully initiated adult members of the church. Notice that the assumption at work here is the one presented earlier in this chapter as something that is true of all rituals, namely, that the meaning is not in the rite but in the minds of the participants. But the proponents of both interpretations are under the illusion that putting ideas in the heads of the participants will make the ceremony meaningful.

Unfortunately, this is not where the primary meaning of a transition ritual comes from. The ritual shape of the confirmation ceremony is a rite of passage, and rites of passage derive their primary meaning from changes in the lives of those who undergo them. In tribal cultures, puberty rituals literally turn children into adults: boys are given men's responsibilities and treated as such, and the girls likewise pass into the world of womanhood. Their experience of themselves and those around them is different before and after their initiation, their understanding of who they are changes, and they can now make decisions that as children they were not allowed to make. The meaning of their initiation therefore draws from all three dimensions of meaning, not just one. This same pattern can be found in many secular rites of passage. For example, people who become naturalized citizens pass from being aliens to being people who have the full protection of the law, who have both the right and the responsibility to vote, and who can travel under their new country's passport. Although the change is not as dramatic, it is just as real: people's experience changes, their self-understanding changes, and the range of their decision making changes. In addition, they themselves made the decision to become naturalized citizens and to give up citizenship in the land of their birth. For most people, this is a big decision.

A third example might be an inauguration into public office. A fourth might be entrance into the armed forces, followed by advances in rank, and each of these transitions stems from a personal decision, leads to new experiences (e.g., new duties and privileges), new understandings (e.g., one's role in the organization), and new powers of decision making (e.g., to do things that require the authority to do them). In each of these cases, and in every case of a genuine rite of passage, the meaning of the ceremony comes from three dimensions of meaning that were inhabited in one way before the ceremony and in another way after the ceremony.

A meaningful transition such as this does not happen in confirmation today. The main difference that children perceive if they are confirmed before first communion is that they can now go to communion with the big people in church; otherwise, their status remains unchanged. Adult Catholics are aware, moreover, that one can make one's first communion without having been confirmed first, since that was the experience of most of them, so they do not perceive confirmation as enabling their children to receive communion, even though they may have been told this by the religious educators in their parish. Adolescent confirmation is even worse, for being confirmed as a teenager makes absolutely no difference in their lives as Catholics. Although some parishes may wisely extend privileges such as being a eucharistic minister or being on the parish council to their confirmed teenagers, this sort of attempt to make confirmation more meaningful is not widespread, and it is not general church policy.

Confirmation in the Catholic Church could be made meaningful only if it were a ritual celebration of actual changes in the lives of those who participate in the sacrament. In this respect, it would be no different from ordination or marriage: the participants would have to make a decision before the ceremony, and afterwards they would have responsibilities and privileges they did not have previously.

The traditional understanding of confirmation is that it is a sacrament of initiation and that it marks the completion of the initiation process. In one respect it is similar to the current ordination process in that men are ordained deacons before they are ordained priests, so one could say that they are partly initiated into clerical ministry in one ceremony, and then they are fully initiated in a second ceremony. After the first ritual, they have certain duties and privileges (e.g., celibacy and preaching), and after the second, they have additional ones that are primarily related to sacramental ministry. Analogously, one could regard baptism and confirmation as two steps in Christian initiation: the first step makes one a member of the church, bestowing the right to the church's spiritual support in one's religious journey[13] and the responsibility to grow in the faith, and the second bestowing the right to engage in all ministries except those reserved for the ordained, as well as the responsibility to contribute to the life of the community by committing to some form of lay ministry, which could also be thought of as part-time ministry or non-professional ministry.

Confirmation would thus be a genuine sacrament of initiation, for it would be required of any Catholic who wanted to be of service in the parish or who wanted to work in the world on behalf of the church. Such service would be different from employment, which could be open to people of any faith or no faith, just as it is now, and Catholics who are employed by the institutional church would not necessarily fulfill their requirement to engage in lay ministry by having such a job (for example, working in a Catholic hospital or being the parish bookkeeper). Moreover, the theology of confirmation calls it the completion of baptism, and rethinking confirmation along these lines would bring practice into line with theory. Arguably, one's initiation into the church is not complete until one has become a follower of Christ in deed as well as in creed, until one has realized that Christians are called not to sit but to do, and until one has moved from being the object of ministry to being a ministering subject. The faith that was received in baptism would thus be truly confirmed when one decided to put that faith into action by ministering to others on a regular basis.

13. This used to be called the right to receive the other sacraments.

Traditionally, baptisms have been confirmed only once in a person's lifetime, but today there is no necessity to retain that rule. In the ancient and medieval worlds, where there was no social mobility, there was no need to baptize or confirm or ordain more than once. Under the influence of thinking that sacraments were things that could be received, the theory of the indelible character provided a rationale for not confirming more than once. Now that the theory of the *sacramentum et res* has been deconstructed, however, it can no longer be used as a justification for confining the ceremony to once in a lifetime. Just as the earlier practice gave rise to the notion of unrepeatability, a change in practice would alter that part of the theology of confirmation.

In some churches, this has already been done. The Episcopal and Lutheran churches changed their confirmation policies in the 1980s, making it a repeatable sacrament. Teenagers can ask to be confirmed when they feel ready to make a mature acceptance of the faith in which they were raised after their baptism as infants, but adults can also ask to participate in the rite if they feel a need to reaffirm their faith at some point later in life.[14] In the first instance, the rite is called confirmation; in the second, it is referred to as affirmation, and its purpose varies. Some adult participants may be returning to church membership after having been absent for a number of years, while others may want to publicly celebrate a conversion process or spiritual growth that they have recently experienced. The flexibility of this practice, combined with the absence of a theology that claims that the rite bestows something permanent on the recipient, make it possible for the sacrament to mean what the participants want it to mean, within some general parameters.

The difference between this policy and the one being proposed for Catholicism is that the Protestant policy puts the emphasis on faith and membership, both of which can be rather passively accepted, and the proposal described earlier in this section puts the emphasis on ministry, which is necessarily active. Baptized Catholics who never felt a need to serve others in or through the church would never be confirmed, and the lack of confirmation would signify that their initiation into the Christian way of life was incomplete. But it could also happen that those who were confirmed as teenagers, and who participated in various ministries for a while, later drifted away from church. At some point in the future, if they wanted to return, their recommitment to a life of service to others could be celebrated in a slightly modified confirmation ritual. Such a ceremony would not only mark their transition back into the faith community, but the ceremony's emphasis on service would be a reminder to the rest of the community that commitment to Christ necessarily entails ministry.

---

14. See Robert L. Browning and Roy A. Reed, *Models of Confirmation and Baptismal Affirmation: Liturgical and Educational Issues and Designs* (Birmingham, AL: Religious Education Press, 1995), 81–99; Paul Turner, *Confirmation: The Baby in Solomon's Court* (Mahwah, NJ: Paulist Press, 1993), 37–53.

No mention has been made here of the eucharist as a sacrament of initiation because it is not really a sacrament of initiation, despite the recent habit of calling it one. Before the Second Vatican Council, the eucharistic liturgy was called the sacrifice of the mass, and it had nothing to do with baptism. The research that led to the redesign of the baptismal liturgy, especially its expansion into the Rite of Christian Initiation of Adults, revealed that in the early patristic period, the initiation of pagans into the Christian community culminated in the neophytes' first participation in the Lord's supper. Even in the fourth century, when the imperial approval of Christianity led to a rapid increase in the number of catechumens, those who were not yet baptized were ushered out of the liturgy before the anaphora or eucharistic prayer began. During the first centuries, therefore, it would have been correct to call the eucharistic liturgy a sacrament of initiation because only those ready to witness the sacred mysteries and receive holy communion were allowed to attend it.

This is no longer the case today. Non-Catholics are not barred from attending mass, and converts to Catholicism have often attended the entire eucharistic liturgy even if they have not received communion. Not until they enroll in the RCIA and officially become catechumens do they join a group that leaves the assembly after the scripture readings to "break open the word" with their catechists during the Liturgy of the Eucharist. If perchance they miss the mass set aside for catechetical instruction, they can attend the entire liturgy (for example, if they go to church with their spouse) even if they refrain from communion. It is simply not true that catechumens' experiences, understandings and decisions are clearly different before and after their baptism. It is simply not true that the Liturgy of the Eucharist is something that they encounter for the first time at the Easter Vigil. So it is simply not true that the eucharistic liturgy is a sacrament of initiation even if the first reception of communion culminates the initiation ceremonies.

c. Baptism

When talking with the Masai about their acceptance of the gospel, Vincent Donovan took for granted that the proper ritual for doing this was baptism, which in the 1950s would have entailed the pouring of a little bit of water on the head of each initiate. Given what has been said earlier about liturgical inculturation, other rituals of initiation might be culturally appropriate, and once we give up any magical connection between ritual actions and metaphysical effects, it is easy to imagine how other types of ceremonies besides water rituals could be used to initiate people into the Christian community. Protestants churches that delay baptism until children are capable of professing their faith in Jesus often celebrate the birth of members' children with a naming ceremony or some other ritual of acceptance into the community.

Given what we have seen about the lack of inherent meaning in any ritual, however, one could argue that a water ritual is more appropriate than any other ritual for symbolizing what baptism traditionally symbolizes. A ceremony's meaning is not in the words that are said and the actions that are performed, but rather it is in the minds of the participants and in the minds of those who see that the lives of the candidates before their initiation were different from what they will be afterward. Nevertheless, baptism in some form or another is so traditional in Christianity—and also so unique to Christianity—that it seems proper to retain it as a unifying symbol even if it is done differently in different churches and different cultures. Indeed, through the centuries, baptisms have been performed in a great variety of ways: full immersion in water, pouring lots of water on the head of someone standing in water, pouring a small amount of water on the head, and sprinkling with water. But the fact that baptizing is mentioned in the New Testament (even if it is never described) makes it a common point of reference to all those who have heard the scripture stories before deciding to join the Christian community. Indeed, if a particular community decided not to initiate with a water ritual, its absence is something that would need to be explained to any newcomers who were familiar with the conversion stories in the book of Acts, for example.

The same cannot be said, however, about the words of the rite, which are not always the same even in the New Testament, which suggests baptism in the name of Jesus and baptism in the name of the Father, Son and Holy Spirit as both appropriate. No one notices today there is a linguistic anachronism in both of these forms: the words, "in the name of." If someone in today's society does something in the name of someone else, it means that they are doing it on the other person's behalf, such as accepting a prize. It could also mean that they are doing something with the backing of a higher authority, such as making an arrest in the name of the law. In ancient Hebrew usage, however, the name represented the reality of the one named, the way that a national flag represents the nation to such an extent that desecrating the flag is identified with dishonoring the nation. This understanding of names also lies behind the concept of blasphemy in traditional religions, and also behind laws in some monarchies even today, where speaking irreverently about the king is a criminal offense. So baptizing in the name of Jesus or the Trinity still makes sense in some places and cultures, but not in ours. And yet we do it, for the meaning of the ritual comes not from the words of the ritual but from the people who participate in it.

Thus the traditional words can be and are used in baptisms today, even though they do not make sense in most modern languages. Probably most of the traditional symbols included in the Catholic ritual can also be retained for the same reason: a lighted candle, anointing with oil, and new clothes or a new outer garment. But since these have no foundation in New Testament baptism stories, they cannot claim to be as symbolically necessary as water is. Therefore it is theoretically possible to design initiation rites that do not utilize these symbols, as in fact most Protestant baptisms do not. If Catholics in other cultures were free to design their own initiation rites, they could include symbolic elements that are culturally appropriate, even if they looked strange to Europeans and Americans.

What would be constant in Catholic but culturally diverse initiation rituals would not be the symbols but what is symbolized. In the case of adult baptism, it should be the decision to quit a lifestyle that is incompatible with Christian values and ideals, and to adopt one that is. What counts as incompatible and compatible is going to vary from culture to culture and from society to society. In a tribal culture, for example, it may mean renouncing practices such as blood revenge and stoning. In a consumer culture, it may mean adopting a simpler lifestyle, and recycling rather than throwing things away. In an industrial society, it may mean giving up foods produced by industrial agriculture in favor of locally grown foods. In a city with great disparities in wealth, it may mean working to improve schools in poor neighborhoods, working to reduce gang violence and police violence, or working to reduce economic exploitation by pawn shops and payday lenders. More internally focused community activities have already been described, such as adult Bible studies, religious education for children, social activities for youth, emotional and financial support groups for members in distress, and so on. What is crucial is that becoming a Catholic should not just be a matter of sitting in a different building for one hour a week.

In order to accomplish such a change in lifestyle, the catechizing that is done in RCIA programs (or something parallel) would come closer to that practice of the second-century *Didache*, which focused almost exclusively on matters of behavior and morality: rejecting the way of death and choosing the way of life.[15] Although doctrines and other Catholic beliefs would not be excluded, they would not be the focus of catechetical attention. Above all, detailed explanations of canon law and expositions of the catechism would be avoided because these church documents have little direct bearing on the way people live their lives. The same could be said about the documents of the Second Vatican Council and about papal encyclicals. If anything, the study of such writings should come after a person has joined the church.

Above all, the parish that is inviting newcomers to live in a different way must already be living in a way that is different, at least to some extent, from the surrounding secular culture. This is not to suggest that middle class parishes in the United States need to close down their RCIA programs until the parishes themselves are radical examples of gospel living, but it does strongly suggest that parishes need to look at what they are doing, and at what they are inviting outsiders into, if they are going to put them through an initiation process. For the structure of genuine rites of passage demands

15. See above, page 74. This is not the place to argue that a simpler and somewhat countercultural lifestyle is more in keeping with gospel values and ideals, or that working for social justice is demanded by prophetic writings in both the Old and New Testament. These arguments have already been made by others. See, for example, Gustavo Gutiérrez, *A Theology of Liberation: History, Politics, and Salvation* (Maryknoll, NY: Orbis Books, 1973); Kathryn Tanner, *The Politics of God: Christian Theologies and Social Justice* (Minneapolis : Fortress Press, 1992); Jim Wallis, *The Call to Conversion: Why Faith Is Always Personal but Never Private* (San Francisco: HarperCollins, 2005).

that people's lives be different after initiation from what they were before. Otherwise there may be a lovely ceremony without any actual initiation or new beginning. To say it in another way, if a transition ritual does not mark a true transition from one state in life to another, it does not celebrate anything real. It is an empty ritual.

At the very least, therefore, the lives of people in a Catholic parish ought to be somehow different from the lives of unchurched people in the neighborhood. All adult members of the parish ought to be expected to be part of at least one ministry that serves other church members or people outside the parish. This requires that the parish support enough ministries that it can honestly say to new initiates that their service is needed, and the catechumenate ought to include a process of discernment and decision making about where they will serve after they are baptized and confirmed. The same would also be true of those who were baptized as infants and later seek to complete their initiation by being confirmed in the church. To the extent that a parish cannot offer initiates a new life, references in the rite to new life will have no concrete meaning.

Finally, something needs to be said about infant baptism. When he first proposed baptism to the Masai, Donovan wanted to baptize only the adults who showed that they had understood what he had been teaching. But the elders disagreed, and they insisted that the slow-witted should be baptized with all the other adults in the tribe. Donovan came to see that the elders were right. People who were physically adults but mentally like children should be allowed to participate in the life of the Christian community as fully as possible, so that they could learn through participation what they could not learn through hearing.

A similar insight lies behind the contemporary pastoral practice of not automatically baptizing children. When the theology of original sin dominated Catholic thinking about baptism, priests baptized infants whenever they were asked to do so, in order to give the children a chance of getting into heaven even if their parents were not church goers. The same kind of magical thinking led Catholic midwives and nurses to baptize infants who were stillborn or in danger of dying, sometimes even when the parents were not Christians. Around the time of the Second Vatican Council, however, a rethinking of humanity's relation to God in many areas of scholarship (scriptural, moral, ecumenical, etc.) led to a reconsideration of the church's policy of always baptizing whenever asked. Pastorally, it did not seem advisable to baptize a child who was not going to be raised by practicing Catholics because, without parental support, he or she would be unlikely to grow in the life of faith. And doctrinally, the Catholic Church affirmed that children who die without baptism are not necessarily condemned to hell, but rather they are entrusted to the mercy of God.[16]

From a ritual perspective, asking parents to be churchgoers if they want their children to be baptized is a minimalist policy at best. Very often the request for baptism from unchurched parents comes from either a magical or cultural mentality: either the

---

16. See *Catechism of the Catholic Church*, 1261 and 1283.

parents think the child will derive some automatic spiritual benefit from the ritual, or they want to satisfy the demands of grandparents and others who want to see that the child gets baptized. Too frequently, however, the entire involvement of Catholic parents in the life of a parish is attendance at Sunday mass, and this is not enough to introduce children to a new life, to expose them to the light of Christ, or to infuse them with a holy spirit. Parents need to be, as Pope John Paul II insisted, a domestic church, and at the very least this implies that families ritualize their faith in ways that children can understand: saying grace before meals, reading Bible stories, saying prayers at night, and having religious art in the home. Above all, parents need to explain their own behavior and family routines in religious as well as secular terms; for example, supporting charities because Jesus asked us to help the least of his brothers and sister, or recycling because God made us stewards of the earth. Children also need to see their parents involved in more church activities than Sunday worship if they are going to grow up thinking that being a Catholic means more than church attendance.

In order to make this happen, the parish needs to have programs that support the involvement of parents and children. Women who give birth, whether married or not, should expect parishioners to be there for them, preparing meals, helping with house-cleaning, and coping with newborns especially if this is their first child. Parishes ought to eliminate so-called crying rooms at the back of church, and instead they should provide baby-sitting so that mothers can actually engage in worship. They should also provide pre-school activities for children who are too young for religious instruction, and lectionary based catechesis for grade school children during the Liturgy of the Word. In addition, parishes need to provide quality religious instruction, social activities and service opportunities for children in elementary school and teenagers in high school. They should also be attentive to the needs of young people who live at home while attending college or who try to earn a living after graduating from high school, especially offering them opportunities for service and inviting them to fill adult leadership roles in the parish. Activities such as these are not optional unless the church (at both the parochial and diocesan levels) is willing to lose its young people and shrink in size until it is little more than a religious club for senior citizens. Sociologically, such thoroughgoing ministerial activity is the only way to grow a church. Theologically, the paschal mystery is an abstract belief unless people experience it in serving others. Ritually, unless the church offers people new life in a way that they can see and feel it, baptism's promise of new life remains unfulfilled.

d. Marriage

The sacrament of marriage offers special challenges because marriage means different things in different cultures, and because its meaning is changing in post-industrial societies. One of the great historical struggles in European Catholicism was to reconcile the marriage customs and beliefs of ancient Rome with those of the Germanic tribes that converted to Christianity during the early Middle Ages. By the twelfth century, the church had acquired a more or less unified rite and a rather uniform theology, both of which were solidified in the Tridentine reforms of the sixteenth century. This culturally European construct of marriage was then imposed on non-European converts to Catholicism during the church's missionary expansion until well into the twentieth century.

Some elements of this construct are that the marriage ritual is a rite of passage from celibacy to socially sanctioned sexual intercourse, that marriage itself is monogamous, and that the marital bond is indissoluble. Young men and women were expected to be virgins prior to getting married, although this expectation was laid more heavily on girls than on boys. Divorce was socially unacceptable, remarriage after divorce entailed excommunication, and annulments were so rare that few Catholics even understood the concept. Moreover, this construct was believed to be found in the Bible and it was understood to be ordained by God. When Christianity was carried into other cultures, therefore, missionaries regarded non-European sexual and marital practices as immoral, and those who converted to the faith also had to convert to European marital norms. This was the case for Protestant as well as Catholic converts.

That Christian marriage has undergone cultural changes is evident from history.[17] In ancient Israel marriage was polygamous, at least for royalty and possibly the wealthy. Marriages were arranged by parents for their children and the virginity of women was highly prized, as it is in most tribal and agrarian societies. The gospels say nothing directly about marriage, and although Jesus does condemn divorce, he does not say that divorce is impossible. Rather, he condemns it as sinful, and the Gospel According to Matthew includes an exception if the wife has been immoral, but the text does not specify which type of immorality. The Epistle to the Ephesians holds forth an ideal of husbands taking care of wives as well as they take care of their own bodies, and of women obeying their husbands just as the church obeys Christ. In the Roman Empire, marriage was monogamous but divorce was legal. Among Christians, marriage was likewise monogamous and divorce was possible, even though it was regarded as sinful unless a woman had committed adultery. Most marriages were arranged, but under Roman law two adults could marry each other without their parents' consent.

Marriage was not yet regarded as a sacrament when Christian missionaries carried the gospel into northern Europe in order to convert the so-called barbarians to the faith. The missionaries did not impose Roman marriage practices on their converts, but instead the traditional Germanic marriage practices continued to prevail. Marriages were arranged by parents, sometimes years in advance of a wedding, and the betrothed couple was considered truly married when they had their first act of sexual intercourse. As Christian Europe became more integrated, Roman and Germanic marital customs clashed, especially when young people tried to thwart their

17. For a summary, see Martos, *Doors to the Sacred*, ch. 11. For greater detail, see Schillebeeckx, *Marriage*, and Mackin, *What is Marriage?*

parents' arrangements by claiming they had married someone else by vowing fidelity to a different partner. Roman law did not even require witnesses for a marriage to be legal, so people could marry without any witnesses. Over time, church authorities passed laws requiring all marriages, even clandestine ones, to be recorded. Gradually, marriages began to take place near or in a church where the records were kept, and eventually priests replaced parents as the ones who presided over weddings. By the middle of the twelfth century, marriage had become a religious matter rather than a strictly familial matter, a Christian wedding ceremony had been devised, and marriages became regulated by canon law rather than civil law. The existence of a liturgical wedding ritual prompted marriage to be regarded as a sacrament, and the New Testament ideal of fidelity was translated into a theological assertion of indissolubility. Divorce became impossible, and the legal process of annulment, once reserved for civil courts (e.g., in cases involving impotence) became a canonical process through which aristocrats might seek to terminate an undesirable marriage (e.g., by claiming that they were too closely related to their spouse).

This is the form and theology of marriage that was enshrined in the Council of Trent's doctrines in the sixteenth century, and that was carried by Catholic missionaries throughout the world until the twentieth century. After Vatican II, for a variety of cultural and theological reasons (e.g., regarding the unbaptized as being in the hands of God rather than in the clutches of Satan), Rome ceased its concerted efforts to convert all the pagans of the world to the Catholic faith. Although the magisterium has not considered the possibility of revisiting the theology of marriage, the historical record demonstrates enough cultural relativity to warrant an exploration of what a wedding ceremony might look like and what it might mean in the twenty-first century.

Issues that suggest themselves for exploration are the timing of the wedding, its desirability and necessity, the relation of sexual activity to marriage, liturgical forms other than the Roman rite, and the possibility of plural and same-sex marriages. What will enable us to address such disparate issues with some coherence is an understanding of marriage that is not bound to any particular culture or society.

In post-industrial societies and perhaps in others, the time for the wedding is changing from before a couple live together to after they have lived together for a while. In the United States at present, about half of the couples who marry have shared the same residence for some time before they decide to marry, and this percentage has been steadily increasing since the 1960s.[18] Many people cohabit in order to test the relationship before they make a legal and lifetime commitment, and recent research suggests that the impact of cohabitation on marital longevity is hard to determine.[19]

18. See Gail Risch, "Cohabitation: Integrating Ecclesial and Social Science Teaching," in Todd A. Salzman, Thomas M. Kelly and John J. O'Keefe, eds., *Marriage and the Catholic Church: Scripture, Tradition and Experience* (New York: Crossroad Publishing, 2004) 159. Risch cites statistics from Larry Bumpass and Hsien-Hen Lu, "Cohabitation and Implications for Children's Family Contexts in the United States, *Population Studies*, v. 54, n. 1 (March 2000) 29–41.

19. Risch refers to a number of studies measuring the effects of various factors on cohabitation

Regardless of the success or failure of this social experiment, the fact is that the wedding ritual is no longer a rite of passage from being single to being married. Today, not only do many couples live together as though they were married, but living together has become more socially accepted by their family and friends. In this context, what happens to the meaning of the wedding, especially if it is a religious wedding ceremony?

Fortunately for Catholics, the rite of marriage makes no reference to the couple's lives before and after marriage. Instead, it focuses on what they are promising to each other at the present moment, and it holds forth a vision of their lives together in the future. This was true even in the Tridentine rite, so we can say that in the past the wedding functioned as a rite of passage from singlehood to married life even though it did not specifically mention the couples' past and only referred to the present and their future together.[20] From this perspective, then, a formal wedding is still a new beginning, even if it is not the beginning of a sexual relationship.

It seems likely, therefore, that the meaning of a wedding for the couple and those who know them has shifted, but it has not substantially changed. Whether or not a couple formally marry before they live together, it means that they feel secure enough in their relationship to declare their love for each other in a public ceremony, to promise to be faithful to each other, and to accept all the rights and responsibilities of being a married couple. When the two individuals are Catholics, and when they are more than nominally Christians, they are possibly aware of various New Testament teachings about marriage and divorce, and they probably have been made aware of the traditional Catholic doctrine that marriage is indissoluble. From having witnessed the dissolution of other Catholic marriages, however, they are liable to believe that the doctrine has little relation to reality.

Conservative Catholics sometimes rail against people who marry with the self-centered and short-sighted idea that they can get a divorce if the marriage does not work out. While this may be true of some who marry civilly, it is not generally the case, and it is especially not true of Christians, Jews, Muslims and others who marry in religious ceremonies.[21] So one can suppose that, apart from beliefs that are specific to different religions, the meaning of a religious wedding ceremony is very similar for most people who marry.

Most Catholic dioceses insist that couples who intend to marry attend some sort of marriage preparation program prior to the wedding ceremony. While this is better than nothing, it does not seem to dissuade ill-prepared people from marrying, and

---

and marriage in "Cohabitation," 162–165. See also David DeVaus, Lixia Qu, and Ruth Watson, "Premarital Cohabitation and Subsequent Marital Stability," *Family Matters*, 65 (Winter 2003) 34–39.

20. As a matter of fact, most rites of passage are similarly structured.

21. See, e.g., Evelyn Lehrer and Carmel Chiswick, "Religion as a Determinant of Marital Stability," *Demography*, v. 30, n. 3 (August 1993) 385–404; Michael Lawler, "Religion Good for Marriage, Research Says," *America*, v. 182, n. 11 (April 1, 2000) 4.

there is no evidence that it has a significant long-term effect on the marital satisfaction or divorce rate of Catholics.[22] And while many express appreciation for the program after going through it, most think of it beforehand as a bureaucratic hurdle to be overcome if they want to get married in a Catholic church. Were church leaders genuinely interested in the welfare of married Catholics, they would do much more than require a few hours of preparation before marriage, for they would insist that parishes offer much more assistance for married couples during the months and years following the wedding. Support groups for newlyweds and new parents could meet monthly to share experiences and to learn from marriage counselors or older married couples how to get through the rough spots of the early years. Volunteers could meet weekly or more regularly with women who had just given birth, offering meals, help with housekeeping, ideas from their own experience, and perhaps even financial assistance from a parish fund specially set up for this purpose. If emotional and spiritual counseling were generally available to parishioners, husbands and wives could take advantage of it whenever they hit rough spots in their relationship, as always happens from time to time. Not every parish would be able to offer day care, but parishes could make day care and pre-school financially possible for parents who could not otherwise afford it. When children enter school, when they need help with their homework or a place to stay while their parents are still at work, and especially when they become teenagers, parents often need help understanding child and adolescent psychology, working through changing relationships, and handling the stress related to their teenagers' sexual or drug-related activity. With so much support at the parish level, Catholic marriages could become more stable and long lasting than the national average.

Even with such support, however, divorces would happen, and people need as much help through the breakdown of a relationship as they do for the maintenance of a relationship. Once the decision to divorce has been made, people often need legal and emotional guidance if they cannot find it on their own or get it from their family and friends. Very often one or both partners move out of the parish, but if they stay, it would be good to develop some kind of ritual for helping them and the other members of the parish make the mental move from regarding them as married to regarding them as single. A ritual of this sort could be a healing experience for the person who has gone through the divorce, helping him or her to experience acceptance and affirmation from the people in the parish. Divorce, like sin, is often experienced as failure and loss, so such a ritual could help with the grieving process and facilitate personal and social reintegration.

If divorce is accepted as a social reality that sometimes happens even though it is undesirable, as it was during the first millennium of Christianity, then annulment could be returned to the civil realm for such cases as legally require it (e.g., bigamy),

22. A study by the Center for Marriage and the Family, *Marriage Preparation in the Catholic Church: Getting It Right* (Omaha: Creighton University Press, 1995) showed that such programs can have an immediately positive effect, but long-time effects are hard to determine.

and Catholic marriage tribunals could be dismantled. Today, annulments are sought only by about 15 percent of U.S. Catholics who divorce and want to remarry, and fewer than half of these petitions are granted.[23] Since about 93% percent remarry without an annulment, either civilly or in another church, eliminating religious annulments would have no significant effect on the number of Catholics who divorce and remarry. As has been shown,[24] the doctrine of marital indissolubility was based on a mistaken interpretation of biblical and patristic texts, so unless the Catholic Church wants to maintain doctrines that have no basis in scripture and early church tradition, it has to admit that the canonical requirement that Catholics obtain a decree of annulment before remarrying is a relatively recent tradition that was given the force of law. Like the requirement of celibacy for priests, it is a law that could be stubbornly clung to, but laws that are out of touch with reality tend to be detrimental both to the institutions that issue them and to the people to whom they are meant to apply. In this case, the annulment requirement does not prevent divorced Catholics from remarrying; rather, it causes people to leave the church who would probably remain if the magisterium took a more pastoral approach to marriage, and it causes the magisterium to lose credibility as a religious authority.

Consider the fact that sacramental doctrines have historically reflected sacramental practices of the time. The doctrine of baptismal unrepeatability reflected the Roman practice of not rebaptizing in the fourth century, the doctrine that confirmation is a separate sacrament reflected the separation of the bishop's blessing from the baptismal rite in the early Middle Ages, and the doctrine that extreme unction is a sacrament for the dying reflected the fact that a ninth-century healing ritual had become, by the twelfth century, an anointing for people at the point of death. Likewise, the doctrine that marriage is a sacrament and is indissoluble reflected the fact that, in the twelfth century, the Catholic hierarchy gained complete control of the civil aspects of marriage and could therefore declare divorce to be impossible.

Now, consider what might be the case if marriage had not appeared on Peter Lombard's list of sacraments, just as the coronation of monarchs and the consecration of churches did not. While the Catholic understanding of marriage during the modern period might not have looked much different than it did in historical fact (except that it would not have been regarded as a sacrament), the church would have made it into the twentieth century without a theology of marriage that was dogmatically bound to the marriage practices of the Middle Ages. Consequently, the Catholic theology of marriage could have changed to fit contemporary social realities, just as Protestant theologies of marriage have done. More likely, today there would be a number of Catholic and Protestant theologies of marriage, just as there is a variety of ways of understanding the church.[25] Nevertheless, there would be no theology of marriage

23. See the CARA study cited above in footnote 6, *Marriage in the Catholic Church*, 92.

24. See above, pages 156–57, 206–209.

25. See, for example, Avery Dulles, *Models of the Church* (Garden City, NY: Doubleday, 1974).

that regarded marriage as indissoluble, for since the late twentieth century it has been clear that marriages dissolve at a statistically regular rate. A conservative Catholic theology of marriage might regard all divorce as a sin, as some conservative Protestant theologies do (based on a literal reading of Jesus' condemnation of divorce), but no one would say that people who divorce are still married. Yet this is the position that the magisterium is obliged to adopt because it retains a theology of marriage that reflects the social realities of the twelfth century rather than one that reflects the social realities of the twenty-first century.

The social meaning and purpose of marriage has changed through the centuries, and today most people in America and Europe marry for companionship—what is sometimes called companionate marriage. Although married people may want to have children, they do not marry in order to have children, as was the case in the Middle Ages when children were needed to work the farm, care for elderly parents, and inherit property. Today, people who want to have children can adopt them or produce them biologically without being married. Thus it is no longer true to say that the purpose, or even one of the purposes, of marriage is to have children. For most people, the purpose of marriage is to cement a relationship with a life partner by celebrating it publicly and binding it legally. When a relationship between two people develops to the point that they want to celebrate what they have found and what they hope will last, that is the time for a wedding, and if the couple are religious, that is the time for a religious wedding ceremony. Whether or not they have lived together before the ceremony is quite beside the point.

If it is true that people today in the post-industrial world marry mainly for companionship, how should this be understood theologically? Ask marriage counselors what makes for a healthy and happy marriage, and the first thing they will name is good communication. But good communication entails listening, and listening requires setting aside personal preoccupations and attending to what the other is saying. The second most significant characteristic of a happy and healthy marriage is cooperation, but this too implies setting aside personal preferences in order to do what the other person needs to be done. If one were to go through the list of things that make for a satisfying and lasting marriage, one would find that most of them are some form of caring behavior. In other words, most of them are forms of self-giving love, unconditional love, or what the New Testament calls ἀγάπη.

One could make the case that companionate marriage is closer to the teachings of Jesus than the type of marriage described in Ephesians 5:22–33, where the husband is exhorted to take care of his wife but the wife is told to obey her husband. Both involve self-surrender, but not in the same way, since marriage in a patriarchal culture is an inherently unequal relationship. In today's society, however, marriage is more egalitarian, and so both partners are called to care about and take care of each other, which involves sensitivity to the other's needs and a responsiveness that goes beyond obeying orders. Both are called to live the Johannine call to discipleship and service:

"Take care of each other, just as I have cared for you. None are more caring than those who give their lives for their friends" (Jn 15: 12–13). In this "new command," Jesus tells his followers to take care of each other, to minister to one another's needs. He tells them to be friends in the classical sense of someone who is concerned with the welfare of another person. But companionate marriage is a union of equals who are primarily friends and secondarily lovers, parents, and so on. To put a sort of Christian label on it, it is a marriage of mutual ministry.

Once friendship and mutual ministry are understood to be the primary characteristics of Christian marriage, homosexual relationships, including marriage, become unproblematic. The central issue is always one of αγάπη, caring, not one of sexual behavior. The main question is whether or not two people are putting the other's needs ahead of their own wants, not whether the two have the same or different body parts. The focus is on living the paschal mystery, laying down one's life for another, not on what one does in bed. Nevertheless, this orientation implies that the focus in sexual activity should be on pleasing one's partner, not on self-gratification.

By extension, the same could be said of polygamy, whether polygyny or polyandry. When Christianity was preached to the natives of Africa, those who wanted to join the church were told that, before they could be baptized, they had to put aside any additional wives they might have. African culture at the time was very patriarchal, so companionate marriage would have been culturally inappropriate. A polygynous marriage lived according to the ideal of Ephesians 5 might have been appropriate, but the European insistence on monogamy tore up extended families instead of healing them. Today, as people around the world move from tribal to agricultural to industrial and post-industrial societies, plural marriage is less culturally appropriate. Polyandry, the practice of women having more than one husband, has always been a rarity on this planet, but theologically such marriages would fall under the same norms as all Christian marriages, namely, caring for and caring about the other members of the marriage in ways that are fitting for that society.[26]

A final word about the marriage rite. In the years immediately after Vatican II, Catholics who wanted to marry were given great latitude in choosing the place of the ceremony, the wording of the wedding vows, and other trappings of the ritual. Since the 1980s, however, the guidelines for Catholic weddings have become more restrictive in the apparent belief that uniformity is more important than inculturation. Nevertheless, marriages around the world are still celebrated in ways that are culturally suitable, even if Catholic couples and their families do not have the same freedom in designing nuptial rites that others in their society might have. Perhaps in the future, Catholics may once again have such freedom, if the Vatican realizes that the meaning of a wedding comes from the people who participate in it and not from the words and rubrics in a ritual book.

26. On the moral possibility of same sex and plural marriage, see Margaret A. Farley, *Just Love: A Framework for Christian Sexual Ethics* (New York: Continuum, 2006), esp. 263–64, 271–96.

e. Reconciliation

Like marriage rites, rites of repentance have varied greatly in Christian history. When first century Christians were told to forgive one another, they undoubtedly did it in an informal way that expressed their sincerity. When someone offended the whole community, the offender was ostracized for a while and then readmitted after an acceptable demonstration of repentance.[27] In the second century, a way had to be found to reconcile apostates and others who willfully quit the community, and a strict regimen of public repentance under the supervision of bishops gave such individuals a second chance. When Christianity was legalized and officially approved in the Roman Empire, the canonical penance system fell first into abuse and then into disuse. After the fall of the empire, the monastic practice of confessing sins and receiving moral guidance spread beyond monastery walls and became a form of repeated private confession. Those who heard such confessions, imposed penances and declared God's forgiveness might have been monks or nuns (especially abbots and abbesses) or priests, but eventually the practice was given a canonical form and reserved to the clergy. The *sacramentum penitentiae*, as it was known since the Middle Ages, was a legal and moral forum in which individuals were judged to be repentant and absolved from their sins without necessarily having to make restitution or engage in reconciliation with others. In the late twentieth century, as people's understanding of sin became less legalistic, the official sacrament of penance fell largely into disuse except among the more devout.[28]

As with the spittle of forgiveness among the Masai, rituals of repentance and reconciliation are meant to facilitate the seeking and receiving of forgiveness between individuals and groups. Although they are not clearly rites of passage the way initiation ceremonies are, such rituals in fact help move people from a negative relationship with others to a positive relationship with them. Psychologically, they can also help people to move from shame and self-hatred to self-forgiveness and self-acceptance. Theologically, they also help people to move from God's judgment to divine forgiveness.

One of the problems with the modern sacrament as it was practiced from the Council of Trent to Vatican II is that it had become ritualistic, magical, and separated from any experiences of actual reconciliation with others. The confession of sins was primarily a prerequisite for receiving communion and secondarily a requirement for getting into heaven. The most easily committed mortal sins were breaches of ritual purity by missing mass on Sunday or eating meat on Friday, for example. Next most common (for males) were sins against sexual purity in thought, word or deed, for all sexual offenses were regarded as gravely sinful. In all cases, however, what was

---

27. See 1 Cor 5:1–13 and 2 Cor 2:5–11.

28. For a summary of the history, see Martos, *Doors to the Sacred*, ch. 7; also Ladislas Orsy, *Evolving Church*, Kenan Osborne, *Reconciliation and Justification: The Sacrament and Its Theology* (New York: Paulist Press, 1990), and Sean Fagan, *Does Morality Change?* (Collegeville, MN: Liturgical Press, 1997).

required was remorse for having committed the sin and a resolve not to commit it again. If a confessor judged these two to be present, he could absolve the sin and assure the penitent of God's forgiveness. Sins of theft required restitution (of money or property, or of reputation if the loss was incurred through calumny or slander), but others could be forgiven at the confessor's discretion. No interaction with those who had been sinned against was needed, with the exception of having to pray to God, but even here only the fear of divine punishment was needed and not a deep sorrow for having offended God. As a rite of passage, then, private confession became a means of removing individual guilt without fostering genuine reconciliation between the sinner and those who had been sinned against.[29]

If the Catholic church is to develop rituals of genuine reconciliation in the future, it must begin with a vision of what kind of reconciliation it wants to bring about, and it must then develop appropriate procedures to foster it. These will not be liturgical procedures, but as in the Rite of Christian Initiation of Adults, various steps or moments in the process could be celebrated ritually.

Moreover, those who preside over these procedures will need to be skilled and they will need to be professional, but they will not need to be ordained priests. Certainly there may be priests who are trained in reconciliation, and ordained liturgical ministers may be invited to preside over rites of reconciliation, but ordination to the priesthood should not be viewed as automatically bestowing a power of reconciliation. Considering the broadened concept of ordination discussed earlier, the church could consider ordaining ministers of reconciliation who would not be liturgical ministers but who would be more like family counselors or dispute mediators.

Where are the needs for reconciliation in the church and in the world today, at least the needs that could be ministered to in parishes and dioceses?

First, individuals are sometimes in need of self-reconciliation or forgiveness. Sometimes it is easier to forgive others than to forgive ourselves, and sometime it is hard to believe that God forgives us for what we have done. For centuries, private confession served the function of promoting self-reconciliation and reconciliation with God, but in the Latin tradition the procedure was governed by legal definitions and canonical norms. In the Greek and other Orthodox traditions, by way of contrast, the procedures were and still are more pastoral and more concerned with spirituality. Today, skilled confessors already employ methods that are akin to pastoral counseling or spiritual direction, and it would perhaps be more honest to regard the first and second forms of the current Roman rite of reconciliation as counseling rather than as confession.

The second most likely place to find people in need of reconciliation is within the family. Husbands and wives, parents and children often go through periods of stress caused by misbehavior or miscommunication or both. Many people do not have the

---

29. This way of conceiving sin and forgiveness enabled priests to confess having committed pedophilia without having to face the children who had been harmed, and it enabled bishops to seek the silence of parents in exchange for assurances of priests' repentance.

skills needed to negotiate emotional standoffs or to soften hardened attitudes, many do not have the money to seek secular professional help, and some still regard seeking such help as a sign of weakness or failure that should not be admitted to outsiders. A church that actively promoted family reconciliation, especially one that periodically celebrated stories of reconciliation with personal testimonies and prayers of thanksgiving, could be a beacon of reconciliation to its members and a means of their seeking and obtaining forgiveness in the family.

The third place where reconciliation is both needed and feasible is in the community. Children, teenagers and adults can be alienated from other children, teenagers and adults in the community, leading to psychological warfare, physical fights and legal battles. Today there are few realistic alternatives to police action, civil and criminal detention, and court-ordered mediation when people are hurt and rights are violated. The so-called criminal justice system too often tries to address one injustice by imposing another injustice such as lengthy imprisonment, and the department of corrections is too often a euphemism for human warehousing. Schools and neighborhoods are perfect places for alternative practices such as restorative justice, which is much more biblical than the punitive justice that is so prevalent in society. Churches that actively engaged in mediation between teenagers and police, between rival gangs, between racial and ethnic minorities, and between other antagonists would be public signs that reconciliation is possible and that God's forgiveness is available to all.

In an active context of community, family and individual reconciliation, sacramental celebrations of reconciliation begin to make sense. For there would be actual instances of reconciliation to celebrate, and so rituals of reconciliation would draw their meaning from the experiences of reconciliation—from the acts of forgiving and the awareness of being forgiven—that have already occurred or that are in the process of occurring in people's lives.

Such celebrations would incorporate words and gestures of reconciliation that are already current in a given culture. In European and American culture, words such as "Please forgive me" and "I'm sorry" are already found in informal rituals of reconciliation, as are actions such as shaking hands and hugging. In non-western cultures, other words and gestures would be proper, even the spittle of forgiveness. Certainly scripture stories of reconciliation and admonitions to forgive would put such words and gestures into a Christian context, but the meaning of the liturgies would come not from the scripture passages but from the experiences of the participants.

f. Anointing of the Sick

Meaningful caring for the sick is much easier to visualize than meaningful reconciliation because it is already being done in our society. Not only is secular medical treatment a common occurrence, but hospital chaplains and parish nurses already attend to the spiritual needs of the sick and the elderly both formally and informally.

Therapeutic touching can convey healing energy, and active listening can facilitate emotional sharing of the same sort that ritual anointing and religious confession are meant to do. Although Protestants are generally better than Catholics at praying with the sick (in contrast with praying for them), this is a skill that can be learned and one does not have to be an ordained minister to do it.

For about eleven centuries now, only priests have been allowed to perform the spiritual ministry of praying over and anointing the sick, due primarily to a misinterpretation of James 5:14–15 as applying to a priestly ritual. Moreover, the medieval theory of priestly powers led to the conclusion that no one but a priest could administer the sacrament when sacraments were said to be "administered" and "received." Given the declining number of priests today, however, the restriction of this sacrament to priests effectively denies this ministry to a large number of Catholics who might otherwise benefit from it. And since the scholastic notion of a sacramental reality (*sacramentum et res*) has been deconstructed, the sacrament's theology does not require the minister of anointing to have a special power to administer it. All that is required is authorization from the church and pastoral skill on the part of the minister.

Restricting the anointing of the sick to priests is consequently not a metaphysical limitation but one of history and tradition. It can be changed, and what it could be changed into is limited only by the church's liturgical imagination. In fact, a number of rites could be envisioned:

- A communal rite to be performed by an ordained minister in the context of a liturgy in which the theme and the focus are healing.

- A communal rite to be performed by an ordained minister without an accompanying eucharistic liturgy.

- A formal ritual to be performed by an ordained minister or unordained chaplain for individuals in hospitals or homes.

- An informal ritual to be performed by parish nurses and lay ministers who regularly visit the sick.

Within recent Catholic history, and in the longer Christian tradition, there have been individuals with the personal charism or gift of healing, as mentioned in 1 Corinthians 12 and as evidenced in the charismatic movement among Catholics and Protestants alike. Parishes and dioceses could seek out individuals who demonstrate this gift, which is often exercised with a laying on of hands and speaking in tongues rather than with an anointing. They could approve this ministry, and they could look for ways to make it available to all Catholics who might benefit from it, not just those in charismatic prayer groups. The charismatic ministry as it is usually practiced often aims not so much at physical healing as at spiritual or emotional healing, so the number of people it could reach is potentially different from those who are physically ill. Moreover, charismatic healing rituals are essentially spontaneous, so it would be a mistake to compose a healing rite for charismatics. Thus this practice would remain a sacrament in the broad sense of a ritual that enables people to experience God's presence and power, and it would not be a sacrament in the strict sense of a formal rite.

g. Eucharist

The eucharistic liturgy and the consecrated elements referred to as the Eucharist or the Blessed Sacrament are two major sacraments in Roman Catholicism, although by convention they are thought of as different aspects of a single sacrament. During the first centuries, when Christians met in the evening for the Lord's supper or in the morning for a meal of thanksgiving (εὐχαρίστειν), the emphasis was on the ritual of sharing a meal in the presence of the Lord, θυσία in Greek and *sacrificium* in Latin. In the Christian Roman Empire, this simple ritual became an elaborate public ceremony (λειτουργία), and great emphasis was put on the divinity of Christ as well as on Christ's presence in the eucharistic bread and wine. During the Middle Ages, the ritual was greatly simplified in the Latin west, the idea of its being a liturgy was lost, and it was called the *missa* or the mass, and it was believed to be a sacrifice. The concept of sacrifice had changed, however, from what it had been during the patristic period, and the medieval concept was that of an offering made by a priest for the expiation of sins. What was offered was the Eucharist or the consecrated elements, understood to be Christ himself under the appearances of bread and wine. The priest was understood to be *alter Christus*, another Christ, and so the mass was interpreted as Christ offering himself in sacrifice to God the Father for the salvation of humankind. None but the priest usually partook of the consecrated elements during the mass, but consecrated bread was reserved in a special receptacle known as a tabernacle, and the Eucharist was adored as Christ present in the world. After the Reformation, Catholic reverence for the Blessed Sacrament intensified to offset Protestant denials of the real presence, but the reception of holy communion remained rare until Pope Pius X early in the twentieth century began to encourage more frequent communion. After the Second Vatican Council, Catholic worship was redesigned so that it more closely resembled the patristic liturgy, and although it was still called the mass, it was talked about more as a eucharistic meal than as a sacrifice. In addition, recovery of the concept of liturgy resulted in a call for greater participation by those in attendance. As a result of this shift in theology, most Catholics receive communion at every mass, and their sense of divine presence in the Blessed Sacrament has somewhat diminished. In its place, there is a sometimes greater awareness of Christ's presence in the worshiping community and in the action of the liturgy itself.[30]

---

30. For an expanded summary, see Martos, *Doors to the Sacred*, ch. 8.

As an act of ritual worship, the official meaning of the eucharistic liturgy has shifted from being a sacrifice offered by a priest on behalf of the people to being a communal meal shared by the people under the leadership of a priest. The actual meaning (or meanings) of any particular mass is hard to pin down, however, since the ritual is used to celebrate events in the life of Christ (Christmas, Easter, etc.), to celebrate the lives of the Blessed Mother and the saints, (Feast of the Assumption, St. Patrick's Day, etc.), to celebrate diocesan and parish events, to celebrate school openings and closings, to celebrate anniversaries and deaths (i.e., funerals), and to amplify sacramental celebrations that would otherwise be fairly short (baptisms, confirmations, weddings, ordinations, and anointings). In addition, there is the phenomenon discussed earlier, that the actual meaning (or meanings) of any particular ritual is found in the minds of those who are participating in it. Finally, eucharistic worship is so frequent and common in the lives of practicing Catholics that it tends to get invested with meanings derived from the circumstances under which it takes place. Thus the meaning of a daily mass attended by devout believers is likely to be different from the meaning of a Sunday mass attended by people who think about religion only once a week, and both will be different from the meaning of a mass attended by those who have just completed an intensive retreat such as a Cursillo.

Even within the mass, there are many opportunities for meaningful events. There are two scripture readings on weekdays and three on Sundays, and various individuals are apt to find meaning in any of these. A homily follows the readings, and both the priest and the listeners hope that something meaningful will be said. The liturgy also contains psalms and hymns, long prayers whose form is set (such as the Eucharistic Prayer) and short prayers that vary from day to day, the Lord's Prayer, and actions such as the greeting of peace (usually a handshake) and the receiving of communion. Since the relatively unchanging parts of the liturgy are repeated so often, it is often difficult for participants to find them especially meaningful in themselves. For most Catholics, then, the meaning of any particular mass tends to come not from the words and actions of the rite but, as suggested above, from the meaningful activities of the community and groups within it that have been going on prior to the mass itself.

Given what has been said above about new possibilities for ordination, and given the deconstruction of both priestly powers and real presence in the preceding chapter, there is no metaphysical need for an ordained priest to preside at all eucharistic liturgies. Given the length of the Catholic tradition, however, it would certainly be appropriate to reserve the leadership role in eucharistic liturgies to ordained priests and bishops. In addition to theology and spirituality, their professional preparation should include training in liturgical leadership and ceremonial performance, as well as homiletics. Moreover, given the shortage of priests caused by the current requirements for ordination (years of post-secondary education, celibacy, lifetime commitment, and total obedience to a bishop), it might be advisable to return to the earlier practice of ordaining (i.e., initiating into a ministerial position) individuals to perform specific ministries in specific communities. Those so ordained would be chosen because they have gifts for ministries such as administration, preaching, or liturgical leadership, they would be ordained for a particular parish or local community, and their ministerial status would last only as long as they continued to minister in that community. In this respect, they would have roughly the same status as that enjoyed by lay parish administrators today, that is, they serve for a while in a particular place, and when they leave that place, they become former parish administrators. The division of ministerial duties among individuals called to serve a community strongly suggests that community members should have a voice in selecting those who will be ordained to serve them, as was the case in the early church, even if selections need to be approved by a higher authority such as a bishop for the sake of regional harmony in the larger church.

Following the Pauline practice of leaving the design of religious rituals to the communities he founded,[31] Vincent Donovan allowed the Masai to find their own way to celebrate the message of Jesus and their new way of life. Paul and Donovan both realized that what is essential to any celebration is the reality that is celebrated and not the celebration itself.[32] Just as someone can express the same idea in different languages, just as appreciation can be expressed in different kinds of gifts, and just as affection can be expressed in a kiss, a hug or a handshake, so the same meaningful reality can be expressed in different types of rituals. What is important are the spiritual realities that are being celebrated, not in the abstract but concretely in the lives of individuals and in the life of the community within which the celebration takes place. If those realities are present, then the ritual is meaningful; to the extent that they are absent, it is more likely to be experienced as meaningless.

In religious traditions, such spiritual realities are generally referred to as mysteries, although very often the symbols of the mysteries also get called mysteries and are thought of as more important than the mysteries themselves. In Christianity, Jesus gets celebrated more than what he taught and how he lived, and in traditional Catholicism, the same happens to Mary and the saints. Even the Buddha complained that when he pointed to the moon, people focused on his finger instead of lifting their eyes to the moon, which is to say that they were discussing what he said instead of looking for what he was talking about. Too often organized religion gets caught up in symbols and loses sight of what the symbols point to. Good preachers can use stories about Jesus, Mary and the saints to talk about spiritual realities, just as Jesus used parables to talk about caring, forgiveness, and prayer. But dogmatists insist on preserving church doctrine even if they have to violate the teachings of Jesus to do it. And liturgists have yet to realize that the words and actions of religious rituals are not about liturgy but about what liturgy points to, symbolizes and celebrates.

31. Remember that Paul's complaint with the Corinthians was not that they used the wrong food or said the wrong prayers at the Lord's supper, but that $\alpha\gamma\acute{\alpha}\pi\eta$ was missing from their relationships.

32. In the case of the Masai, if unity was lacking among the households on a particular Sunday, there could be no ecclesial celebration of community life on that day.

The words and actions of the liturgy should not be thought of as being about Jesus or the Incarnation or God or the Trinity, for those too are symbols. None of them are experienced directly; rather, they are talked about. The same too can be said of the teaching that the mass is a sacrifice, that the scriptures are the Word of God, that worshipers are the People of God, and that Christ is present in the Eucharist. To the extent that they are talked about as realities in themselves, as things in a spiritual realm to be pondered and appreciated, as realities that cannot be experienced but have to be accepted on faith, to that extent the discussion is about symbols and not about the symbolized. Although doctrines such as those just named are often called mysteries, they are actually beliefs that cannot be fully explained with regard to how something is the case or how it relates to people's lives. How can the infinite God become a finite human being? How can there be three Persons in one God? How did Jesus' death on the cross effect the salvation of the world? How can Christ's resurrection, his ascension into heaven, or the descent of the Holy Spirit on Pentecost be explained? How can other biblical miracles be explained? In each of these cases, the *explicandum* or that which is in need of explanation is a belief—an idea or a set of ideas that are represented in words or images.

Although people usually assume that what they believe is somehow real, the fact is that what is real for human beings always has a foundation in experience. This is true of the material objects that we take to be real (as opposed to imaginary things that we can think about and make pictures of, even though no one has ever actually experienced them), it is true of the physical objects and laws that scientists take to be real (for there must always be some verifiable evidence for them), and it is true of the spiritual realities that make human life bearable, meaningful and enjoyable (such as justice, love, community, honesty, forgiveness, and so on). The things that are real for human beings—and this is true of both material realities and spiritual realities—are always things that are experienced in some way and at least partly understood.

With regard to the physical things around us, we usually understand enough about them that we do not regard them as mysteries. Artists and poets, however, are often aware of the mysteriousness of the world around us—flowers and birds and clouds and sunsets are typical examples—and they can depict these in such a way that we too begin to sense the wonder of them. Even spiritual realities are not often called mysteries, and we do not usually regard them as mysterious until something goes wrong with a relationship, until we experience rejection, until we lose a loved one, and so on, at which point we wonder what went wrong? Again here, artists and poets are often more sensitive to spiritual realities, and they are able to describe them with songs and stories and images in which we can recognize what we perhaps felt but were unable to articulate about infatuation, friendship, courage, compassion, fidelity, and so on.

It has been the contention of this work that sacramental theology, when it is done correctly, is a reflection on and articulation of spiritual realities that have been experienced by Christians at certain places and times. Those experienced realities are initially understood in terms of ideas in the culture of the period and in terms of stories and symbols from the past that are available in sacred writings. Thus baptism was understood in terms of new life because it was an immersion in a new lifestyle, and it was said to bring about the remission of sin because membership in a supportive community enabled people to get rid of destructive behaviors. Thus the laying on of hands in the book of Acts was interpreted as bestowing a holy spirit because people who had hands laid on them started behaving in strange but godly ways. In the Middle Ages, Augustine's concept of an indelible character helped theologians interpret the social fact that some sacraments were not repeated. In addition, it helped them to understand why Christians were seen as different from pagans and Jews, and why priests were experienced as different from lay people. Also in those days, married people were not able to divorce, and the concept of indissolubility both explained and enforced this social reality. Likewise the doctrine of the real presence of Christ in the Eucharist both prompted the devout to experience a spiritual presence in bread and wine, and it helped them to understand that presence when they experienced it.

Many religious rituals are rites of passage, and in the present context, this can be understood as creating spiritual realities and enabling people to perceive them. Baptism (in Catholic theology, for there are others) makes someone a member of the Christian community, and confirmation confirms that spiritual reality (or at least it is supposed to). Marriage turns single people into married people and ordination turns men into deacons, priests and bishops. They are experienced as different before and after the ritual that transforms them. People sometimes describe the cleansing they felt after receiving absolution or the comfort they felt after being anointed, so here too the theology of the sacrament both reflects people's experience and prompts their experience of spiritual realities. The eucharistic liturgy is not a rite of passage, but traditional eucharistic theology interpreted the consecration of the elements as causing a transformation of bread and wine into the body and blood of Christ, and traditional eucharistic spirituality enabled people to look at the elements and see bread and wine before the consecration, and then to look at the same elements and perceive the presence of Christ after the consecration.

Since the eucharistic liturgy is not a rite of passage, it does not enable and prompt people to experience a change in spiritual realities, but rather it invites them to more intensely feel spiritual realities of which they are already aware. A child's birthday party does not make anyone a year older, but it helps children and parents appreciate growing up. A Thanksgiving dinner may or may not help anyone feel more thankful for life's blessings, but it almost always helps people feel like family. An Independence Day celebration does not make people free, but it arouses feelings of patriotism and pride. In the same way, a eucharistic celebration helps the people in a particular religious community (a parish, a school, a monastery, etc.) experience more deeply the spiritual realities that are already found in that community. Note that the claim is not that the liturgy automatically celebrates certain spiritual realities, but rather the claim is that, to the extent that various spiritual realities are present and operative in a group, to that extent the awareness of them can be heightened and the appreciation of them can be deepened.

Some other things can be noted. First, in a large group such as an American parish of a thousand to five thousand households, no one knows everyone else, and people tend to cluster into subgroups such as people of similar ages, people with children, people in the same parish organization, people who attend the same mass every week, and so on. So the meaning found in the mass by different subgroups and different people within them will be unavoidably different with regard to particulars. Second, despite the best efforts of liturgy planners and parish ministers to emphasize gospel values and religious ideals, some people are going to have a negative experience of worship. Teenagers whose parents force them to attend may feel resentful the whole time, and a person who sees in church someone who has wronged them may have a hard time letting go of the animosity they feel. These are simply facts. We cannot make everyone find the same meaning in the liturgy.

Nor can we specify the meanings that people actually find in public worship, for that is an empirical question that could only be answered by extensively surveying worshipers. But we can set forth general principles regarding the types of meanings that eucharistic worship ought to evoke and resonate in the minds of the participants. First and foremost would be the meaning of ἀγάπη or caring for others, for the liturgy is primarily a celebration of the love of God—not the affection of a transcendent being for us, but our love for others modeled on the love of God and the love of Christ as revealed in the scriptures. Whenever we take care of others, whenever we put their needs ahead of our wants, whenever we act selflessly rather than selfishly, our behavior is modeled on the biblical example of God's love. As the schoolmen would have explained it, when we act with charity (*caritas* being the Latin translation of ἀγάπη), we participate in the love of God. Therefore, whether parishioners are greeters or lectors or communion distributors, whether they decorate the church or sing in the choir, whether they prepare coffee and donuts or organize pot luck suppers, whether they are Girl Scout or Boy Scout leaders, whether they help in the RCIA or marriage preparation program, whether they coach or help sports teams in other ways, whether they are catechists or religious educators, whether they are in the parents' association or are teachers' assistants in the parochial school, whether they channel financial assistance to the poor or bring social services to the needy, all those who are engaged in volunteer (or sometimes minimally paid) charitable activities under the auspices of the church are, from a theological perspective, participating in God's love, or to say it more scripturally, they are bringing Christ's love to others. Put more simply, when people act in a caring manner toward others, they embody God's love for others. For all these people then, and also for the recipients of their Christ-like behavior, the Sunday mass can be a celebration of God's love, for it is an opportunity to experience more intensely with others the spiritual reality of caring, which they have been doing and feeling during the week.

Beyond ἀγάπη is the paschal mystery. Here too, however, this mystery is often projected on to Jesus' death and resurrection. If those biblical events are thought of as having happened long ago and far away, they are nothing more than stories, images and beliefs in the mind. One reason why evangelical preachers get a reputation for being good is that they can arouse emotions in their audience. For example, they can help people sense the suffering of Jesus, the pain of his crucifixion, and the desolation of his apparent abandonment by the Father. Then they arouse feelings of dependency and gratefulness by emphasizing that Jesus did it for them, and that they could not be saved without his love and sacrifice on their behalf. Finally they arouse feelings of relief and jubilation by recounting Jesus' resurrection and assuring the audience that they too will rise to lasting glory on the last day. Preachers do this because they know instinctively that words and symbols are not truly meaningful unless they connect with something that is real in the minds of their listeners, which in this case are thoughts and feelings that the audience has had beforehand, and which therefore can be evoked by helping them connect scripture stories and religious doctrines with those feelings.

But all that is quite beside the point. It is talking about the finger rather than about the moon, it is talking about the story rather than about what the story represents, it is talking about the symbol rather than about what is real. Just as the love of God is not primarily something that is going on in God quite apart from us, so also the paschal mystery is not primarily something that Jesus underwent two thousand years ago in a faraway land. A mystery is not something that is thought and not fully understood, but something that is experienced and not fully understood. So if the liturgy is a celebration of the paschal mystery, it has to celebrate the paschal mystery that has been experienced by the participants in the celebration.

But when in the lives of ordinary people has this happened? Most of us never get a chance to act heroically, to suffer and die on behalf of others. Nor do we need to. For self-giving love does not have to be heroic and dramatic; it just has to be caring for others. Caring and self-giving can be overdone to the point of exhaustion, and then it results in burnout or giving up. Ordinarily, however, caring is curiously rewarding. Even the care we devote to our job or profession, to fixing up our house or decorating our apartment, to preparing meals for family and company, or to hobbies such as gardening or quilting is often rewarding. This emotional reward is even stronger when we help people. Whether we answer someone's question, help a child learn to read, paint a room for a friend, volunteer for disaster relief, bring meals to a shut-in, or lend a listening ear to someone who is grieving, we ourselves feel somehow energized and spiritually enlarged after doing it. Jesus recognized the phenomenon, and he talked about it in terms of losing life and finding it.[33]

33. This metaphor is found in all four gospels. See Mk 8:35; Mt 10:39, 16:25; Lk 9:24, 17:33; Jn

One way to think about life (ζωή in Greek) is as a way of life, a lifestyle. One of the earliest non-scriptural Christian works is the *Didache*, which tells those who would become followers of Jesus that they must choose between the way of life and the way of death.[34] The document greatly simplifies the choices that people have in front of them by distinguishing sharply between living in a way that makes things better and living in a way that makes things worse, between a constructive way of living and a destructive one, between a healthy and an unhealthy lifestyle. It would seem to make sense, therefore, that Jesus in the gospels talks to his followers about finding life, he is talking about life in a spiritually positive sense, that is, he is talking about a good life, a healthy life, a happy life. Moreover, his advice regarding the way to arrive at this positive outcome is to give up life, but here the life he is talking about is clearly something negative. In general terms, it might be called a destructive or unhealthy lifestyle, and if this is the case, then Jesus is teaching the same thing as the *Didache*, although historically the *Didache* was an expansion of the earlier teaching of Jesus.

But what is an unhealthy and destructive lifestyle, one that makes things worse rather than better? Contemporary psychologists would probably agree that in one way or another it is one that is self-centered and self-seeking. Pushed to extremes, it is narcissism, but more commonly it involves self-gratification through food or drink or sex drugs or self-satisfaction through the acquisition of wealth and power. Wanting to have one's needs met is a natural orientation from infancy to adolescence, but if one remains psychologically a child even in adulthood, the use of what gives pleasure or satisfaction easily becomes an abuse of those things, even an addiction. Moreover, other people get seen primarily as means to one's selfish ends, so they too get used and abused. Within such an outlook, there are no boundaries: everything is mine or ought to be mine, so I have a right to take what I want and to use any means to get it. Society can tolerate a certain amount of this behavior, but not much, for if too many people lead extremely self-centered and self-seeking lives, the social fabric begins to unravel in animosity and conflict. And individuals who lead such lives in an otherwise healthy society tend to hurt themselves and others to a greater or lesser extent.

For this reason, Jesus in the gospels is seen urging his listeners to stop being self-centered and self-seeking (what the *Didache* calls the way of death)—in other words, to lose that life—if they want to reach more than temporary pleasure and satisfaction (what the *Didache* calls the way of life). Put in psychological terms, Jesus is preaching altruism over narcissism, compassion over indifference, and caring over apathy as the best way to live. And it is quite reasonable to imagine that if a group or community subscribed to this ideal (and if they were able to live accordingly), it would be a psychologically and socially healthy environment. Put in spiritual terms, Jesus is urging his listeners to turn away from the pursuit of physical pleasure and material

---

12:25. The Greek text speaks of losing and finding one's ψυχή or life force. The word is usually translated as soul in older translations and as life in more recent translations.

34. See above, pages 74–78.

satisfaction and instead choose the spiritual realities of acceptance, caring, trust, fidelity, truth, forgiveness, and so on.

More than the synoptic gospels, the Gospel According to John plays on the theme of life. In chapter 3, Jesus talks with Nicodemus about being born again, and in chapter 6 he delivers what is called the bread of life discourse. Both of these were given metaphysical interpretations by Christian thinkers in the Greco-Roman world, but in the Semitic world of the evangelist, they more likely referred to things that people could experience. Evangelical Christians probably come close to what the Johannine Jesus is referring to when he talks about being born again, and being born of water and the spirit: it is an experience of inner transformation, a spiritual renewal associated with baptism into a community committed to the way of life revealed by the one sent by God. Likewise, eating that one's flesh and drinking his blood is more probably about chewing on the words of Jesus and drinking in his teaching than it is about the Eucharist, since Jews had a prohibition against drinking blood. Being nourished by the word of God, which John identifies with Jesus himself, is the way to new life.

One phrase that appears in the synoptic gospels, but most frequently in John's gospel, is ζωή αιώνια, usually translated as eternal life and interpreted metaphysically as everlasting existence after death.[35] But if ζωή means life in the sense of lifestyle or way of living, it can be stretched metaphorically to mean liveliness, just as *vita* in Latin can refer to life and also to vitality. Since Jews at the time of Jesus (except for the Pharisees) did not believe in life after death, it seems unlikely that Jesus would have been promising his disciples a post-mortem existence for being good. Now it is true that Paul was a Pharisee and he preached that those who died with Christ would rise with him (presumably to live forever) at his second coming, so it is quite conceivable that ζωή αιώνια came very soon to mean living forever. Originally, however, it may have meant something more like unbounded liveliness or limitless vitality. In fact, many of the texts that speak about ζωή αιώνια in John's gospel easily lend themselves to this interpretation, as do the discussion with Nicodemus and the bread of life discourse. John 3:36 says that those who believe in the son have ζωήν αιώνιον, not that they will have it in the future. John 4:14 promises that the living water that Christ gives becomes a fountain of ζωήν αιώνιον in the present. Jesus in John 5:24 says that those who heed his words cross over from death to life and have ζωήν αιώνιον. At John 6:54, the bread of life discourse says that those who eat and drink of the son have ζωήν αιώνιον now, and they will be raised up on the last day. Peter in John 6:68 says that Jesus has the words of ζωήν αιώνιον, which is more credibly taken to mean that the teaching of Jesus opens up the possibility of unbounded vitality, instead of taking it to mean that is teaching makes it possible to live forever. Thus at the last supper, Jesus in John 17:2 thanks the Father for enabling him to give this limitless vitality to others. The texts in the synoptic gospels that speak of ζωήν αιώνιον can also be interpreted in

35. See Mk 10:17; Mt 19:16, 19:29, 25:46; Lk 10:25, 18:18; Jn 3:36, 4:14, 4:36, 5:24, 5:39, 6:40, 6:54, 6:68, 10:28, 17:2.

this way, but the referent is often less clear; that is, many of them could also be taken as referring to endless life.

What then is the source of this unbounded vitality? Theologically, the source is God, from whom all good things come. In John's gospel, it comes from believing the one sent by God. This is not a gnostic believing in Christ, which is to say, accepting the idea that Jesus is the messiah, the son of God, or whatever. That can be done without changing in the least the way one lives. In fact, Christians believers of diverse life styles do that all the time. Rather, it is a matter of actually believing Jesus, accepting his teaching, and putting it into practice. As Matthew 7:21 puts it, "Not everyone who calls me Lord will enter the kingdom of heaven, but only those who do the will of my Father in heaven." Entering God's kingdom is a metaphor for doing God's will, and God's will as revealed through Jesus is that people should take care of one another.

Living a life of αγάπη leads to experiencing the paschal mystery, being inwardly renewed, discovering the possibility of boundless vitality. According to psychology, one of the rewards of altruism is an increase in endorphins, but the writers of the gospels knew nothing of endorphins. Yet they did know that caring for others made people feel good; it gave them an emotional reward and gave them the spiritual energy to maintain that lifestyle. Instead of being caught in the vicious cycle of selfishness, those who lived the way Jesus taught were caught up in a virtuous cycle of mutual caring, and their benevolence toward one another gave them a spiritual energy that felt like it would never stop. To them it was ζωήν αιώνιον.

Just as a picnic during courtship celebrates a romantic relationship, just as a family cookout celebrates a complex web of close relationships, and just as a formal banquet celebrates business or political or sports relationships, so also the eucharistic liturgy, like any intensification ritual, helps people to feel more deeply the relationships that they already experience with one another. If the relationships embody the spiritual realities of acceptance, trust, honesty, self-giving, and so on, the liturgy itself is an affirmation of and a reinforcement of those realities. And if the relationships are rewarding and energizing, the liturgy can amplify such feelings and motivate people to continue living to improve the lives of others.

6. Sacraments and Sacramentality

For centuries, the Catholic Church insisted that there are seven sacraments, but the sacraments to which this doctrine referred were not religious rituals but metaphysical entities, what the schoolmen called the *sacramentum et res* that is brought into being whenever a sacramental rite is properly performed. In the 1960s, however, the Second Vatican Council stretched the meaning of the term and spoke about Christ as the sacrament of God and the church as the sacrament of Christ. By doing so, the council's bishops introduced the possibility of thinking about sacraments in a phenomenological rather than in a metaphysical frame of reference.

Undoubtedly the bishops were thinking metaphysically of Christ and the church as substantive sacraments, analogous to the way Catholics for centuries had thought of the Eucharist as Christ substantially present under the appearance of bread and wine. But the new usage suggested, just as its proponents had, that there is a phenomenological dimension to sacramentality.[36] Understood as representative phenomena, symbols enable those who look at them to perceive what the symbols represent, which is why Christians, for example, can look at an image of Jesus and perceive divinity. Whereas a metaphysical analysis does not allow for the possibility of deception, however, a phenomenological analysis does. Thus in Aristotelian metaphysics, one perceives the substance of a tree because it is out there in the world to be seen, and in scholastic theology, one perceives the presence of Christ because he is there in the consecrated elements to be found by those who have the eyes of faith. A philosophical analysis of phenomena, however, reveals the possibility that appearances can be deceiving, that what one sees may not be out there at all.

Consider stage props and movie sets. They are constructed to give the appearance (one might say the illusion) of reality while not really being what they seem to be. A small town in a movie western set in the 1870s may look as though it has a hotel and a saloon and a general store, but in fact they are facades that give the appearance of being buildings. Looked at from a phenomenological perspective, what the eye sees is only the surface of things, in other words, outward appearances, sense data, or visual phenomena. Using this information, the mind constructs, as it were, the entire object, and perceives the whole thing even though what is seen is only its surface, and indeed only the surface that is facing the viewer. Looking at a baseball, for example, we see only half of its surface, but we assume that it has a side that we do not see, as well as a solid interior that we never see.

A phenomenological analysis is helpful for understanding why Christians can look at an image of Jesus and see God, while non-Christians do not. It is not as though non-Christians reject the truth of Christ's divinity; rather, they literally do not see it. The same can be said of gospel stories and Christological doctrines, for these are linguistic symbols analogous to visual symbols such as pictures and statues. Simply stating that something is the case does not guarantee that others will perceive the truth of what you say.

But a phenomenological analysis also raises the possibility of symbolic deception. Just as one can speak words that do not represent the truth, and just as one can draw pictures of things that do not exist, one can perform rituals that do not correspond to reality. This possibility raises the issue of symbolic honesty and, in the present context, of sacramental honesty.

In the past, it was assumed that when sacramental rites were properly performed, they always produced their effects. The traditional understanding was that sacraments are effective *ex opere operato*, that is, through their valid performance. And as long

36. See Edward Schillebeeckx, *Christ the Sacrament* and Karl Rahner, *Church and the Sacraments*.

as Catholic culture remained relatively stable, as it did from the mid-twelfth century to the mid-twentieth century, the effectiveness of the sacraments was manifest. The baptized were Christians for life, the married were married for life, and the ordained were ordained for life. Confession was needed for the forgiveness of sins, and sins that were absolved were felt to be truly erased from the soul. Consecration of the Eucharist made Christ truly present, and his presence could be perceived in the Blessed Sacrament. Catholic canon law still operates within this conceptual system, and so it regards the baptized as still Christians even if they become Jews or Muslims or atheists. Likewise, canon law regards people as married even after they have divorced if they have not gotten an annulment. And it regards the ordained as priests forever even if they are laicized. Catholic doctrine regards the integral confession of mortal sins as necessary for their forgiveness, which is why Pope John Paul II put a stop to the practice of offering general absolution without personal confession. It also regards receiving the Eucharist as a sign of unity with the pope, which is why the hierarchy have insisted that non-Catholics and public dissenters should not receive communion at mass.

This last example is an indication that the church's leaders recognize that there is such a thing as sacramental honesty, but they define honesty in terms of ecclesiastical or institutional meaning, not in terms of what going to communion might mean to the ones seeking to receive the sacrament. The same is true of rules governing the sacrament of penance, which required that mortal sins be enumerated before they could be forgiven, and did not consider what receiving general absolution might mean for people who had very limited access to priests. From an institutional point of view, therefore, sacramental honesty is a matter of following the church's rules about the sacraments.

Phenomenologically, however, sacramental honesty calls for a correspondence between a ritual and what is actually going on in the minds, hearts and lives of the participants. The baptism of a child whose parents do not practice their faith may be canonically valid, but it is a ritual falsehood since the child is not really becoming part of any Catholic community. The confirmation of a teenager who regards the sacrament as the way to get out of religious education classes is likewise a ritual lie because the rite says one thing and the youngster's intention is something quite different. People who marry do not intend to divorce, but today they know that many marriages do not last, so to insist that marriage is indissoluble when in fact it is not seems out of contact with reality. Likewise, the claim that ordination is forever at a time when many have left the priesthood seems less than honest. Restricting the ministry of healing to priests is questionable when people have found forgiveness and comfort through the ministry of chaplains, counselors and caregivers who are not ordained. Insisting that the Eucharist is the body and blood of Christ when the revised liturgy does not support that perception makes the traditional doctrine open to question. Even calling the church a sacrament of Christ seems a bit unreal when the institution presents a public face of condemning birth control and concealing child abuse.

For the seven Catholic sacraments to be recognized as sacramental in contemporary society, they need to exhibit ritual honesty. Baptism has to be for people (including infants) who are actually joining a church community, and the community for its part needs to make the lives of those who join it different from the lives of people who do not. Confirmation has to be for people (whether adolescents or adults) who have accepted the spirit of Christ as their own, and the church needs to both insist on and provide opportunities for them to demonstrate that by engaging in service to others. Reconciliation needs to be reconfigured so that it promotes genuine reconciliation between people in addition to giving assurance of forgiveness by God. Anointing of the sick in its current form is ritually honest, but it is historically dishonest to claim that only priests have the power do it. The church cannot insist that marriage is indissoluble when in fact marriages regularly, if regrettably, dissolve in our society; and if society allows people of the same sex to marry, it is somewhat dishonest not to recognize such relationships as marriages. Likewise, it cannot honestly insist that only celibate males can be priests when there is both historical evidence to the contrary and theological justification for ordaining women and married men. Lastly, the eucharistic liturgy is honestly sacramentally when it celebrates the community's experience of the paschal mystery in its caring for others and the spiritual energy generated by such service.

In order for sacraments to be credible today, they have to be in touch with reality, that is, with people's lives and with what is going on in local church communities. When people's lives do not reflect what the sacraments are supposed to celebrate, the sacraments cannot mean what they are supposed to mean, since the actual meaning of any ritual is found in the minds and lives of those who participate in it. Likewise, when local communities such as parishes do not embody and support what the sacraments are supposed to celebrate, the sacraments do not celebrate anything, for the mysteries to which they point are primarily the spiritual realities of acceptance and belonging, community and fellowship, forgiveness and reconciliation, healing and strengthening, self-giving and regeneration.

On the other hand, if the spiritual realities that the sacraments celebrate are found in Catholic communities, if those communities are demonstratively welcoming of strangers and supportive of members, if they are reaching out to the poor and the sick, if they are meeting the material and emotional needs of individuals and families, if they facilitate reconciliation and healing on many levels, if they oppose systemic injustice and promote social justice, if they engage all their members in service to others, and if they allow for the appropriate cultural expression of beliefs and values, then regardless of what those rituals look like, they will be honest and authentic sacraments.

A Summary of the Argument

SOME READERS OF THIS book when it was still in manuscript form complained that parts of it were so dense and technical that they could not follow the argument. For the sake of other readers who may find the book hard to follow, I offer this condensed version so that it can be comprehended in a single sitting.

Essentially, the argument is that Catholic sacramental theology evolved through a series of cultural settings (Judeo-Palestinian, Greco-Roman, and medieval European) in which the uncritical use of texts from earlier eras was customary. Reviewing that theological evolution today, however, it becomes apparent that earlier texts were often misinterpreted by later writers. From a historical-critical perspective, therefore, the medieval Catholic theology of sacraments, although plausible in its day, is no longer acceptable.

At the beginning of the modern era, the Council of Trent gave magisterial approval to what it believed to be Catholic doctrine from time immemorial, and in doing so it couched the official teachings of the church in the conceptual framework of Aristotelian scholasticism. If it can be shown, therefore, that scholastic sacramental theology is based on faulty premises, the same is implicitly true of Catholic sacramental doctrine.

Even today, Catholic canon law assumes that the metaphysical assertions of sacramental doctrine correspond to reality: that baptized Christians are ontologically different from unbaptized pagans, that married Catholics are spiritually bonded to one another even if they are legally divorced, that priests receive supernatural powers when they are ordained, and so on. Demonstrating that the church's sacramental doctrine rests on highly questionable premises has the potential to free Roman Catholicism from its medieval mindset and to enable Catholics in the future to develop sacramental rituals that are both culturally appropriate and ritually honest.

Introduction and Chapter 1

The habit of speaking about sacraments as administered and received is unique to Roman Catholicism. Most Catholics (including theologians and canonists) assume that when they say that sacraments are administered and received, something actually happens that corresponds to this language. In reality, however, this is only a manner of speaking that has been taken as being factual even though it is not. Historically, speaking of the sun rising and setting led to a theory of planetary motion which assumed that the sun revolved around a stationary earth. Similarly, talking about giving and receiving sacraments led to a theory of church rituals which assumed that something called a sacrament was given and received whenever certain church ceremonies were properly performed.

Chapter 1 demonstrates that the language of giving and receiving sacraments is intrinsic to scholastic sacramental theology and to Catholic sacramental doctrine. It also deconstructs the scholastic concept of grace as a supernatural additive to the human soul that makes Christians able to do what the unbaptized cannot do. Although a credible concept in the closed society of medieval Christendom, this conception of grace has neither plausibility nor verifiability in a pluralistic and globalized culture.

The *sacramentum et res* is a prime example of a supernatural effect that was regarded as an ability, a virtue or a power, depending on which sacrament was being analyzed within the Aristotelian conceptual framework. Aquinas and other schoolmen determined which categories could be applied to each sacrament by reflecting on the medieval church rituals in the light of scripture and patristic quotations (interpreted uncritically) and their effect on people in their Christian culture. Thus, for example, they could say that baptism bestows virtues that gives Christians the potential for sanctity (a potential denied to Jews, Muslims and pagans), and that ordination bestows powers that make priests able to change bread and wine into the body and blood of Christ (a power denied to lay people). Their beliefs were informally verified by what they observed in the society around them.

The chapter concludes by showing that Catholic sacramental doctrine has been expressed in scholastic terminology in church documents issued after the Second Vatican Council, and so scholastic theology cannot be dismissed as something that disappeared with the liturgical revisions that followed the council.

Chapter 2

Catholics generally have a naïve understanding about the origins of their sacraments. Whether they are misinformed and believe that the sacraments can be traced back to the early church or to Jesus himself, or whether they are aware that their church's rituals evolved over the centuries, they have a sense that there is something basically correct about having seven sacraments. Books like *Doors to the Sacred* support this misconception by showing how each stage of liturgical and theological development made sense at the time when those developments took place. Read carefully, however, that book reveals the interdependence of liturgical practice and sacramental theology in a historically conditioned dialectic.

When Catholics disagree with the magisterium about the sacraments, it is often because the rules regarding them do not seem appropriate for contemporary culture. They are not aware that the church's inability to change is rooted in the hierarchy's belief that many aspects of sacramental life are divinely ordained. The church's leadership clings to the notion that dogmas correspond to reality and therefore cannot be changed.

Chapter 2 sketches the main lines of the development of sacramental practice and theology in a way that justifies the changes in belief and understanding that took place at each stage of cultural development. Early bishops explained their ritual practices by assuming that the church was guided by the Holy Spirit and by using scripture passages as proof texts to buttress their arguments. Medieval schoolmen explained drastically different ritual practices by appealing to the same texts and by citing church fathers as authorities, who actually wrote about rituals that were much different from those in the Middle Ages. For the most part, the schoolmen did not have access to the large corpus of patristic literature written in Greek, so they relied heavily on a few Latin fathers, especially Augustine. The Council of Trent validated the medieval developments by appealing to scriptural, patristic and scholastic texts in the same uncritical manner, which was intellectually defensible at the time.

The chapter also shows how Catholic sacramental doctrine became inextricably connected to Aristotelian concepts that were used by the schoolmen to explain the practices of the medieval and Tridentine church. These explanations made complete sense within the ecclesiastical culture that perdured until the mid-twentieth century. Before then, no one considered the possibility that church rituals were culturally conditioned or that the scholastic analysis was historically relative.

Chapter 3

Historical consciousness and critical analysis are prerequisites for doing theology in a credible fashion today. Biblical texts have long been subjected to scholarly criticism, but not patristic writings, scholastic theories or Catholic doctrines, which are usually taken at face value. Moreover, contemporary scholarship often fails to ask questions that would undermine religious assumptions. Louis-Marie Chauvet, for example, does not analyze scholastic theology but dismisses out of hand the caricature of it that he found in the French equivalent of the Baltimore Catechism, and he does not question the truth of the doctrines that he attempts to recast in postmodern categories.

One fundamental question regards the origin of ideas for which there are no textual precedents. On what did Paul the Apostle, for example, base the theological claims he makes in some of his epistles if those ideas cannot be found in earlier writings? Or how did Augustine of Hippo conclude that baptism has to bestow on the baptized something that cannot be lost? Or how did Thomas Aquinas know how to apply Aristotelian categories accurately to his explanations of the sacraments?

Bernard Lonergan, both in his analysis of Aquinas' presentation of classical psychology and in his own cognitional theory, argues that original ideas arise from insights into sense data given in experience. Reconstructing the process through which original thinkers such as Paul, Augustine and Aquinas came up with new ideas can never be conclusive, but it can reach a high degree of probability. For example, given that Augustine was looking for a way to justify the Roman practice of not repeating baptism, and given that he inherited the practice of speaking about receiving the sacrament of baptism from his North African predecessors (which originally meant receiving the water), it is quite plausible that he interpreted the word *sacramentum* (which could refer either to a symbol or to a mystery) as a mysterious spiritual reality that was received through the rite of baptism and could not be lost, analogous to a tattoo or a brand mark.

Chapter 3 traces the development of sacramental theology in the Latin west from the earliest biblical texts to the texts that were gathered by Peter Lombard in his *Book of Sentences*, which, in addition to the Bible, was a prime source of theological information in the thirteenth century. Every single text in which the words for sacrament, baptism, eucharist, marriage, ordination, penance and anointing appear in all their cognate Latin forms, as well as the verbs for giving and receiving that are associated with those nouns, were examined through the use of electronic databases that are now available on CD-ROMs. Arranging those texts in chronological order shows a clear evolution of theological language from the metaphorical use of words in the earliest texts to a metaphysical interpretation of those words in later texts. For example, the seal of the spirit about which Paul wrote was arguably the outward manifestation of a spiritual conversion, but centuries later, when becoming a Christian did not entail a dramatic change in lifestyle, it was interpreted as a metaphysical reality that was imprinted on the soul by the rite of baptism.

Some of the more significant findings of this and earlier research can be summarized her, section by section.

First, here is what can be learned from the New Testament:

- The noun *baptisma* does not appear in New Testament writings, except in reference to the ministry of John the Baptist, until late in the first century. In contrast, the verb *baptizein* is used quite often. This suggests that the early followers of Jesus thought of what they were doing as symbolic immersing, not as performing a ritual that had a proper name. Paul's understanding of the meaning of this symbolic immersion came out of his own experience and that of others. The pledge or down-payment of the spirit is plausibly a reference to the experience of charismatic gifts, with the expectation that there is more to come. The images of a body, of immersion or plunging, and of dying and rising can all be interpreted as referring to changes in group membership, in attitudes and in behaviors that were experienced by Paul and other early members of the Jesus movement. Likewise, the charisms or gifts of the spirit listed in 1 Corinthians and Romans all have experiential counterparts in charismatic or pentecostal communities.

- The Lord's supper described in 1 Corinthians is best understood as a communal meal to which many people brought food. There is no indication that the so-called words of institution were spoken during the meal; rather, those words of Jesus are given as the rationale for the meal. The body of the Lord to which the text refers is more likely the local community than what was later called consecrated bread.

- Jesus' words over the bread and wine, as recounted in the synoptic gospels, cannot be used as proof texts for later Christian eucharistic beliefs because the copula "is" would not have been used in Aramaic. Likewise, the bread of life discourse in the fourth gospel can be interpreted symbolically, as Protestants have done since the Reformation. In other words, there is no reason to take these passages literally except in the interest of supporting later Catholic doctrines.

- In the majority of cases where the words *pneuma hagion* appear in the New Testament, the definite article is lacking, suggesting that what the writers had in mind was a holy spirit and not the Holy Spirit. Just as an evil spirit was thought to cause bad behavior, a holy spirit was thought to cause good behavior. Whenever the definite article is used, *to pneuma hagion* can usually be understood as referring to the holy spirit mentioned earlier in the text. That holy spirit would have been identified experientially.

- In the teaching of Jesus, forgiving the sins of others is something that is to be done by all of his followers, not just by designated ministers.

- The reference to anointing by elders in the Epistle of James cannot be used to justify an ecclesiastical ritual that only priests are allowed to perform.

- There is no reference in the New Testament to a laying on of hands that can arguably be interpreted as an ordination ritual.

- The supervisors, elders and servers mentioned in the New Testament were not the same as bishops, presbyters and deacons that later emerged in the church's organizational structure.

- The relationship of mutual caring and self-giving between husband and wife is symbolic of the Christ-church relationship. However, the mystery referred to in Ephesians 5 is found in the relationship between Christ and the church.

- In summary, there are no New Testament texts that can be used to support scholastic sacramental theology.

Second, here is what can be learned from ante-Nicene writings:

- As in the New Testament, there are no references to Christian *mysteria* or *sacramenta* in general.

- The *Didache* describes basic baptismal practices, but it offers no theology of baptism except that the immersion is to be done in the name of the Father, Son and Holy Spirit.

- The *Didache* describes communal meals during which prayers of thanksgiving (*eucharistia*) are said, some of which may have been symbolic partakings of bread and wine rather than full meals. There is no reference to the body and blood of Christ but only to spiritual food and drink. The action is called a sacrifice (*thusia*) but the reason for this is not explained.

- Ignatius of Antioch speaks of supervisors (*episkopoi*) as decision makers rather than as presiding elders.

- Ignatius is the first writer to refer to food served in the meal as the flesh (*sarka*) of Christ but he does not explain what is meant by that.

- Justin Martyr describes the process of "being made new through Christ," which entails a washing that is not called baptism. The process can be understood as moral regeneration, abandoning the sins of the past and learning the right way to live. The washing symbolizes this but does not cause it to happen.

- Justin says that the food of the thanksgiving meal is made into the flesh and blood of Jesus for spiritual nourishment, but no explanation of this is given, nor is there any reference to the words of institution.

- Justin characterizes the Christian meal as a sacrifice (*thusia*), most likely meaning a meal shared in the presence of a god, which his pagan audience would have understood. He invokes Malachi 1:10–11 to explain why this meal can be shared in many places and not just at a single shrine.

- Tertullian is the first early writer to speak of baptism as having automatic spiritual effects. He is also the first to speak of giving and receiving baptism, which most likely refers to the water that is poured during the ritual.

- There is evidence that by the mid-third century, the meal could also be shared in the morning, and that water was substituted for wine in some places.

- *The Apostolic Tradition* describes a well-developed rite of Christian initiation, but it offers no theology of the rite itself.

- During the controversy about whether to rebaptize those who renounced their faith during persecution, Ephesians 4:5–5 was interpreted as meaning that people can be baptized only once, which is not the original meaning of that text.

- Addressing the issue of apostates in North Africa, Cyprian of Antioch speaks about giving and receiving grace, as well as giving and receiving the Holy Spirit, through baptism. His language strongly suggests that these effects of baptism are automatic if the baptizing minister is a member of the one true church; baptism has no immediate connection with moral conversion or living a Christian life.

- Cyprian also shows evidence of ritualistic thinking with regard to the symbolic meal when he argues that water cannot become the blood of Christ because Jesus at the last supper told his followers to use wine.

- The Latin word *sacrificium* could refer either to the ritual meal or to the food that was offered to a deity, and Cyprian speaks of the symbolic food as a sacrifice in the sense of its being an offering to God.

- During this era, a process of public repentance allowed repentant apostates and other sinners to return to full membership in the church under the supervision of the local bishop. It was universally understood that the penitent was forgiven by God, not by the bishop.

- Anointing of the sick was a lay, not a clerical, practice.

- Through the third century, there is no direct evidence of ordination in the sense of being inducted into a clerical order. At most, there is evidence that approval and blessing were symbolized by a laying on of hands.

- Through the third century, marriage was a family affair, arranged by parents for their children or contracted by adult couples for themselves. There was no Christian wedding ceremony.

- In summary, by the end of the third century, we see the beginning of ritualistic thinking with regard to Christian rituals. This is to say that the rituals begin to get thought of as automatically effective as long as they are performed properly. Moreover, in this era, rituals that were later designated as sacraments either did not exist or they were lay practices.

Third, here is what can be learned from post-Nicene writings:

- In the fourth century and later, the sacramental theologizing of the Latin-speaking church followed the lead of the north Africans, Tertullian, Cyprian and Augustine, in speaking about sacraments as given and received. The Greek-speaking theologians developed understandings of church rituals that did not adopt this terminology.

- The Greek word *mysterion* could refer to either a religious ritual, or to the mystery that it signified, or both. The Latin word *sacramentum* initially had this ambiguity, but in the fourth century, the Latin transliteration *mysterium* began to be used for *mysterion* when it meant a spiritual reality or mystery.

- In the writings of both Ambrose and Augustine, however, ambiguities remain, and the intended referent of the word *sacramentum* has to be determined in each instance from the context in which it is used.

- The catechetical writings and mystagogical sermons of Ambrose give no indication that he is basing his remarks on experience. Rather, he uses philosophical ideas and proof texts from scripture to explain what happens when people are baptized or when the words of consecration are spoken.

- Augustine inherited this conceptual approach to theology, searching the scriptures for ideas to address the Donatist and Pelagian controversies. Believing that the Roman practice of not rebaptizing is correct, and not questioning the north African manner of speaking about sacraments being given and received, he borrows an idea from Ambrose and concludes that baptism bestows an indelible mark on the soul. Scripture quotes which he takes to be about the seal of the Spirit confirm this conclusion.

- Likewise, Augustine justifies the practice of infant baptism by appealing to psalm texts that speak of human sinfulness and to Pauline texts comparing the salvation of Christ with the sin of Adam.

- Similarly, Augustine argues for the indissolubility of marriage by appealing to the gospels' condemnation of divorce and to Ephesians' declaration, *Hoc enim est magnum sacramentum*, in its treatment of marriage.

- It must be admitted that, due to the ambiguity of the word *sacramentum*, we cannot be certain whether Augustine was thinking of the baptismal seal, the priestly character and the marital bond as a sign, a mystery, or both, when he called the spiritual reality received in those rituals a *sacramentum*.

- Nevertheless, both Ambrose and Augustine clearly engage in ritualistic or mechanistic thinking when they attribute automatic invisible effects to the performance of church rituals.

- The same can be said about their understanding of the Eucharist: they took Christ's words of institution literally, and after those words were used to consecrate bread and wine during the liturgy, the body and blood of Christ were believed to be and were perceived to be present on the altar.

- As Christian basilicas replaced pagan temples, it was natural for laity and clergy to think of the eucharistic liturgy in sacrificial terms. And as church leaders looked in the Old Testament for examples of sacrifice, Christian worship was increasingly interpreted as an offering to God in atonement for sins.

- As the number of converts grew, it was impossible for bishops to preside over all of the annual baptisms, so bishops in the Latin church gave priests authority to preside over baptisms, but they reserved the final blessing to themselves.

- In discussing the process of public repentance, some writers in this period begin to speak as though bishops and priests have the power to forgive, although others continue to speak of forgiveness as coming from God when a sinner is truly repentant.

- The oil used for anointing the sick begins to get viewed as a *sacramentum*, but there is as yet no clerical rite of anointing.

- Ecclesiastical ministry becomes organized into sacred orders, primarily the episcopate, the presbyterate and the deaconate. Initiation into these orders is accomplished through a rite of ordination that inducts a person into a local office but does not bestow power that can be exercised in other places.

Fourth, here is what can be learned from what was written during the centuries following the collapse of the Roman Empire:

- The age for baptism goes down until it is practiced primarily for children. When Augustine's theory of original sin becomes widely accepted, the time for baptism moves from once a year to shortly after birth. The rite used for infant baptism is used even for adults when entire tribes are converted to Christianity.

- The cultural understanding of baptism becomes essentially magical, that is, the ritual is understood to wash away original sin and all other past sins as long as it is properly performed.

- The bishop's post-baptismal blessing becomes a separate rite of confirmation, but it is largely ignored by parents and bishops alike. Frankish reformers fabricate the so-called false decretals, in part to prove that early popes encouraged the use of the sacrament, saying that it provides strengthening by the Holy Spirit.

- The elaborate patristic liturgy is simplified and becomes the mass, which can be said by one priest without other liturgical ministers if necessary.

- The purpose of the mass is understood to be to confect the Eucharist, that is, to turn bread and wine into the body and blood of Christ, which are then offered to God for the redemption of the world. It is an unbloody sacrifice that spiritually participates in the mystery of Christ's sacrifice on the cross.

- Some theologically inclined monks offer various explanations of how the bread and wine became the body and blood of Christ.

- Private confession evolves out of the practice of spiritual direction by monks and becomes a widespread ritual. The understanding is that God forgives the sins of those who repent, but confessors also absolve penitents from having to do works of penance if they get sick and die before completing them.

- The same Frankish bishops who tried to encourage confirmation also create a clerical rite of anointing the sick. Over time, it becomes an anointing of the dying and is known as extreme unction.

- Apart from ordained monks, most priests are married (as they were in ancient times) and earn a living by farming or some other trade. Their main duties are to offer the sacrifice of the mass and to preside over baptisms and funerals. Some priests also hear confessions and administer extreme unction.

- The clergy slowly become involved in marriages, first serving as public witnesses, and later offering a blessing, but there is no church wedding ritual. Bishops become increasingly involved with adjudicating marriage cases.

Fifth, here is what can be learned from writings of the schoolmen in the High Middle Ages . . .

. . . about sacraments in general:

- By the middle of the twelfth century, many church rituals develop into forms that are culturally and pastorally appropriate for medieval Christendom. Babies are baptized shortly after birth. Children and adolescents are confirmed according to local custom. The sacrifice of the mass is offered daily by priests, sometimes with no one in attendance. Confession is usually to a priest, but sometimes to a monk or nun. Extreme unction is available but not easily accessible because the sick have to be brought to church. Candidates for the priesthood proceed through a sequence of holy orders, each of which is received in a ceremony called ordination. Weddings take place in a church and are presided over by a priest, but clandestine marriages are still considered valid.

- Perhaps around 1140, Hugh of St. Victor writes *The Sacraments of the Christian Faith*, using a broad Augustinian definition of sacrament as a sign of a sacred thing, and so it treats not only church rituals but also the incarnation, the church, religious feast days, liturgical symbols and vestments.

- Around the same time, the canonist John Gratian writes *The Agreement of Disagreeing Canons* in an attempt to reconcile or at least organize a wide variety of canon laws, many of which dealt with church ceremonies. He treats confirmation, penance, ordination and marriage, but he gives the name sacrament only to baptism, chrism, and the Eucharist.

- For both Hugh and Gratian, there are two aspects or dimensions to a sacrament: an outer or visible aspect such as a ritual, and an inner or invisible aspect that is a grace, which is sometimes called the *res* or *virtus* of the sacrament.

- Following the usage of Augustine and Cyprian, Gratian speaks of sacraments besides the Eucharist being given, administered, conferred and bestowed, and also received, accepted and taken. He says that baptism and marriage are had by those who receive them, and that they cannot be lost.

- Around 1150, Peter Lombard writes *Four Books of Opinions*, commonly called the *Sentences*, and in Book IV he treats the seven church rituals that he believes should be called sacraments. He defines sacrament more narrowly than did Hugh, perhaps because he is primarily interested in those rituals that are said to be causes of grace.

- Whereas in earlier ages grace had been a predicate (something was said to be a grace or gift from God), the schoolmen treat it as something substantive— something, a *res*, that can be classified into different types such as actual grace, habitual grace, sanctifying grace, and so on.

. . . about baptism:

- According to Hugh, the sacrament of baptism is the water that is poured. Gratian talks about giving and receiving baptism, but he does not explain what is given and received. He states that baptism effects the remission of sins, but he does not explain how this happens. He does say that baptism should not be repeated because it cannot be lost, but he does not clarify what it is that cannot be lost.

- According to Lombard, baptism is an inner washing that takes place when the outer washing is properly performed. When he says that the sacrament is received, he does not clarify what he is talking about, but he is not referring to the water. Nor does he mean the *res* or thing or grace that is received. So the status of the received sacrament is left unclarified in the *Sentences*.

. . . about the scholastic method:

- Lombard's *Sentences* is literally a text book or book of texts to be used by students who are studying theology systematically. He wants to pose all the important questions, and to include all the relevant information, but he is not concerned to provide all the answers.

- Like previous authors who wrote about Christian rituals, the medieval schoolmen write about what they see going on in the society around them, but they uncritically apply earlier texts written about different matters to the church ceremonies of their day.

- Besides observing visible ceremonies, the schoolmen also perceive invisible effects such as infants being saved from hell, sins being forgiven, people being married, and men becoming priests. Those who are devout also perceive Christ's presence in the Eucharist. Thus they know from experience, as it were, both the sacraments and their major effects.

. . . about confirmation:

- Both Gratian and Lombard accept the theology of confirmation that they find in the false decretals of the ninth century, and which will later become the basis for the theology of confirmation in Tridentine Catholicism.

. . . about the Eucharist:

- There is textual evidence that in developing their theology of the eucharist, some schoolmen are reflecting on spiritual experience as well as on traditional beliefs. If this is the case, the theory of transubstantiation agrees not only with the traditional belief that bread and wine become the body and blood of Christ, but also with what they perceive when they look at the consecrated elements.

- It is natural for the schoolmen to speak about the Eucharist being given and received, but they also talk about it as being confected and consecrated, dispensed and administered, eaten and drunk, and offered as a gift to God.

- The term *sacramentum et res* is at first introduced only with regard to the Eucharist. The schoolmen call it the body and blood, or the flesh of Christ, but from what they write about it, they sometimes seem to be talking about an experience of spiritual presence that they identify as the real presence of Christ.

. . . about the mass:

- To the schoolmen, the consecrated Eucharist is a sacrament. The mass is not a sacrament but a sacrifice.

- The schoolmen draw their understanding of sacrifice primarily from the Old Testament, developing a picture of the bloody death of an animal on the altar so that it can be burned and offered to God. Thus the mass is called an unbloody sacrifice that makes Christ's bloody sacrifice on Calvary present at the altar when the elements are consecrated and the Eucharist is offered to God the Father.

- Clearly, this is a much different concept of sacrifice than that found in early Christian writings. The word "sacrifice" is the same, but the meaning is now entirely different. Nonetheless, it corresponds with what the schoolmen perceive themselves doing when, as priests, they say mass daily.

. . . about penance:

- As priests, the schoolmen also believe they have the power to forgive sins. This power is understood to have been given by Christ to the apostles, passed down through generations of bishops, and bestowed on priests when they were ordained.

- Since *penitentia* can refer to interior repentance or to exterior works of penance, what the schoolmen write about it and the *sacramentum penitentiae* is sometimes ambiguous.

- Gratian has a very legalistic appreciation of penance, saying that it is for the remission of sins, done by a priest who has the power of the keys to the kingdom of heaven. He seems to be talking about an automatic removal of guilt rather than a conversion from sinful to virtuous behavior.

- Lombard, in contrast, has a rather spiritual appreciation of penance, saying that it is sorrow in one's soul for the sins one has committed, and a firm decision to change one's behavior. Thus he considers the possibility that the remission of sins can be achieved through confession to a lay person as well as to a priest.

- Both Gratian and Lombard develop their theology of penance by reflecting on experience: Gratian on the priestly rite, Lombard on the experience of repentance.

- In time, however, the scholastic theology of penance moves strongly in the direction of legalism, attributing the forgiveness of sins in the sacrament to priestly power.

. . . about extreme unction:

- As with penance, there seems to be no standard rite for anointing of the sick in the twelfth century since Gratian mentions no canons about it, and Hugh treats it only briefly and without describing it. Lombard lists it as *extrema unctio* because he knows it is administered at the end of life.

- Also as with penance, the scholastic theology of extreme unction is a reflection on the ritual practice of the day.

. . . about ordination:

- Until the twelfth century, the word "ordination" is applied to any religious ritual through which a person enters into a position of service to a community of monks, nuns or laypeople. Thus the ordained could be men or women, laity or clergy.

- Beginning in that century, however, ordination begins to be interpreted as a bestowal of power rather than as a conferral of responsibility, and the word is used only in reference to clerical offices. Henceforward the installation of abbots, abbesses, and others in positions of authority or service is no longer called an ordination.

- Hugh is one of the last to ask whether someone can be ordained without appointment to a specific community. The interpretation of ordination as giving power in an Aristotelian sense implies that once power was given, it is received as a spiritual reality residing in the soul of the recipient. The idea of a priestly power to confect the Eucharist and forgive sins fits this paradigm perfectly.

- The fact that ordinations are never repeated supports the idea that the ordained receive something that cannot be lost.

- Not only does Lombard list seven sacraments in the *Sentences*, but he also lists seven clerical orders whose distinct powers are received through seven separate ordinations. Although he calls the making of bishops and archbishops ordinations, he regards those rituals as bestowing offices rather than priestly powers, thus reflecting the practice of his day.

. . . about marriage:

- Hugh calls marriage a sacrament that was instituted by God in the Garden of Eden when he gave Adam and Eve the duty to increase and multiply. Ephesians calls the husband-wife relationship a sign of the relationship between Christ and the church, so marriage fits Augustine's broad definition of a sacrament as a sign of something sacred.

- Gratian agrees that God instituted marriage but not that it was a sacrament from the very beginning. His analysis reflects the canonical opinion of his day that consent is needed to contract a marriage, but he believes that a marriage is not ratified until it is consummated by sexual intercourse.

- Gratian speaks not so much of the sacrament of marriage as of a sacrament in marriage, which for all intents and purposes is the marriage bond. Following the lead of Augustine and others who took the gospel prohibitions of divorce literally, he argues that the bond cannot be dissolved by anything except the death of one of the spouses.

- Lombard agreed that marriage is a divinely ordained institution, but he sees the husband-wife relationship as the sacrament rather than the marriage contract or bond. He understands the *sacramentum* in Ephesians to be a sacrament rather than a mystery, and he applies it to the marital relationship rather than to the Christ-church relationship, thus doubly misinterpreting that passage.

- To establish that marriage is a sacrament, the schoolmen also appeal to the fact that Augustine had written that the three benefits of Christian marriage are fidelity, offspring and sacrament.

- It can be argued that in the scholastic theology of marriage, experience trumps logic. Logically, if the husband-wife relationship is indissoluble because it is a sacrament of the indissoluble Christ-church relationship, then such a relationship should remain in existence even after the death of one of the spouses since both partners still exist, one in the earthly life and one in the afterlife. But in medieval society widows and widowers were free to remarry, so the logical implications of indissolubility were never brought up.

Conclusions and Transition

What conclusions can be drawn from this analysis?

The primary conclusion is that scholastic sacramental theology was a reflection on and a reflection of Christian ritual practices in medieval Europe. What the schoolmen wanted to understand were the religious practices of their day: the rites themselves, certainly, but also the effects of those rites.

The rites they knew from their own experience. As Catholics, they had seen them, and as priests, they had performed most of them. The effects they also knew, in the same way that we in our secular society know that getting a driver's license makes one a legal driver, that graduating from high school makes one eligible to apply to college, that going through a civil wedding makes a couple married, and that being sworn in to an office makes one a public official. In the same way, the schoolmen knew that sacraments were given and received, and that some sacraments could be received only once. They knew that baptism was required in order to receive other sacraments, that receiving absolution from a confessor gave forgiveness for sins, that Christ was present in the Eucharist, that people could have only one spouse at a time, and that priests had supernatural powers.

What they did not know, and what they wanted to understand, was how the rituals that they saw and performed caused the effects that they perceived. By using the analytical concepts provided by Aristotelian science, they were able to explain quite plausibly how the sacraments produced their effects. For assistance in this analysis, they drew upon the wisdom of the past: God's revelation in the scriptures, and the writings of the church fathers. The result was a coherent and plausible explanation of Christian rituals in the Middle Ages.

From the perspective of the human sciences today, however, scholastic sacramental theology suffered from two shortcomings that were inherent in the schoolmen's methodology. The first is that they assumed that the biblical and patristic texts they used meant what they thought them to mean. That is, the schoolmen operated under the assumption that what they understood the ancient texts to mean was what those texts meant when they were written. In other words, they took their proof texts literally, and it is clear to critical scholarship today that they misunderstood and misinterpreted many of those texts. The second is that they assumed that the explanations they developed were universally true in the same way that basic philosophical explanations are true: if people do things, they must have the ability to do them; every effect has a cause; most things undergo changes and remain essentially the same, but some things change completely into something else; and so on. In other words, the schoolmen assumed that their sacramental theories were true for the whole Christian world and that they would remain true forever. They did not realize that their explanations were historically conditioned.

Nor did the bishops at the Second Vatican Council. They thought that what was true about the sacraments would remain true even if the sacraments were changed in some ways to make them more appealing to contemporary Catholics. For this reason they allowed the rites to be translated into a wide variety of languages that are spoken around the world, and they invited liturgical scholars to redesign the rites so that they would more closely correspond to earlier Christian traditions. Thus the position of the altar was changed so that the celebrant could face the assembly, people were invited to stand and not always kneel, and communion was given in the hand rather than on the tongue. Thus confession was made to look and feel more like spiritual direction than like telling secrets in the dark. Thus extreme unction was renamed anointing of the sick and Catholics were invited to seek the anointing whenever they were seriously ill. Other changes could be mentioned here, but these suffice to make the point.

Within a short while, Catholics' experience of their sacraments changed much more than anyone had anticipated. For example, hearing the words of consecration spoken aloud, receiving communion in the hand, and singing during the communion rite made it difficult if not impossible to experience the presence of Christ in the Eucharist as a felt reality. Conservative Catholics complained that the changes had taken the mystery out of the mass, but liberal Catholics who had received their spiritual formation prior to the council argued that fuller participation in the liturgy compensated for that loss. But the next generation of Catholics did not remember the Latin mass and the experience of mystery, so belief in the real presence of Christ in the Eucharist began to wane.

Meanwhile, Catholics' experience of themselves in the world was also changing. More of them were going to colleges and universities, becoming more educated and more accustomed to thinking for themselves. The church's positions on birth control, divorce and clerical celibacy began to seem out of touch with what was going on in the real world. Many men left the priesthood and many women left the convent, not only to marry but also to enter professions that were less ruled by authoritarian structures. In the name of embracing modernity, theologians themselves contributed to the cultural shift that was taking place. Moral theologians argued that categorizing sins as mortal and venial was untenably simplistic, and Catholics stopped going to confession shortly after the new rite of reconciliation was introduced. Scripture scholars pointed out that much in the Bible should not be taken literally, and church historians admitted that parts of papal history were seriously scandalous. Canon lawyers argued that full commitment in marriage was more difficult than previously believed, and people felt freer to seek annulments of broken marriages as the Catholic divorce rate rose to meet the national average. The ecumenical movement brought Catholics into contact with other Christians and even with people of other faiths, dispelling the uniqueness they had been taught to feel during the Tridentine era.

These changes in Catholic society resulted in changes in the perceived effects of the sacraments. It was harder to keep believing that only the baptized could be saved. It was easier to admit that confirmation did not have any discernable effects. Marriage was no longer seen as indissoluble, and men were seen leaving the priesthood even though they had been ordained as priests forever. Confession was no longer thought to be as necessary as it once had been, and anointing of the sick was increasingly unavailable due to the shortage of priests. As mentioned earlier, belief in the real presence of Christ declined, and the teaching that the mass is a sacrifice became hard to understand.

The church's leadership has yet to admit that its sacramental doctrine, inextricably connected to scholastic theology, is intellectually bankrupt. Around the time of Vatican II, well-intentioned theologians tried to translate scholastic doctrines into non-scholastic frames of reference—existentialism, phenomenology, process thought and postmodernism, to name a few—but none of these theologies was able make the church's sacramental doctrines more plausible. The problem is that sacramental theology is, properly speaking, a reflection on sacramental practices, but the sacramental theologies produced after the council were based on sacramental doctrines. The explanations of Christian rituals developed by Paul, the fathers of the church and the medieval schoolmen grew out of thinking about the rituals themselves in the context of their times. The explanations of the Catholic sacraments developed by Schillebeeckx, Rahner, Chauvet and others, however, were each an apologetic for traditional doctrines rather than an explanation of contemporary practices. The earlier ones, such as those proposed by Schillebeeckx and Rahner, were developed before the liturgical changes mentioned above, and so they were quite plausible at the time. But once the changes were made, and once the sacraments no longer had the perceived effects that they had had for centuries, even the most sophisticated theologies were no longer tenable.

If Catholicism is to remain a vibrant faith in the future, therefore, it must rethink its ritual policies and allow for the rethinking of what happens in and through its religious rituals. Otherwise it is destined to become a church of beautiful ceremonies that have little relation to the lives that people actually live.

Chapter 4

Most theories of meaning focus on objects—words and other symbols—to which meaning is ascribed, or which human beings know how to interpret. Much of the analysis in the previous chapter is implicitly based on such an understanding of meaning: that a text has a meaning which can be correctly or incorrectly interpreted.

The analysis presented in this chapter focuses instead on subjects, on human beings who express meaning in symbols or who find symbols meaningful. It is not a theory of meaning, but it is loosely based on Bernard Lonergan's cognitional theory. It assumes that when human beings "find" meaning in symbols they are engaged in meaning-making—either ascribing meaning to what they perceive or expressing meaning in symbols (words, pictures, gestures, etc.) that others can perceive.

Lonergan's theory is based on the fact that it is possible to verify that acts of meaning occur in human consciousness. Although most acts of meaning occur simultaneously with acts of sensing, meaning-making or insight is actually a pre- or non-verbal activity. If you find the words that you are reading meaningful, for example, the meaning occurs as you look at the sequence of words on the page. Were you looking at words written in a language with which you are not familiar, however, you would look at them and not find any meaning "in" them. More accurately put, you would look at the words and no acts of meaning would occur in your mind.

Chapter 4 opens with a brief description of a Catholic missionary's work among the Masai people in Africa. Instead of trying to teach them Christian doctrines, he told them stories about Jesus and about what Jesus said about God's way of living. Whenever he finished a life lesson, he would ask the elders if they accepted the teaching. If they did, he would go on to the next lesson; if they did not, they would discuss the matter among themselves.

If and when a village agreed to the way of life taught by Jesus, he baptized them all and charged them with remembering what they had accepted. Like the missionary apostle Paul, he allowed them to find their own way of remembering Jesus once a week, to ritualize forgiveness, to celebrate coming of age as a follower of Jesus, to marry, and so on. They took the meanings of community, forgiveness, strengthening, fidelity and so on, and either created their own meaningful rituals or adapted rituals they already had.

When a sentence is first written, the meaning is present in the mind of the writer before the words are put on the page. Likewise, when a ritual is first created, the meaning is first present in the minds of those who are designing it. Then, when others participate in the ritual, the intended meaning hopefully occurs in the minds of the participants. It is much easier for this to happen when people participate in rituals than when they merely attend them, for in the latter instance their minds may wander while the ritual is going on.

Most of the religious rituals in the lives of Christians today are rituals that they attend rather than participate in (unless they are going to confession, becoming married, etc.). In these cases especially, the meaning—or, better, the meaningfulness—of the rituals comes not from the ceremony itself but from events that precede the ceremony. At a wedding, for example, the meaning that it has for the parents of the couple will be more complex and intense than the meaning that it has for a distant relative who has had little contact with the couple.

Since meaning, as already indicated, is non-verbal, the meanings that are felt by those in attendance can be many and varied, even though they are not conceptualized or spoken. These meanings can be quite different from the meaning of the rite, which can be determined by examining the text and rubrics of the rite. Hopefully, at least some of the actual meanings that occur in the minds of the attendees coincide with the meanings that can be found in the rite when it is read and not being performed.

As a general rule, the more understanding that people bring to a performance, the more meaning it will have for them, or the more meaningful it will be. Someone who does not understand the language of a ceremony will find it less meaningful than someone who does. Someone who knows little about classical music will find it less meaningful than someone who understands music theory, or who knows the life of the composer, or who is familiar with the history of music. Someone who is involved in a church and its ministries and who knows others who are present will find a service more meaningful than someone who stepped into the building out of curiosity.

Meaning can also be quantified, as it were, according to its extension. A symbol or ritual can have personal meaning for a single individual, it can be a meaning that is shared by some but not all of the attendees, or it can be a meaning that is shared by all in attendance with greater or lesser intensity.

Shared meaning can be qualified, as it were, according to the level of consciousness on which it occurs. People who have shared experiences or who have had similar experiences can find common meaning in symbols that evoke feelings about those experiences, for example, a memorial service for the victims of a past disaster. People who have similar ideas about religion, politics or sports can find common meaning in activities that promote those ideas, for example, demonstrations on either side of the issues of abortion or gun control. People who have made similar decisions in their lives can find common meaning it rituals that result from having made those decisions, such as deciding to attend a rally in support of underpaid workers or undocumented immigrants, which can be done for a variety of different reasons.

If a symbol or ritual evokes meaning on two or three levels of consciousness, people will find it more meaningful that those who find it meaningful only on the level of experience, only on the level of understanding, or only on the level of decision making.

Meaning is real, but it is not a physical reality. In a fundamental but obvious sense, it is a spiritual reality. Meaning cannot be weighed, measured or photographed. (Here, "spiritual reality" refers to something that is experienced, such as love, forgiveness, trust, fidelity, and so on. In ancient and medieval times, the term referred to metaphysical entities that were not experienced but were believed to be real, such as grace or the Holy Spirit.)

Meaning can be abstract or concrete. Abstract meaning is disassociated from any concrete experiences. It is like the meaning that is found in a dictionary, giving synonyms for a word or telling how the word is used. Concrete meaning is associated with actual experiences. In the case of civil and religious rituals, it is a meaning that is shared with others on the basis of common experiences, common understandings or common decisions.

For rituals to be truly meaningful to people, the symbols must evoke or refer to concrete meanings, that is, meanings that were lived prior to the ritual performance. For example, one can know that the abstract meaning of a *bar mitvah* or *bat mitzvah* is a Jewish coming of age ceremony for adolescents. But one can know its concrete meaning only if one has lived through the process of coming to age in a Jewish community and has begun to assume adult responsibilities in that community. Likewise, one can know that the abstract meaning of anointing of the sick is healing. But one can know its concrete meaning only if one has been ill and has experienced physical or emotional healing through being anointed.

Knowing the concrete meaning of a ritual is the same as knowing a spiritual reality: it is a meaning that is found in a concrete experience. In other words, knowing the concrete meaning of a ritual is knowing what the ritual is about.

If one does not know what a ritual is about, one can still know its abstract meaning if one understands the words and symbols used in the ritual.

Sacramental rituals are meaningful to people to the extent that they have experienced what the rituals mean prior to the symbolic event. That is, sacraments are meaningful to the extent that the meanings have been found in the concrete experiences of people's lives. This implies that the same ritual can have various meanings for different people who participate in or attend a sacramental ritual (and which is often the case).

Conversely, a concrete meaning or spiritual reality can be expressed in any language or culture in which that reality is found, that is, in which that meaning is lived.

Therefore, except for desiring to associate a current ritual with a biblical precedent (e.g., baptizing with or in water), any words, symbols or gestures that are culturally appropriate can be used to express spiritual realities.

Further, a concrete meaning or spiritual reality can be celebrated in any community in which that reality is found, that is, in which that meaning is lived.

Such celebrations are symbolically honest, for they celebrate meanings that are real in the life of the community or in the lives of individuals who are members of the community.

If sacramental celebrations are not symbolically honest, they are experienced as meaningless and not connected with life. If they celebrate meanings that are abstract and not concrete, they are not symbolically honest. For example, the baptism of a child whose parents are not members of a community and who do not intend to raise the child in the Christian faith is not symbolically honest. This is so for the six sacraments that are transition rituals or rites of passage.

The eucharistic liturgy is not a transition ritual, and it celebrates the spiritual realities that are being lived by the community and its members. It does this explicitly when reference is made to concrete realities such as events in the lives of individuals, groups, or the community as a whole. It does this implicitly when people bring to the liturgy the memories of relationships and activities in which they are involved.

A parish with a vibrant community life can enjoy a meaningful liturgy even if it is done simply. Conversely, an elaborate liturgy may not be meaningful to people (except as a performance) if they are not involved in parish activities or in each others' lives.

Liturgy is not made more meaningful by increasing the quality of the performance. Rather, it becomes more meaningful as people share experiences of caring for others within and beyond their community.

NOTE: The summaries of chapters 1, 2 and 3 follow those chapters fairly closely. The argument summarized for chapter 4 covers the same points but in a very different order from the one found in the chapter.

Bibliography

Ancient and Medieval Works

Ambrose of Milan. *Abraham* (*De Abraham*)

———. *Cain and Abel* (*De Cain et Abel*)

———. *Commentary on Luke's Gospel* (*Expositio evangelii secundum Lucam*)

———. *Commentary on Psalm 37* (*Expositio psalmi XXXVII*)

———. *Commentary on Psalm 118* (*Expositio psalmi CXVIII*)

———. *Commentary on Twelve Psalms* (*Enarrationes in XII psalmos Davidicos*)

———. *The Death of Valentinian* (*De obitu Valentiniani consolatio*)

———. *A Dialogue between Job and David* (*De interpellatione Job et David*)

———. *Elijah and Fasting* (*De Elia et jejunio*)

———. *An Explanation of the Prophet David to the Emperor Theodosius* (*Apologia Prophetae David ad Theodosium Augustum*)

———. *The Faith* (*De fide ad Gratianum Augustum*)

———. *The Holy Spirit* (*De Spiritu Sancto*)

———. *Jacob and the Blessed Life* (*De Jacob et vita beata*)

———. *Letters* (*Epistolae*)

———. *The Mysteries* (*De mysteriis*)

———. *The Mystery of the Lord's Incarnation* (*De incarnationis Dominicae sacramento*)

———. *Paradise* (*De Paradiso*)

———. *Repentance* (*De poenitentia*)

———. *The Sacraments* (*De sacramentis*)

———. *The Six Days of Creation* (*Exameron*)

———. *Widows* (*De viduis*)

The Apostolic Tradition (*Traditio Apostolica*)

Aquinas, Thomas. *Commentary on Book IV of the Sentences* (*Super IV Sententiarum*)

———. *Summa Theologica*, Book III

Augustine of Hippo. *Adulterous Marriages* (*De conjugiis adulterinis*)

———. *Against Cresconius, a Donatist Teacher* (*Contra Cresconium grammaticum Donatistam*)

———. *Against the Letter of Parmenian* (*Contra epistolam Parmeniani*)

———. *Against the Letters of Petilianus* (*Contra litteras Petiliani*)

———. *Baptism, Against the Donatists* (*De Baptismo contra Donatistas*)

———. *Catechizing the Uninstructed* (*De catechizandis rudibus*)

———. *The City of God* (*De civitate Dei contra paganos*)

———. *Commentaries on the Psalms* (*Enarrationes in Psalmos*)

———. *The Good of Marriage* (*De bono coniugali*)

———. *Handbook on Faith, Hope and Charity* (*Enchiridion de Fide, Spe et Caritate*)

———. *Letters* (*Epistolae*)

———. *The Literal Meaning of Genesis* (*De Genesi ad litteram*)

———. *Marriage and Concupiscence* (*De nuptiis et concupiscentiae*)

———. *Merit and the Forgiveness of Sins, and the Baptism of Infants* (*De peccatorum meritis et remissione et de baptismo parvulorum*)

———. *The Proceedings of Pelagius* (*De gestis Pelagii*)

———. *Questions about the Heptateuch* (*Quaestionum in Heptateuchum*)

———. *Treatises on the Gospel of John* (*In evangelium Ioannis tractati*)

———. *Sermon to Catechumens on the Creed* (*De symbolo ad catechumenos*)

———. *Sermon to the People of the Church of Carthage* (*Sermo ad populum Carthaginiensis ecclesiae*)

———. *Sermons* (*Sermones*)

———. *A Summary of the Three-Day Conference with the Donatists* (*Breviculus collationis cum Donatistas in tres diebus*),

———. *To the Donatists after the Conference* (*Ad Donatistas post collationem*)

———. *Treatises on the Gospel of John* (*In evangelium Ioannis tractatus*)

Chrystostom, John. *On the Priesthood* (περί ιερωσῦνης)

Clement of Alexandria. *The Instructor* (Παιδαγωγςός)

———. *Miscellanies* (Στρωματέων)

Cyprian of Carthage. *An Address to Demetruianus* (*Liber ad Demetruianum*)

———. *Exhortation to Martyrdom, Addressed to Fortunatus* (*Epistola ad Fortuantum de exhoratione martyrii*)

———. *The Lapsed* (*De Lapsis*)

———. *Letter to Quirinus* (*Testimonia ad Qurinum*)

———. *Letters* (*Epistolae*)

———. *The Lord's Prayer* (*Liber de oratione dominica*)

———. *The Unity of the Church* (*Liber de unitate ecclesiae*)

Didache (Διδαχὴ κυρίου διὰ τῶν δώδεκα ἀποστόλων τοῖς ἔθνεσιν)

Gratian, John. *Decretum* or *The Agreement of Disagreeing Canons* (*Concordia discordantium canonum*)

Hermas. *The Shepherd* (Ποιμὴν τοῦ Ἑρμᾶ)

Hugh of St. Victor. *The Sacraments of the Christian Faith.* (*De sacramentis christianae fidei*)

Ignatius of Antioch. *Letter to Polycarp* (Πρός Πολυκάρπον)

———. *Letter to the Smyrnaeans* (Σμύρναιοις)

Irenaeus, *Against Heresies* (*Adversus haereses*)

Justin Martyr, *Dialogue with Trypho*   (Πρός Τρυφώνα Ιυδαίον διάλογος)

———. *First Apology* (Απολογία πρωτη ὑπερ Χριστιανων)

Lombard, Peter. *Sentences* or *Sententiarum libri IV* (*Four Books of Opinions*)

Tertullian. *Against Marcion* (*Adversus Marcionem*)

———. *Against the Valentinians* (*Adversus Valentinianos*)

———. *Letters* (*Epistolae*)

———. *Baptism* (*De baptismo*)

———. *The Crown* (*De corona militis*)

———. *Modesty* (*De Pudicitia*)

———. *Patience* (*De patientia*)

———. *The Prescription of Heretics* (*De praescriptionibus adversus haereticos*)

———. *Repentance* (*De poenitentia*)

———. *The Soul* (*De anima*)

———. *To the Nations* (*Ad nationes*)

Church Documents

The 1917 or Pio-Benedictine Code of Canon Law: In English Translation with Extensive Scholarly Apparatus, edited by Edward N. Peters. San Francisco: Ignatius, 2001.

Catechism of the Catholic Church. Città del Vaticano: Libreria Editrice Vaticana, 1994.

The Catechism of the Council of Trent. Translated by Rev. J. Donovan. New York: Christian Press Association, c. 1830.

Clarkson, John F., et al., eds., *The Church Teaches: Documents of the Church in English Translation.* St. Louis, MO: B. Herder, 1964.

Code of Canon Law: Latin-English Edition. Washington, DC: Canon Law Society of America, 1983.

Codex Juris Canonici. Città del Vaticano: Tipografia Poliglotta Vaticana, 1926.

Denzinger, Henricus, and Adolfus Schönmetzer, eds. *Enchiridion Symbolorum: Definitionum et Declarationum de Rebus Fidei et Morum.* Freiburg: Verlag Herder, 1963.

The Documents of Vatican II: In a New and Definitive Translation with Commentaries and Notes by Catholic, Protestant and Orthodox Authorities, edited by Walter M. Abbott. London: Geoffrey Chapman, 1966.

Hünermann, Peter, Helmut Hoping, Robert L Fastiggi, Anne Englund Nash, and Heinrich Denzinger, eds. *Compendium of Creeds, Definitions, and Declarations on Matters of Faith and Morals.* San Francisco: Ignatius, 2012.

The Rites of the Catholic Church. Collegeville, MN: Liturgical, 1990.

The Rites of the Catholic Church, vol. 2. Collegeville, MN: Liturgical Press, 1990.

Schroeder, H. J., ed., *Canons and Decrees of the Council of Trent.* St. Louis: B. Herder, 1941.

Translations of Philosophical and Theological Texts

Ardens, Radulphus. *The Questions on the Sacraments.* Toronto: Pontifical Institute of Medieval Studies, 2010.

Bradshaw, Paul, Maxwell E. Johnson, L. Edward Phillips, and Harold W. Attridge. *The Apostolic Tradition: A Commentary.* Minneapolis: Fortress, 2002.

Deferrari, Roy J., ed. *Hugh of St. Victor on the Sacraments of the Christian Faith*, Cambridge, MA: Medieval Academy of America, 1951.

Dix, Gregory, ed. *The Treatise on the Apostolic Tradition of St. Hippolytus of Rome, Bishop and Martyr.* London: SPCK, 1937.

Donna, Rose Bernard. *The Fathers of the Church: A New Translation*, vol. 51. Washington, DC: Catholic University of America Press, 1964.

Lombard, Peter. *The Sentences, Book 4: On the Doctrine of Signs.* Translated by Giulio Silano. Toronto: Pontifical Institute of Medieval Studies, 2010.

McKeon, Richard. *The Basic Works of Aristotle.* New York: Random House, 1941.

Milavec, Aaron. *The Didache: Faith, Hope, and Life of the Earliest Christian Communities, 50–70 C.E.* Mahwah, NJ: Paulist, 2003.

Palmer, Paul F., ed., *Sources of Christian Theology: Sacraments and Forgiveness.* Westminster, MD: Newman, 1959.

———. *Sources of Christian Theology: Sacraments and Worship*, Westminster, MD: Newman, 1957.

Roberts, Alexander, James Donaldson, and A. Cleveland Coxe, eds. *Ante-Nicene Fathers*, 10 vols. Peabody, MA: Hendrickson, 1994.

Modern and Contemporary Works

Bradshaw, Paul F. *The Search for the Origins of Christian Worship.* New York: Oxford University Press, 2002.

Cooke, Bernard. *Ministry to Word and Sacraments: History and Theology.* Philadelphia: Fortress, 1976.

Dix, Gregory. *The Shape of the Liturgy.* London: Dacre, 1945.

Donovan, Vincent J. *Christianity Rediscovered.* Chicago: Fides Claretian, 1978.

Ferguson, Everett. *Baptism in the Early Church: History, Theology, and Liturgy in the First Five Centuries.* Grand Rapids, MI: William B. Eerdmans, 2009.

Jungmann, Josef. *The Mass of the Roman Rite: Its Origins and Development (Missarum Solemnia).* New York: Benziger, 1950.

Leeming, Bernard. *Principles of Sacramental Theology.* Westminster, MD: Newman, 1956.

Lonergan, Bernard. *Collection: Papers by Bernard Lonergan.* New York: Herder and Herder, 1967.

———. *Grace and Freedom: Operative Grace in the Thought of St. Thomas Aquinas.* New York: Herder and Herder, 1971.

———. *Insight: A Study of Human Understanding,* London: Longmans, 1958.

———. *Method in Theology.* New York: Herder and Herder, 1972.

Mackin, Theodore. *Divorce and Remarriage.* Mahwah, NJ: Paulist, 1984.

———. *The Marital Sacrament.* Mahwah, NJ: Paulist, 1989.

———. *What is Marriage?* Mahwah, NJ: Paulist, 1982.

Macy, Gary. *The Banquet's Wisdom: A Short History of the Theologies of the Lord's Supper.* Mahwah, NJ: Paulist, 1992.

———. *The Hidden History of Women's Ordination.* New York: Oxford University Press, 2008.

Martos, Joseph. *Doors to the Sacred: A Historical Introduction to Sacraments in the Catholic Church.* Liguori, MO: Liguori, 2014.

———. *The Sacraments: An Interdisciplinary and Interactive Study,* Collegeville, MN: Liturgical, 2009.

Milavec, Aaron. *To Empower as Jesus Did: Acquiring Spiritual Power Through Apprenticeship.* New York: Edwin Mellen, 1982.

Milner, Austin. *The Theology of Confirmation.* Notre Dame, IN: Fides, 1971.

Orsy, Ladislas. *The Evolving Church and the Sacrament of Penance.* Denville, NJ: Dimension Books, 1978.

Ott, Ludwig. *Fundamentals of Catholic Dogma.* Translated by Patrick Lynch. St. Louis, MO: B. Herder, 1962.

Piaget, Jean. *The Construction of Reality in the Child.* New York: Basic Books, 1954

——— and Bärbel Inhelder, *The Psychology of the Child.* New York: Basic Books, 1969

Poschmann, Bernhard. *Penance and the Anointing of the Sick.* New York: Herder and Herder, 1964.

Rahner, Karl. *The Church and the Sacraments.* New York: Herder and Herder, 1963.

Rosemann, Philipp W. *The Story of a Great Medieval Book: Peter Lombard's Sentences.* Peterborough, ON: Broadview, 2007.

Schillebeeckx, Edward. *Marriage: Human Reality and Saving Mystery.* New York: Sheed and Ward, 1965.

———. *Ministry: Leadership in the Community of Jesus Christ.* New York: Crossroad, 1981

Index of Names

n = *appears only in the footnotes*

Ambrose of Milan, 51–52, 54, 124–29, 131, 132n, 134, 136, 139–41, 147–48, 179, 194, 289

The Apostolic Tradition, 48, 49n, 93, 104, 120–21, 134n, 137, 151–52, 201, 287.

Aquinas, Thomas, 2–3, 16, 18, 24, 25n, 29–30, 57, 60, 61n, 68, 182, 204, 216, 283, 285.

Augustine of Hippo, 4, 18, 21–22, 24, 27, 40, 43, 51–53, 55, 56, 58, 61, 65, 100, 104, 107, 124, 129–35, 136, 139–41, 143–44, 148–50, 153n, 154, 155–59, 160, 161, 172, 173, 174, 176n, 179–82, 183, 189–92, 194, 203, 205–12, 222, 273, 284–85, 288–91, 295

Catechism of the Catholic Church, xv, 3, 32, 33–39, 69, 256n

Catechism of the Council of Trent, 3, 12–13, 15, 18, 20, 32, 68

Chauvet, Louis-Marie, 216, 284, 298

Chrysostom, John, 55, 138, 139, 142–43, 147, 148, 150n, 153, 163

Clement of Alexandria, 42n, 50, 118, 119

Clement of Rome, 94n, 118n

Code of Canon Law (1917), 3, 13–15, 16, 27n, 30, 33

Code of Canon Law (1983), xv, 3, 31–33, 34, 69

Cooke, Bernard, 93n, 153n, 168n, 213,

Cyprian of Carthage, 49–51, 54–55, 105–107, 115–17, 124, 129, 131, 132, 136, 288, 291

Donovan, Vincent J., 220-21, 223–24, 243, 253, 256, 271

The *Didache,* 48, 55, 74, 101, 102, 104, 110–111, 113, 115, 121, 135, 255, 276, 287

Gratian, John, 172, 174–75, 180, 183, 187–89, 196–97, 200, 202–209, 211, 291–95

Hermas. 87, 118–19

Hugh of St. Victor, 4, 172–74, 176, 178–80, 81n, 183, 186-87, 189–91, 196, 200, 202–204, 206, 208, 210–11, 291–95

Ignatius of Antioch, 42, 101–102, 112, 118n, 121, 122, 287

Irenaeus, 55, 102, 115

Justin Martyr, 42, 50, 55, 101–102, 112–15, 116n, 121, 136, 287

Leeming, Bernard, 3, 4n, 17, 19n, 22–23, 29n, 30, 35n, 59n, 63n,

Lombard, Peter, 4, 16, 18, 57–58, 172–76, 178–79, 180–82, 183–84, 189–94, 197–99, 200n, 201, 202–204, 205, 208–209, 210–11, 262, 285, 291–92, 294, 295

Lonergan, Bernard, 17, 19n, 25n, 60n, 108n, 193, 223n, 230, 231n, 285, 298

Mackin, Theodore, 97n, 122n, 155–56, 157n, 158n, 169n, 170n, 213, 258n

Macy, Gary, 58n, 165n, 166n, 169n, 185n, 187n, 194n, 202n, 213, 248n

Milavec, Aaron, 48n, 111n, 128n

Ott, Ludwig, 3, 4n, 17, 18n, 19n, 20–21, 25n, 26, 27n, 28n, 29n, 30, 35n

Piaget, Jean, 117n

Rahner, Karl, 17, 216, 218, 238n, 279n, 298

Schillebeeckx, Edward, 17, 22, 93n, 97n, 122n, 152–53, 154n, 205n, 206n, 208n, 216, 218, 258n, 279n, 298

Tertullian, 49–51, 53–55, 103–105, 107, 119, 120, 122, 131, 136, 149n, 179, 287–88

Trent, Council of, ix, 1–3, 6–12, 15–16, 17, 26, 27, 28, 30, 34–35, 39, 43, 64–67, 69, 70, 91, 194, 210, 217, 242, 259, 265, 282, 284

Vatican II, Council of, xv, 3, 10, 15, 17, 22, 26n, 29, 31, 33, 35, 37, 38, 43, 69, 90–91, 163, 186, 197, 210, 216, 218, 235, 240, 241, 242, 244, 249, 253, 255, 256, 259, 264, 265, 269, 278, 283, 296, 298